Stagecoach

Rare Views of the Old West
1849-1915

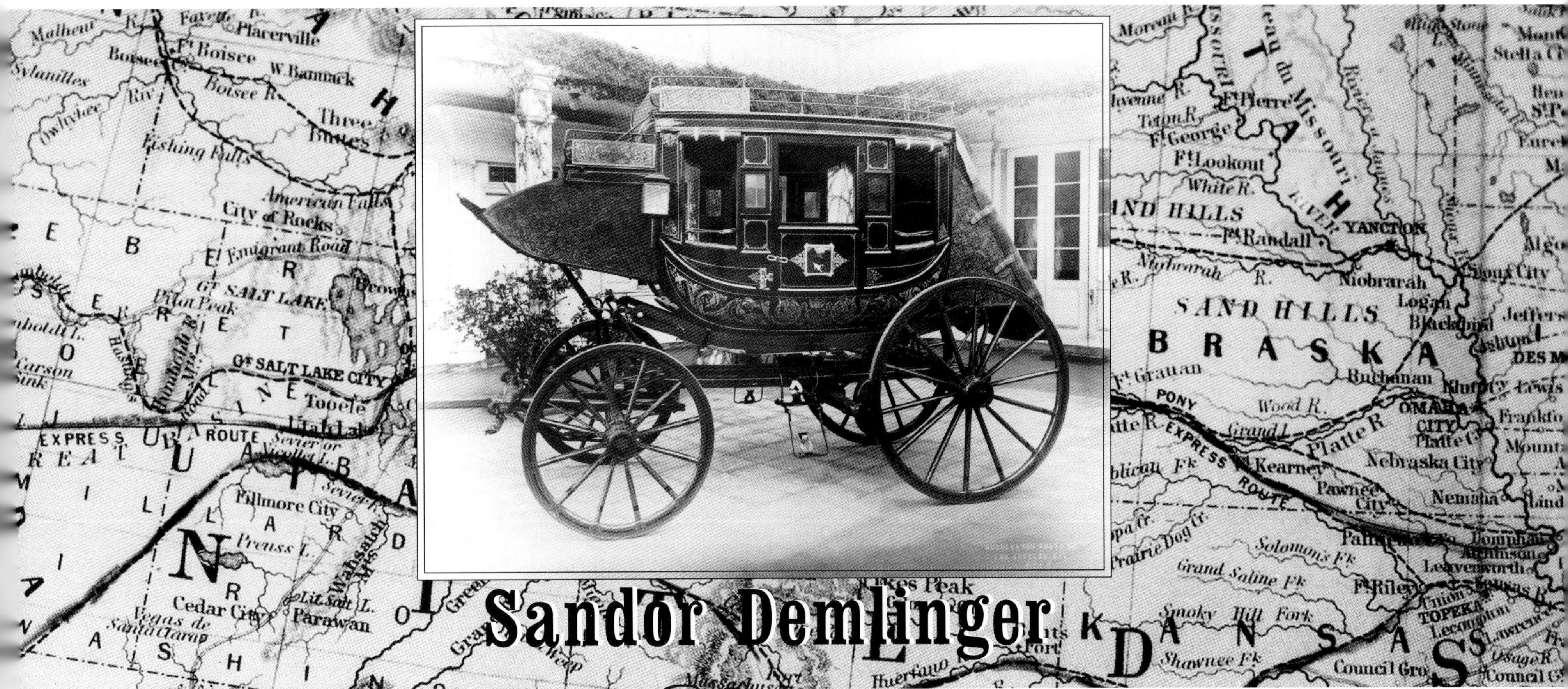

Sandor Demlinger

Schiffer Publishing Ltd®

4880 Lower Valley Road, Atglen, PA 19310 USA

Dedication

To my loving and helpful wife Reva, my sons Keith,
Msc.D. and Glenn, O.D., and my daughter Chef Allyson

Library of Congress Cataloging-in-Publication Data

Demlinger, Sandor.
Stagecoach : rare views of the Old West, 1849-1915 / by Sandor Demlinger.
p. cm.
ISBN 0-7643-2124-2 (large print : pbk.)
1. Frontier and pioneer life—West (U.S.)—Pictorial works. 2. Overland journeys to the Pacific—Pictorial works. 3. Stagecoaches—West (U.S.)—History—Pictorial works. 4. Pioneers—West (U.S.)—History—Pictorial works. 5. Immigrants—West (U.S.)—History—Pictorial works. 6. West (U.S.)—Social life and customs—Pictorial works. 7. West (U.S.)—History—Pictorial works. I. Title.

F596.D46 2004
978'.02'0222—dc22
2004015492

Designed by Mark David Bowyer
Type set in Korinna BT

ISBN: 0-7643-2124-2
Printed in China

Published by Schiffer Publishing Ltd.
4880 Lower Valley Road
Atglen, PA 19310
Phone: (610) 593-1777; Fax: (610) 593-2002
E-mail: Info@schifferbooks.com

In Europe, Schiffer books are distributed by
Bushwood Books
6 Marksbury Ave.
Kew Gardens
Surrey TW9 4JF England
Phone: 44 (0) 20 8392-8585; Fax: 44 (0) 20 8392-9876
E-mail: info@bushwoodbooks.co.uk
Free postage in the U.K., Europe; air mail at cost.

Contents

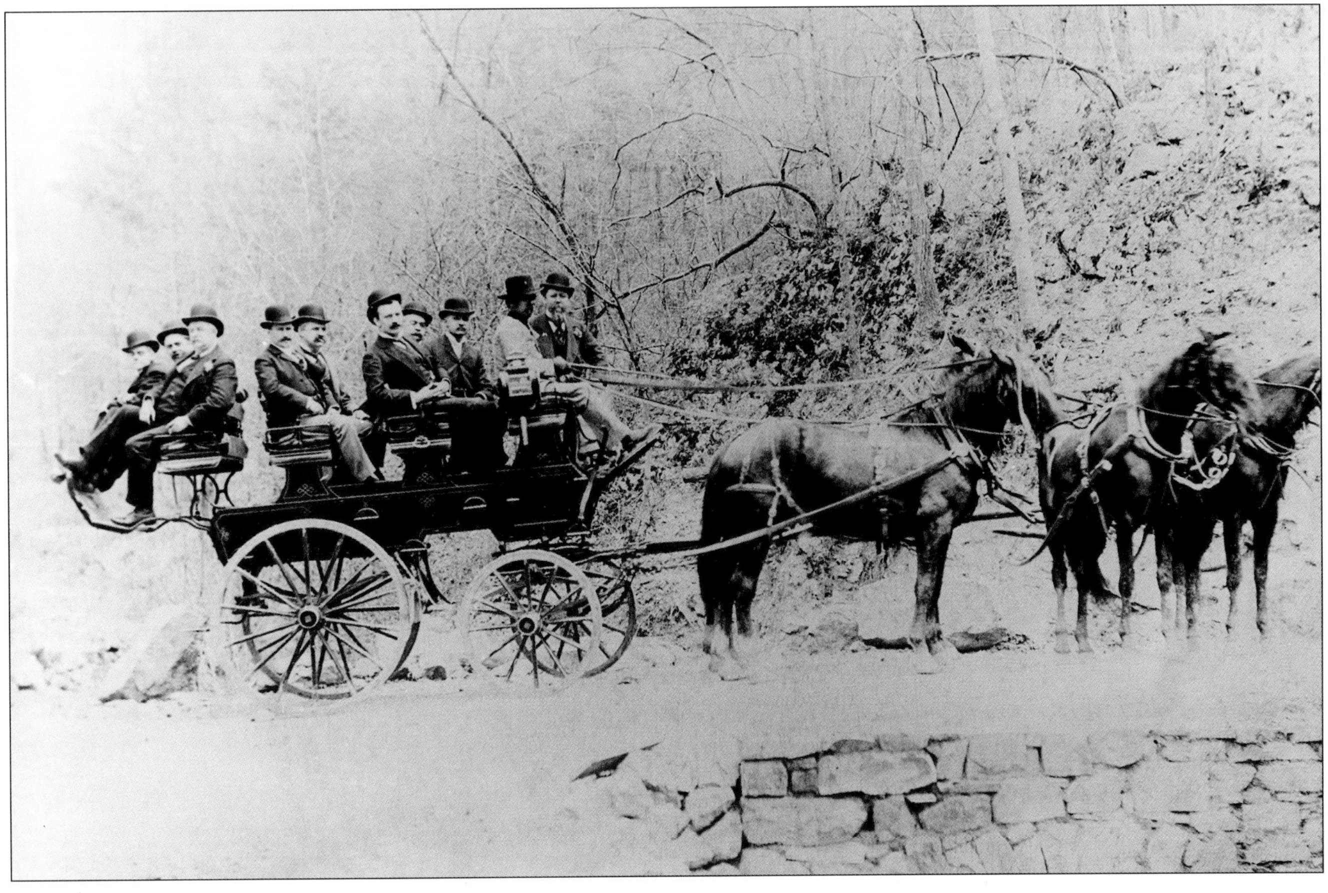

Introduction

In 1848 President James Polk announced that the stories about huge amounts of gold being discovered in California were, indeed, true. With that a gold fever struck the entire nation and unleashed a tidal wave of people heading west. Traveling by ship around the Horn, crossing over through Mexico and Panama, or going over land through the American West's deserts and mountain ranges, it didn't deter the emigrants seeking their fortunes.

For those who dreaded the travel by ship to California, which meant weeks on the ocean, facing winds and storms that might sink their ship, and who didn't mind taking the overland route through wild and unexplored regions, the trip to the West by stagecoach was a great attraction. The thoughts that they would see actual Indians made the trip even more exciting.

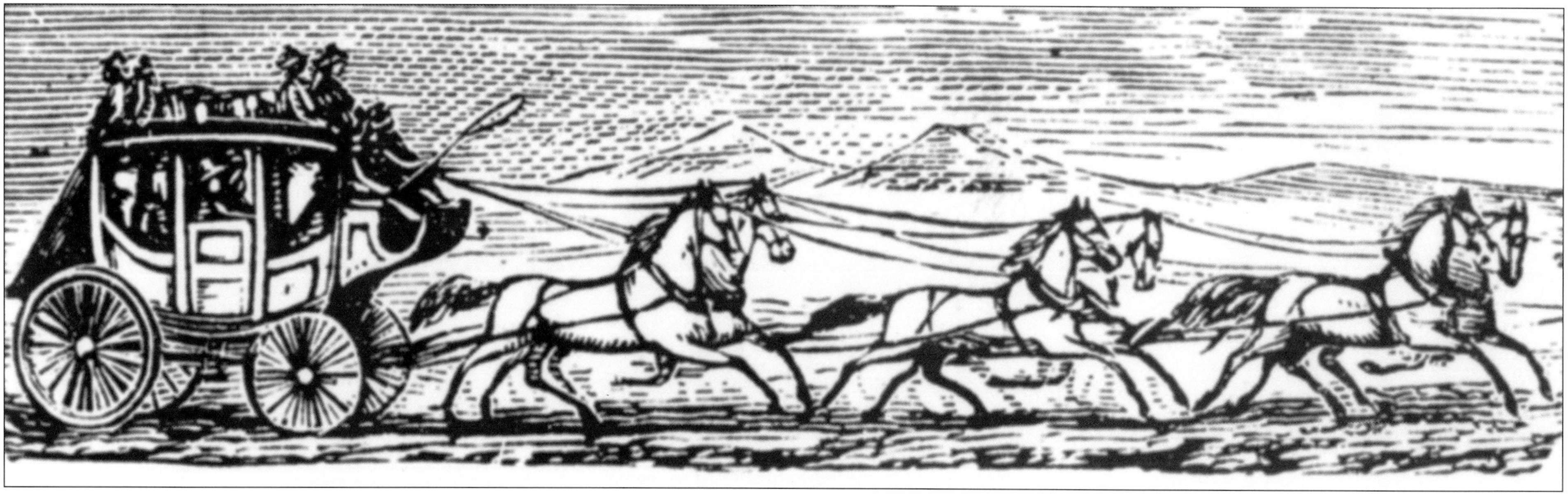

Chapter 1

Emigrant Routes and U.S. Government Surveys

On May 17, 1850, a report was issued from the Secretary of War, George W. Crawford, including reports from the Tenth Military Department that Lieutenant G. H. Derby had made a survey of the upper Sacramento. His survey included maps and topographical sketches of the area, noting the resources and the number of Indians (distinguishing between "tame" Indians and the "wild" Sierra Indians). It also showed where he had set up his command at Johnson's Rancho, on Bear Creek, away from the Indians of the Sierra.

The Truckee emigrant route saw hundreds of wagons and emigrants pass on the way to the Yuba mines and to the Feather River "dry diggings." "Within three or four miles of our post, gold is found in small quantities in the ravines running toward the creek," wrote Lieutenant Derby in his report. Earlier he had recruited ten helpers to help him with his survey.

Returning to his encampment Lt. George Derby found a disturbing incident had happened. Manuel Montano, a servant who had been with him more than two months, had deserted. But before doing so, he cut a hole in Derby's tent and stole a box containing $425 of public funds, a gold pencil, a gold watch, a pistol, and other articles of value. In addition he also took his room mate's money and then left on the best horse in the camp. Derby asked for volunteers to bring him back, and a Mr. Kemp took up the chase. "I am sad to report I have not heard from either man since." From this report a general sense of gloom settled over the little party of five.

It was late October when the rains came and the area was a swamp. Many miners came into camp and declared it impossible to mine as the weather had changed so fast they could have frozen to death. There were two rancherias of Indians above "Butte Creek," living on fish and wild grapes.

This ended a long stay in the Bear Creek area by Lieutenant George Derby who produced a map of the Sacramento Valley and the main route for the emigration.

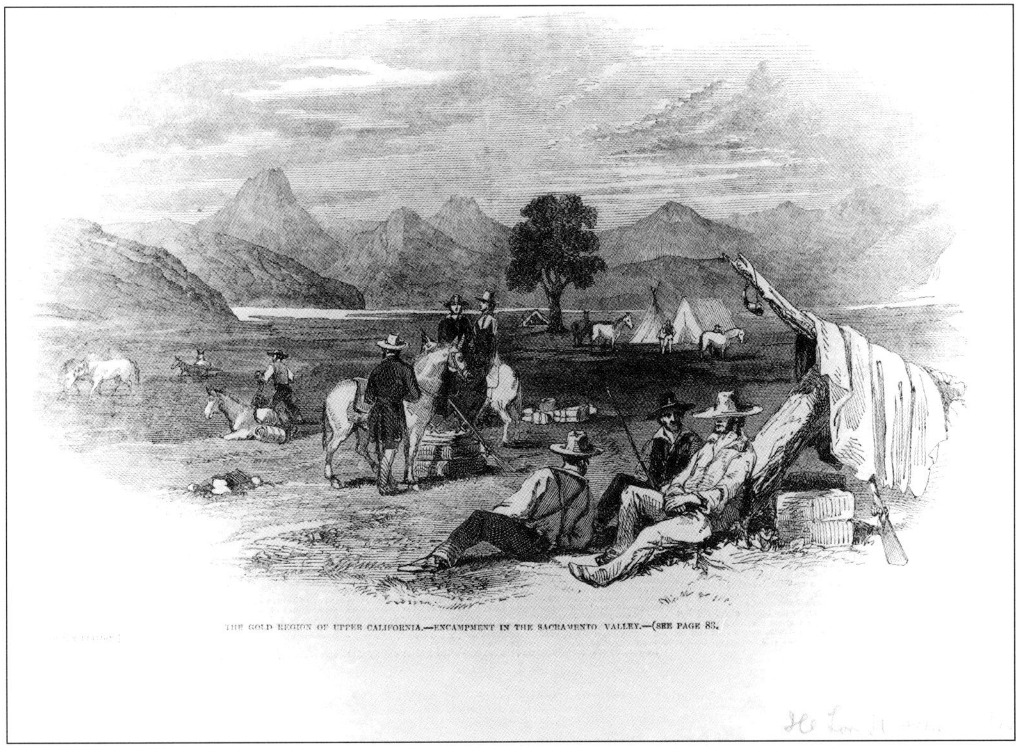

The gold region in upper California, showing an encampment in the Sacramento Valley. The engraving is an illustration from *Gleason's Pictorial Review*.

The Army's Corps of Topographical Engineers continued to explore the vast regions of California and sent a force of four officers and eighty men into upper California. A report dated December 1, 1849 from the Tenth Military Department. Monterey, California, reads:.

> In compliance with your instructions and arriving at camp Anderson, near Sutter, California, I reported to Captain H. Day, who I found had relieved Major Kingsbury. Since I had not received special orders No. 44, dated September 4, and having no information of the duties assigned to me I was not prepared with instruments or funds for this duty. Orders were issued to Captain W.H. Warner and his corps of engineers to explore the upper Sacramento, across the Nevada, to the Humboldt River, with the main object being to discover a railroad route through that section of the country. At the moment Captain Warner had done so he was soon murdered by the Indians.

The reports mentioned in this briefing were from the U.S. Armies from September, 1849, through 1850. Much more can be read from these reports, but it gives the reader an idea what was a very dangerous trip to the upper California.

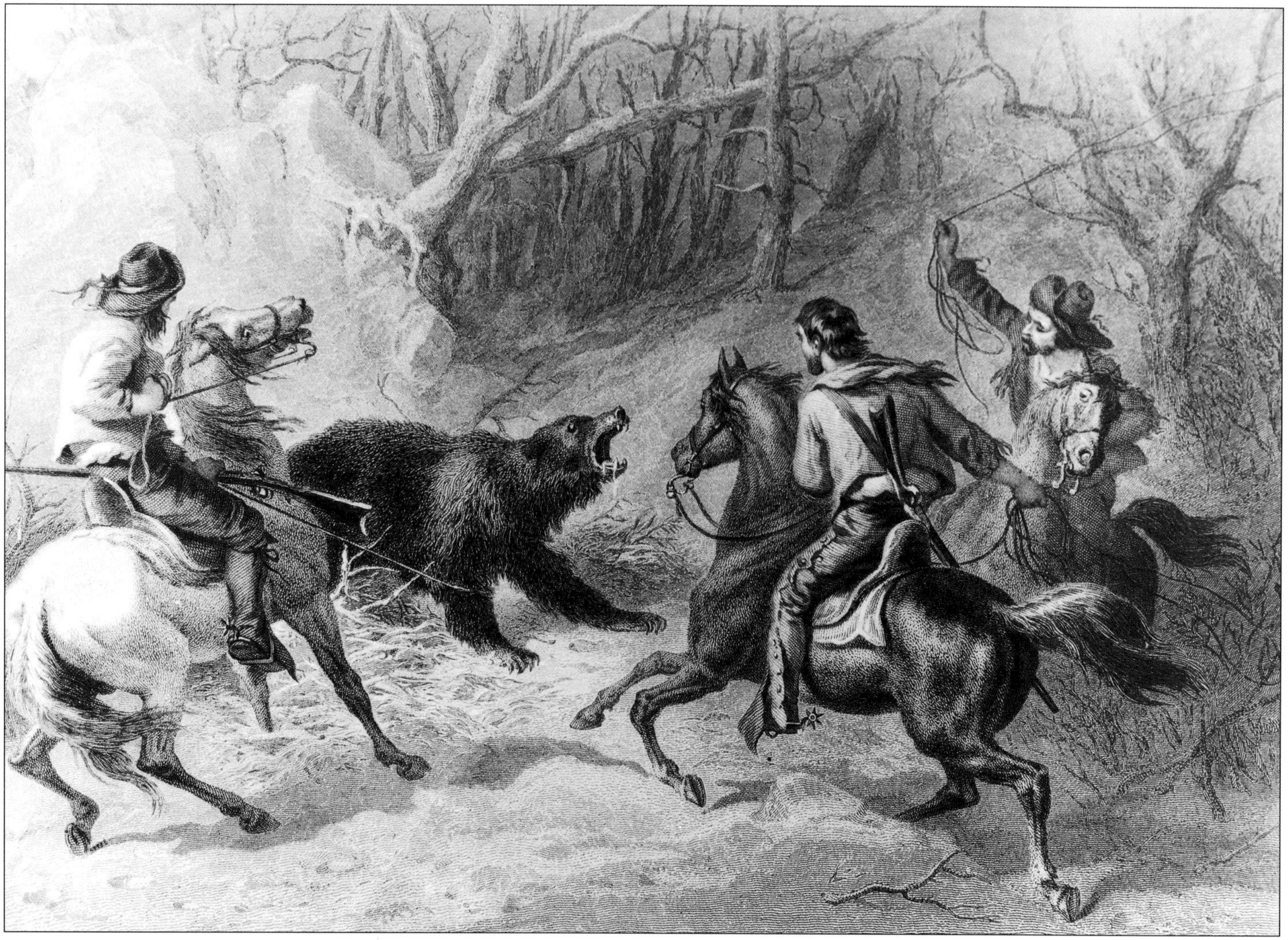

Early Californians capturing a bear. Engraving from *Gleason's Pictorial Review*.

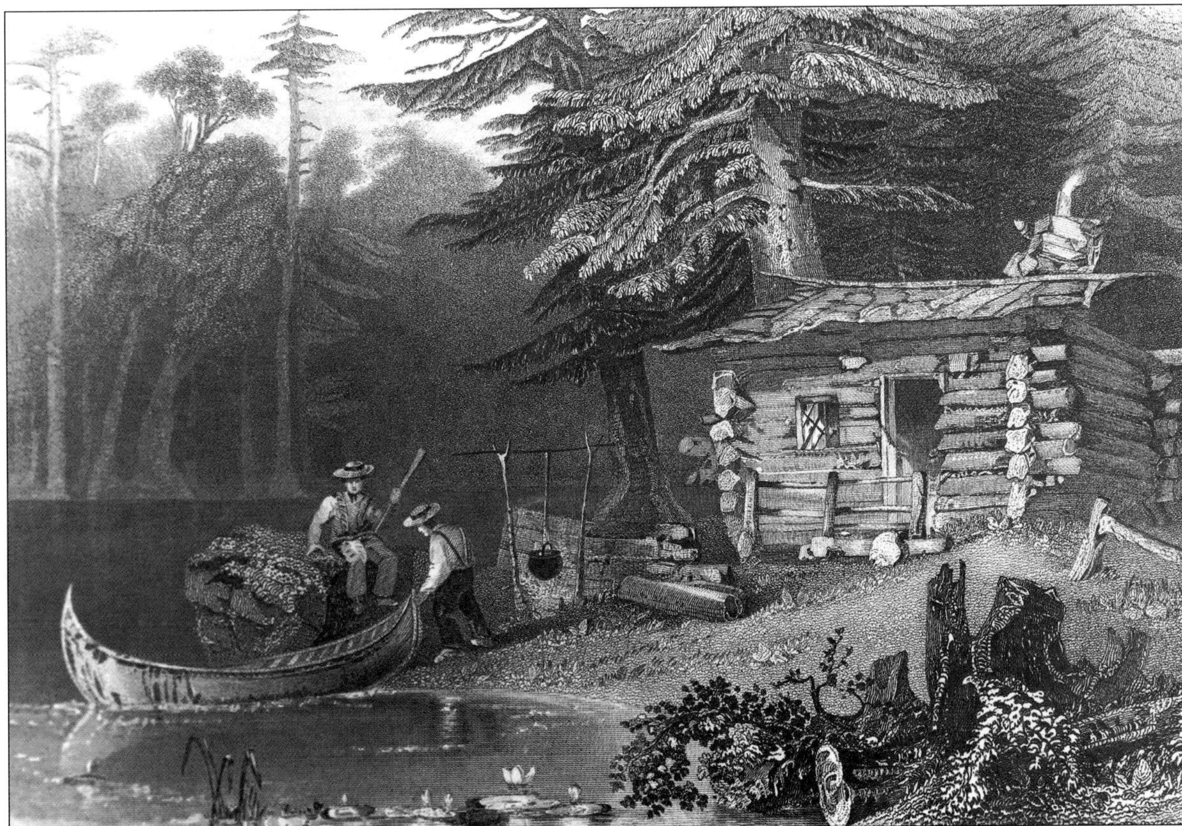

W.H. Bartlett's 1844 steel engraving of a very early log cabin and two hunters, deep in a redwood forest.

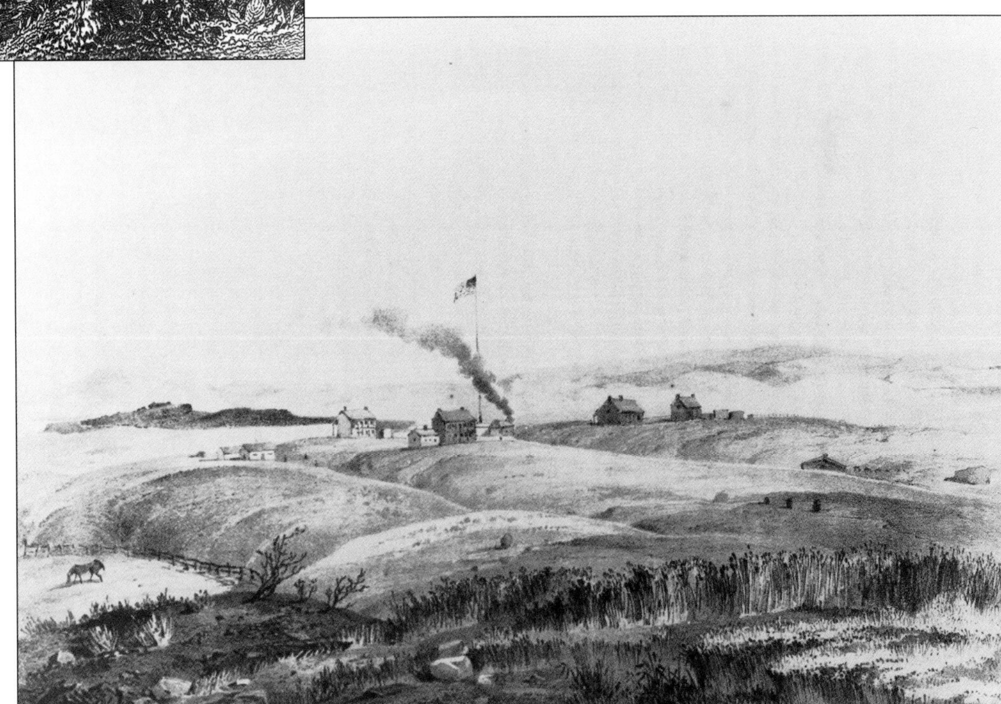

Benicia, a U.S. military post. The view is from an artist's rendering for the *U.S.P.R.R. Survey in California*.

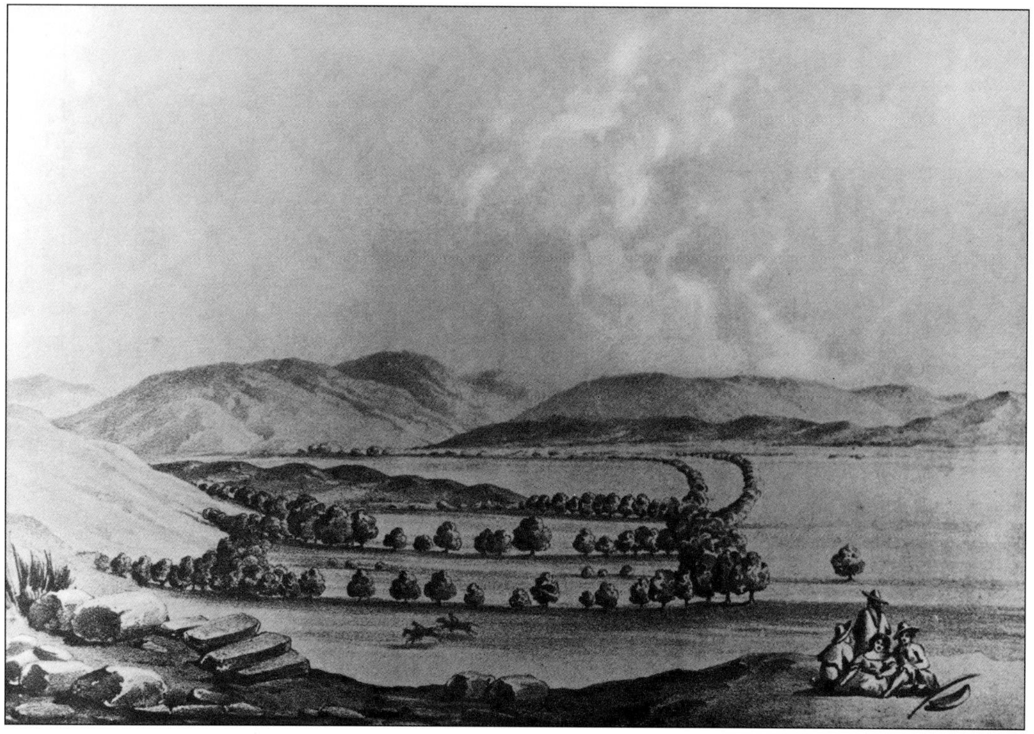

A U.S. Survey drawing showing the entrance of the Tejon Pass and a portion of the Tejon.

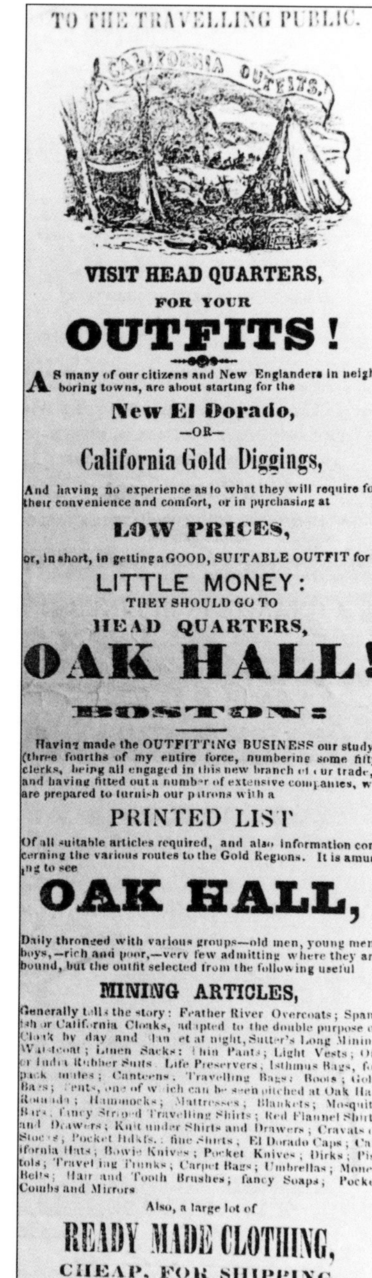

Businesses in Boston and other large eastern cities would sell thousands of dollars in equipment with full column advertisements like these.

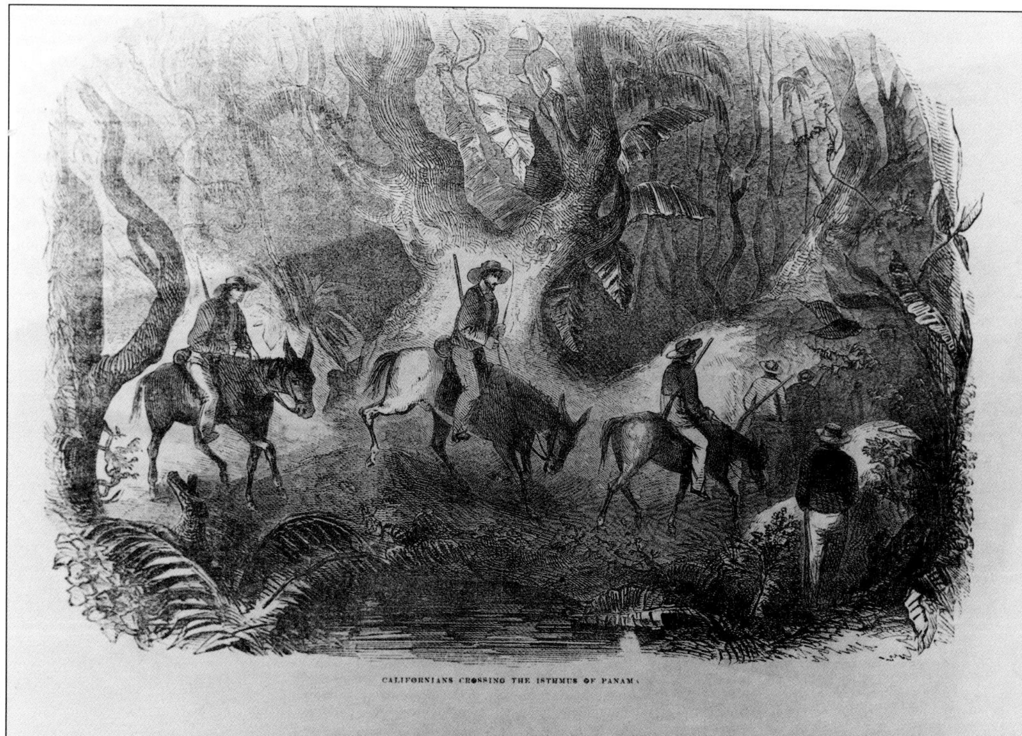

Gleason's Pictorial Review printed this illustration of travelers crossing the Isthmus of Panama.

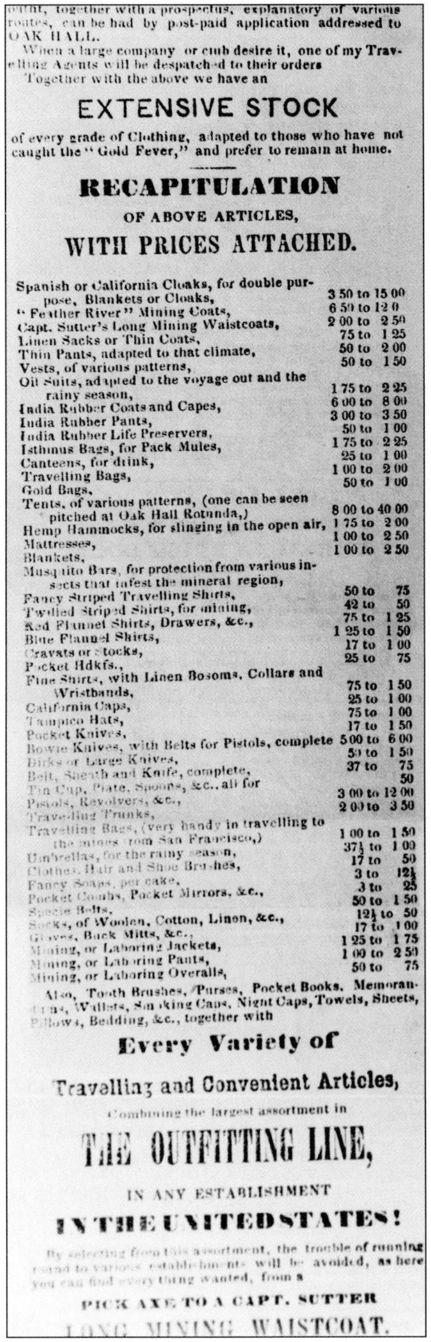

…outfit, together with a prospectus, explanatory of various routes, can be had by post-paid application addressed to OAK HALL.

When a large company or club desire it, one of my Travelling Agents will be despatched to their orders

Together with the above we have an

EXTENSIVE STOCK

of every grade of Clothing, adapted to those who have not caught the "Gold Fever," and prefer to remain at home.

RECAPITULATION

OF ABOVE ARTICLES,

WITH PRICES ATTACHED.

Spanish or California Cloaks, for double purpose, Blankets or Cloaks,	3 50 to 15 00
"Feather River" Mining Coats,	6 50 to 12 0
Capt. Sutter's Long Mining Waistcoats,	2 00 to 2 50
Linen Sacks or Thin Coats,	75 to 1 25
Thin Pants, adapted to that climate,	50 to 2 00
Vests, of various patterns,	50 to 1 50
Oil Suits, adapted to the voyage out and the rainy season,	1 75 to 2 25
India Rubber Coats and Capes,	6 00 to 8 00
India Rubber Pants,	3 00 to 3 50
India Rubber Life Preservers,	50 to 1 00
Isthmus Bags, for Pack Mules,	1 75 to 2 25
Canteens, for drink,	25 to 1 00
Travelling Bags,	1 00 to 2 00
Gold Bags,	50 to 1 00
Tents, of various patterns, (one can be seen pitched at Oak Hall Rotunda,)	8 00 to 40 00
Hemp Hammocks, for slinging in the open air,	1 75 to 2 00
Mattresses,	1 00 to 2 50
Blankets,	1 00 to 2 50
Musquito Bars, for protection from various insects that infest the mineral region,	
Fancy Striped Travelling Shirts,	50 to 75
Twilled Striped Shirts, for mining,	42 to 50
Red Flannel Shirts, Drawers, &c.,	75 to 1 25
Blue Flannel Shirts,	1 25 to 1 50
Cravats or Stocks,	17 to 1 00
Pocket Hdkfs.,	25 to 75
Fine Shirts, with Linen Bosoms, Collars and Wristbands,	75 to 1 50
California Caps,	25 to 1 00
Tampico Hats,	75 to 1 00
Pocket Knives,	17 to 1 50
Bowie Knives, with Belts for Pistols, complete	5 00 to 6 00
Dirks or Large Knives,	50 to 1 50
Belt, Sheath and Knife, complete,	37 to 75
Tin Cup, Plate, Spoons, &c., all for	50
Pistols, Revolvers, &c.,	3 00 to 12 00
Travelling Trunks,	2 00 to 3 50
Travelling Bags, (very handy in travelling to the mines from San Francisco,)	1 00 to 1 50
Umbrellas, for the rainy season,	37½ to 1 00
Clothes, Hair and Shoe Brushes,	17 to 50
Fancy Soaps, per cake,	3 to 12½
Pocket Combs, Pocket Mirrors, &c.,	3 to 25
Specie Belts,	50 to 1 50
Socks, of Woolen, Cotton, Linen, &c.,	12½ to 50
Gloves, Buck Mitts, &c.,	17 to 1 00
Mining, or Laboring Jackets,	1 25 to 1 75
Mining, or Laboring Pants,	1 00 to 2 50
Mining, or Laboring Overalls,	50 to 75

Also, Tooth Brushes, Purses, Pocket Books, Memorandums, Wallets, Smoking Caps, Night Caps, Towels, Sheets, Pillows, Bedding, &c., together with

Every Variety of

Travelling and Convenient Articles,

Combining the largest assortment in

THE OUTFITTING LINE,

IN ANY ESTABLISHMENT

IN THE UNITED STATES!

By selecting from this assortment, the trouble of running round to various establishments will be avoided, as here you can find every thing wanted, from a

PICK AXE TO A CAPT. SUTTER

LONG MINING WAISTCOAT.

Another example of advertisements for equipment and supplies for the emigrants who were traveling west.

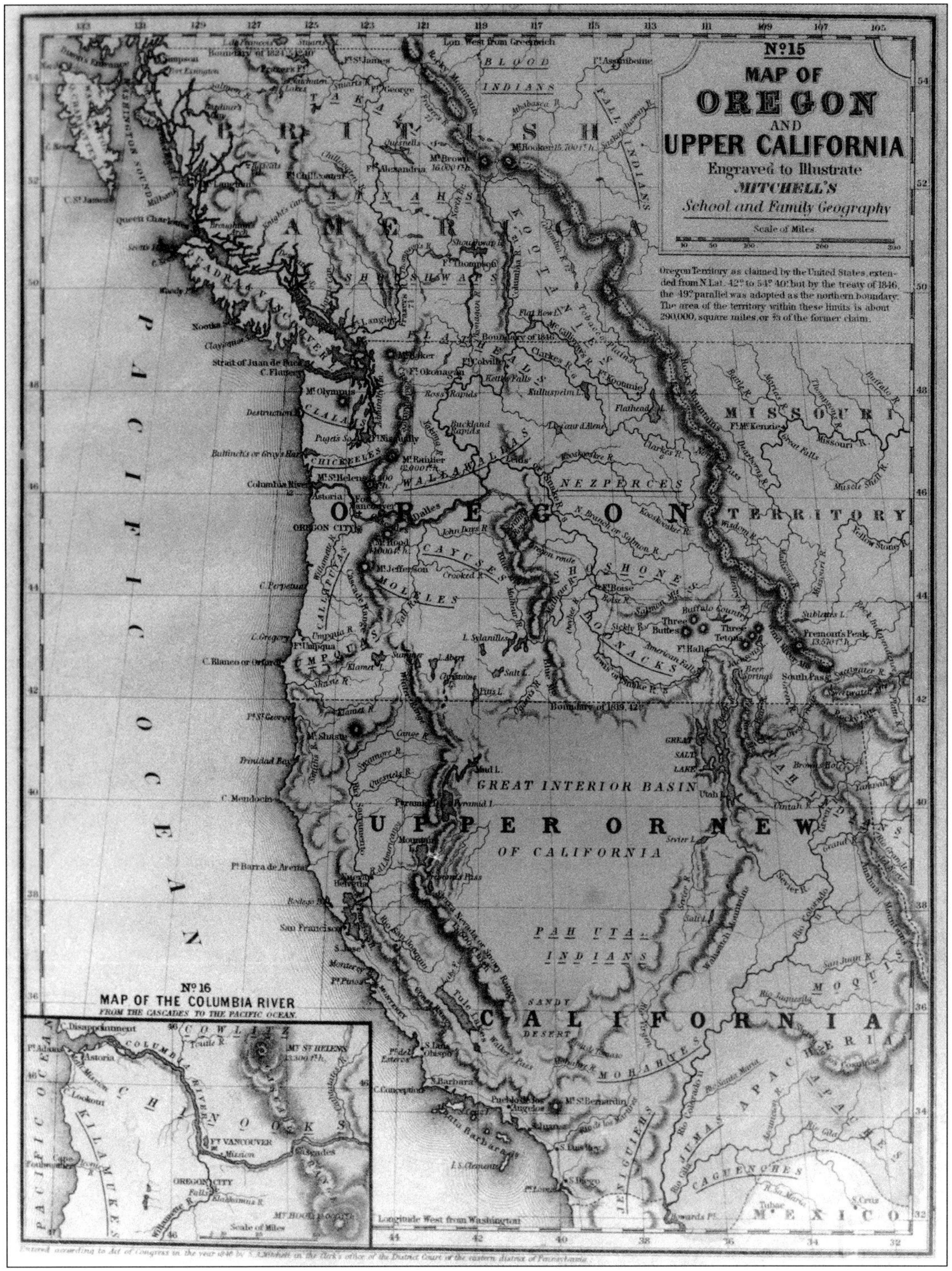

A map of Oregon and Upper or New California in 1846.

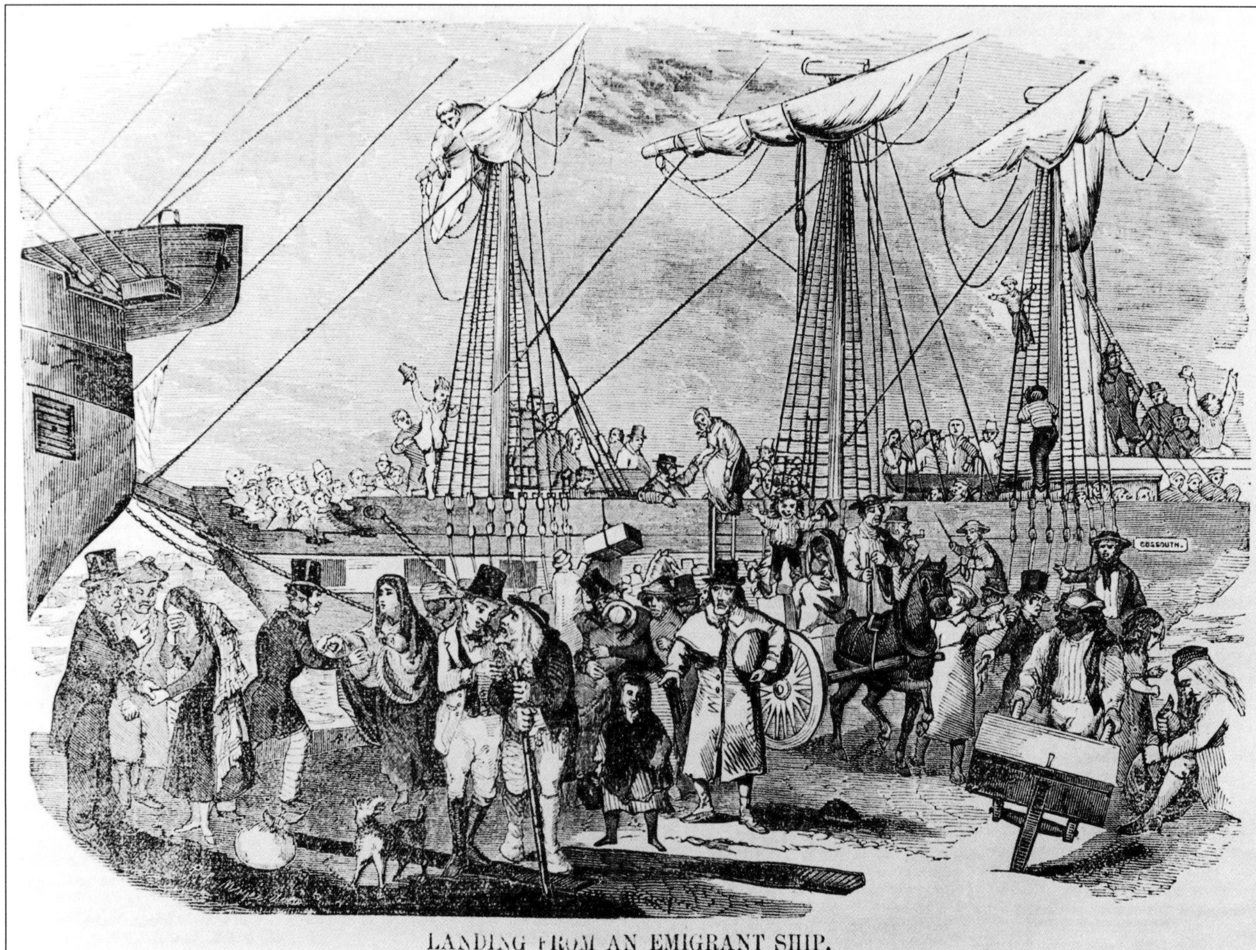

A steel engraving from *Gleason's Pictorial Review* provides us with a fine look at emigrants landing by ship.

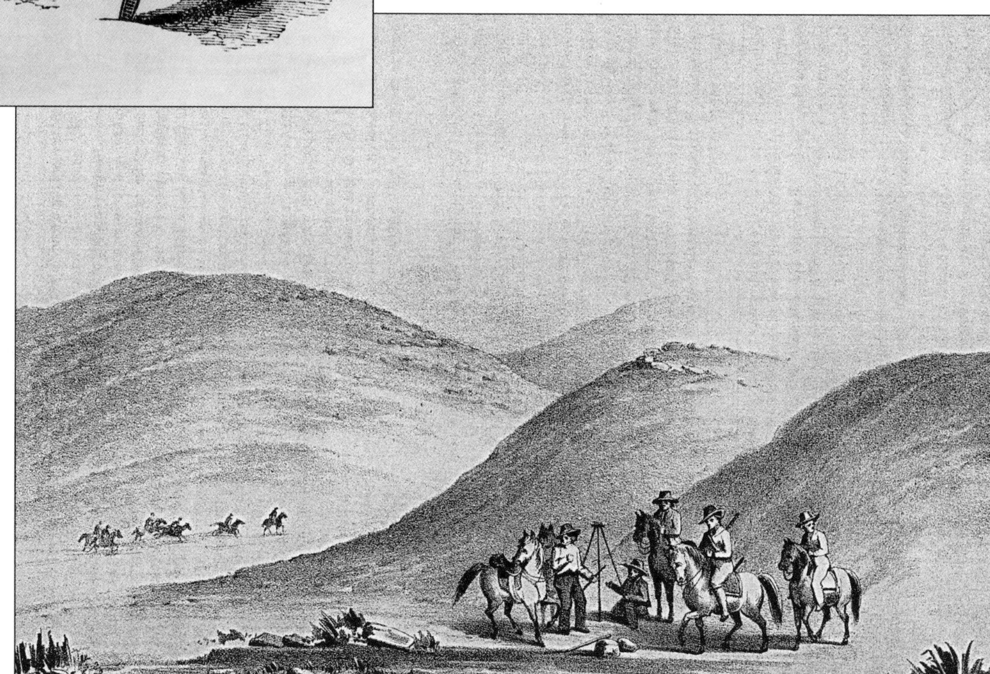

A U.S. Survey drawing showing the entrance to Livermore Pass

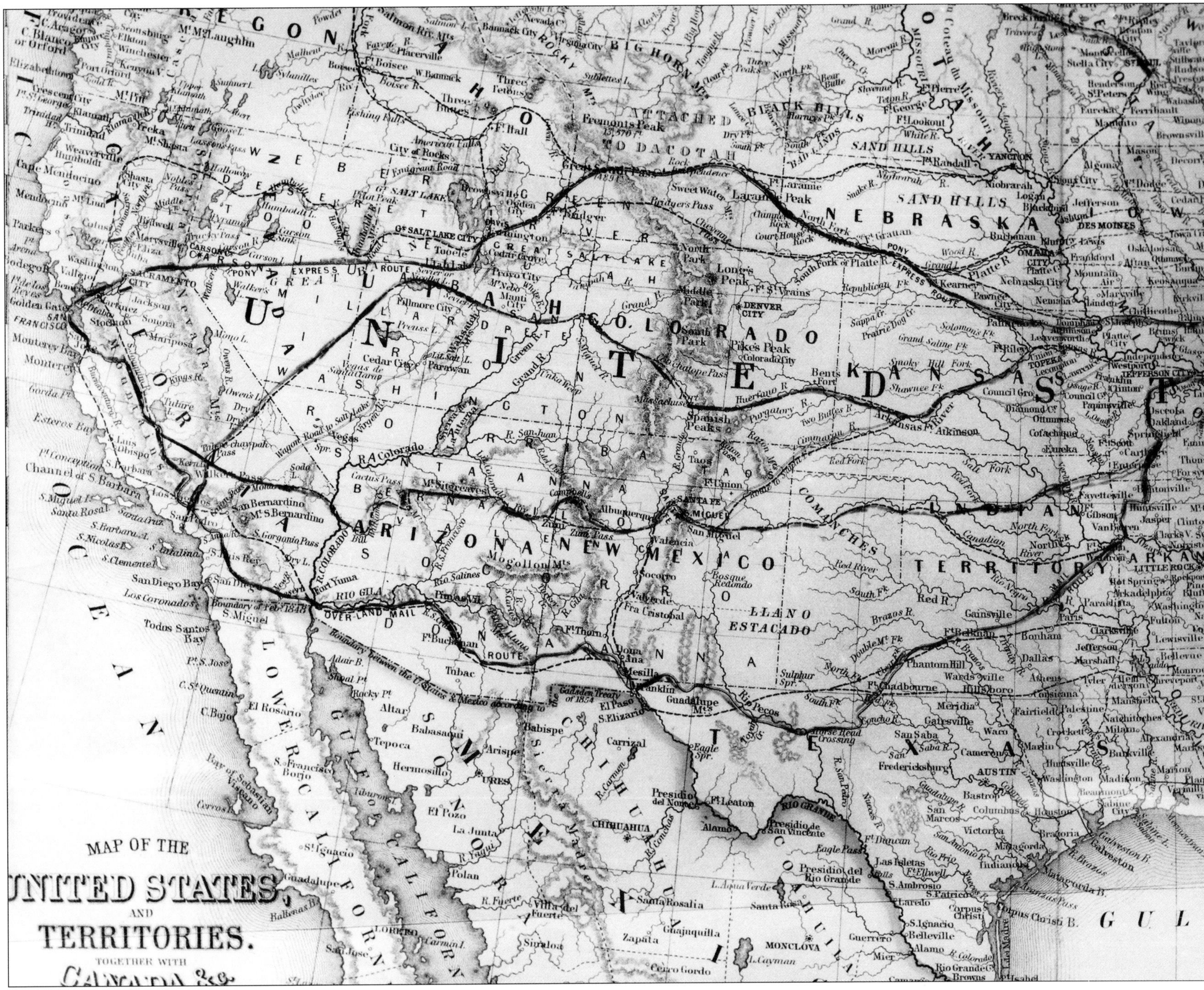

A map of the United States and Territories showing main routes of the Overland Mail Route (to the south), The Pony Express Route (to the north), and several other routes west to California, all going through Indian territories.

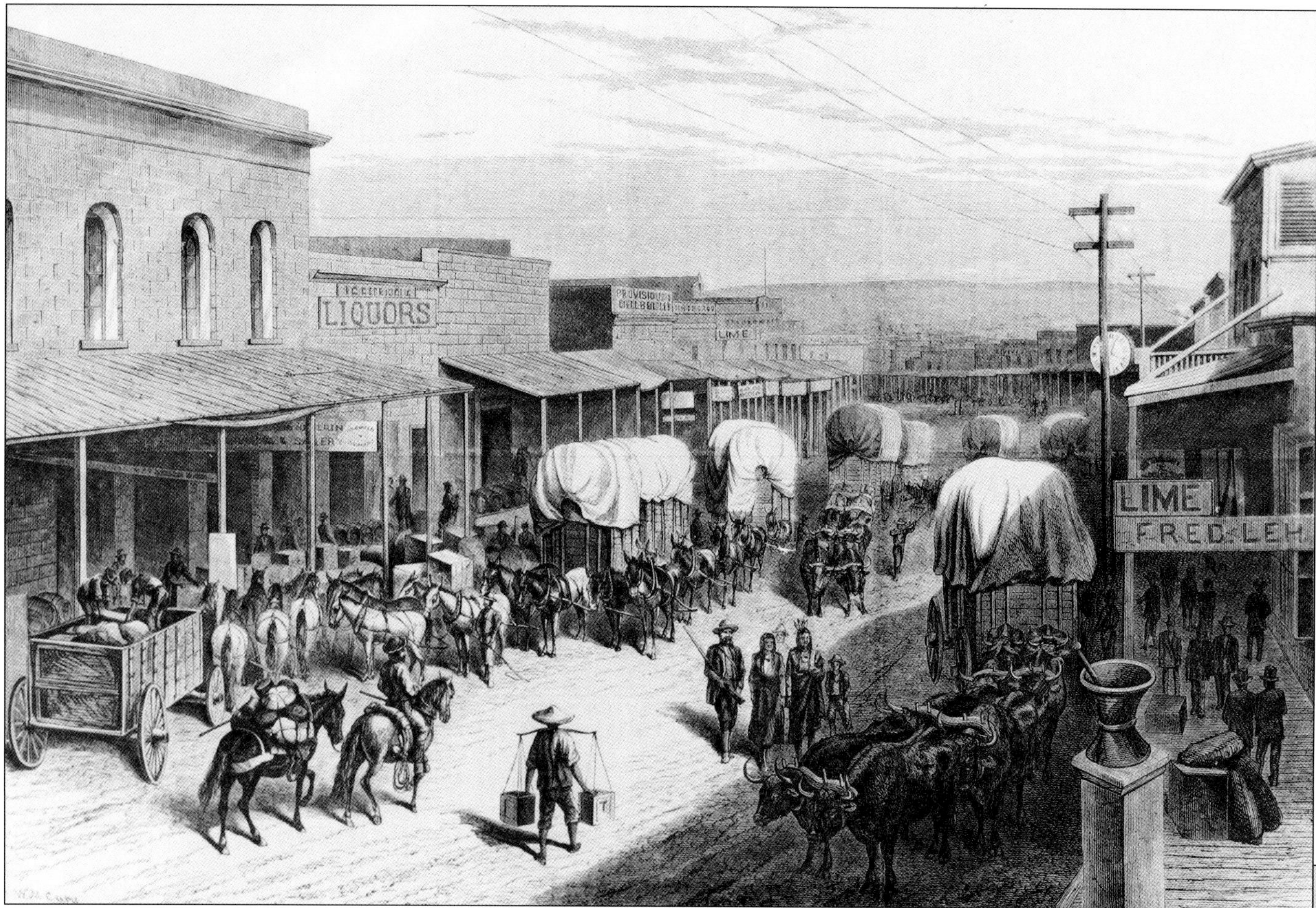

Harper's Weekly provided a fine engraving of wagon trains at Helena, Montana.

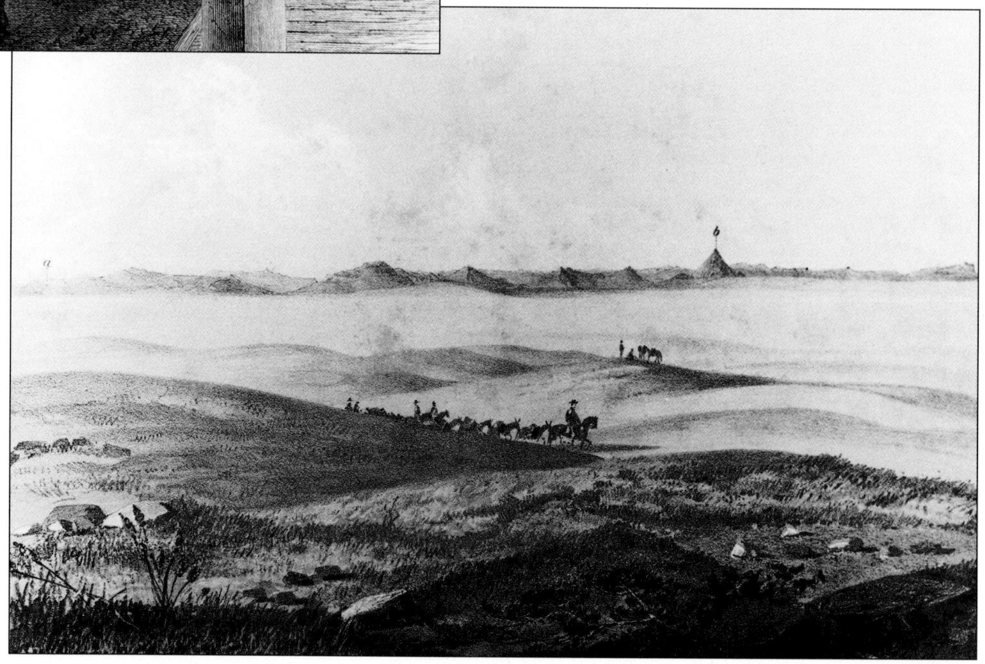

U.S. Survey lithograph of the Rocky Mountains, looking westward from the Lewis and Clark Pass.

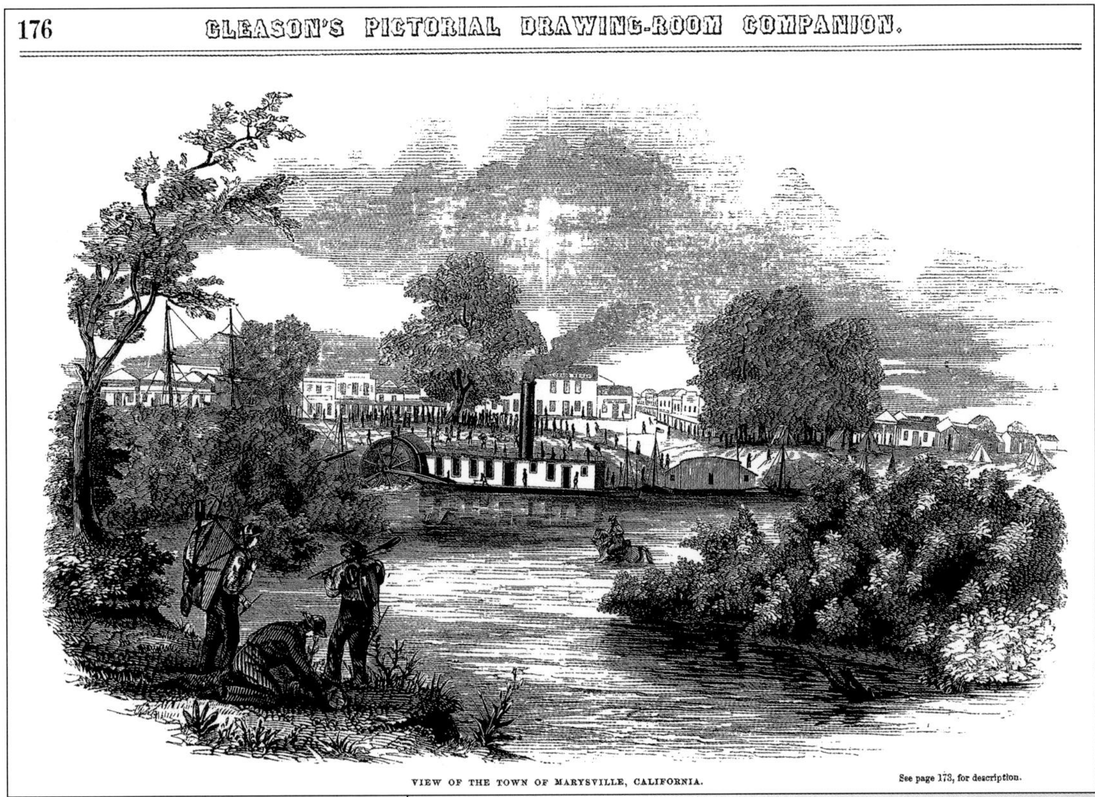

Gleason's Pictorial Review engraving of Marysville, California.

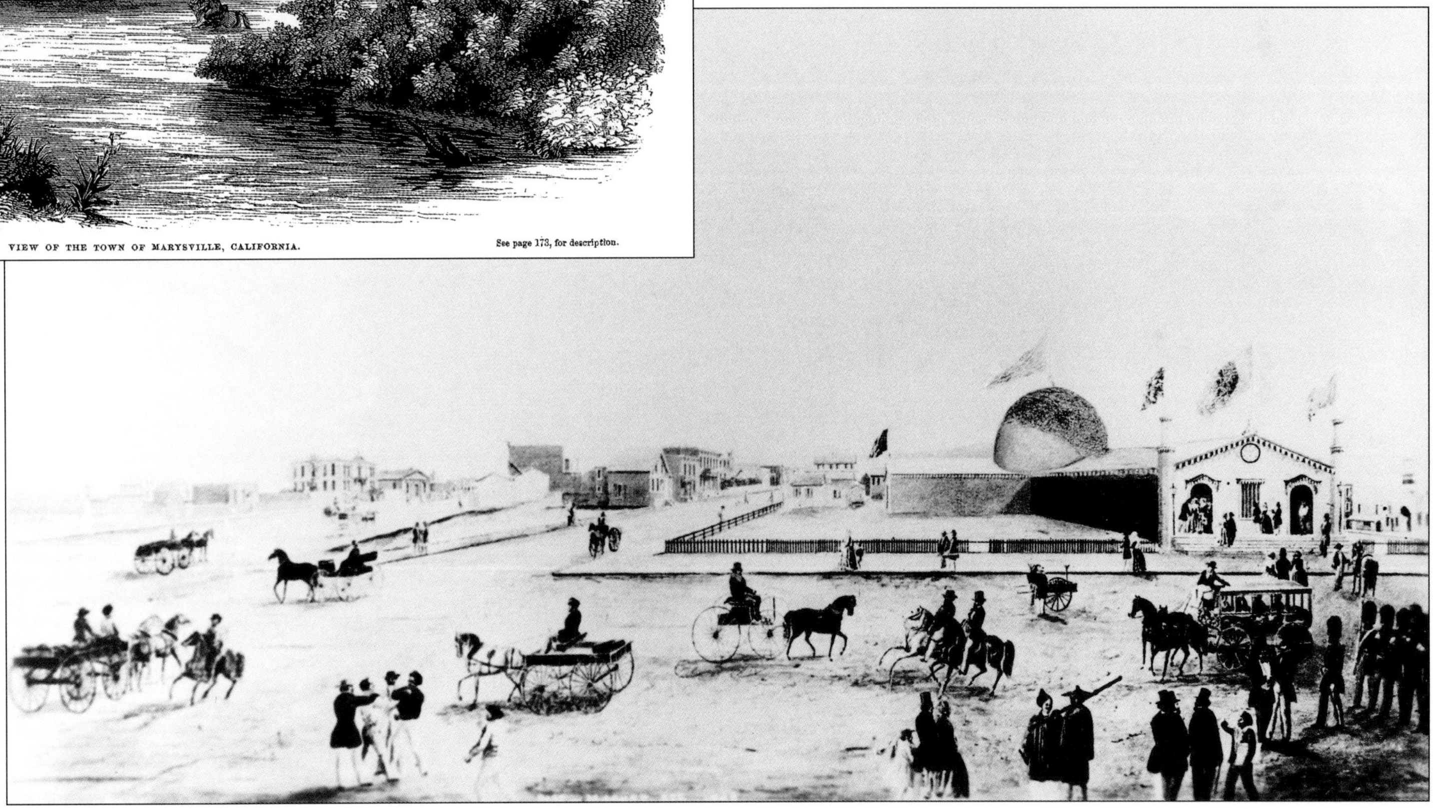

This early drawing of San Francisco in 1850s is identified on the back: "#1. Flat Iron Point-site of Crocker Building, #2. Church of Saint-Patrick, grounds on present site of Palace Hotel, #3. First National Bank site, #4. First Mechanic's Pavilion.

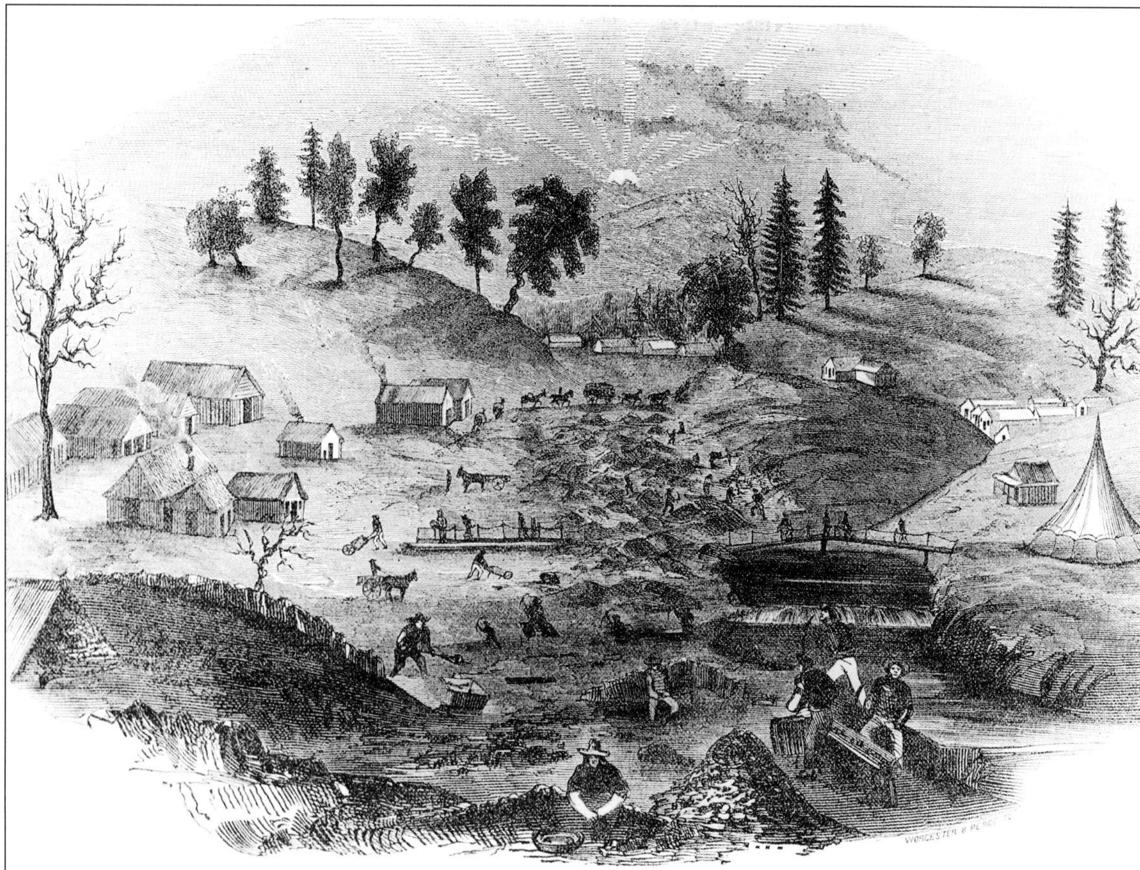

SOUTH MINES, JAMESTOWN, CALIFORNIA.

An early engraving of the South Mines in Jamestown, California.

An early engraving with a view of Boston Ravine, Grass Valley, California. This drawing was taken from a sketch drawn on the spot. It includes the market owned by Holis and Baxter, and the Eagle tavern kept by John West. The gold hill that serves as the background was named Boston Hill, after a Negro who discovered a quartz vein on it.

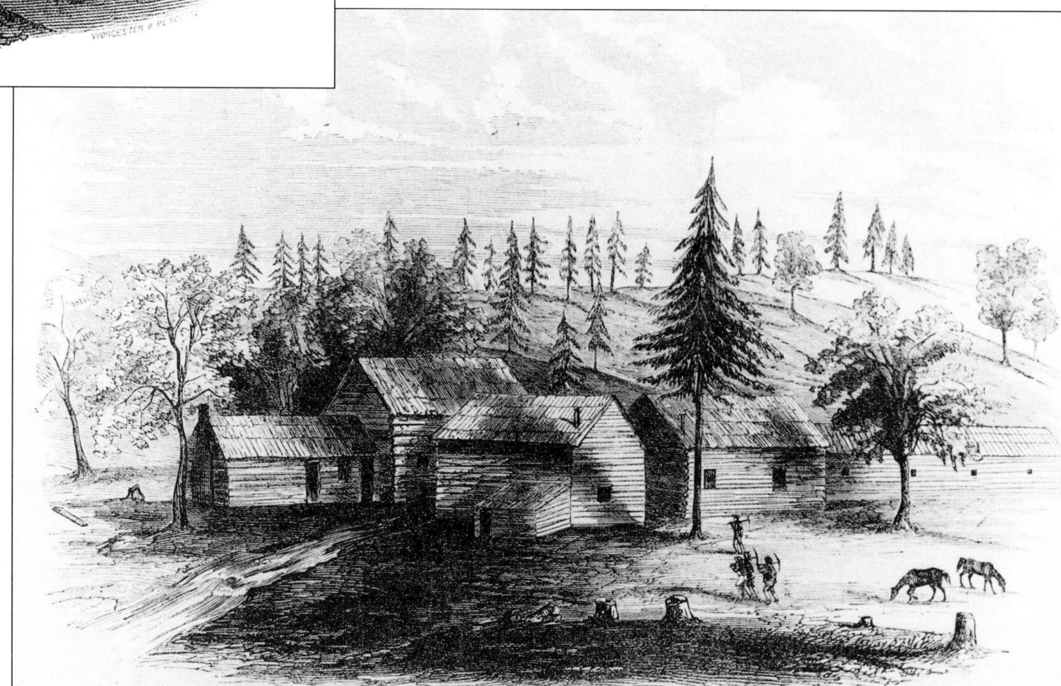

VIEW OF BOSTON RAVINE, GRASS VALLEY, CALIFORNIA.

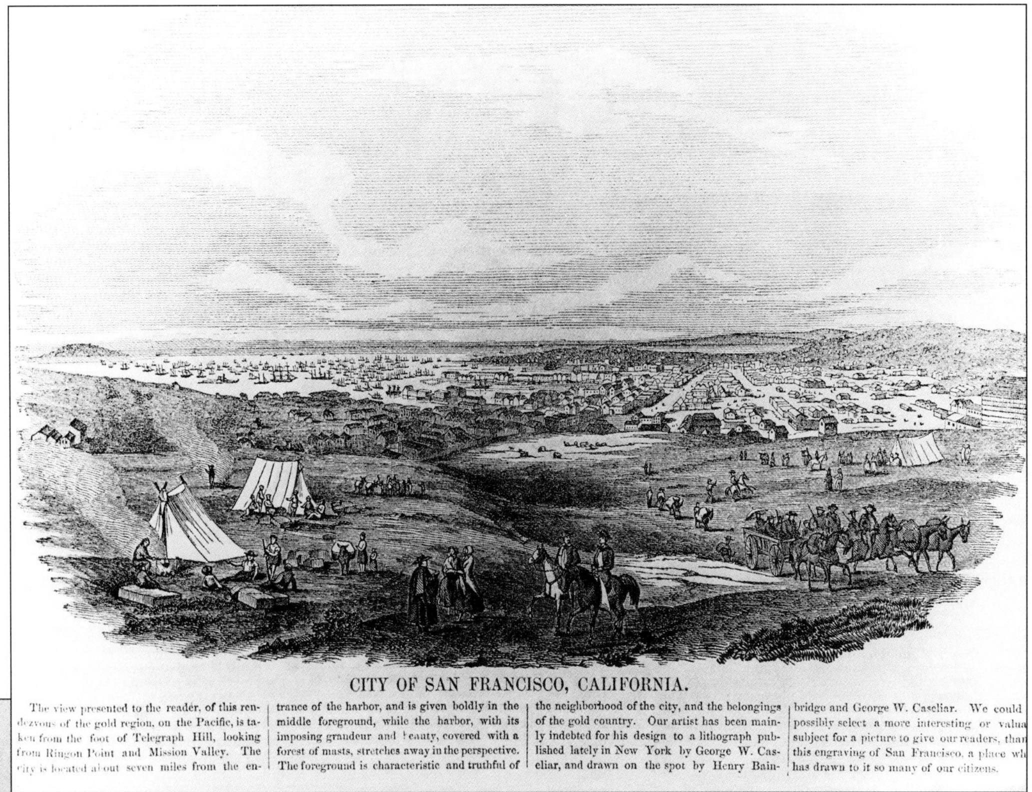

CITY OF SAN FRANCISCO, CALIFORNIA.

The view presented to the reader, of this rendezvous of the gold region, on the Pacific, is taken from the foot of Telegraph Hill, looking from Ringon Point and Mission Valley. The city is located about seven miles from the entrance of the harbor, and is given boldly in the middle foreground, while the harbor, with its imposing grandeur and beauty, covered with a forest of masts, stretches away in the perspective. The foreground is characteristic and truthful of the neighborhood of the city, and the belongings of the gold country. Our artist has been mainly indebted for his design to a lithograph published lately in New York by George W. Casliar, and drawn on the spot by Henry Bainbridge and George W. Casliar. We could possibly select a more interesting or valua subject for a picture to give our readers, than this engraving of San Francisco, a place wh has drawn to it so many of our citizens.

An early engraving of San Francisco, California, showing the harbor below and a few miners heading toward the hills.

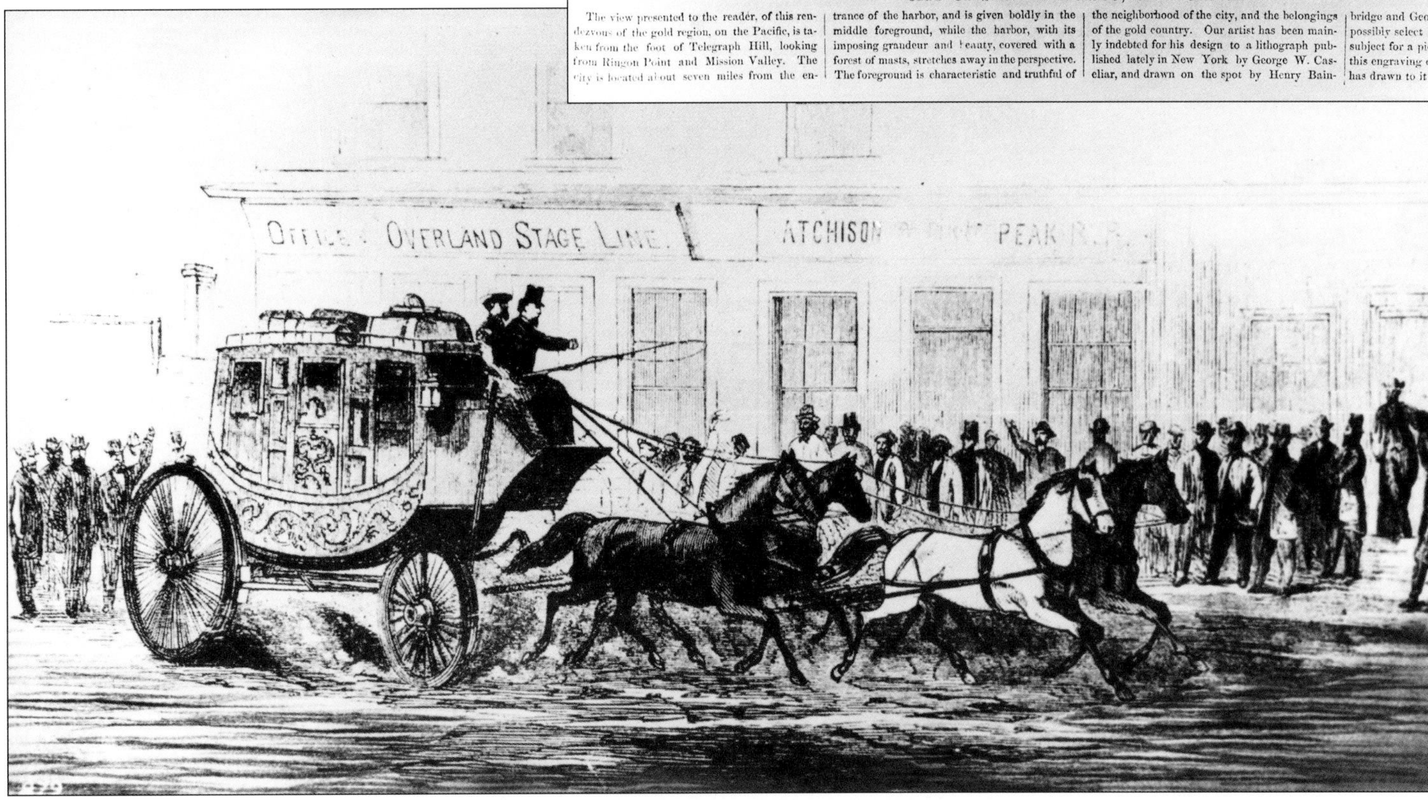

An early drawing of a stage arriving in San Francisco.

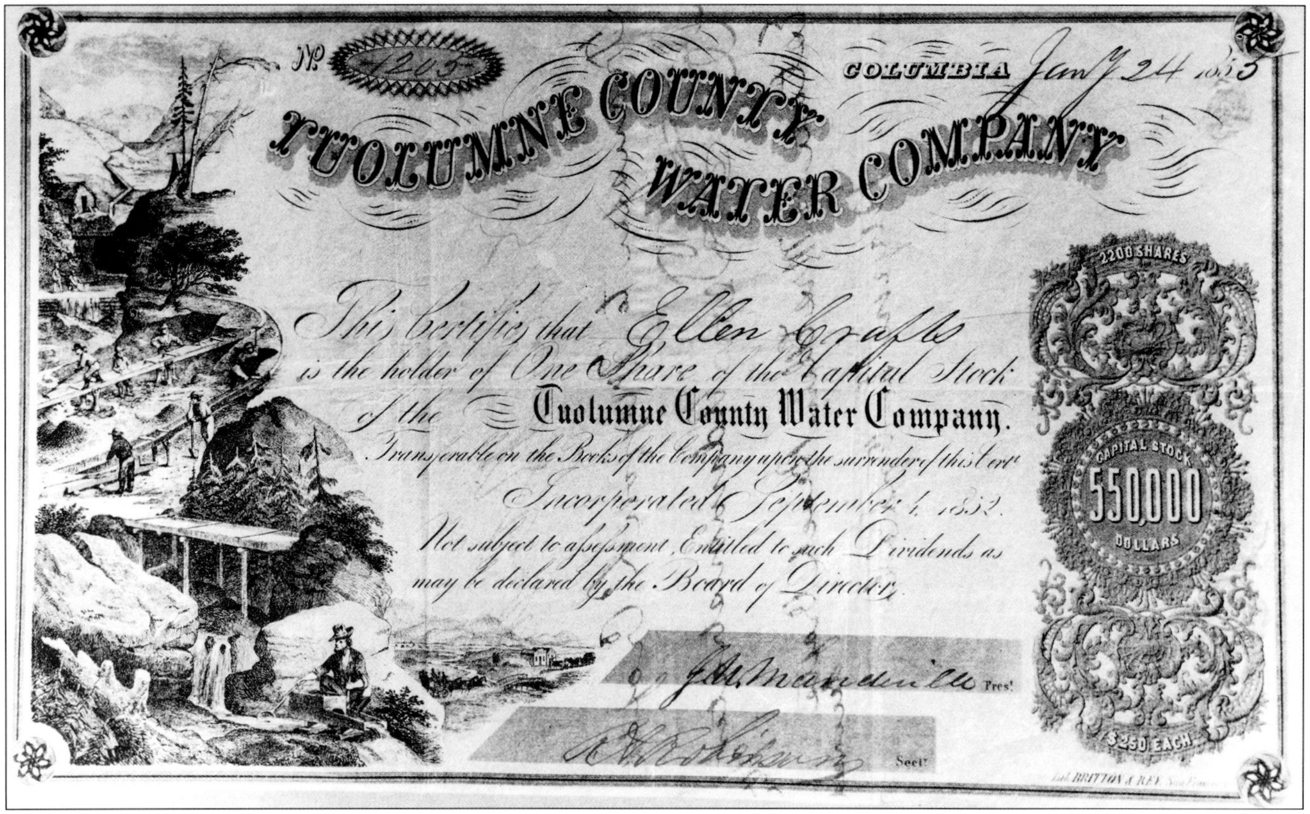

The stock certificate of The Tuolumne County Water Company in Columbia, California. This is a fine example of the art of the engravers who decorated these early mining stocks.

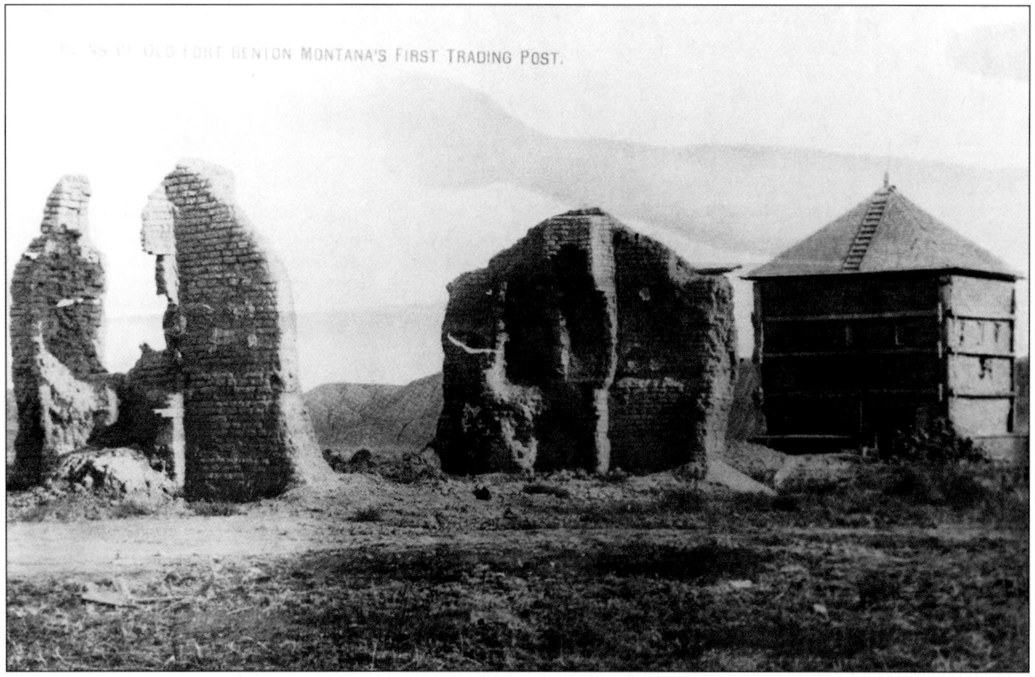

The crumbling remains of Fort Benton, Montana. This was the first trading post in the state of Montana.

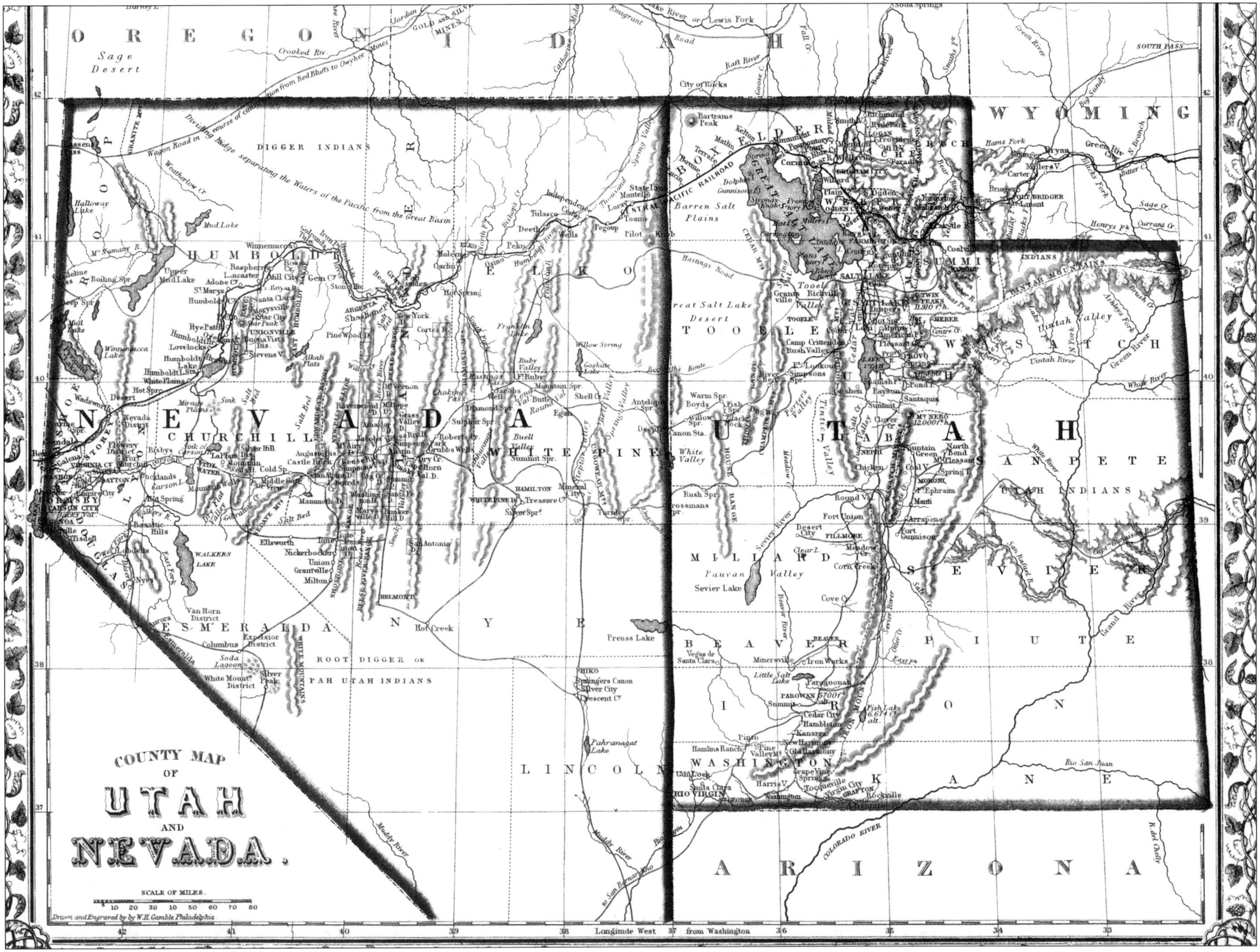

An early map of Utah and Nevada.

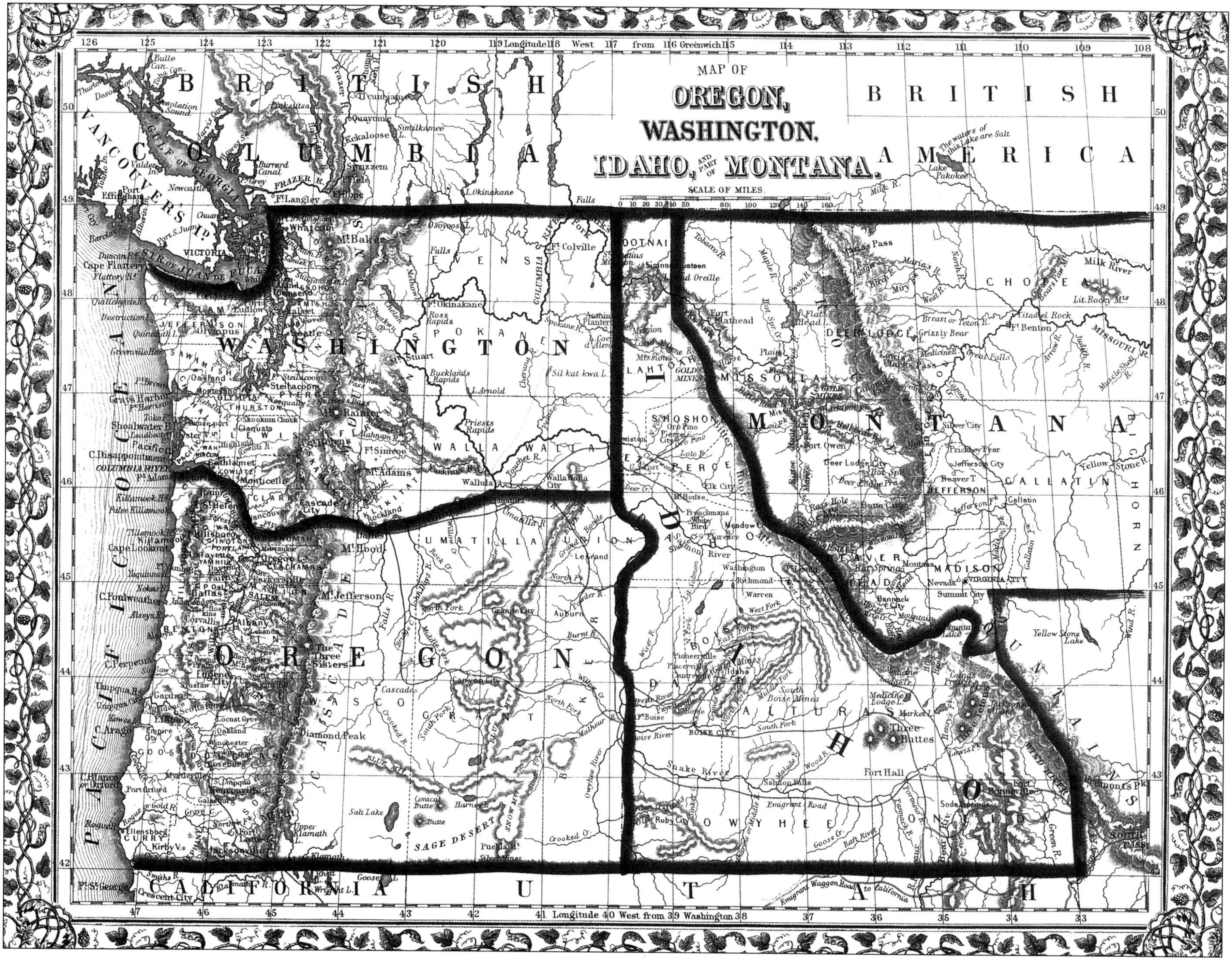

An early map of Oregon, Washington, Idaho, and Montana.

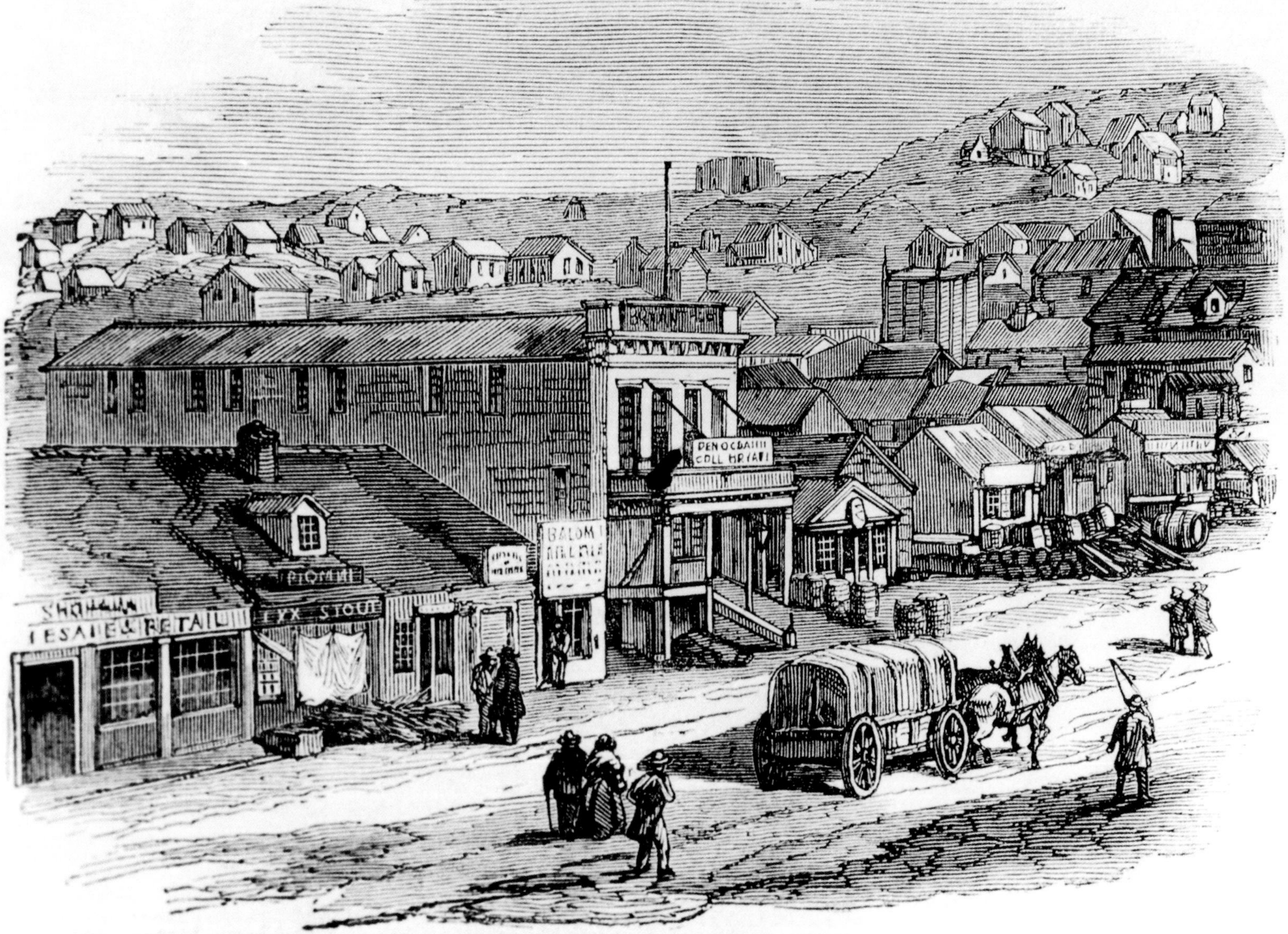

BLAY-PLACE, SAN FRANCISCO.

A street scene in San Francisco, called Blay-Place, looks pretty bleak in this *Harpers* illustration.

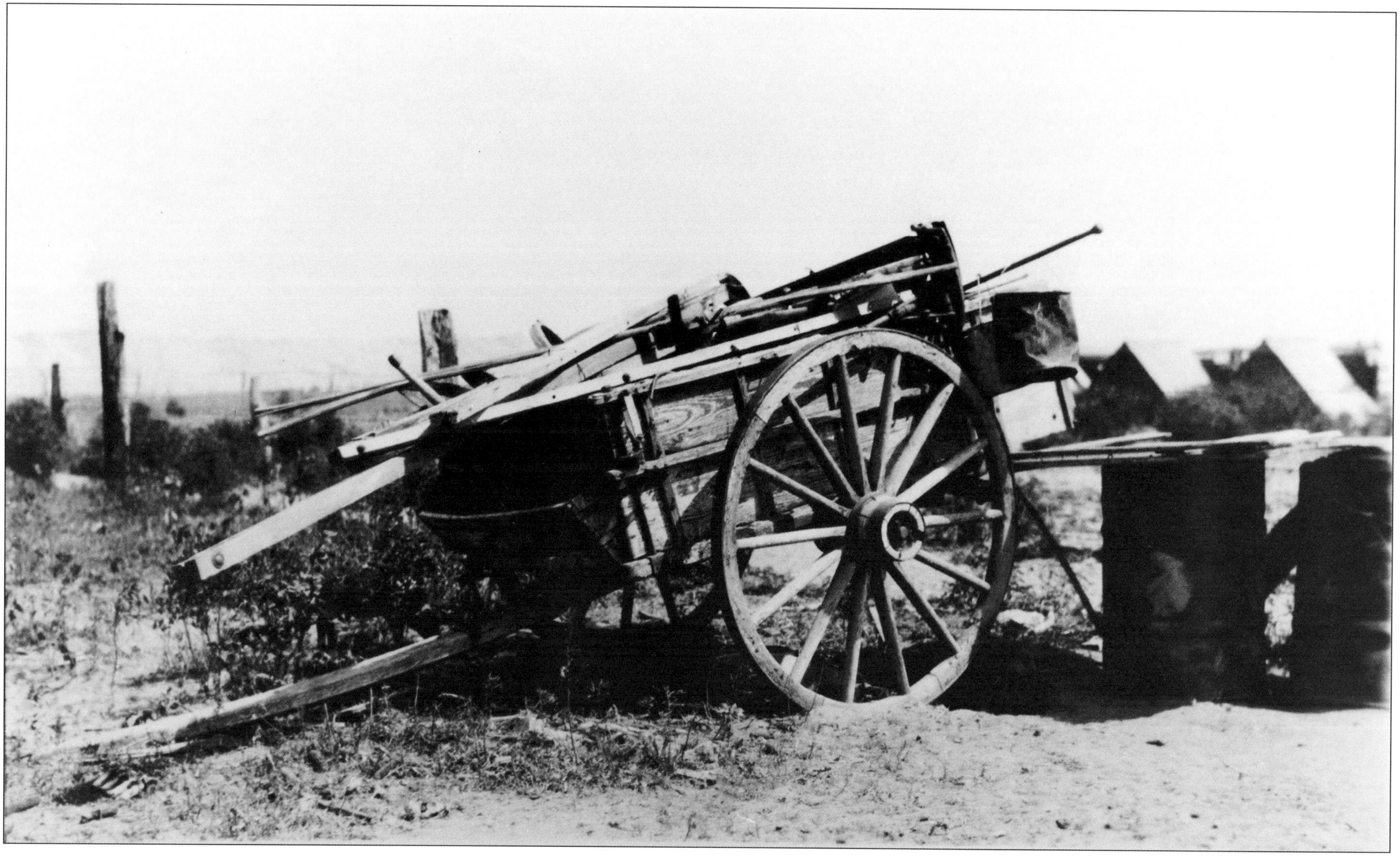

This old army cart stood at Fort Sidney, Nebraska. It is now in the possession of the Nebraska Historical Society at Lincoln Nebraska. The photo is by Emil Kapac in 1931 who is from Oshkosh, Nebraska.

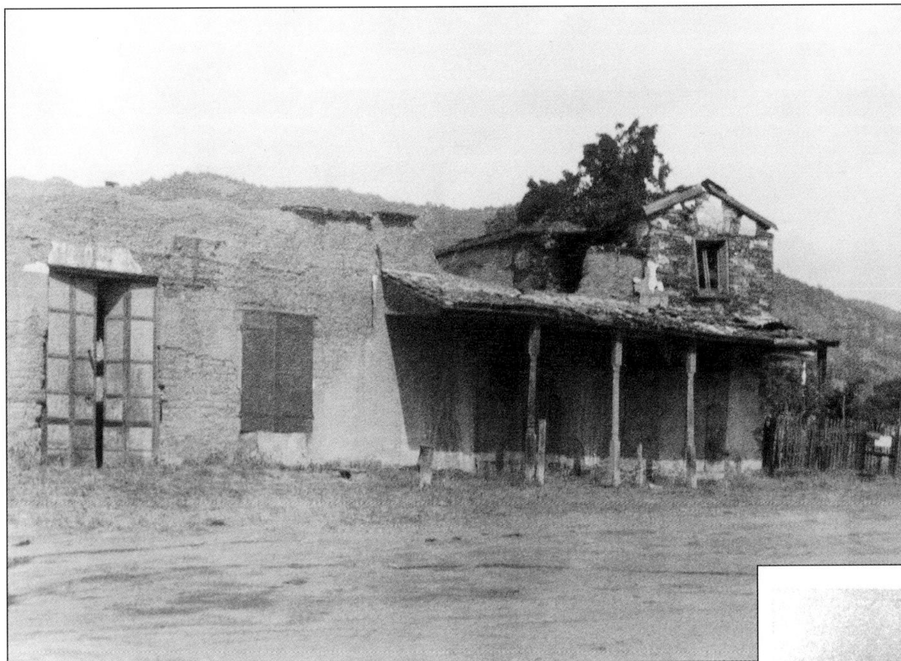

The crumbling buildings in early Bear Valley, California. Notice the heavy steel doors on the windows and door.

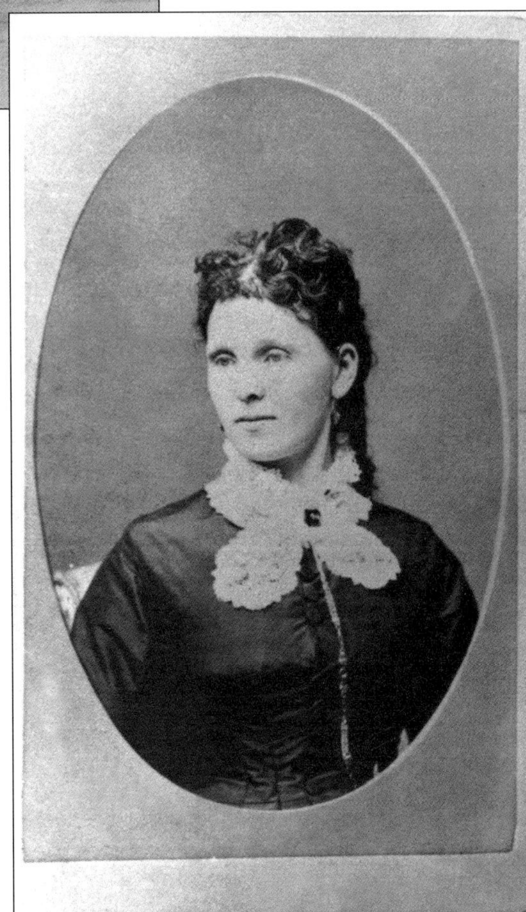

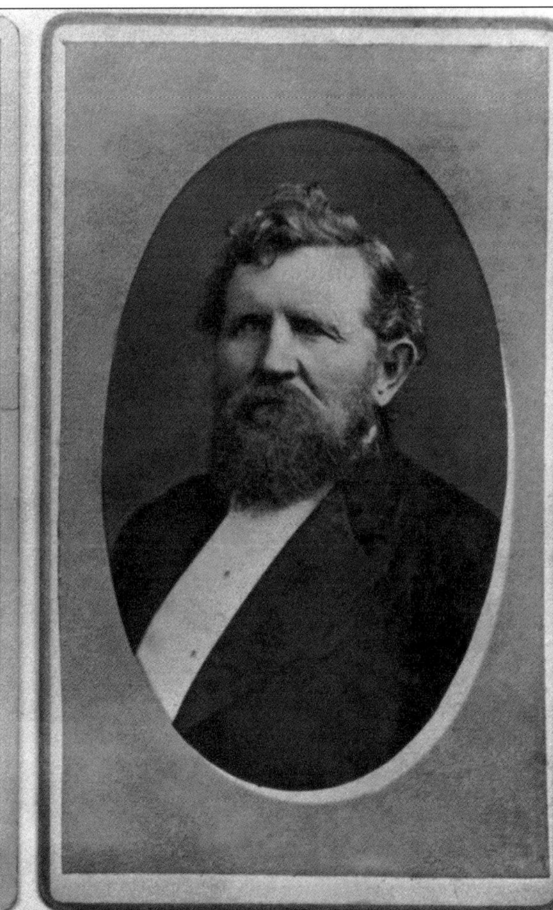

Photos of Henry Van Sickle and his wife, Julia Van Vleck. These were early citizens and builders of Genoa, Nevada, where they operated a hotel and blacksmith shop. Julia came across the plains to Placerville, California, to meet Henry. They both died in 1894.

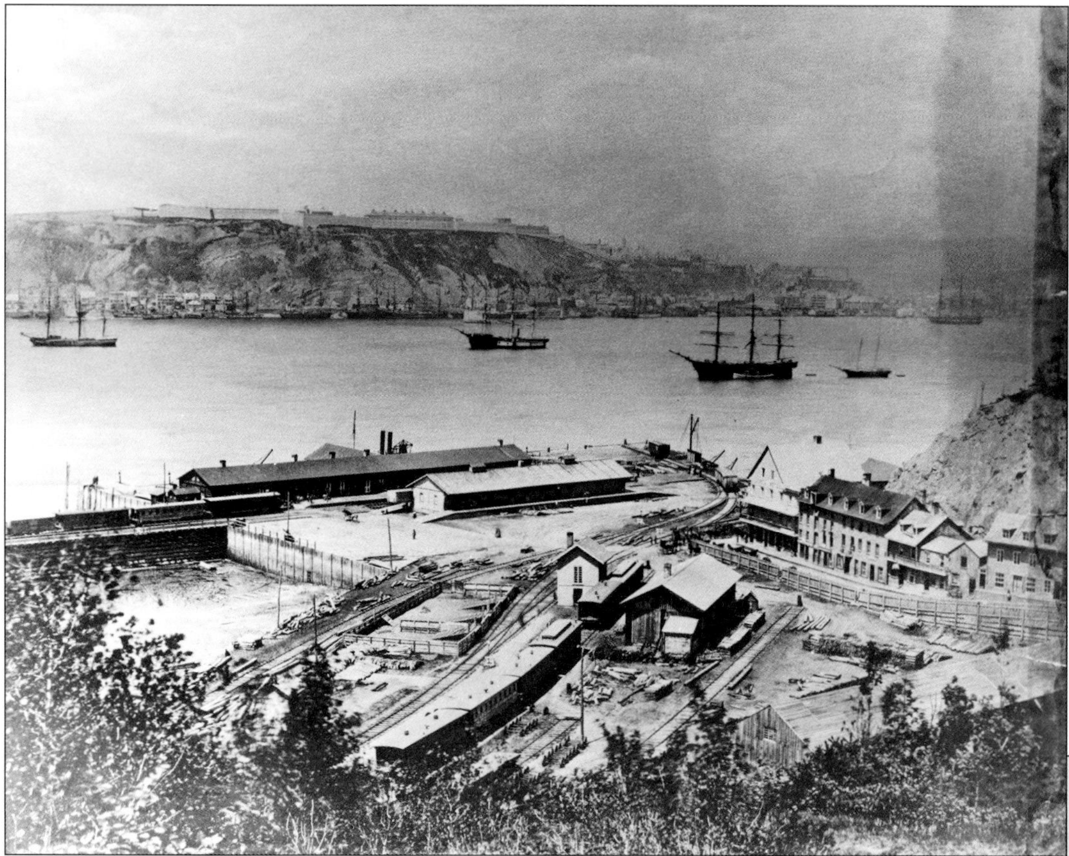

An albumen photo of the harbor where Great Lakes shipping took place around Port Huron, Michigan. They are hard to see, but there is a lineup of stages along the street on the right.

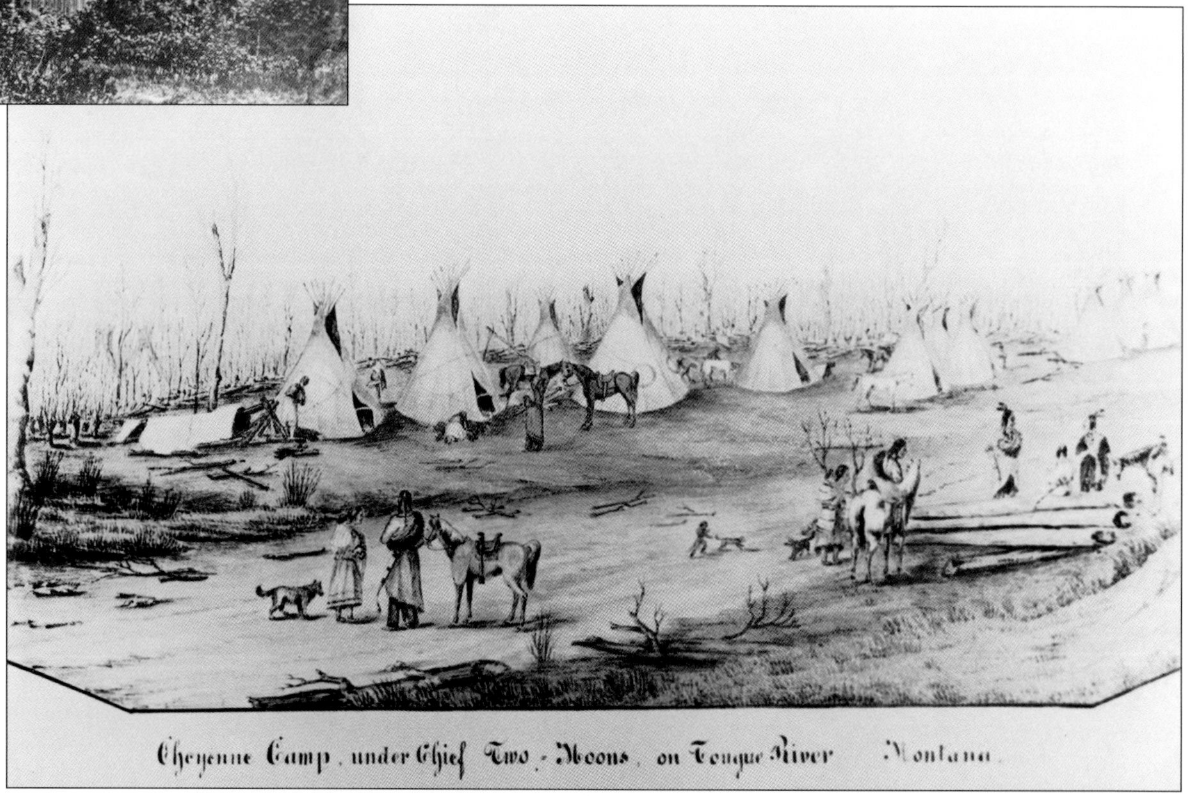

A Cheyenne camp under Chief Two Moons, along the Tongue River, Montana.

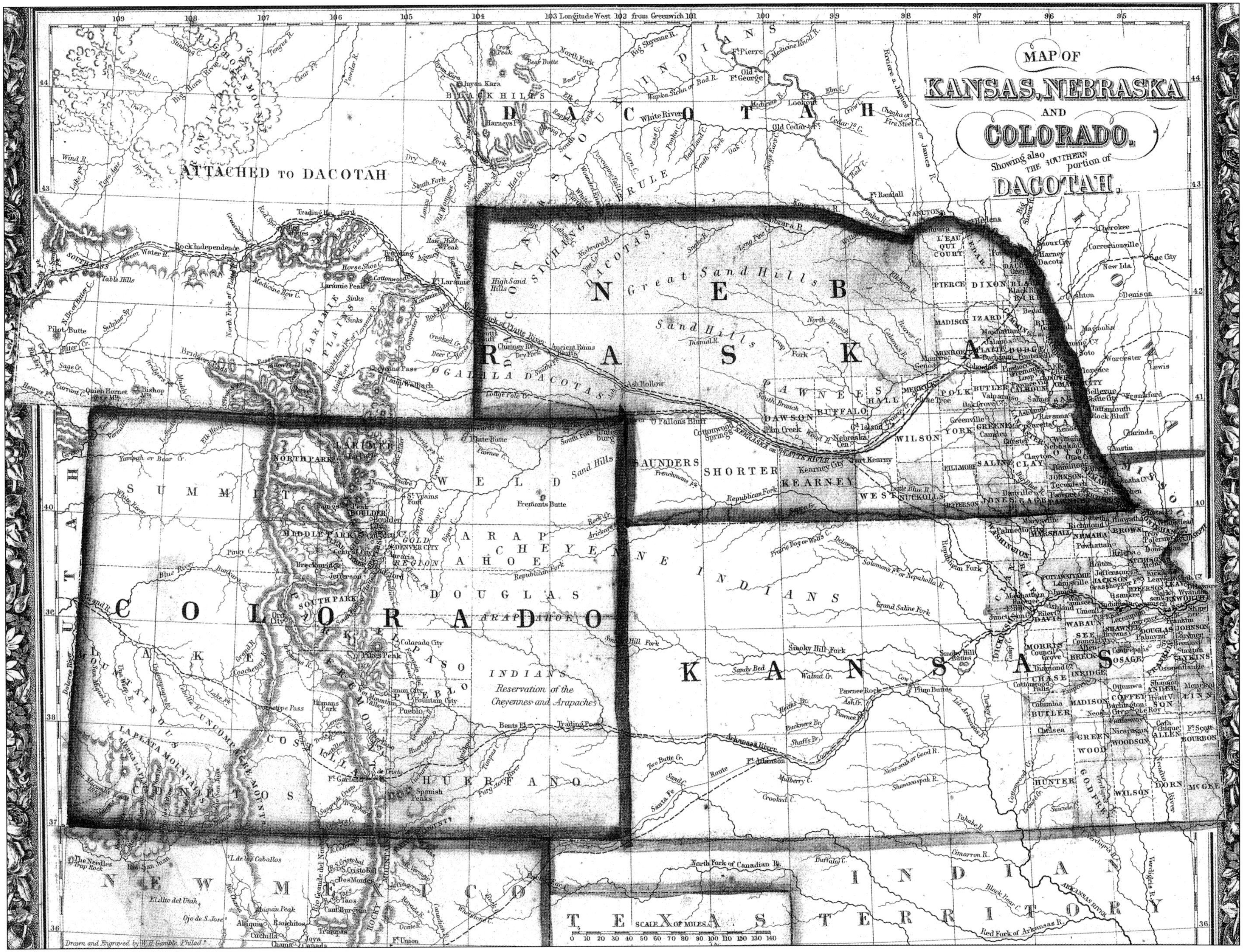

An early map of Kansas, Nebraska, and Colorado showing the state "Dacotah."

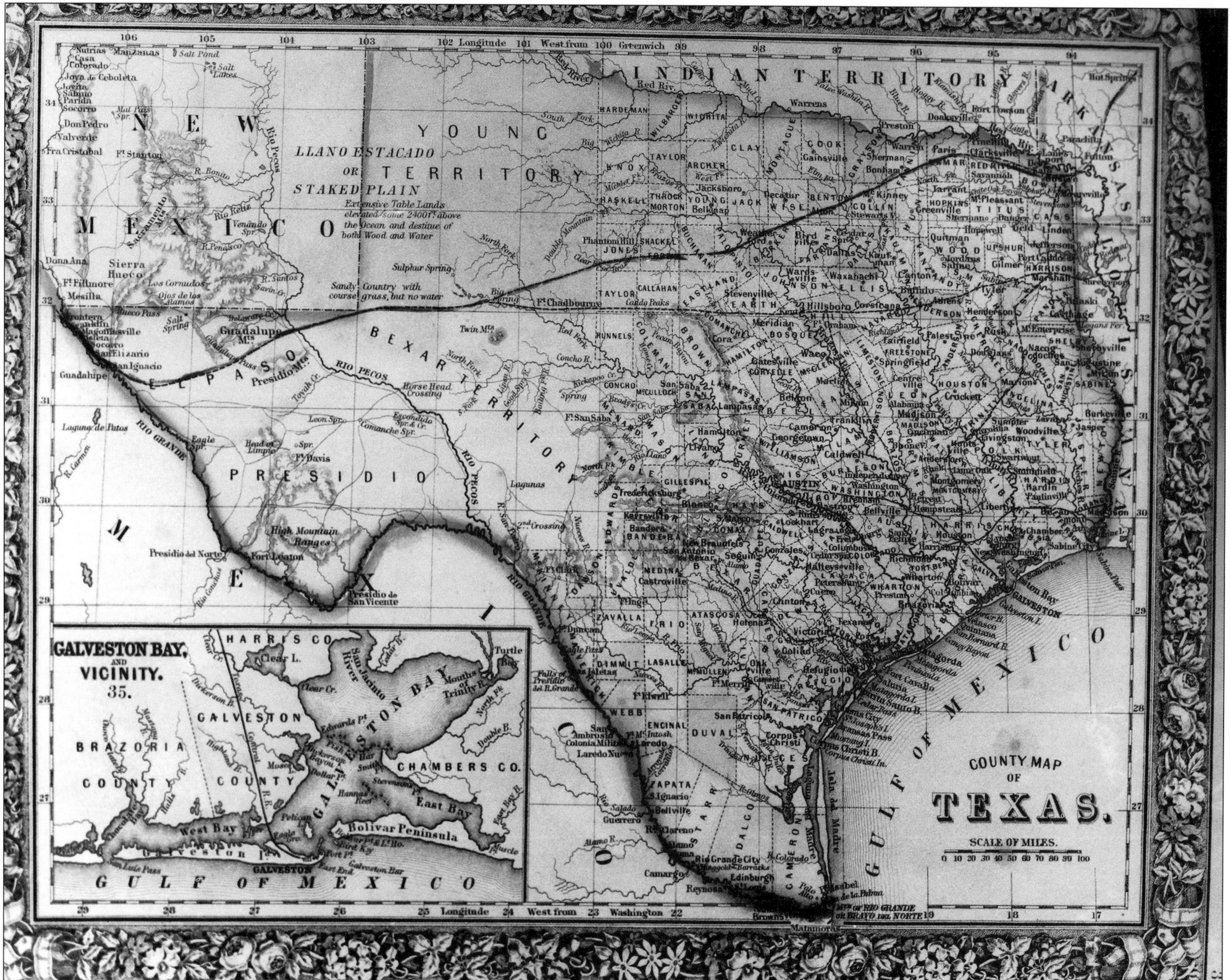

An early map of Texas, showing some of the main routes leading to the West.

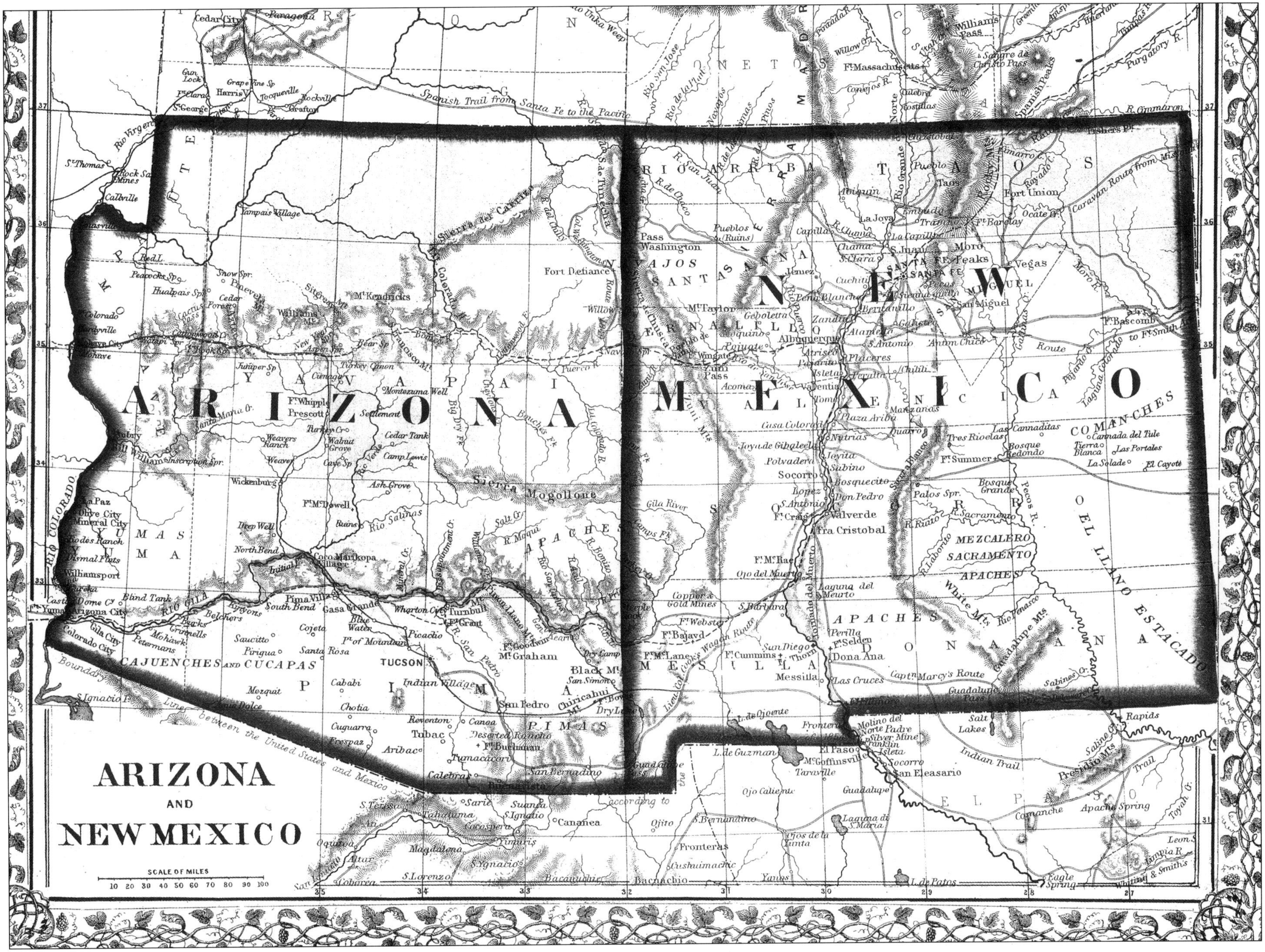

An early map of Arizona and New Mexico, showing the Overland routes through these states.

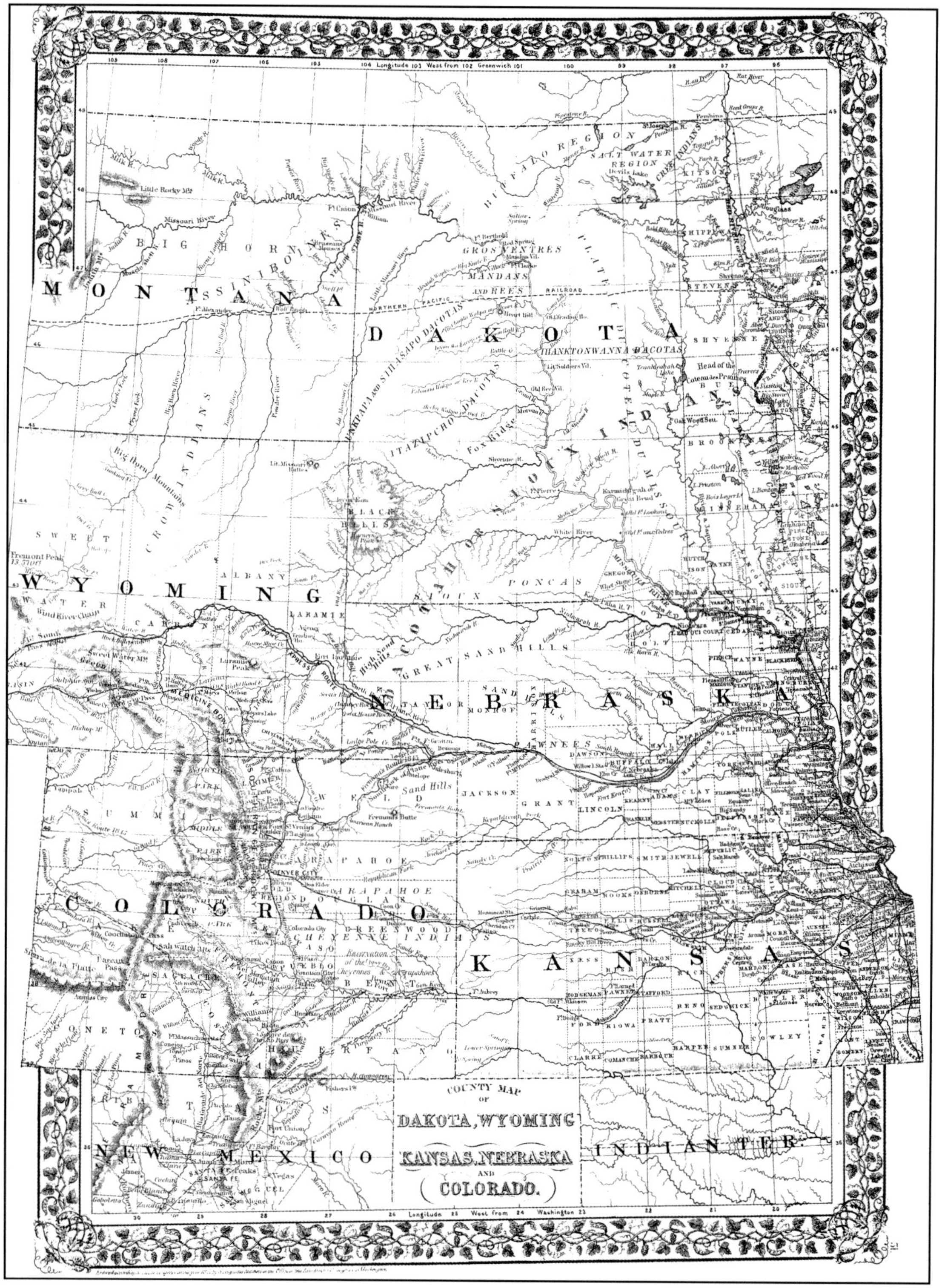

An early map of Dakota, Wyoming, Kansas, Nebraska, and Colorado showing some Overland routes into Indian Territories.

Chapter 2

1849-1860

In the East, the advertising in most of the newspapers was pitching would-be emigrants to buy "outfits" for the New El Dorado. At Oak Hall in Boston, for example, the long list of things needed to get you wherever you were going, took up quarter pages of the local newspaper, with low prices as a come-on. For mining articles the list included mining clothes, jackets, overalls, stout pants, socks, coats, and more. Prices ranged from $3.50 to $15.00 for blankets or coats; $2.00 to $2.50 for Capt. Sutter's long waist coat; $6.00 to $8.00 for India rubber coats and capes; $0.75 to $1.25 for red flannel shirts; $2.00 to $3.50 for traveling trunks; and $5.00 to $6.00 for Bowie knives and a belt for pistols.

Beginning at St. Louis, the stagecoaches took several different overland routes to the West. Butterfield's route went south through Texas at El Paso, through New Mexico to Tucson Arizona, and then to Los Angeles, California, and north to San Francisco. On the Butterfield Stage line, a trip from St. Louis to Los Angeles in 1858 took 22 days and the fare was $90.00.

The Overland route went north using the Oregon Trail to Fort Laramie, to Fort Bridger in Wyoming, and on to many more stage stops and small forts along the way. Continuing the trip west, they would swing up to Fort Hall and then go southwest on the California Trail to Sacramento, California.

These trips were usually on Concord stagecoaches with a conductor and driver on top. Every five hundred miles a new conductor would take over for the tired worker. The passengers were allowed forty pounds of luggage and they could stow more in a handy port manteau or large purse in their lap.

When the Civil War broke out, all travel along the southern route was discontinued. This meant the travelers would be on roads further north going through Indian territory, where stage stops and small forts were farther apart. They had to carry arms, as they would be on roads well scouted by the Indians. In addition, in the fall season the weather would change overnight and they could be stranded in a snowstorm at higher elevations.

During the early expansion into the West it was important that the U.S. Army had built forts to protect the emigrants from the hostile Indians. With the average speed of the wagon trains about 5 miles a day, and the hours it took, it would take days and days to make it to the next stage stop and outpost.

A story out of Oatman Flats, Arizona, illustrates some of the danger the emigrants faced on their sojourn. A family was part of a large convoy of emigrants traveling west when they became separated from the rest. They were attacked by a band of Apaches and the entire family was murdered except for three children. Two young girls who were carried away, and a son escaped. Although badly wounded, he crawled many miles to a ranch where he was helped by local hunters. He later recovered one of his sisters by paying a large ransom, but was told that the other sister had died.

All of the western states had block houses or forts built along the trails for the Overland Stages to rest or to provide protection against the Indians. As early as 1804, forts of log cabins or dug outs were built to protect against attacks.

I have listed some of the important forts and stage stops that the Overland Mail coaches would stop at and the reasons for them being there.

Arizona

- Fort Defiance, built in 1851 in the Navajo Valley. The Navajo kept this fort under siege constantly until it was abandoned in 1861.
- Yuma Depot, was built in 1864 and was used as a supply depot.
- Fort Bowie was built in 1862 and was the site of constant fights with the Apache near Apache Pass. The captured Chief Geronimo and his followers were sent from here to prison in Florida.

California;

- Camp at San Luis Rey, built in 1846. It had a battalion of troops to protect the travelers.
- Camp Stanislaus was built in 1849 at the sight of Knights Ferry on the river, thirty miles from Stockton.
- Fort Sutter, built in 1845, started as a trading post.

• Camp at Warner's Ranch, built in 1850. It was on the emigrants' road and a U.S. Mail route and was protected by the 2nd Infantry.
• Fort Benson, built in 1846. It was established because of land ownership in the San Bernardino area.
• Camp Bitter Sweet, built in 1859. It was a desert outpost on the stage route between Los Angeles and Las Vegas.
• Fort Defiance, built in 1849 to guard the ferry across the Colorado river. It was four miles from Fort Yuma.
• Camp Cantonment, in 1849, had only tents and huts for the soldiers who were stationed there to protect the gold diggers.
• Camp Grant in 1863 was built to protect the U.S. Mail route.

Colorado

Most of the forts built in Colorado were there to protect the prospectors and travelers.

• Fort Davy Crockett was built in 1836 and was a fur trading post.
• Bent's Fort was built in 1832 by the Bent brothers who turned a profit trading with the Indians. This was the first fort built west of Independence, Missouri.
• Fort Collins was built in 1864 to watch over the Utes and the stage route.

Idaho

Many army posts were built along the emigrant trail to protect the settlers from Indians.

• Fort Sherman, built in 1878 and named after the Union Army General
• Fort Boise, was built in 1863 to protect the U.S. Mails and emigrants from hostiles.
• Fort Hall, built in 1870 near the trading post to guard against the Bannock Indians, who had their reservation near by.
• Camp Lander, an 1865 army post near Fort Hall, built to patrol the Oregon Trail.
• Camp Lyon, built in 1865, to keep the peace along the stage routes in southwestern Idaho.

Kansas

Along the Sante Fe Trail men built forts to fight off the attacking Indian raiders.

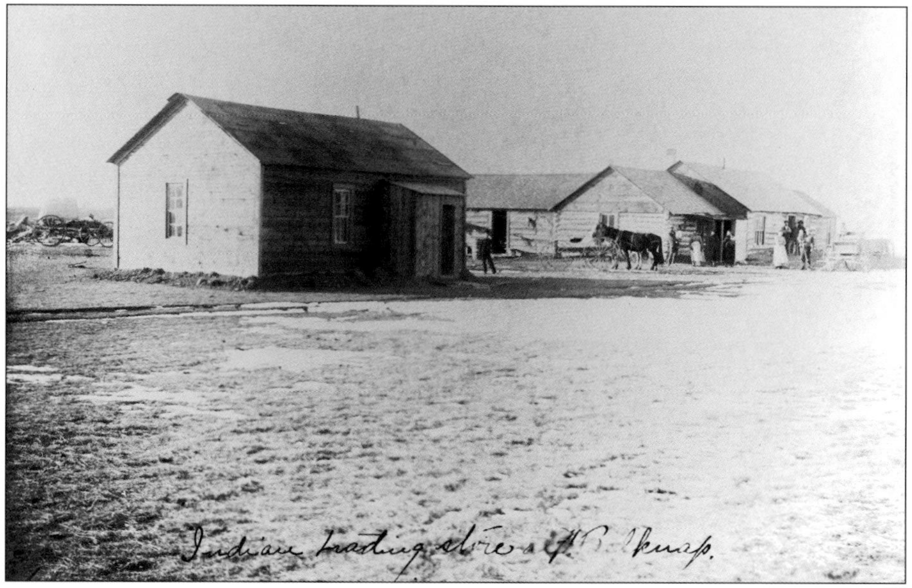

This very early photo was taken at Fort Belknap, Montana, near Yellowstone. The Indian trading cabin in the photo has several children, Indians, and civilians looking toward the photographer, James Mantiath.

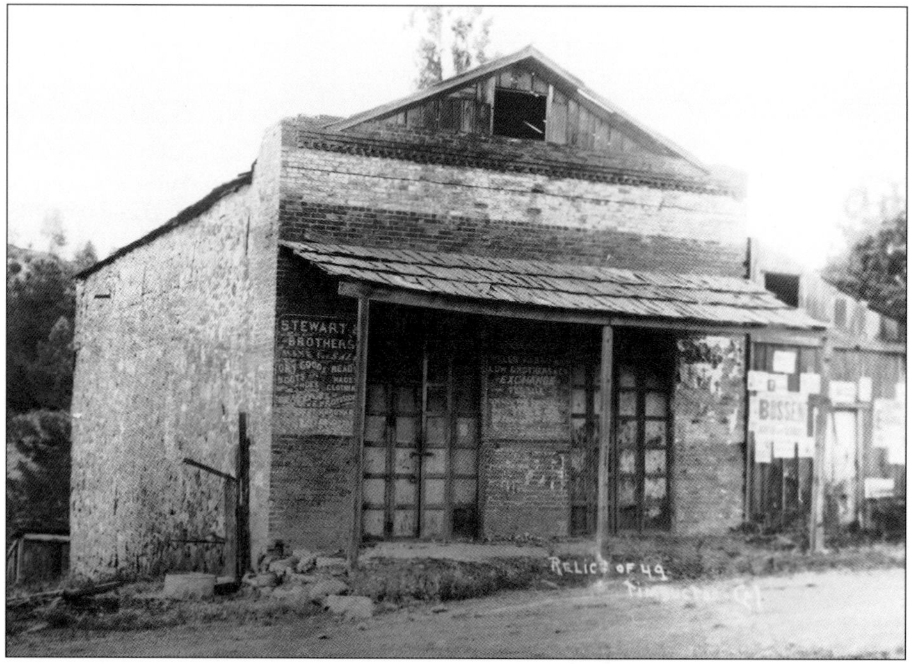

An old store that sold clothing and equipment is all that remains of the town called Timbuctoo, California.

- The detachment at Carlysle Stage station was built in 1865.
- Castle Rocks Creek stage station was built in 1865 for the Smoky Hill stage route.
- Chalk Bluffs Station was built in 1865 and lasted until the Cheyenne attacked, killing all the stock tenders and burning the station.
- Fort Dodge was built in 1864 to fight off the many Indian attacks and stop a riot of civilians at nearby Dodge City.
- Fort Downer was built in 1865 as a stage stop and was used by General Custer until 1867.
- Grinnel Springs station was a short-lived stage stopover.
- Henshaw's Station was built in 1865 and was the first stage stop east of Fort Wallace on the Smoky Hill route.

Montana

- Fort Assiniboine, built in 1879, was the largest military post in Montana.
- Fort Belknap, built in 1871, was a trading post center and named after the Indian agent.
- Fort Benton was built in 1846 as a trading post and to protect the population of the town of Benton, which was the headquarters of Steamboat Navigation Company along the Missouri river.
- Fort Smith was famous for the "hay field fight," when just thirty-one soldiers fought off eight hundred attacking Cheyenne.
- Fort Custer was built in 1877. One thousand soldiers were stationed there to keep the peace after the Custer massacre of 1876.

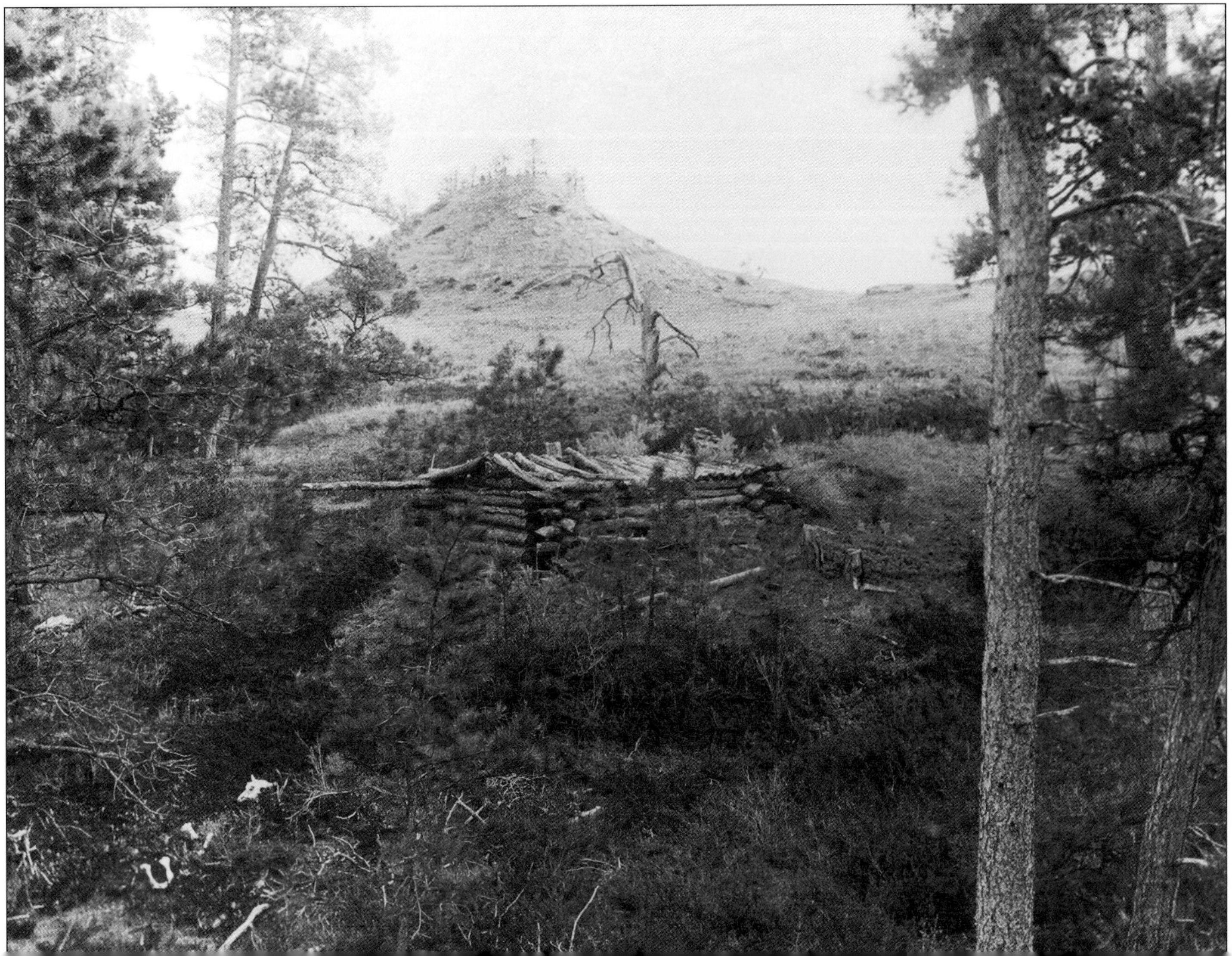

Photographer Huffman of Miles City, Montana, took this photo of an early buffalo hunter's cabin in Hull Creek Brakes.

Nebraska

The Platte River Road wound its way through Nebraska along the Oregon Trail. Troops were stationed at many of the stage stations.

- Beauvais Station was part of the Overland Stage route in 1864. A company of cavalry was stationed there between the Overland road and the South Platte River.
- Gilman Station, an Overland Stage stop.
- Fort Kearny was built in 1846 to protect the Oregon Trail.
- Post Mullaly Ranch. In 1864 it served as a Pony Express and an Overland Mail route stop.
- Post Plum Creek Station was built in 1864, and was located a mile from the stage station and Plum Creek Ranch.
- Fort Robinson, built in 1864, was a post for the Red Cloud Indian Agency. Dull Knife and his warriors died against the bluffs in 1879. Crazy Horse was shot dead near the original guard house here.

Nevada

As most of the troops were scattered about the west, few military posts were maintained in Nevada.

- Antelope Station, was built in 1863 and was manned by volunteers.
- Fort Baker was built in 1855 by Mormons, who also founded Las Vegas. This served as a stage station and had troops posted there when there were Indian scares.
- Deep Creek, a stage stop built in 1864. It had troops stationed there to protect the stage route of eastern Nevada.
- Camp Deep Hole had a detachment of troops in 1865 protecting the stage station.
- Fort McGarry was built in 1865 and was one of the most isolated sites in the west.
- Granite Creek Station.
- Fort Schillboure, built in 1860, was a stagecoach, and Pony Express stop.

New Mexico

New Mexico was struggling with Apache wars and Navajos on the war path, and was in constant war alert. This contributed to the armies use of forts all over New Mexico.

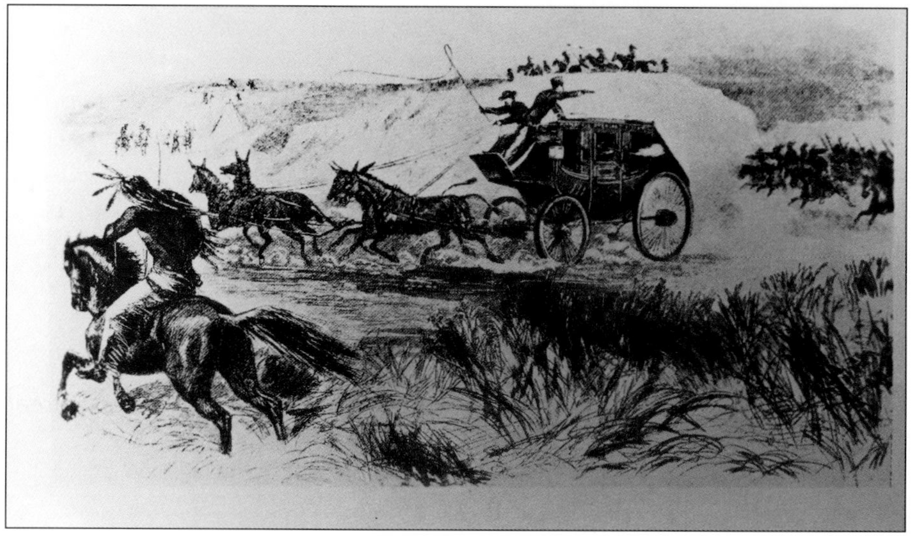

An early drawing of Indians attacking a stagecoach on the prairie. The artist is unknown.

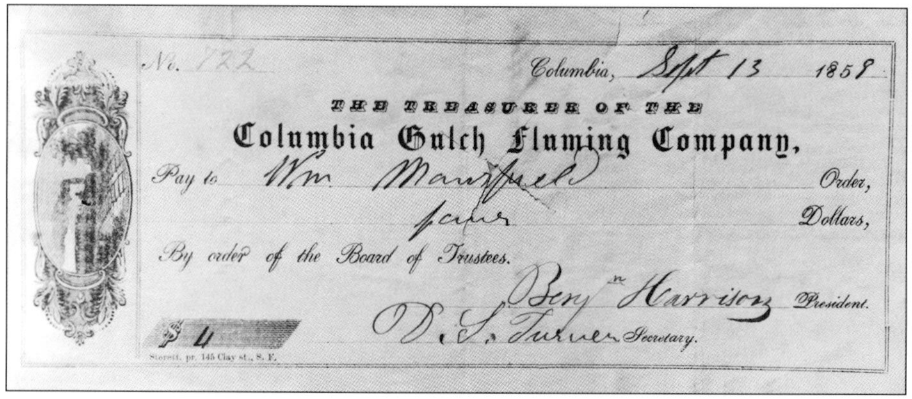

No. 722 Columbia, Sept 13 1858

The Treasurer of the
Columbia Gulch Fluming Company,
Pay to Wm Mansfield Order,
four Dollars,
By order of the Board of Trustees.
Benj.n Harrison President.
D. S. Turner Secretary.
$4

A check from the Columbia Gulch Fluming Company, signed by Benjamin Harrison, who was President of the company. Dated Sept. 13, at Columbia, California in 1858.

- Barclay's Fort , was built in 1848 and was a trading post and stage stop.
- Fort Craig, was built in 1854 and was manned by an army of over three thousand Union Soldiers.
- Fort Cummings, was built in 1862. Its mission was to watch over the stage routes.
- Camp La Joya, built in 1846, had the California Infantry stationed at the outpost on the "Journey of Death." The camp was on the route through the worst sand swept wastelands in the West.
- Fort Union was built in 1851 and used as a headquarters and supply depot.

Oklahoma

The overland travelers faced many Indian nations including the Choctaco in Oklahoma.

- Fort Coffee was built in 1834 and in 1862 was used to curtail whiskey smuggling.
- Camp Nichols was built in 1865. Kit Carson was the founder and commander of this stone fort built to protect the Sante Fe Trail
- Fort Sill was built in 1869 and is one of the most historic western forts. In the Apache cemetery on its grounds is the grave site of the great Geronimo.
- Fort Spunky was a stage stop built in 1880.

Oregon

- Fort Clatsor, built in 1805, was the first U.S. fort on the Pacific coast.
- Camp Day was built in 1860 to provide security for the upper Klammath Road at the time of the Piute Indian war.
- Fort Trask was built in 1855 to protect fur traders and settlers.

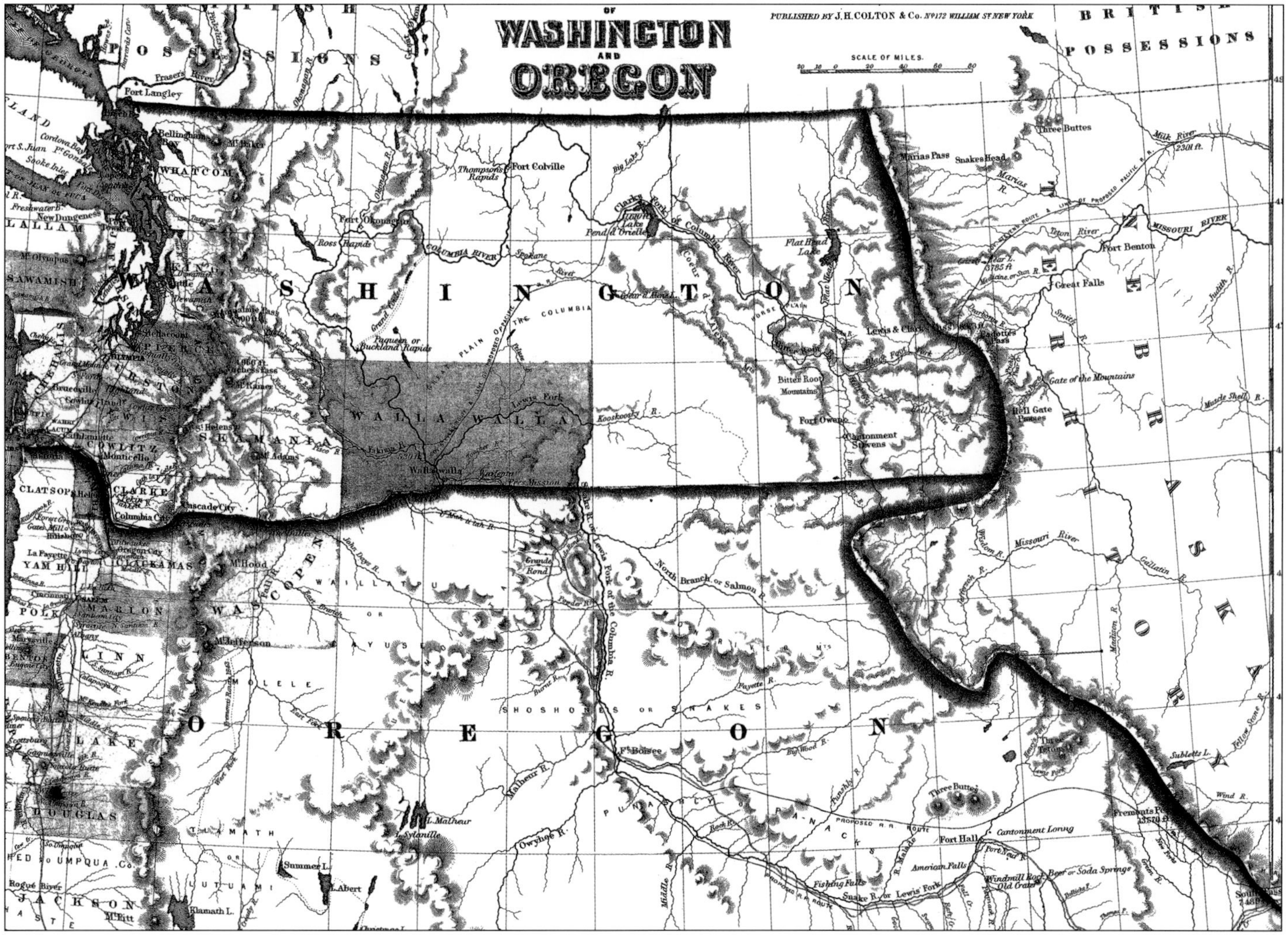

A map of Oregon and Washington in 1853.

South Dakota

The Pony Express ran from Fort Kearny to Brady's Station to Fort McPherson and split at the Platte City Trail.

- Gordon Stockade was built in 1874 to protect the gold fields of the Black Hills. The twenty-eight occupants stayed in their eighty foot square, ten foot high stockade whenever Indian trouble was upon them.
- Fort Meade was a camp at the mouth of the Red Canyon to protect the Black Hills stage route.
- Sidney Stockade was built in 1876 to protect the Sidney Deadwood Stage Lines.

Texas

There were hundreds of forts built in the state of Texas, of which a few are listed.

- Fort Lancaster, 1855-1865, was built to protect the pre-Civil War stagecoach stops. During the war it was occupied by the Confederate army.
- Camp Langtry, built in 1885, was named after the famous Lily Langtry, a popular actress who was the love of Judge Roy Bean. It was built to protect the railroad workers during this period.
- Parker's Fort was built in 1834 by members of the Parker family. Several hundred Indians attacked this fort in 1838 killing five settlers and kidnapping five. One of these was Cynthia Ann Parker who was nine years old. As an adult she gave birth to a child by an Indian, and named him Quanah Parker. He became a smart business man, even running a stagecoach line.

Utah

- Canon Station was built in 1864 and occupied by troops from Camp Ruby, Nevada.. It provided protection at the nearby Overland Stage stations.
- Deep Creek Station was built in 1864. Troops were stationed here to protect the Overland Stage route.
- Fish Springs Station was built in 1864. A garrison was stationed here to protect the Overland Stage station at Canon and Deep Creek. The Fish Springs Station is on the route used by the Pony Express as well as the Overland Mails.

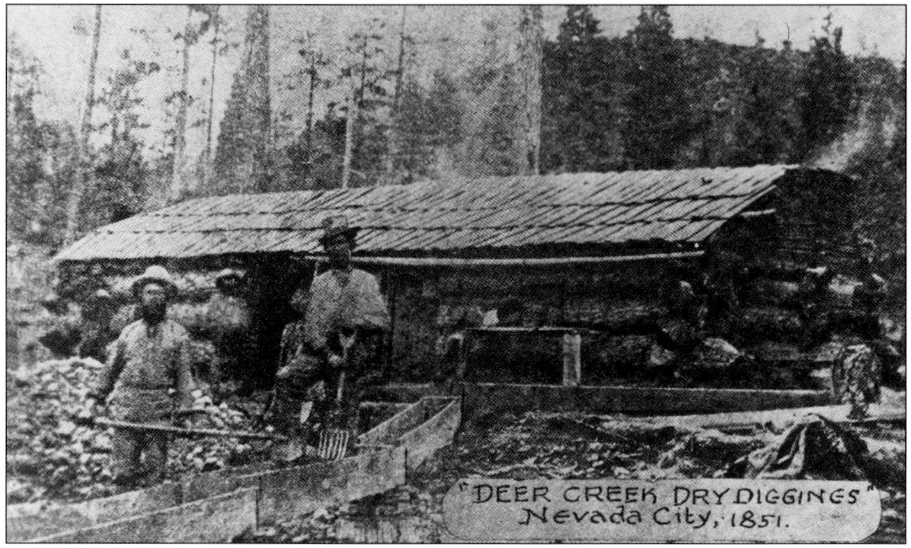

Nevada City was first settled in 1849 and known as Deer Creek Dry Diggings until the spring of 1850 when the name was changed. The miners roamed the area until the gold dust ran out.

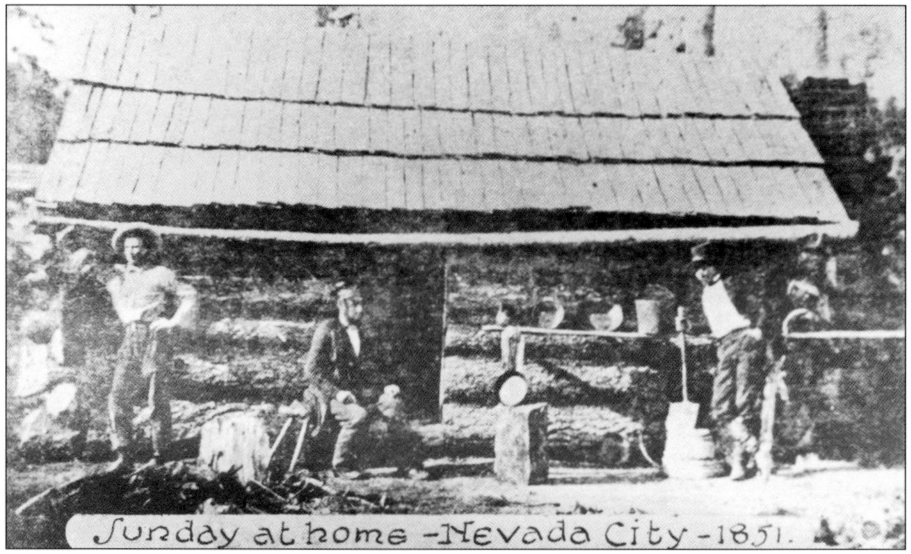

"Sunday at Home" in Nevada City, 1851.

• Fort Pierce, built in 1860, was intended as a stage stop on the road between Virgin Valley and the Pierce Ferry on the Mojave.

Washington

• Fort Colville, built in 1859, was also Harney's Depot.
• Fort Nisqually was a very early fort built in 1843.
• The Hudson Bay Company Trading post.

Wyoming

• Fort Bernard was built in 1845 as a trading post
• Fort Bridger was built in 1842 as a trading post of John Bridger. He left in 1853 when the Mormons took over.
• Deer Creek Station was built in 1862. Troops stationed there watched over the Oregon Trail.
• Camp Dodge was built in 1865 and housed the U.S. Calvary to protect against the attacks of the warring Indian tribes along the Oregon Trail and stagecoach stations.
• Camp Hat Creek, built in 1876, was a stockade and sub-post of Fort Laramie used to protect the Black Hills and stops for the stagecoach route.
• Camp Horseshoe, built in 1862, had a lone lieutenant and thirty eight soldiers assigned to guard weary travelers and the stagecoaches who came from Fort Laramie.
• Three Crossings, built in 1862, was a stage station. At one time a small number of troops had to fight off three to five hundred Indians. Troops from other stations finally arrived in time to rescue them.

These are only a few of the many forts and stage stations that were scattered about the United States during our country's expansion into the West. Although the Overland Stage route didn't follow the same roads as the Pony Express, their paths would cross more then once on any given journey.

During the 1860s or until the Civil War broke out, the ideal route weather wise was the U.S. Mail overland route to Saint Louis using a route that took the stage to stops at Monterey, Santa Barbara, Los Angeles, Fort Yuma, Fort Buchanan, Franklin, Fort Chadbourne, and into the Indian Territories, Fort Belknap, and Fort Smith, then to Jefferson City, and on to Saint Louis.

Most of the mails were very late in arriving, some even took months to deliver. Somehow, against terrible odds, they got through. With the exciting news of all the gold strikes in California most of the eastern newspapers informed the population with day-by-day, week-by-week news updates. Taken exactly as printed, I have copied several of these news flashes with the related stories.

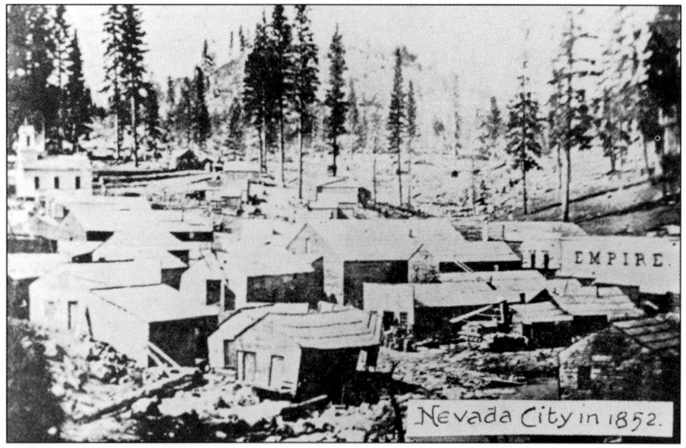

An overall view of Nevada City in 1852 from a early photo drawing.

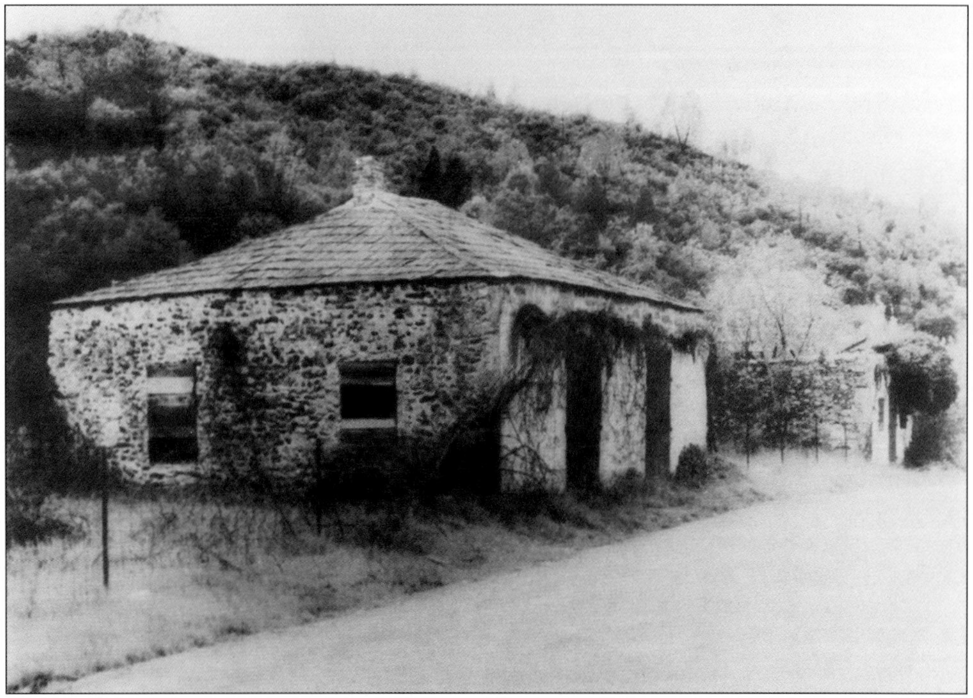

The decaying stores from Bear Valley's earlier days.

San Francisco February 7, 1849

You ask me to give you facts as they are. You shall have a plain statement of matters as they exits. At present there is little or nothing doing in the place of consequence in the immense quantity of snow that has fallen this year.

There are at present two thousand persons at the mines. Some are living in tents, and others are in log houses. Many have perished from exposure to cold and fevers, but such is the excitement and rage for gold that they undergo the most unheard of hardships.

As regards to the richness of these mines, I can only say that the most exaggerated accounts may be believed. A few days ago a man came down from the mines bringing with him $12,000 in gold dust, which he dug out in the space of six days.

All who go to the mines do well, which is the most convincing proof I can give you of their great richness.

Additional from California, Jan 19,1849, St. Louis Mis.

We learn from the San Francisco Journals, received by the Overland Mail , further items of news.

There had been a riot in at Sacramento among some settlers in consequence of the refusal of Judge Terry to grant a writ of error from the State to the Federal court in the case of Ferris against Coover.

The Eliza Anderson, the first Ocean steamer built on the Pacific coast, was launched at Portland Nov. 7th.

The Keeper of the mail station at near Fort Tejon had been murdered by Mexicans, who also stole eight mules. The Mail coach in consequence had to be hauled fifteen miles by one mule.

The Lopez Expedition, 1849

The more light that is thrown upon the Lopez expedition the blacker it becomes.

A recently published statement of a portion of the Contoy prisoners makes it yet the more odious.

The way was cleared for villainess robbery by perfidy as villainess.

It appears that one of the doughtiest heroes of this expedition, Captain Hardy, advertised during April last in a Cincinnati paper, for men to accompany him to California, and labor in his service for a specific time, engaging to pay each person employed four thousand dollars per annum, and also seven dollars a month as a contingent fund. A public meeting was convened by him, at Covington, Ky., at which his proposed route to California, and plans after arriving there, were fully explained. He professed to be the agent of a large and perfectly responsible mining company and made such fair representations as to induce a considerable number of persons to engage themselves to his service.

The party soon rendezvoused at New Orleans, according to agreement, without the least suspicion, as stated, that they had before them any other destination other than California. They embarked on board the bark, Georgiana on the 25th of April, and arrived at the Balize on the 26th. Here arms were brought on board, and the men were coolly informed that their business was not to work in the mines of California, but to liberate the oppressed natives of Cuba. The ship immediately put to sea, and on the 6th of May anchored at the island of Contoy. Refusing to go further, they remained here until the 18th, when they were taken prisoners by the Spanish war steamer, Pizarro.

The fact of the inveiglement of these men by the basest violation of good faith is now no longer a matter of doubt. Thus General Lopez and his confederates proved themselves thoroughbred rascals at the very outset of their undertaking.

Philadelphia, Tuesday April 10, 1849

Adventures on the road to California.

From the MS. Journal of a friend who traveled a few years since to California by the Overland Route, we are allowed to take the following extract, giving a day's adventure on the banks of the Goo-al-pah river. It may be well to mention that while our friends party was still in camp, some Mexicans rode in and stated that they had just been robbed and beaten by the Comanches, who had been out in great numbers, and that there was great danger in proceeding. This occasioned no alarm. The party was unusually strong in numbers and determination; and everyone felt himself able to cope with a dozen antagonists. Immediately after breakfast they formed in line, with outriding scouts in all directions, and took up the march. And now the action of our extract commences.

On went the caravan, nearly a mile in length, while on our right was the Goo-al-pah, growing narrower, foamed and fretted within the rock-bound canon. The scene, the excitement generated by the recent news, and the fresh morning breeze which blew in our faces, tossing our hair and beards, made each man feel some "fever of the mad," which relieved itself now and then (loud noises being forbidden) in a hasty gallop to and fro. Suddenly, having my eyes fixed in front, I saw the rifle of our most foremost scout waved in the air. The order was given to close; a little eminence, about a mile distant, on which a dozen cotton woods–the only trees we had seen for two days– was selected as the standing place; and we had scarcely time to reach it and form our wagons into a ring, with the mules in the center, before our scouts joined us, La Quene de Beuf at their head. He reported a large body of Indians coming down the river path. The mules and horses were made secure by their lariats to the heaviest wagons and the trees; the ammunition wagon was opened; the rifles and pistols examined and freshly capped; and the bowie- knives loosened in their sheaths. The minute after, the form of a single Indian scout made a dark spot on the horizon from the summit of an eminence some miles to the northwest. I examined him with my glass. He was mounted on a horse taken from the whites, as the sized and Spanish equipment proved; was naked with the exception of a breech-cloth, leggins, and moccasins; and armed with a long lance, shield, bow and arrows. He reined up his horse, as though to examine us carefully. I offered the glass to La Queue de Beuf, who pushing it aside with his hand, and muttering the word, "Comanche," divested his head of its ornaments, leaving the scalp-lock bare.

I now saw that serious work was before us, and calling the men together, told them that we must fight or be plundered–perhaps murdered. The odds against us would be probably great; but our position was good, in case they made a onset, which, confident in their superior numbers, they would probably do. If they undertook to lay siege we should attack them, as we could not afford time to remain.

I have just finished my speech, to which the men replied by an enthusiastic shout, when the Indian scout disappeared as suddenly as though he had sank in the earth. A few minutes more passed away, when a body of several hundred horsemen, arrayed in a column about twenty deep, suddenly rode into sight. At about the distance of a mile they halted, while four of them separated themselves from the main body, and rode at a respectable distance half around us, examining the numbers and disposition of our force. Presently they returned. A somewhat animated conference ensued and the whole body remained quiet.

As I thought this to be an invitation to parley, I was about to despatch La Queue de Beuf and Hurley with a white flag, when the tallest of the savages rode about thirty paces in front of the rest, and suddenly wheeling his horse, made a gesture, equally vulgar and significant, which amounted to a declaration of war. My gorge rose at the insult, and observing them to be closely huddled together, I told O'Mears that he had an opportunity of trying the heavy war- rockets, which he had persisted in making at St. Louis. The eyes

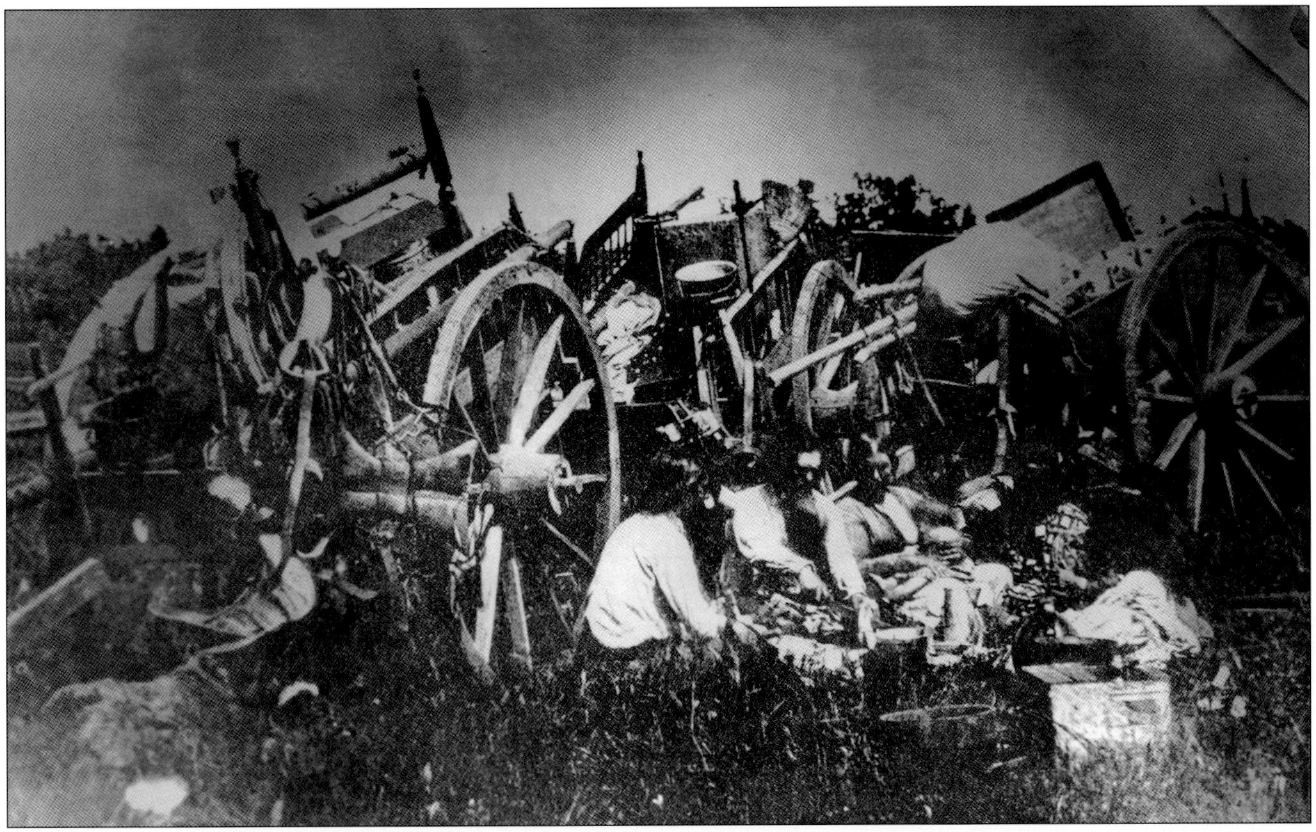

In this grim- looking photo are the survivors of an Indian attack that took place on the prairie.

of the Irishman sparkled at the proposition, and he brought his rocket-stand with a couple of three inch rockets from the wagon. While he was fixing his apparatus La Quene de Beuf touched me on the shoulder; I looked around, and at less than half-mile distance behind us was a band of twenty Indians, armed with rifles, who seemed to be watching us closely. I supposed them to be a division of the Comanches; but La Quene de Beuf rode out to meet them, when the whole part came rushing into camp. They proved to be Cheyennes, headed by Beuf's brother. They had been out beyond their hunting grounds in search of buffalo, when, on their return, they discovered us at bay. Their only chance of safety was to league with us, which they did more readily when they saw who was our guide. I was rather pleased with this addition to our strength, as they were well armed, fierce looking fellows, and brought with them six pack horses, loaded with buffalo meat–quite an addition to the general store.

O'Meara signified he was ready, and bringing a small signal rocket, fired it off to attain the proper elevation. It fell somewhat short, ploughing up the ground in front of the enemy, and scattering the dirt and stones over the foremost. They gave way in a little alarm at the novel missile; and the eyes of the Cheyennes opened wider at the trail of fire made by our messenger in its flight. In a moment the ranks of the Comanches closed up, apparently preparing to make a charge. Our pyrotechnical friend had now his angle of aim correctly ascertained, and lighting the fuse of one of his three inch rockets, it started on its errand of death. Our mules and horses plunged furiously at the unusual spectacle; and one of our Cheyenne friends was nearly unhorsed altogether. The rocket struck directly in the center of a group of savages and exploded with terrific force, scattering the fragments of its head in all directions, and fairly tearing the men and horses around it to pieces. The horses of the surviving Comanches took flight and galloped off, perfectly unmanageable, while our Cheyennes started in pursuit of the fugitives. Our men would have followed but I restrained them.

The spot we finally chose to encamp was in a rocky glen, made by a semicircular indentation in some cliffs of trap and sandstone. I had just swallowed a cup of coffee made for me by Patrick, and no persuasion could induce the Cheyennes to touch after the first mouthful, and Sweetzer had gone to look for his patient in the tent wagon, when Basil Chevier, who, contrary to my orders, had strayed beyond the line of scouts, came in accompanied by Hurley and Queue de Beuf. He reported a large body Indians coming down in chase of a herd of buffalo, one of which he had before he was aware of his proximity to such dangerous neighbors. The camp was put in order for their reception; but Hurley and an old chief assured us that we need be under little alarm. The new comers were Kioways, who, as they had not yet probably heard of our fight with the Comanches, might be rendered friendly, with very little trouble. I was just at the point of sending the chief to hold a parley, when we heard a tremendous explosion up the river, in the distance, accompanied by a series of yells. A horse's feet clattered over the stones and pebbles on the river banks, and up galloped O'Meara, waving his rocket stand in one hand and his rifle in the other, and shouting like a madman. It was some seconds before he recovered breath and informed us of his haste. He had taken a ride up the river side, to pick wild grapes and explore a little, taking a rocket and stand with him.

He saw the scouts ride past him towards camp and noticed the Indians. Taking it for granted that the former were pursued, and the latter must be Comanches, he had fixed his stand, struck a light, and sent a rocket with its explosive compliments among the strangers. The consequence had been that two of the Indians and several buffalos were spared the necessity of earthly cares.

Here was a comfortable prospect about to open. The Kioways are a race far superior in point intelligence and bravery to the Comanches, though they herd with and control the latter; and it was very likely that they would resent this attack, fearfully. Even if we repulsed their charge in the present stance, we would be harassed during the whole journey; and have our men and cattle picked off, one by one, whenever exposed to such depredation. I spoke rather sharply to O'Meara, and I'm afraid wished him and his rockets to much warmer latitude than any they occupied

The mischief had been done, however, and we now had to prepare to meet what ever consequences might ensue. The spot where we had encamped was a strange one; no arrows shot could well reach us from the bluff, and La Quene de Beuf informed us that there appeared to be few rifles among the Kioways. So we ranged our wagons on the bank, and made fitting preparation to fight with foes who by all accounts, were both dauntless and persevering. As we engaged in tying the mules and horses by lariats to such fragments of rocks as were suitable, a shrill whistle from Hurley, the crack of a rifle, and a whizzing like a downward flight of birds caused us to look up. There, directly on the summit of the bluffs, almost to the very brink, were figures of fifty horses, each mounted by a warrior. The arrows had fallen far short, and so had the ball sent from the rifle of one who appeared to lead. We pointed our rifles at them, and they made derisive motions, for they knew the distance to be too great. The Chief put his thumb to his nose, and twiddled his finger, a trick he had probably learned from some of his white traders.

"Ef I had that rifle thar," said Hurley, "I could fetch that chap sure. "

The rifle he alluded to was Vache's, a fine one, made by Wesson, and finished with such accuracy, that it would carry a wedged ball twice the ordinary range. Vache handed him the desired weapon, and Hurley took deliberate aim.

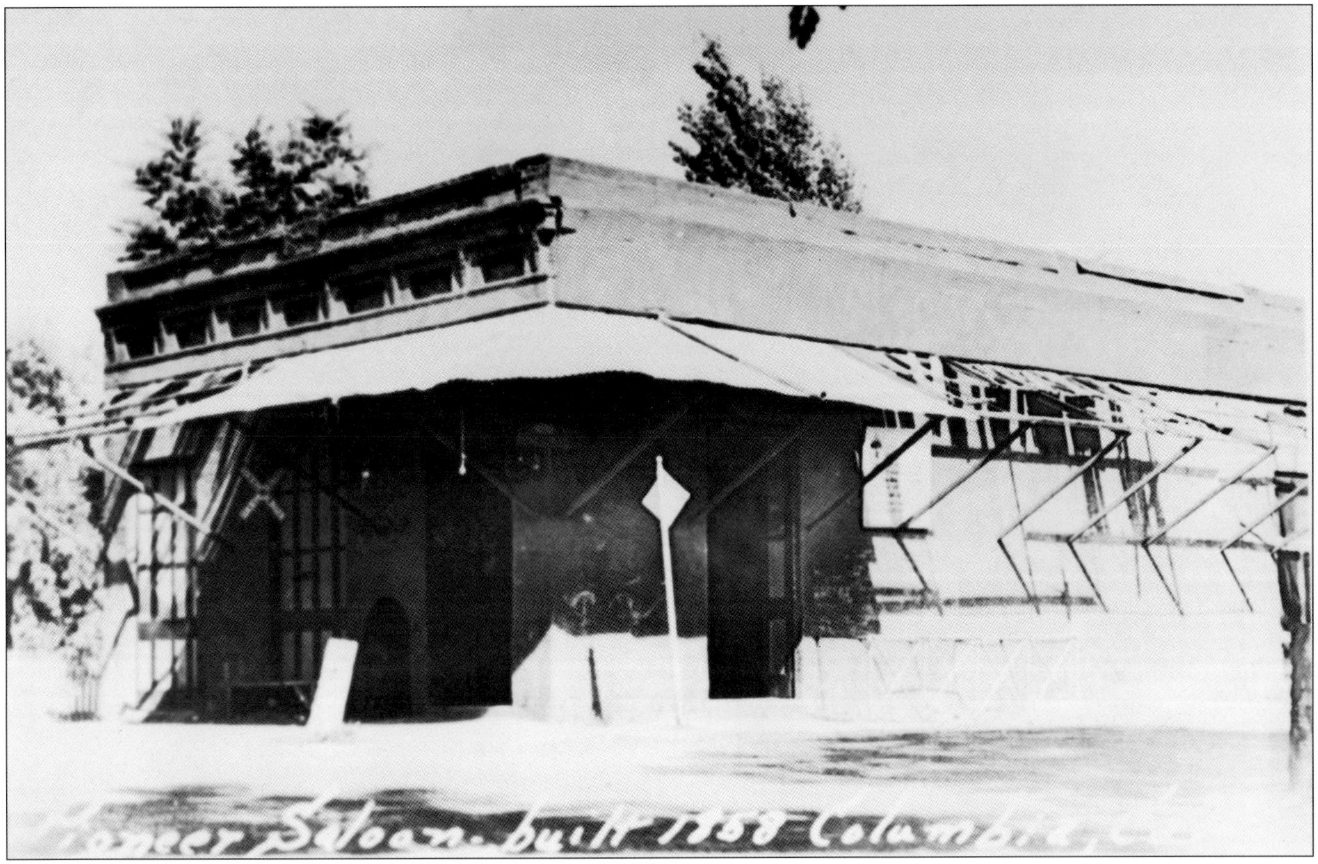

Pioneer Saloon, built in 1858, Columbia, California.

and Sweetzer, regardless of the danger ran out to assist him. Our Cheyennes in the meanwhile, and most of our men, were exchanging shots with the enemy, who feared apparently to charge up to our wagons, and the latter, after losing several of their warriors without doing more then wound Paul Choutteau, our first teamster, in the shoulder, fell back to consult on their next movement.

Poor O'Meara had planted his rocket-stand behind a little projection of rock, and adjusted three of his darling rockets to be fired simultaneously. He then had stepped out to observe the spot where the Kioways must necessarily pass, if beaten back, for they were to near them to render his rockets available, and one of the enemy had found a chance to make a target of him. There was little blood flowing externally as the wound was in his breast. I expressed a hope of his recovery; but doctor Sweetzer merely shook his head and gave the patient some water which one of the men brought from the river. The draught seemed to rally the wounded man; and then I was obliged to leave him, for our enemies had made a new disposition. Their largest number had crossed the creek at a ford we had passed in the morning, and had come up on the opposite side, where the country was more level and low. They had sent small forces by the river bank above and below, so that so that we were in danger of being assailed on three sides at once. They did not give us much chance to think, for along came two wings, while the main body in front of us thundered down, yelling and screaming, to the river brink.

It was now a hand to hand conflict, in which our pistols and Bowie knives did as much work as riles; but it gave the long lances of the Kioways a better chance. Several of our men and two Cheyennes were struck down. Old La Queue de Beuf had a desperate conflict with one of the enemy, receiving an ugly gash on the cheek as he rushed in. They tugged at each other's throats, and their horses entering into the matter with rifles falling to

"Hit the horse, " said I, "that will bring both. "

Hurley brought the rifle down, looked at me a moment, and then laughed. Then raising the gun again, he said, "Whar?"

"In the head," I replied. Hurley fired at the word. The horse plunged, and the Chief threw himself back, but not in time. He was pitched over the head of the animal, and the two came down together into the glen, crushed into mere lumps of flesh. The rest of the band vanished.

A yell from La Queue de Beuf who had been on the lookout, showed us a band on the river bank rushing toward us at full charge. The bluffs at the part they were approaching were so near the water, which at that point was deep, as to only admit ten abreast, and every warrior in the front rank fell before our rifles. The rest halted, and some of them had rifles gave us a volley. Only one of their shots took effect, and that was on O'Meara, he fell,

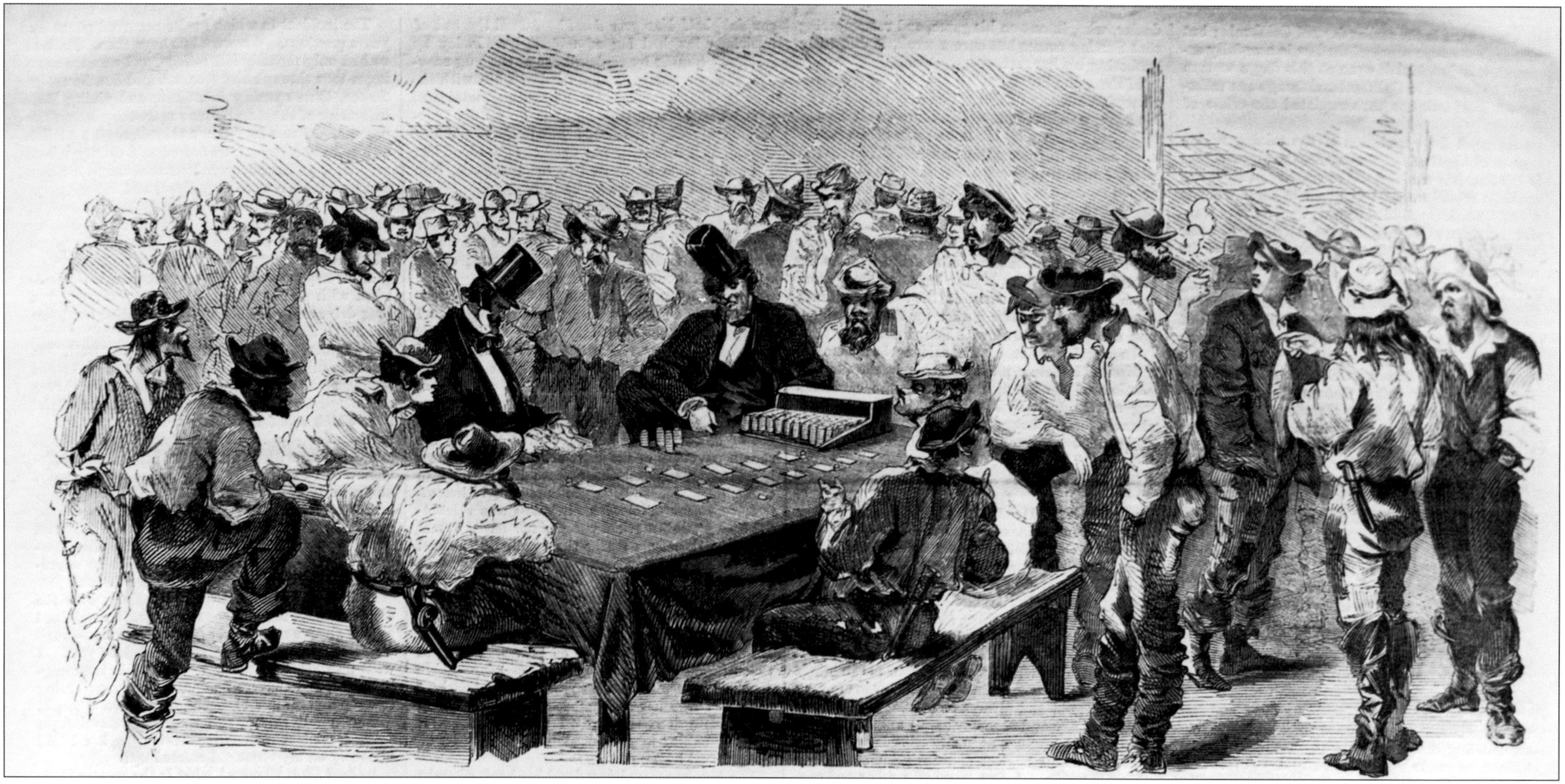

Gambling was just the thing to pass the time. These players are trying their luck in the game of Faro. The fine drawing illustrated an early edition of *Harpers*.

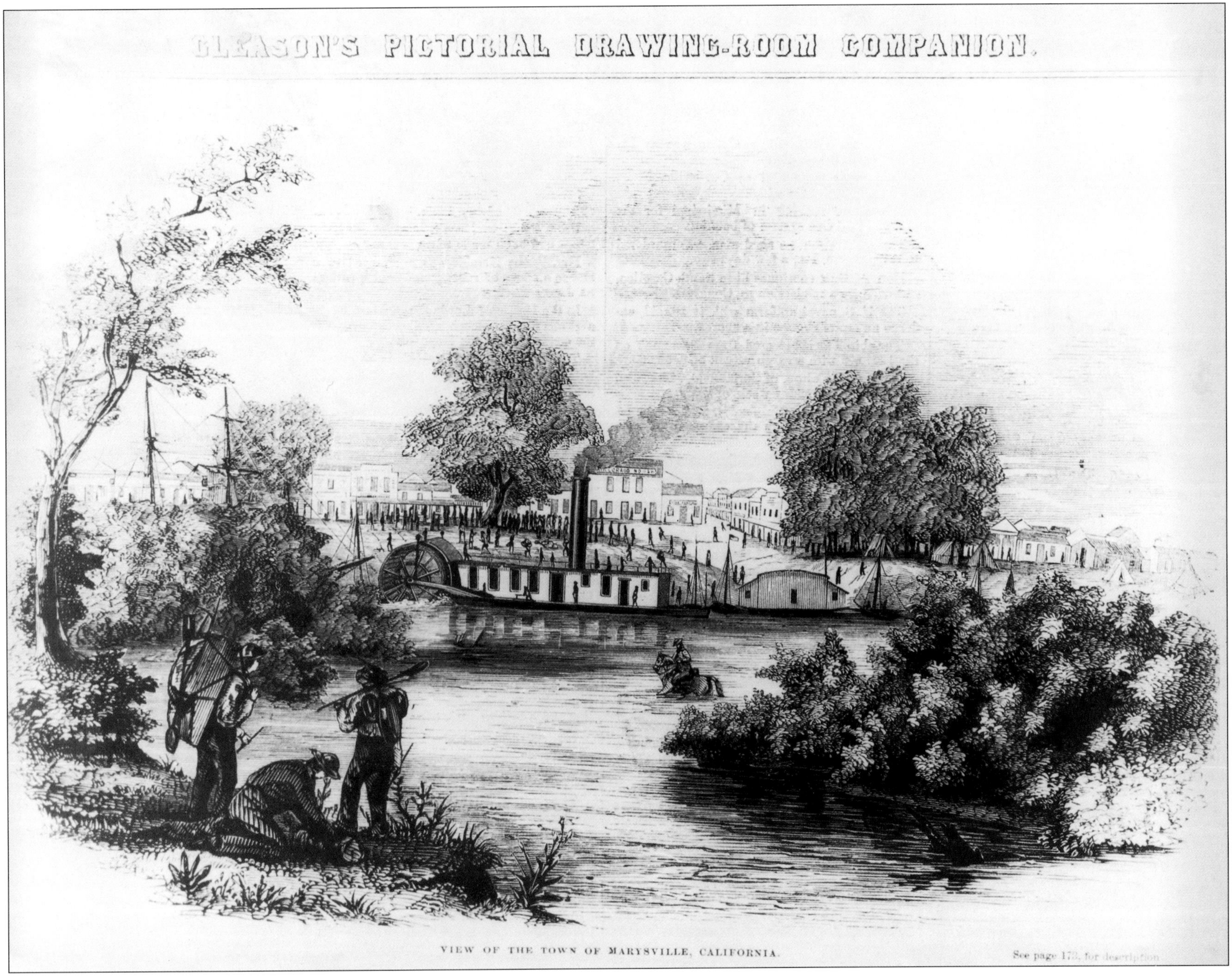

Marysville, California, in the early days, as illustrated in *Harpers*.

the ground. The Kioway was an athletic young man, and was getting the best of our old scout, but Vache, without much regard to the chivalry of the matter, assailed him from behind, and took off his head with his long heavy knife as easily as you would the top of a turnip. I had insensibly stopped to witness this, but, recollecting myself, turned, and just in time to save my life. One of the red skins was within twenty feet of me with his long lance full pointed, coming down as fast as he could, and I had just time to make my horse swerve with the spur to avoid his blow. As it was, the lance found a lodgment in my hunting shirt, and carried off the skirt. He turned and came at me again, with the trophy sticking to the lance; and, as his attention seemed to be getting troublesome, I gave him the contents of my revolver. I was in so great a flurry, that I expended some powder and ball uselessly. One shot could have finished him. He fell from his horse forward, striking his lance in the ground.

After making a vain attempt to cross the current of the river, the main body had gone back to reinforce their comrades, but seeing that we had dispersed or slain our enemies, the larger body drew up a distance for consultation. We could see them in a warm animated discussion; and La Quene de Beuf, who came up to me with a half dozen bloody scalps dangling them from his gun, said they were going to lay siege to us and starve us out. Or attack us when we only got to a place more favorable to their operations. They were evidently bent on our extermination; and directing Hurley to call in all who were in pursuit of fugitives, I proceeded to examine our force. I found that six of the Cheyennes had been killed and eight slightly wounded. Two of our men were severely wounded and seven of them slightly wounded. They were attended to and I turned to see and visit O'Meara, who insisted on staying at the spot where he had been shot. I found him to be very weak, and asked him how he felt.

"Mighty bad, Captain, " said he, "mighty bad, in truth, I can hardly speak; an look what a puddle of blood I've spit up. I wish I had a light I do."

"What for O'Meara?"

"Look at the copper skinned varmints; bad luck to them to shoot a Christian like a buffalo. Do I get me a light, and I think I'll scatter them."

The distance of the Kioways was at least a mile and a half, and although the rockets had nearly a range of two miles, I did not expect O'Meara, in such a situation, to have the judgement necessary for taking the proper angle. It would be a chance business, but I could not thwart a dying man; so I directed a light to be struck. This was done; and the men gathered around to witness the firing. They assisted O'Meara to rise; and the doctor held him on his knees as he adjusted the plane of the rocket-troughs. The Indians were grouped together watching our movements, but ignorant of their intent; and our Cheyennes seemed to have eyes starting out of their heads with wonder.

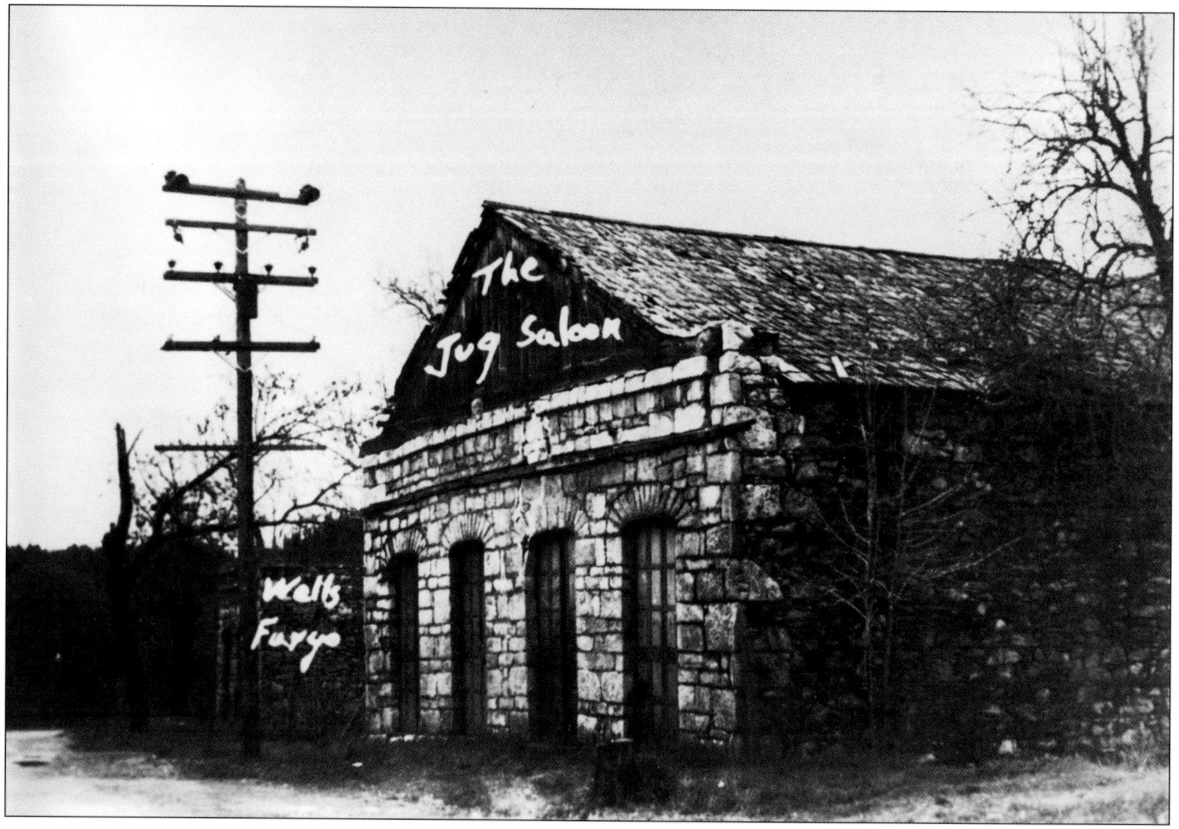

In Volcano, California, the remaining buildings from gold rush days included the Jug Saloon and a wall from the Wells Fargo store

O'Meara applied the light to the fuses. The rockets rose with a whiz that set our horses and mules plunging; and to my utter astonishment, descended directly in the middle of the Kioways, who started too late. Three explosions, distant scarcely a second from each other, ensued, starting the still air-cloud of smoke arose over the spot where the Kioways had stood. It cleared away presently with the breeze. Where several wounded steeds plunged furiously over the buttes; but there were no riders to be seen. Desolation and death had followed the hand of a dying man.

La Quene de Beuf touched my shoulder. I turned and found O'Meara lying with his face forward, in a small pool of blood. We raised him and wiped the gore from his mouth but he was no more.

We buried our dead that afternoon, and put O'Meara in a lone spot, under the shelter of the bluff.

On the next morning, before we started on our journey, Vache, who was somewhat of a sculptor spent an hour or more in carving the letters O'Meara's name upon the rock which overhung his grave. T.D.E.

In reviewing and following the trails to the west and on to California it seems that the most dangerous route were the ones that led south through the desert. With far fewer forts for protection, and less stage stops for water and food. The stagecoach traveler had other worries. Indian attacks could be just over the next hill. On the other hand when the Civil War broke out, the Confederacy took control of many of the area's forts and stage stops. So the stagecoach and Overland routes had to use the Northern routes. Which meant travel could only be done during late spring and early fall, before the snows hit the mountain passes.

The early settlement of Los Angeles had little more than adobe houses and a few larger wooden structures to house what was a growing population. There was a harbor built to receive ships with passengers, people who told of news from all over the world. Early Los Angeles had no telegraph, no railroad, no banks, and consequently they were almost cut off from affairs of the outside world. So, by the time that stagecoaches arrived at the town's two largest hotels, bringing the new arrivals from the ships, there would be much excitement in the town.

Major Phineas Banning and A.W. Timms, were rivals in carrying passengers and freight into Los Angeles. Banning was founder of the Union Club and, eventually, helped to build a railroad into Los Angeles.

Timms would unload his passengers at the Lafayette Hotel across the street from the Union Belle Hotel where Banning would drop off his. There were mad races between coaches though this was not as popular a sport for the passengers as it was with the residents. These stages were far from luxurious, with the harnesses patched up and unreliable and roads filled with rocks and bumps for miles. Nevertheless, the passengers enjoyed the race because they would also pay less for the ride, depending on who got to town first. Charges would be dropped to as little as one dollar per trip for the winner.

There was a time in Los Angeles history that was a black mark against the city. It happened in 1870, in a little place called, "Calle De Los Negros." It was called the "Chinese Massacre" and it plunged the United States into trouble with China, a disturbance settled only with much diplomatic effort. Judge R.M. Widney declared that the cause of the tragedy was the struggle between two Chinese gactions over the possession of a slave woman.

Kidnappers from one Chinese faction kidnapped the woman and drove her as far as Santa Barbara. The other faction swore out an arrest for her on the charge of stealing jewelry, and whe was taken prisoner and returned to Los Angeles. That began the trouble. As she was being driven back to jail in a hack, armed Chinese men from both factions surrounded the hack. Only the intervention of the police force prevented a Chinese battle in the streets.

That evening a police officer named Jesus Bilderain went to the old Coronel Building to make an arrest. This building was the headquarters for the Chinese community in Los Angeles. Bilderain deputized a bystander, Robert Thompson, to assist him in the arrest. As they entered an area called Nigger Alley, the Chinese opened fire, mortally wounding Thompson and shattering Bilderain's shoulder. Dragging Thompson to the street, Bilderain sent for help.

News traveled fast, and before long a crowd had gathered, made up mostly of the poor people who inhabited the area around the Coronel Building. Things grew ominous as the crowd grew to a mob of nearly 3000 mostly armed men, the murmering against the Chinese grew louder and more antagonistic. Around supper time a shot was fired, and in a moment the whole building became a target for the guns and pistols of the crowd.

Judge Widney was president of the Law and Order Party, which substantial citizens had recently organized to suppress crime and violence. He sent word for members of the party to collect at the Arcadia Block, which stood on Los Angeles Street near the Coronel Building. When he went to arm himself, he found both his pistol and revolvers missing. Unarmed, he joined the others offering his service to Sheriff Burns.

But the mood of the mob grew uglier. They were not satisfied with merely shooting the Chinese people. According to courtroom testimony, 20 were hanged by the mob on Los Angeles Street from the gate post at John Goller's wagon shop. Others were hung at the old Thomlinson coral, at Temple and Buena Vista Streets. The mob was demanding the life of every Chinese person in town, man, woman, and child.

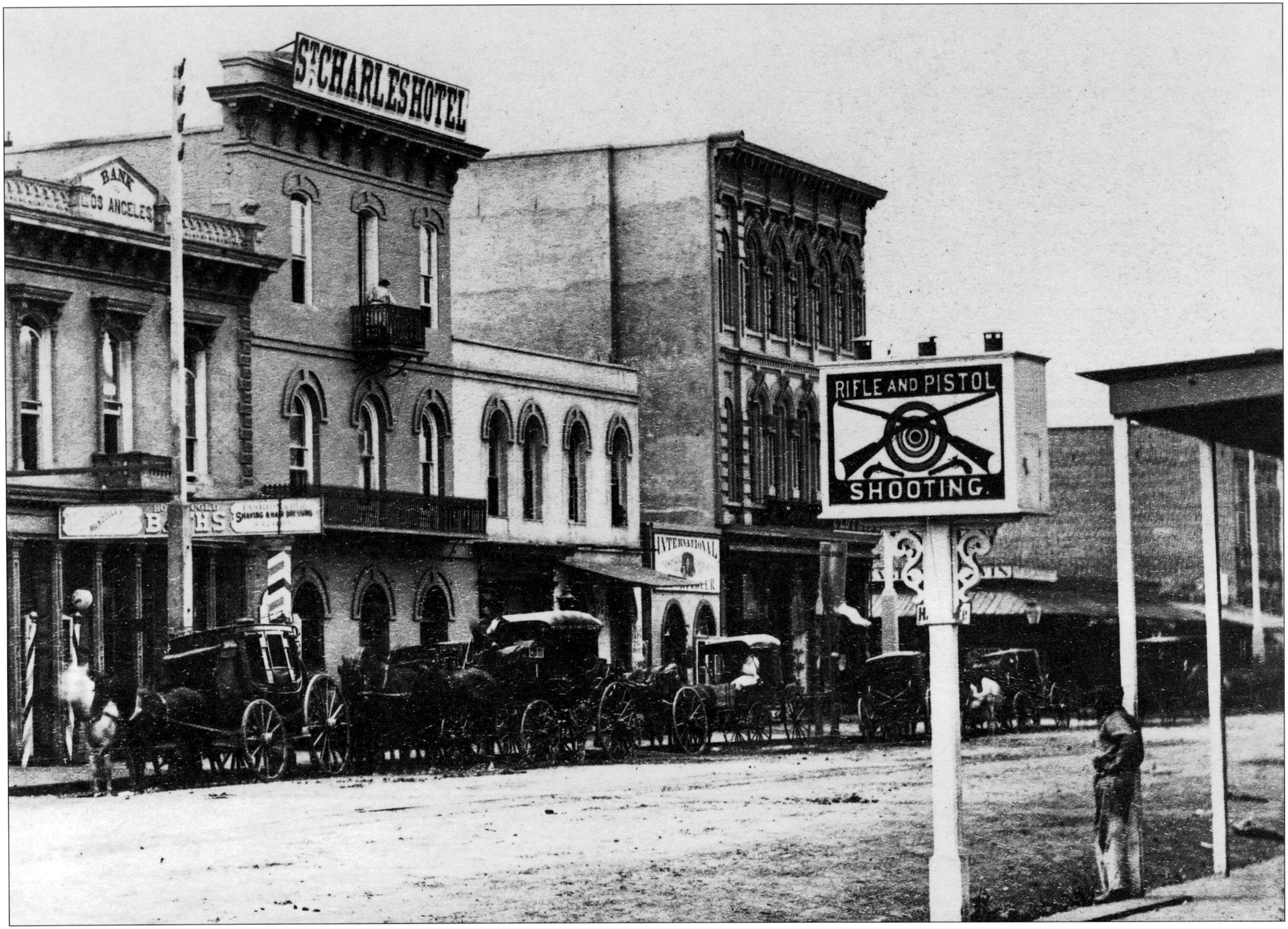

This early Los Angeles photo shows the St. Charles Hotel and other stores. It should be noted that the sign is clearly marked "no rifle or pistol shooting."

At the risk of his own life, Judge Widney organized a rescue party, with John Lazarovich as his assistant. Obtaining a revolver and a one shot pistol, Widney began to disperse small groups of rioters who were dragging people to the gallows. As he rescued them, he placed them in a jail cell for safety until the danger had passed.

This tragic event placed Los Angeles in the public eye as a violent place. The Chinese government protested to the U.S. government and was finally paid a large indemnity for the massacre.

The following story appeared in the Union Newspaper, from Washington, January 23, 1849.

Dear Sir; In answer to your inquires concerning the emigration party from Arkansas to California, which will set off about the 1st of April next, I herewith enclose you a communication from the Adjutant General. With instructions to General Arbuckle that he will furnish an escort of troops for this party, as least as far as Sante Fe. Along with this expedition. Also, as you will see, an officer of topographical engineers has been ordered to make a reconnaissance of the route traveled, and to file a report. The great benefit to our country I anticipate from the movement is the settlement, in great part, at least, of the mooted question, "Which is the shortest and best route to California?"

From Fort Smith, Arkansas, 1848, this story appeared in a local paper.

A company is now forming at this place, intending to proceed to California, taking Gregg's route to Sante Fe and Albuquerque. It has been ascertained, that to leave Sante Fe about seventy miles to the north, and proceed from Albuquerque directly to El Passo, will shorten the distance over one hundred miles; but should any of the emigrants wish to go to Sante Fe, they can go with the company as far as Dry River, about 300 miles from this place, and from thence to Sante Fe.

We have been assured by a gentlemen who is going with the company, and has been as far as Sante Fe on this route, that the distance does not exceed 500 miles to the last mentioned place. Lying every Sunday and with plenty of food and water. It will not be over 100 days in arriving at San Francisco or Monterey.

Every able bodied man will be required to furnish himself with a good gun and plenty of ammunition; also with 150 pounds of good flour, 100 pounds of good bacon, and transportation for the same (horse or mule). Every head of a family was must furnish himself with a good wagon to be drawn by horses, mules, or oxen, to carry over 2,000 pounds. Any person will be permitted to take as much stock as he may wish. Young men could unite, say five or six to purchase a wagon, or might find a job as a teamster.

Every person who wishes to attach themselves to this company must forward his or her name to this company along with the number of wagons in his party. Every emigrant to be at this place on the first day of April next. And commence the march immediately. All letters addressed to the agent must be post paid.

Respectfully,
John J. Dillard, J.R. Kannady, Joan F. Wheeler, AGENTS

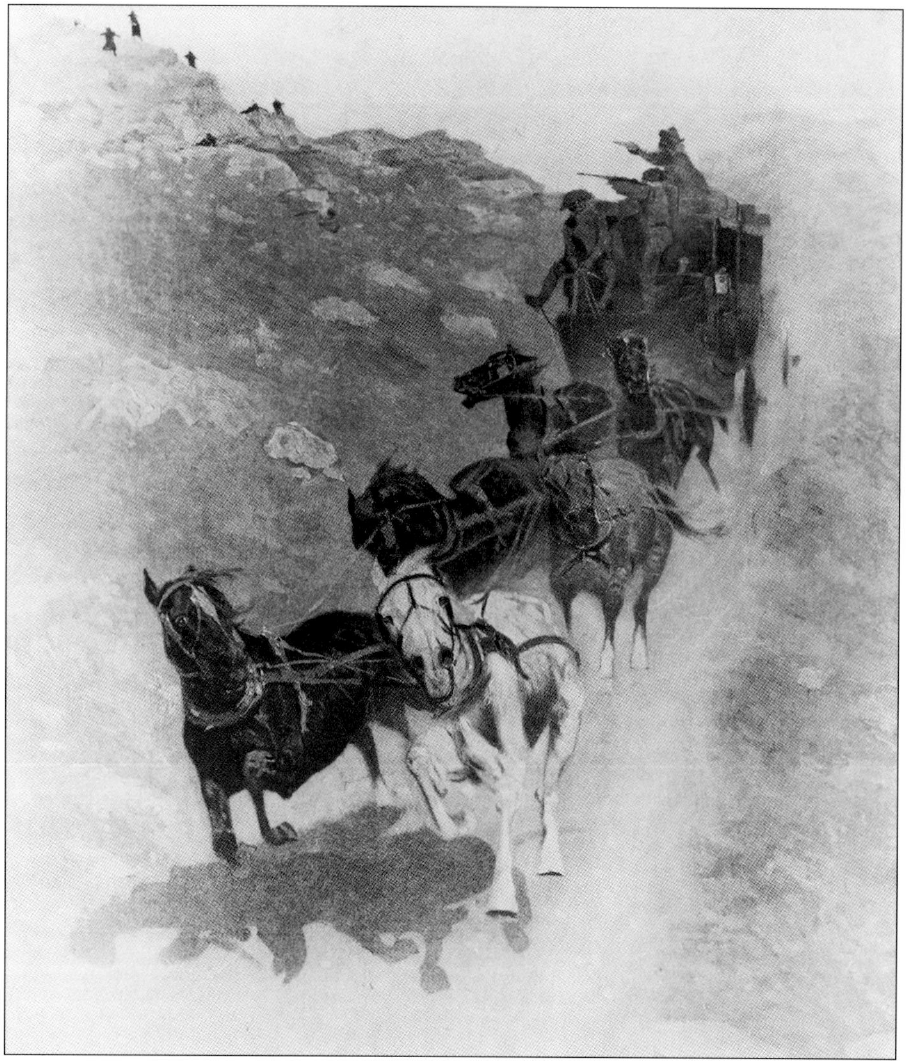

"Mixed Up," based on the great oil painting by R.W. Hanson, has plenty of action.

An early California emigrant stop was called Boston Ravine. In Grass Valley there were rough wooden cabins and houses built at this site. Even a market was set up by Hollis & Baxter. A tavern called the Eagle Tavern was kept by John West. These establishments were set up at the foot of Gold Hill, Boston Ravine. The hill was named for a Negro who first discovered a quartz vein there We have an illustration of Boston Ravine from an early edition of *Gleason's Pictorial Review* of early 1800s.

Early *Gleason's Pictorial Reviews* also had a fine print of the gold region from Telegraph Hill in San Francisco. Showing the camp-like scene and gold seekers marching off to the hills.

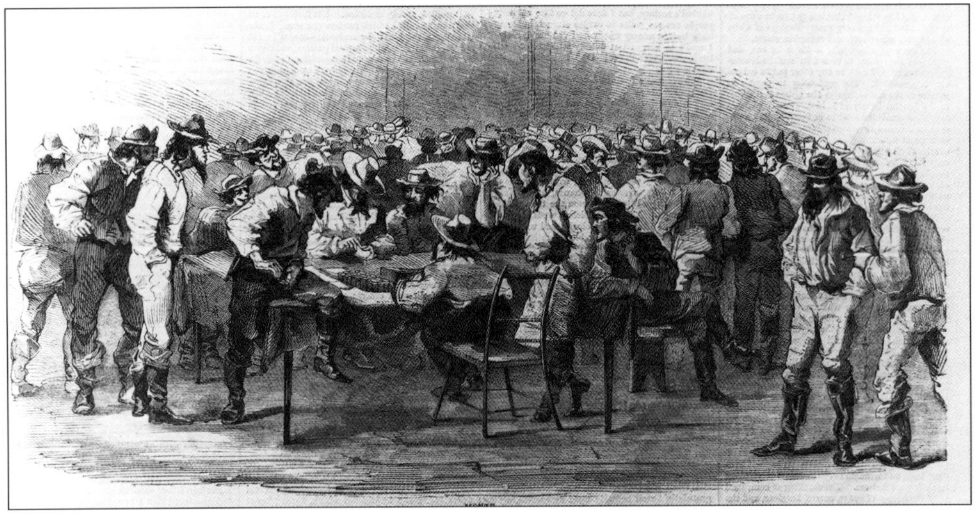

Miners surround gamblers playing the game of Monte. The drawing is from an early *Harpers*.

GUIDE TO BUSINESS HOUSES IN COLUMBIA, TUOLUMNE CO., CAL.

Fallon's Hotel.

O. Fallon, Prop'r. First-Class accommodations. Large Hall with Stage adjoining, for public entertainments. Junction of B'dway and Washington Streets.

Sewell Knapp,

Dealer in Choice Groceries and Provisions, Hardware, Crockery, Flour, Feed, Grain and General Merchandise, cor. Main and State.

G. Wing,

Retal Dealer in Stoves, Tinware, Housekeeping Furniture, &c. Hydraulic Pipe, Made and Repaired. Main Street.

James Wilson,

Manufacturer and Dealer in first quality Ladies', Gents' and Children's Boots and Shoes, also, work made and repaired to order. Main Street.

R. H. Towle,

Watchmaker and Jeweler, Watches and Clocks repaired, Jewelry of every description manufactured from native gold. Main Street.

Siebert & Vassalo.

U. S. Mail Stage Office, Billiard and Wine Hall, choice brands of Imported and Domestic Wines, Liquors and Cigars, cor. Main and Fulton Streets.

H. Childs.

Horse-Shoeing and Blacksmithing, Miner's Tools made to order and repairs neatly executed, cor. Main and Jackson Streets.

Columbia Bakery.

Antone Siebert, Proprietor. Soda, Graham, Wine and Boston Crackers, Bread, Buns, Wedding Cakes, &c. Main Street.

Wm. Jacobi,

Manufacturer of first quality Boots and Shoes. All work made of the best materials. Repairing neatly done. Main Street.

Empire Saloon,

O. F. Strobringe, Proprietor, Choicest Brands of Imported Wines, Liquors and Cigars. Main Street.

N. Y. Restaurant,

Horace Butler, Proprietor. Meals served at all hours with best the market affords. Main St.

H. Kluber's Saloon.

Wholesale and Retail Dealer in Imported and Domestic Wines, Liquors and Choice Havana Cigars, cor. Main and State Sts.

Meat Market.

D. McCormick & Son, dealers in fresh Beef, Veal, Mutton, Pork, Lard, &c., cor. Main and Fulton Streets.

Columbia, Tuolumne Co., Cal.

Of the many beautiful mountain towns in the State, there is probably none that can boast of a more remarkable or romantic history than Columbia.

Gold was first discovered in the Autumn of '49 in very rich deposits near where the main part of the town now stands. The population soon increased to thousands, and the yield of gold grew to immense quantities. It is estimated by our oldest citizens that the amount of gold taken out in this vicinity since its first discovery, will reach $90,000,000 to $100,000,000. Parties have, with only pick and pan, secured as high as $1800 to $2000 in a single day. For the past few years mining has decreased considerably, on account of surface water, thereby preventing the working of shafts to any great depth, compelling the abandonment of mines, which were yielding in proportion to the depth secured. This difficulty is likely to be effectually removed, however, by the construction of a working and drain tunnel, at a depth of 150 feet below the surface, extending to the Stanislaus River, a distance of about one and a quarter miles. This enterprise when completed, will reestablish mining interests on a better basis than ever, and with it, the return of former success and prosperity.

Many valuable discoveries, in Gold bearing veins of quartz, have been made near the place, some of which need but the requisite amount of capital invested to insure success and a handsome dividend to its owners.

Columbia has suffered severly by fires, it being twice entirely destroyed by this element.

Two miles distant from the town exists an extensive Marble Quarry, pronounced to be of a superior quality, by San Francisco dealers. Lime of excellent quality, can also be produced from rock in this section. Plumbago is found in quantities, equal to the requirements of trade, in purity and fineness.

Agriculture is quite successfully followed, and Fruits of nearly every kind grow in abundance. The crops in general are cured and furnished to the coast markets.

There are several church organizations, and three churches, a fine Graded School, Masonic and Odd Fellows Lodges, two Fire Companies, &c. It is thought that the great demand for the contemplated railroad will soon secure its completion. The climate is exceedingly healthy, with a slight fall of snow in winter.

Ed. Elias,

Post Master, Agent W. U. Tel. Co., and dealer in Books, Stationery, Medicines, Notions, Cigars, Tobacco, &c. Main St.

E. E. White,

Justice of the Peace, Notary Public and Conveyancer. Secretary Argentum Gold and Silver Mining Co.

Joel Levy & Son,

Dealers in Dry Goods, Clothing, Furnishing and Fancy Goods, Notions. Main Street.

H. Sevening,

Agent Wells, Fargo & Co.'s Express, Banking and Assay Office. Highest price paid for gold. Main Street.

Diamond Job and Music Print., Oakland.

Tuolumne Water Co.

Jos. Pownall, Secretary, office on Fulton Street.

G. W. Hale,

Dealer in Lumber of all dimensions, Sash, Doors, Blinds, &c. Planing Mill in connection. Work of all kinds furnished to order.

M. Brady,

Dealer in choice family Groceries and Provisions, Wines, Liquors, &c., cor. Broadway and Washington Streets.

Columbia Livery.

Conveyances of every description. Particular attention to parties visiting Big Trees and Yosemite Valley. M. Kelly, Proprietor. Broadway.

L. Brunet,

Dealer in Dry Goods, Clothing, Hats, Caps, Boots, Shoes and Notions, cor. Main & Jackson Sts.

Charles Koch.

Shaving and Hair Dressing Rooms, Hot and Cold Baths. Main Street.

John Richards.

Blacksmithing, Horseshoeing, General Repairing, Miner's Tools made to order and Mill Picks sharpened to order. Broadway.

F. J. Schoettgen,

Butcher and Stock dealer. All kinds of fresh and salt Meats, Sausage, Tripe, &c., Main Street.

M. J. Rehm.

Grower and Dealer in all kinds of California Wines, also, choice Foreign Wines, Liquors and Cigars, cor. Main and Jackson Sts.

J. S. Sullivan,

Inventor and Manufacturer of the Lightning Plum Pitters, saves fruit and does the work in one fourth the time. Orders by mail promptly filled.

Springfield Brewery.

Jas. Schooler, dealer in choice Wines, Liquors, Ales, Imported and Domestic Cigars. State St.

Bornheim's Saloon.

Dealer in Foreign and Domestic Wines, Liquors, Ales and Choice Havana Cigars. Main St.

Columbo Restaurant.

D. Rolleri Proprietor. Meals and Lunches served at all hours. Choice Wines Liquors and Cigars. cor. Main and State Streets.

An early guide to business houses in the town of Columbia, California. Among the establishments are: Siebert & Vassalo, which had a U.S. Mail stage office, billiard and wine hall, and choice wines; Fallons Hotel, which had a stage for entertainment; H. Sevening, an agent for the Wells Fargo & Co. Express; and the famous, Joel Levy & Son, dealers in dry goods, clothing, furnishings, and fancy goods.

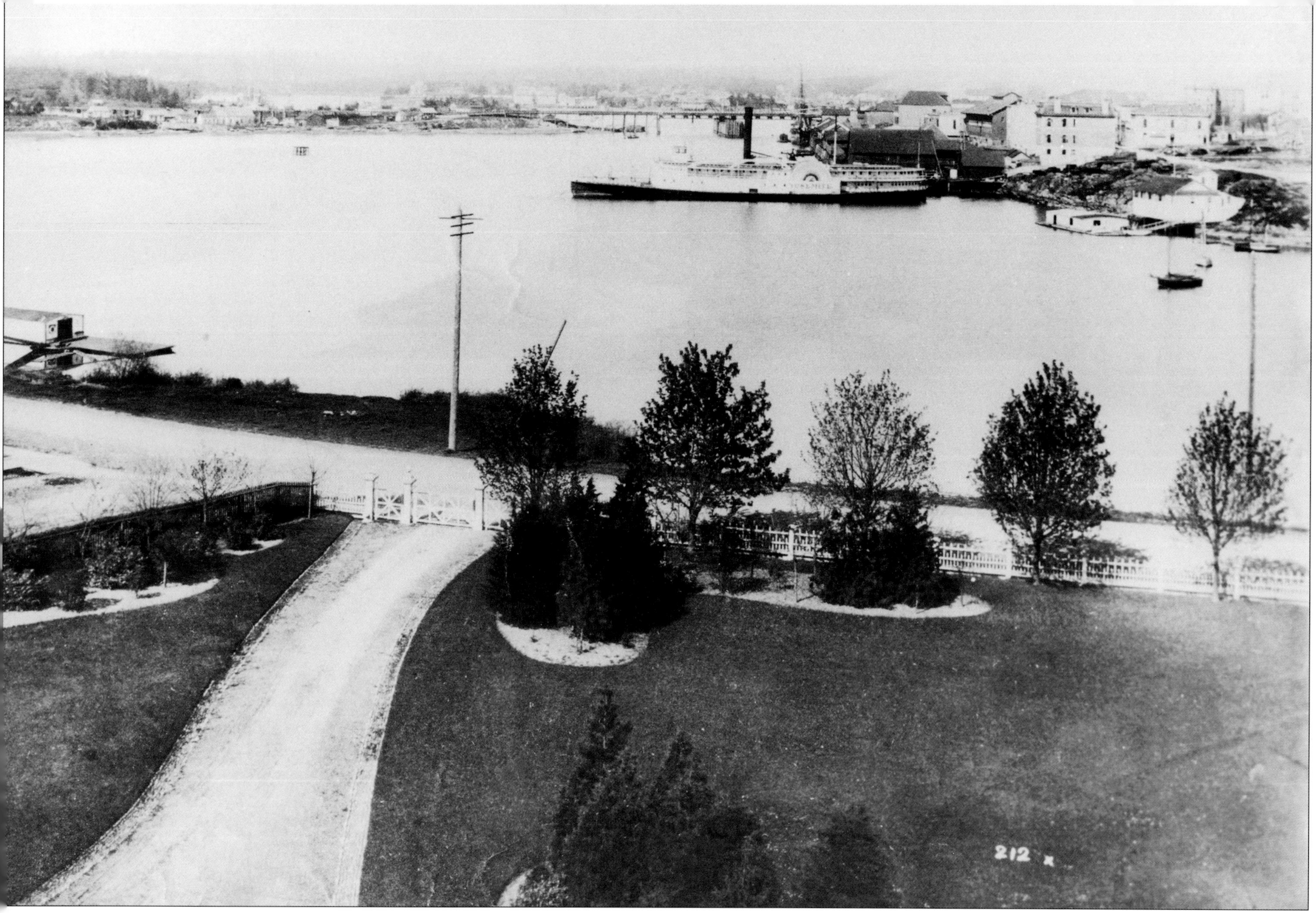

An albumen photo showing the famous Yosemite Steamer, waiting in port to haul both passengers and coaches along the Sacramento River. Made for the California Steam Navigation Company, it was one of the fastest ships of its type. This ship came to a bitter end when its captain, a Mr. Edwards, expected the current to strike the port side and thus throw the ship over to the starboard side slowly. Instead with a rush, the current struck the ship's starboard and threw it onto the rocks, killing everyone on board.

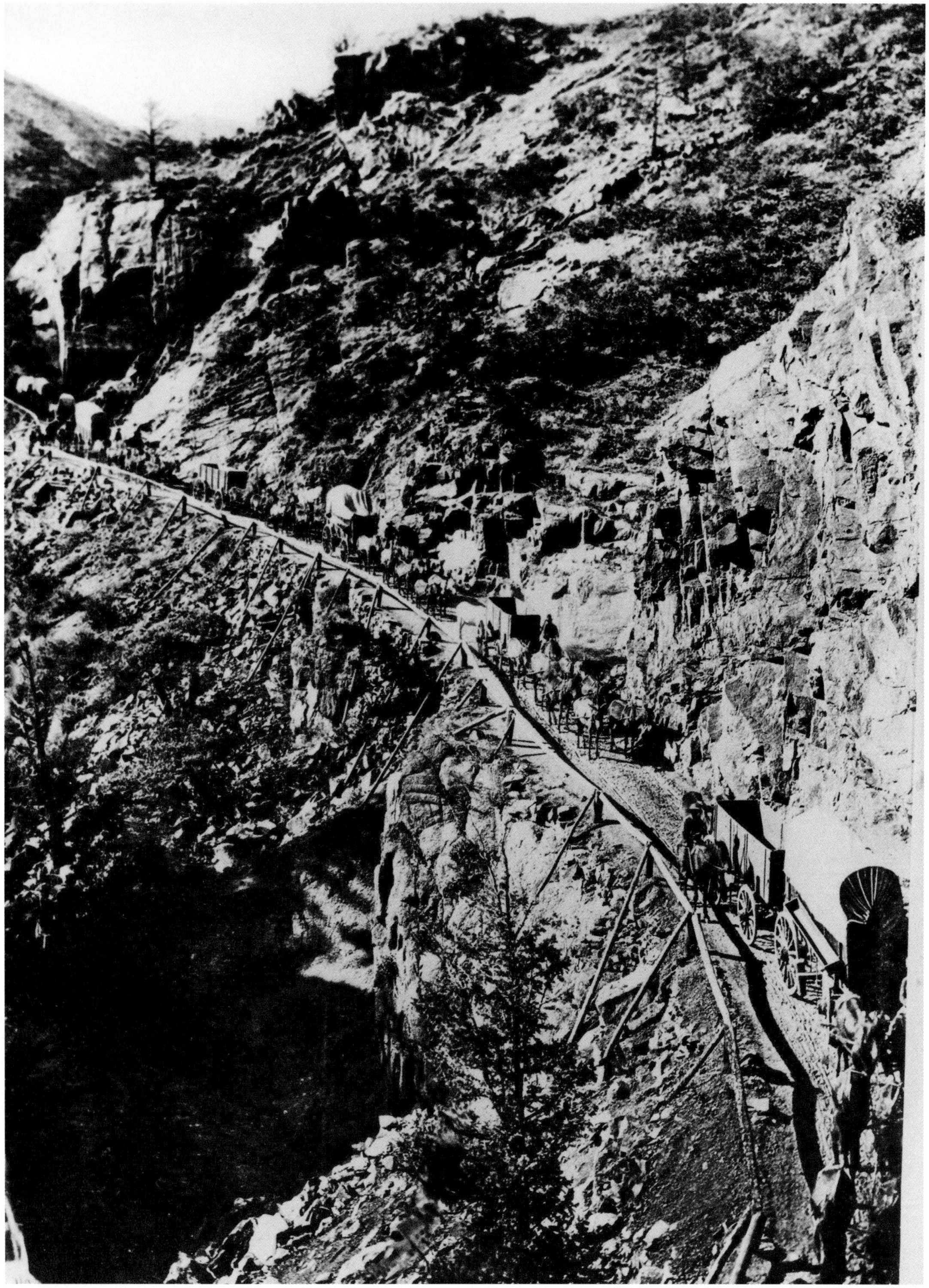

The famous "Ute" Pass, used by the immigrants traveling west. This was the chief pass through the front range and originally used by the Indians. The photo is made from the original glass negative.

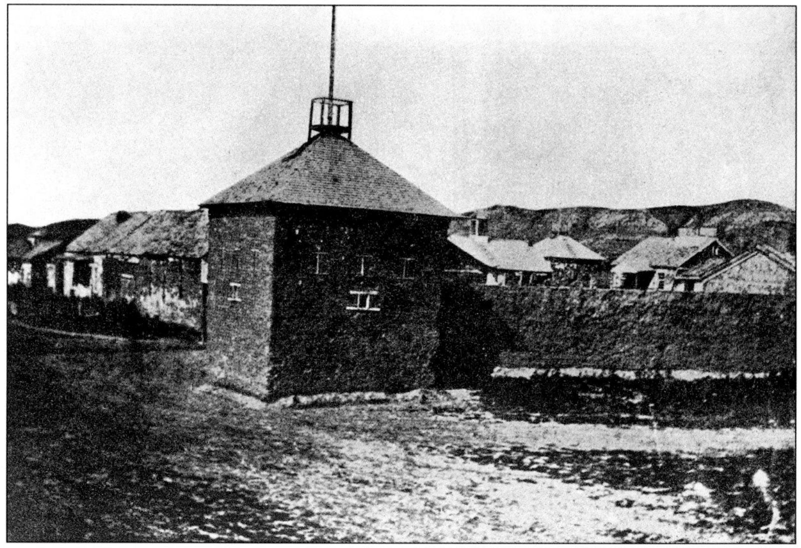

Old Fort Benton in the 1870s, showing the block house wall and buildings inside.

Opposite Page:
Coloma, California was a bustling place during the gold rush, but these deserted buildings are all that is left from that period.

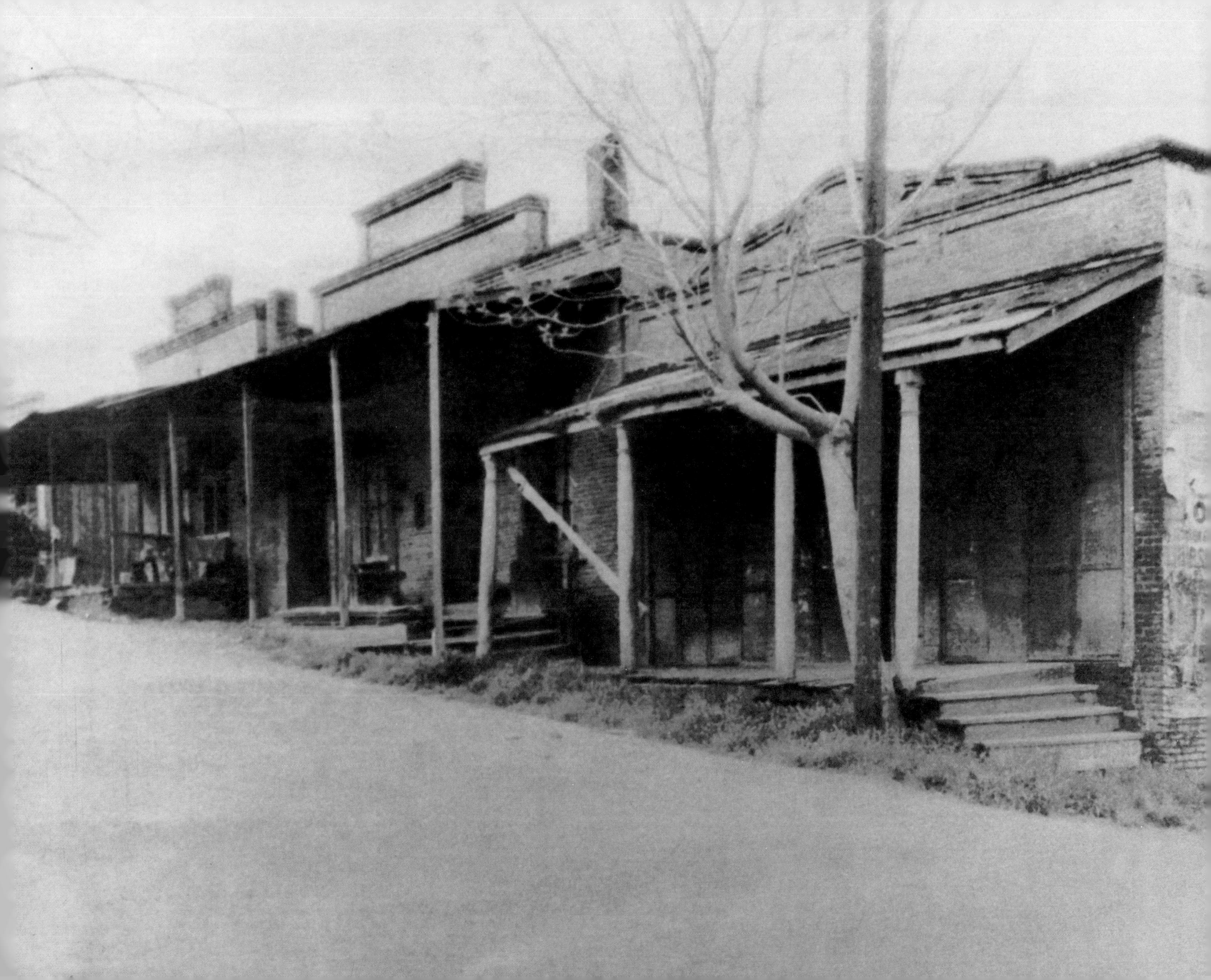

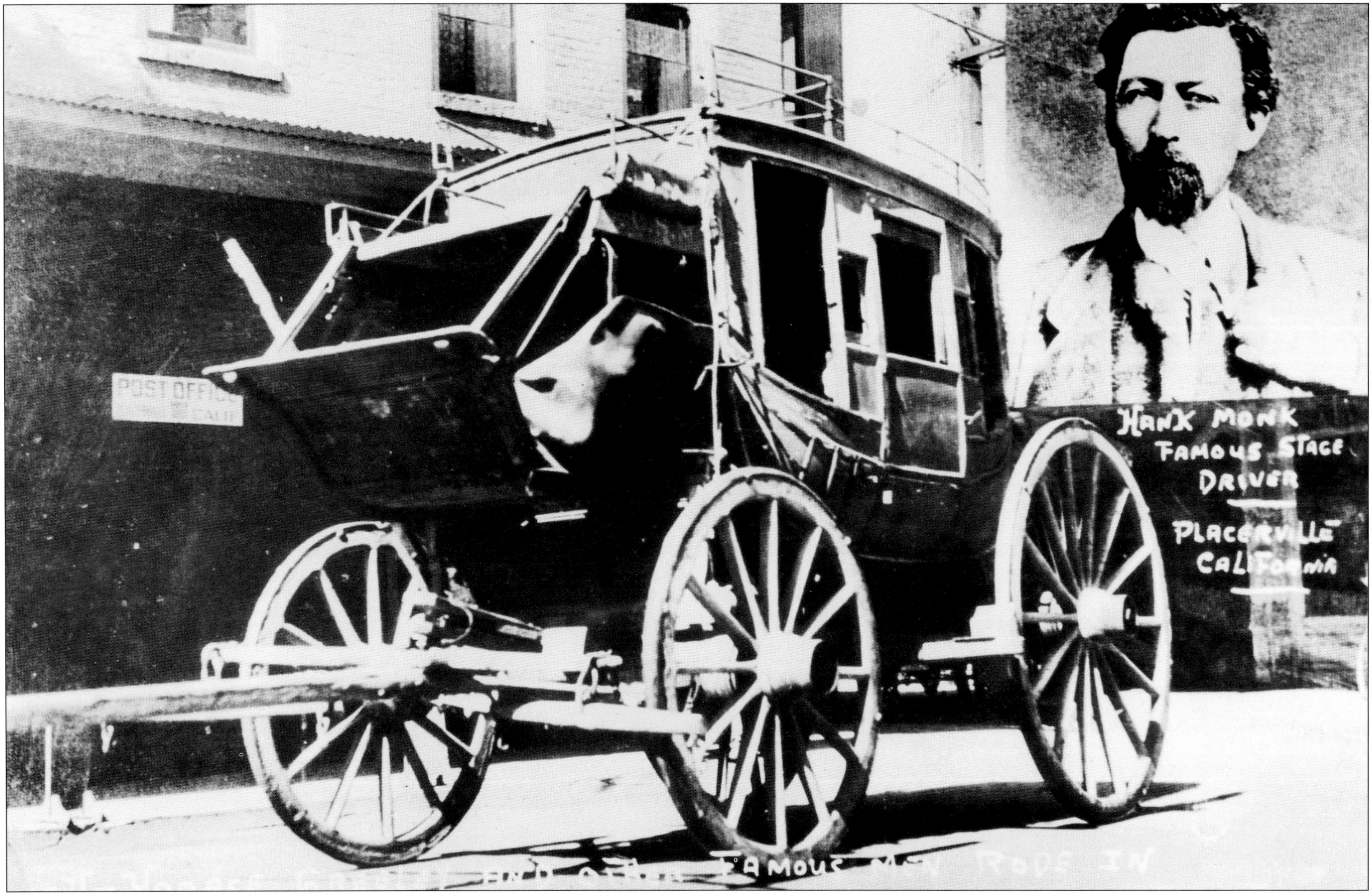

The famous stage driver, Hank Monk, who took publisher Horace Greeley on a long and bumpy ride that made history. The coach is parked outside of Placerville, California's post office.

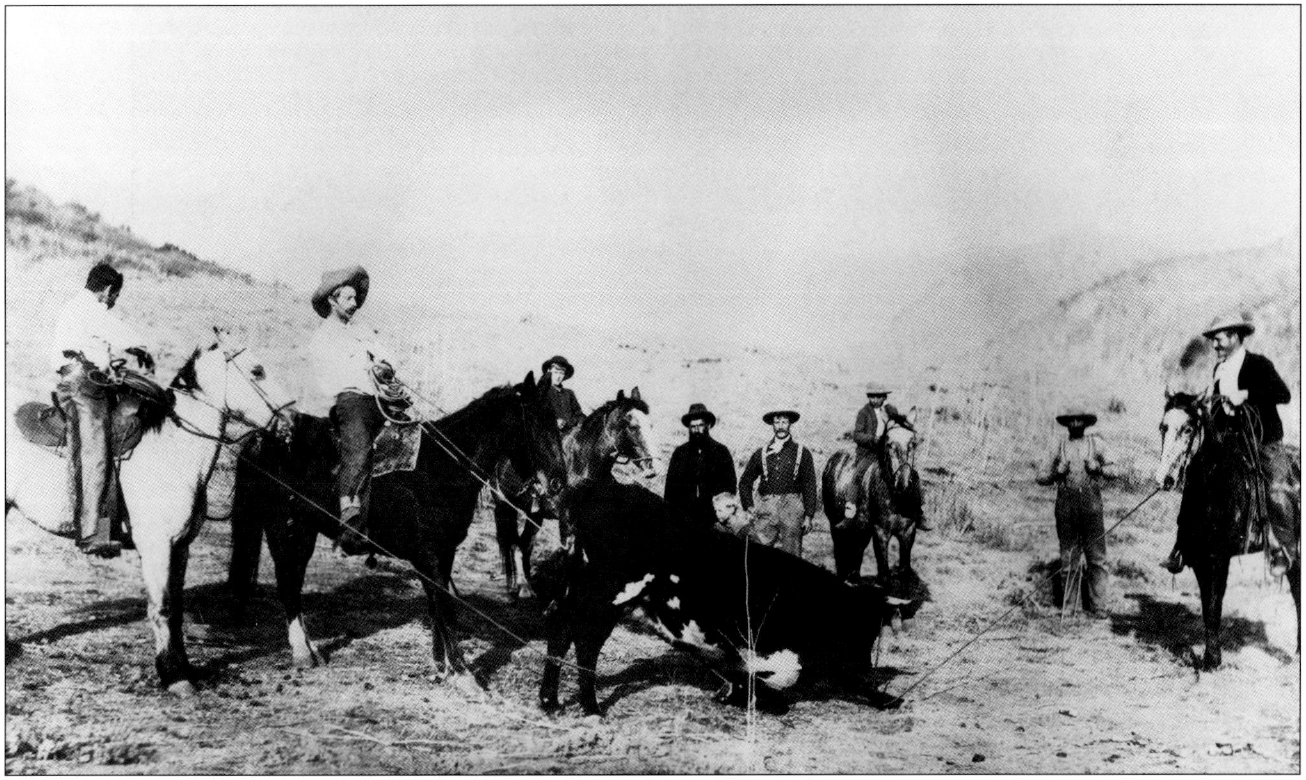

These early California cowboys are ready to throw a steer, while working on Gilibrand's Ranch in Simi Valley. The photo is credited to Garden Photo Co.

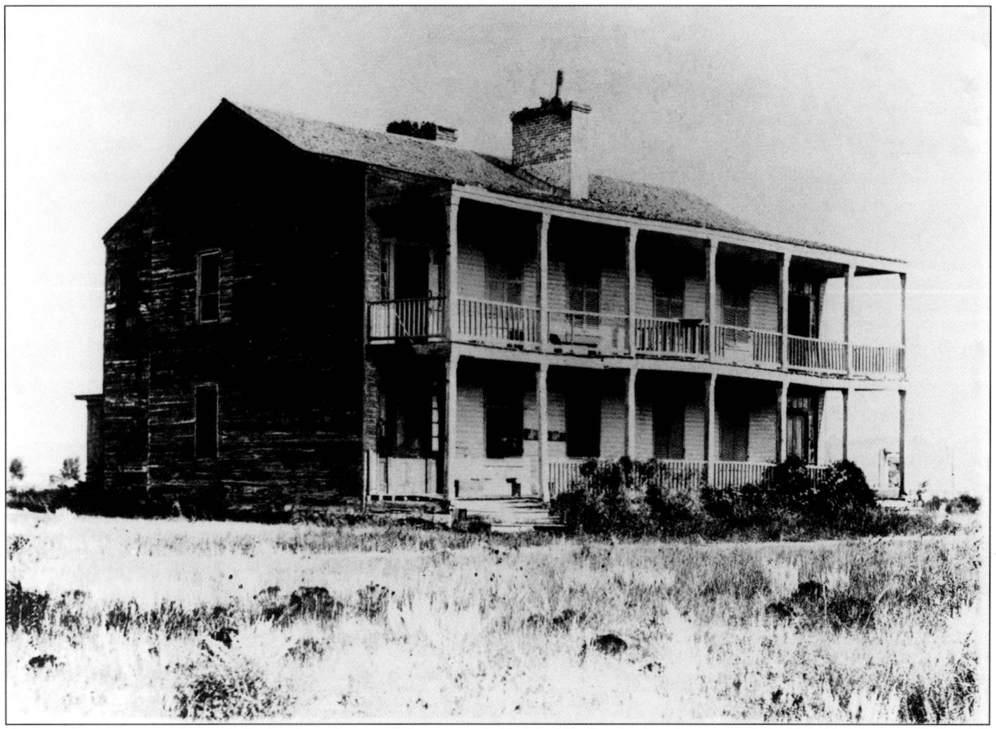

This building was a barracks called "Bedlam." The troops stationed here fought many battles with the Indians.

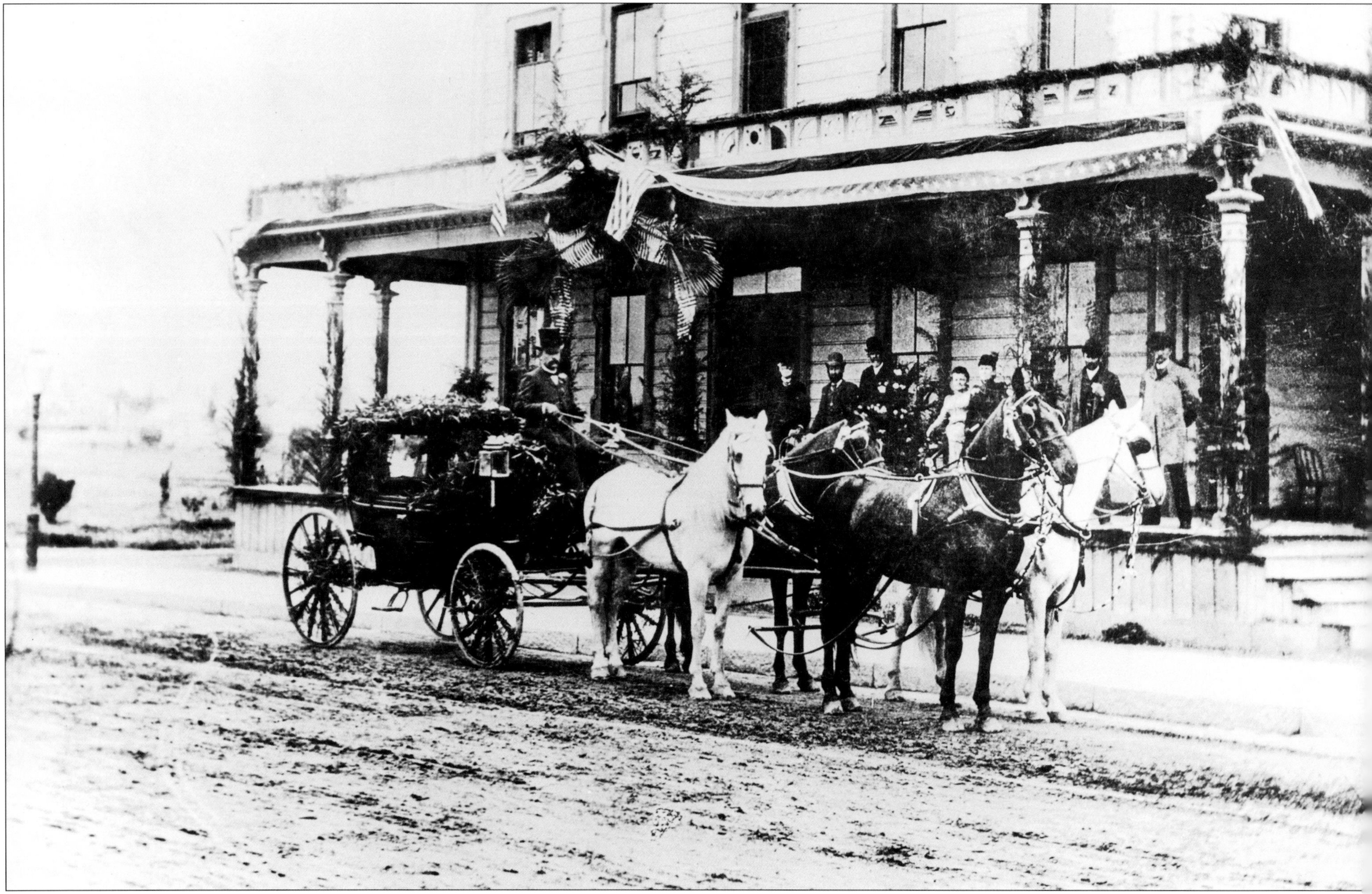

The stagecoach parked outside the hotel where President Harrison stayed in Pasadena, California.

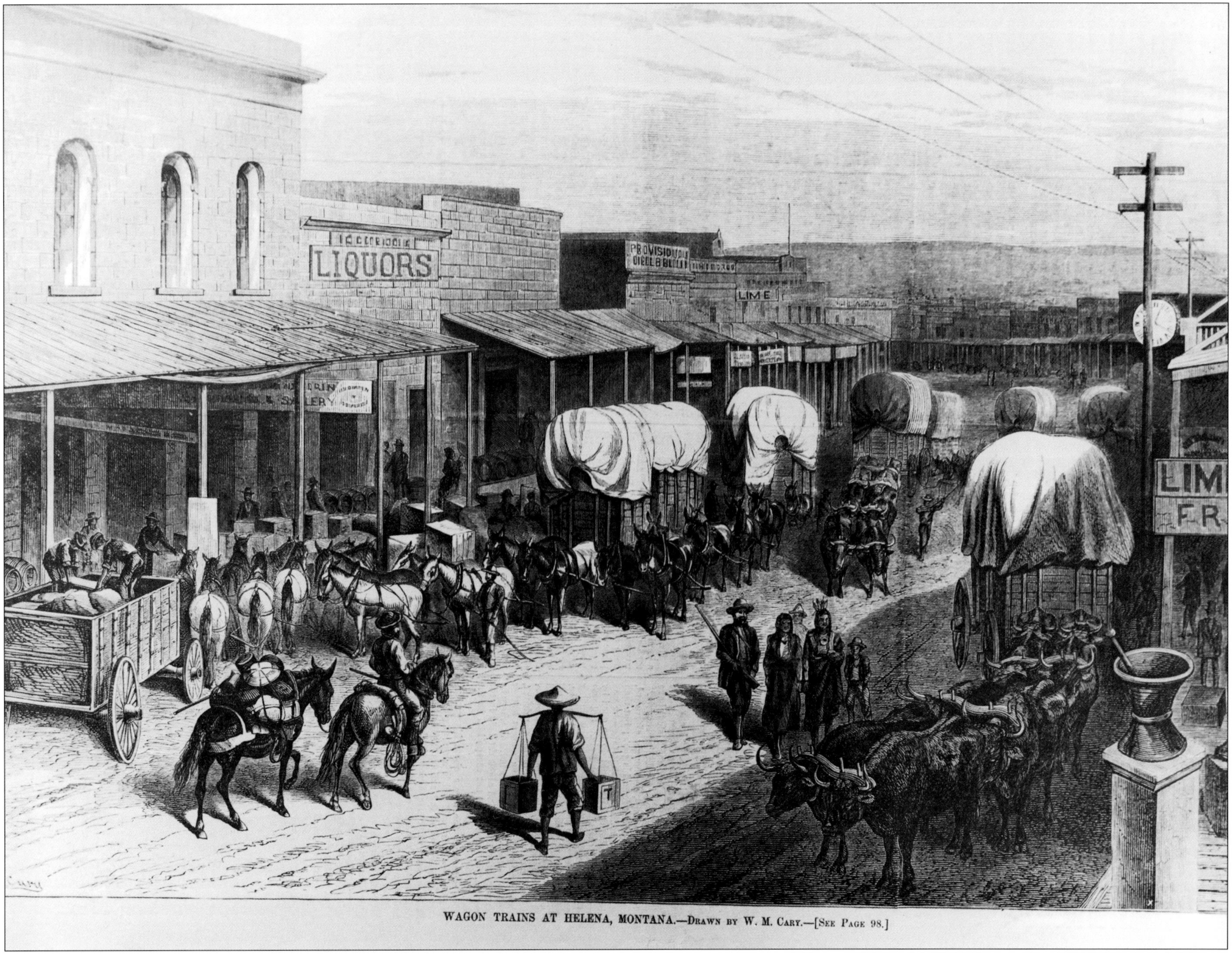

A fine drawing by W. M. Cary, from *Harpers* showing wagon trains at Helena, Montana.

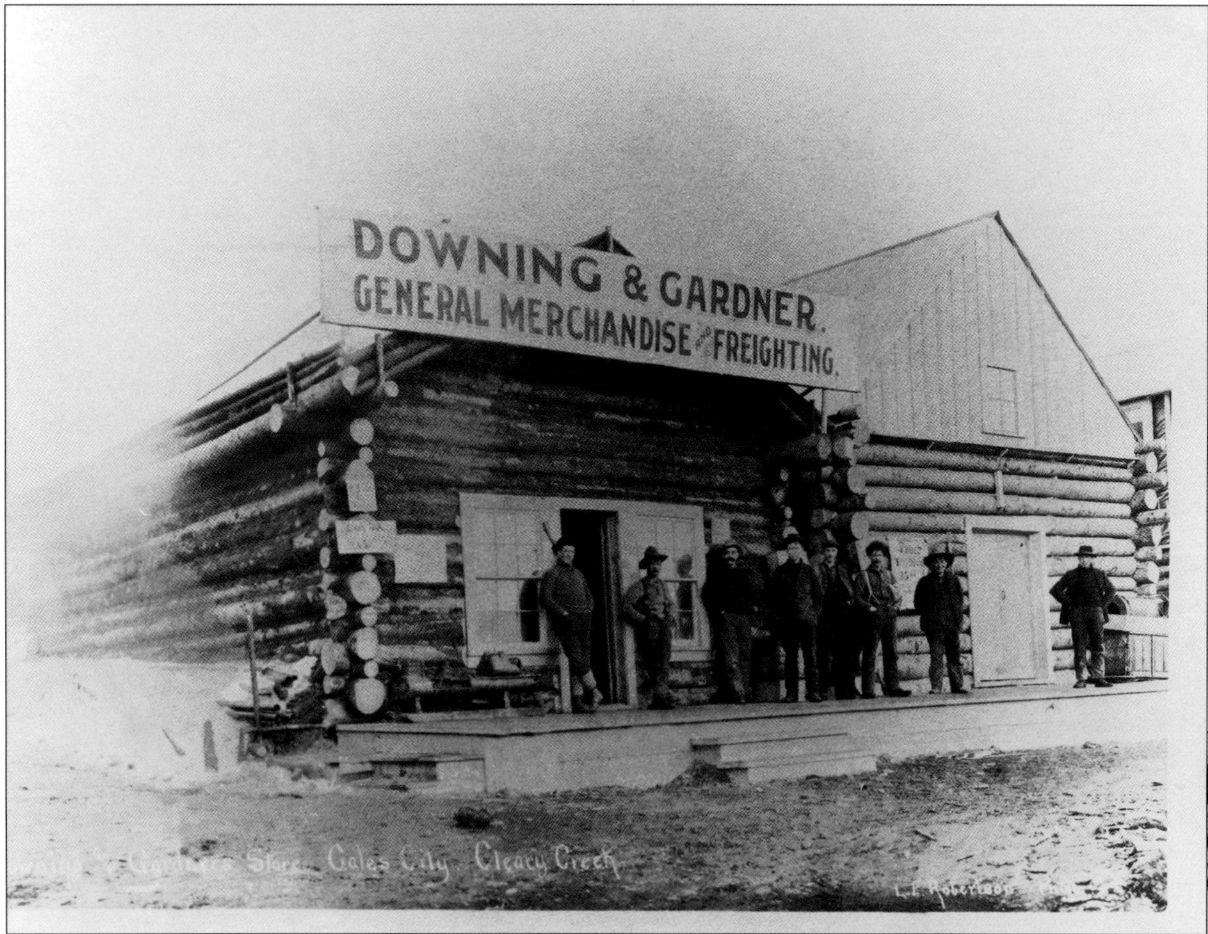

In Gales Creek, Oregon, a group of men pose for their portrait in front of the Downing and Gardner stage stop and freighting store. The photo is credited to L..L. Robinson.

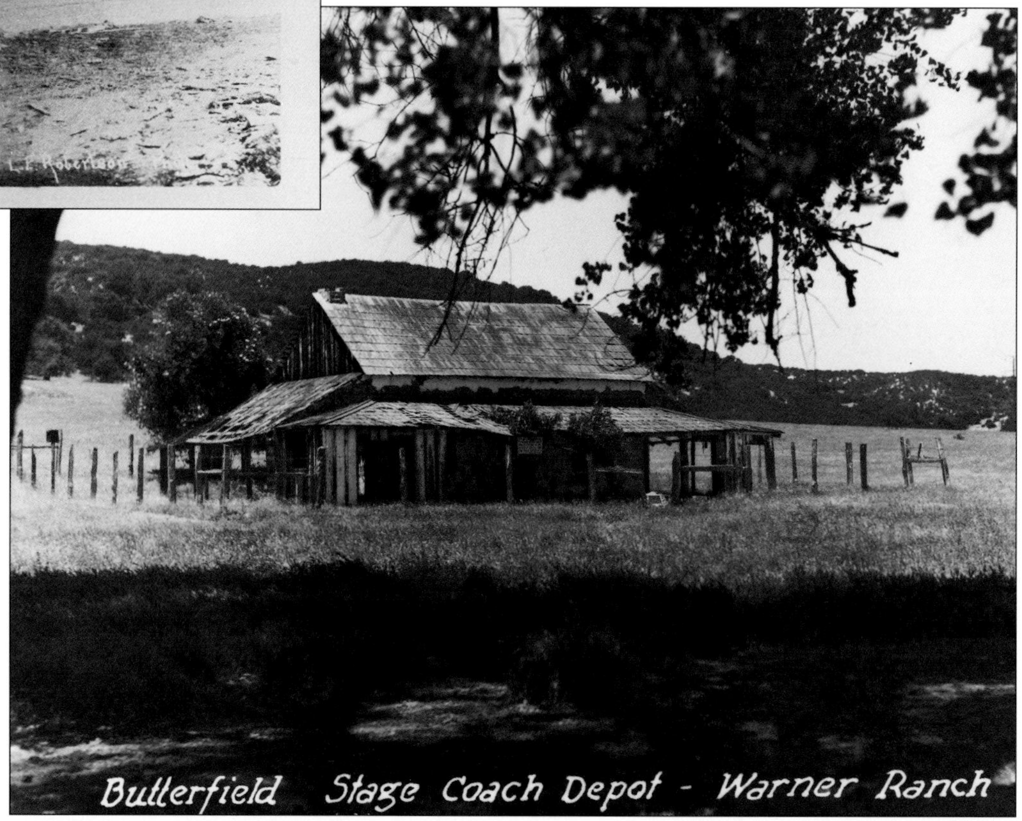

The old Butterfield Stagecoach Depot, at Warner Ranch, California.

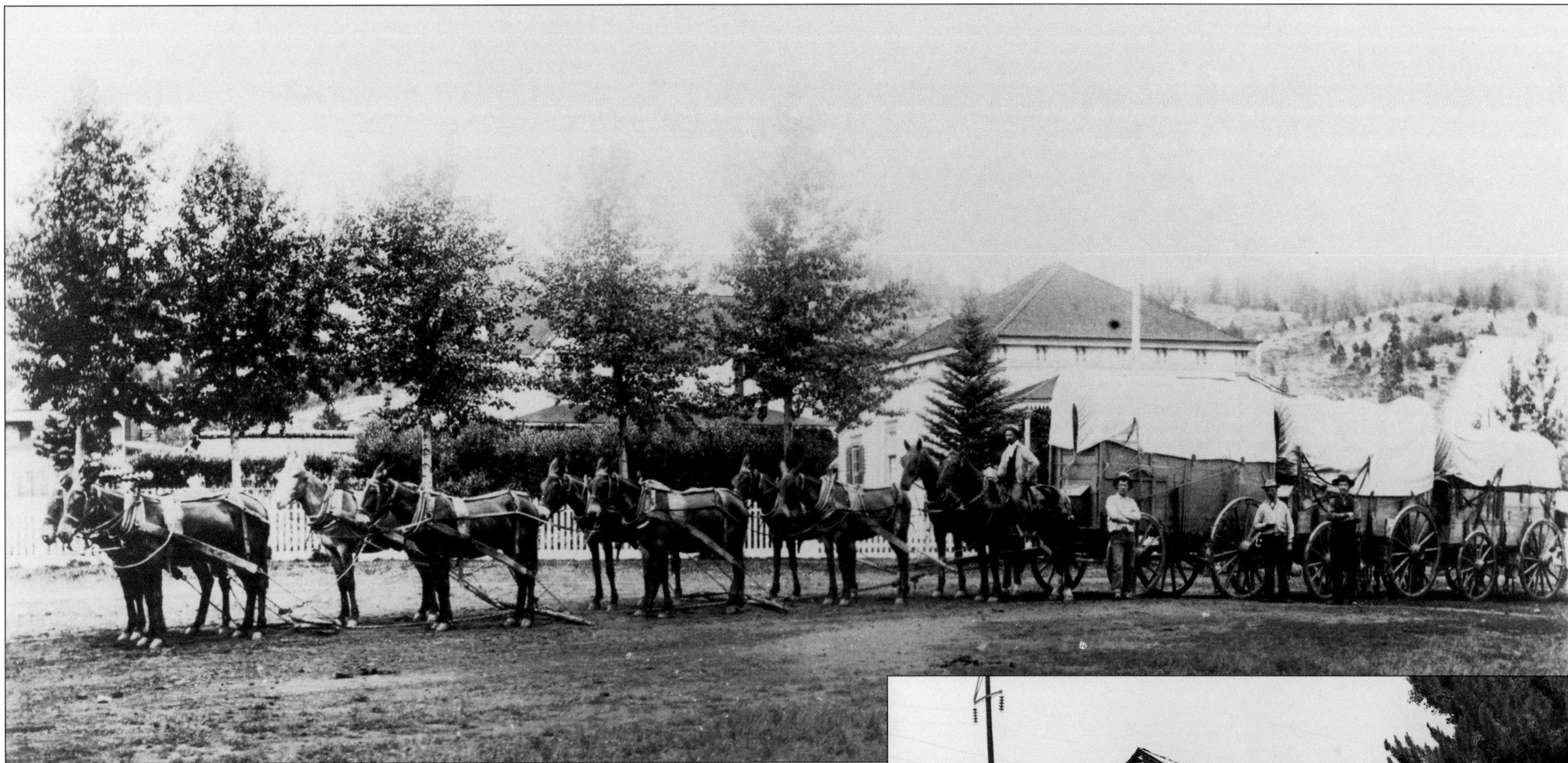

A Wells Fargo team stands for its photograph. This was a supply train that traveled to the different stage stations in 1859. It carried 25,000 pounds of feed in each load. The photograph was from Emile La Forest, a superintendent of Wells Fargo.

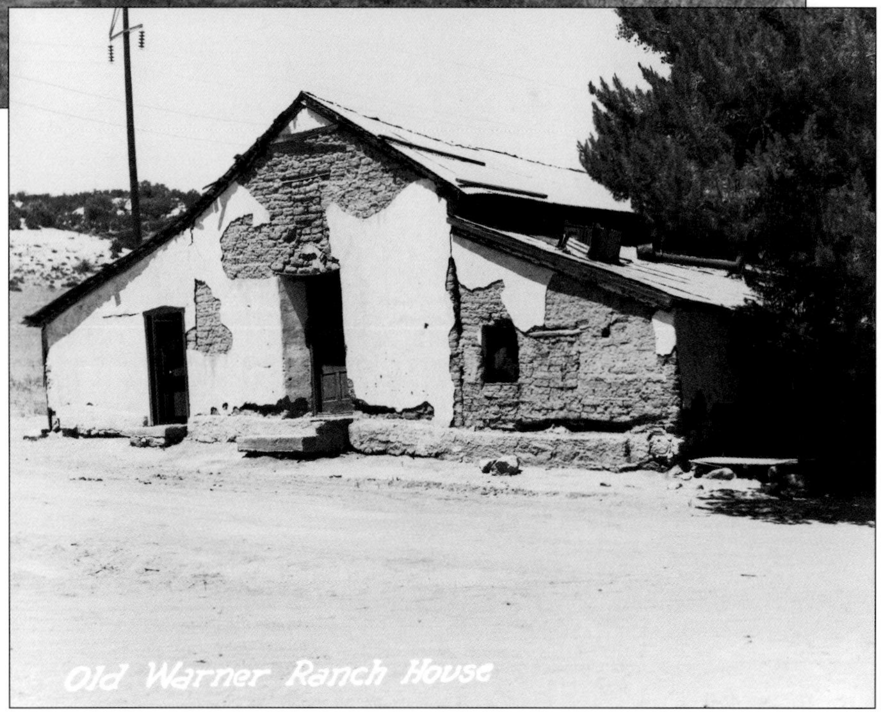

The old ranch house at Warner Ranch during the stagecoach days.

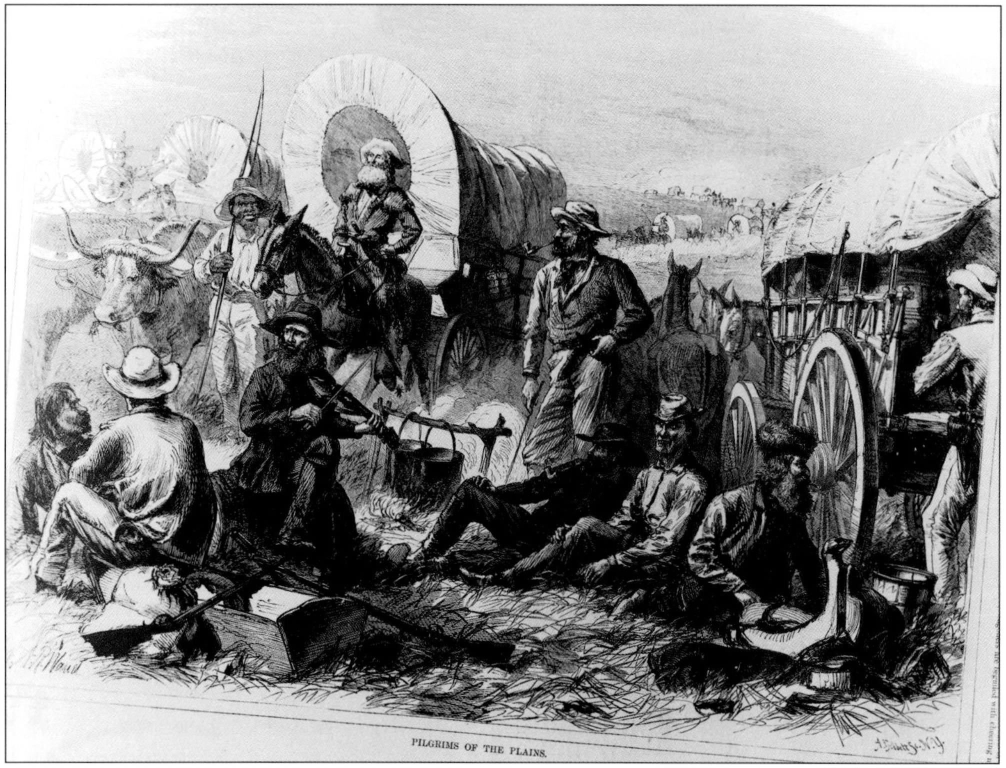

A fine drawing from *Harpers* illustrates a rest period for the "Pilgrims of the Plains."

A mammoth tree stump creates a dance floor for a party of thirty-persons holding a party. A drawing from an early *Harpers*.

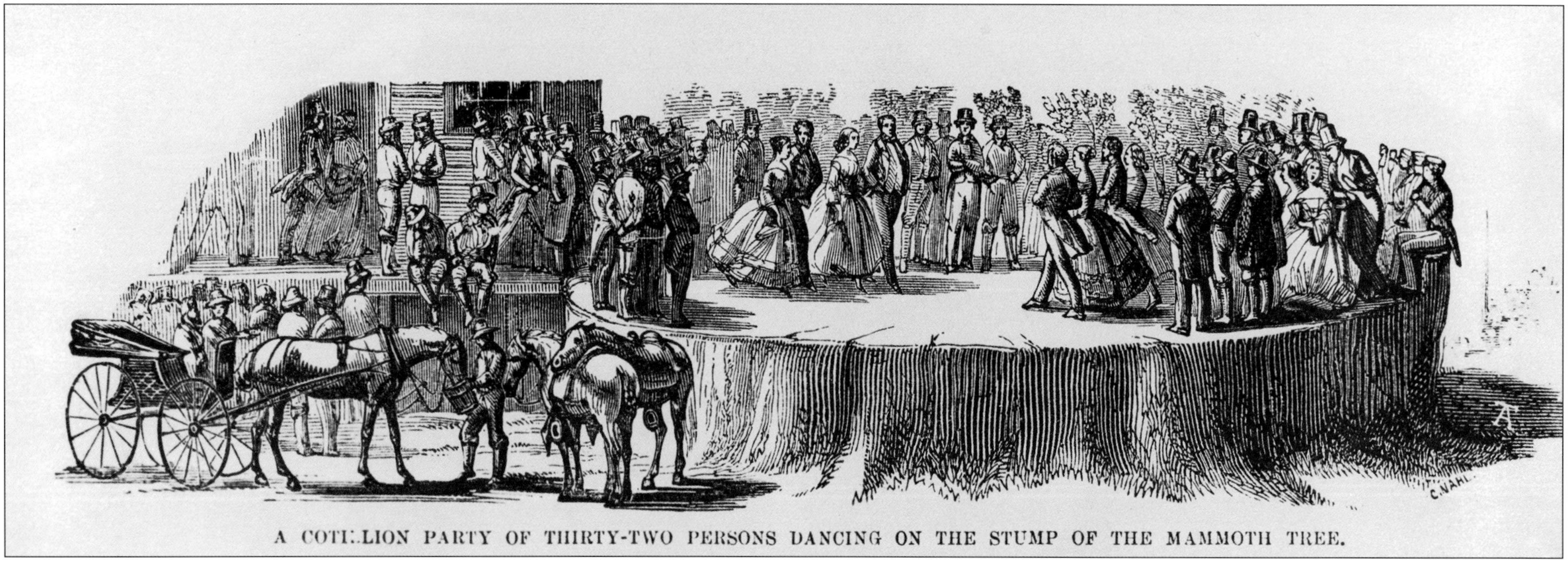

A rare photograph of an interior of a early stagecoach depot. The men are spending the time reading and studying in the middle of winter. The photograph made by flash powder resulted in the white spot at the upper center.

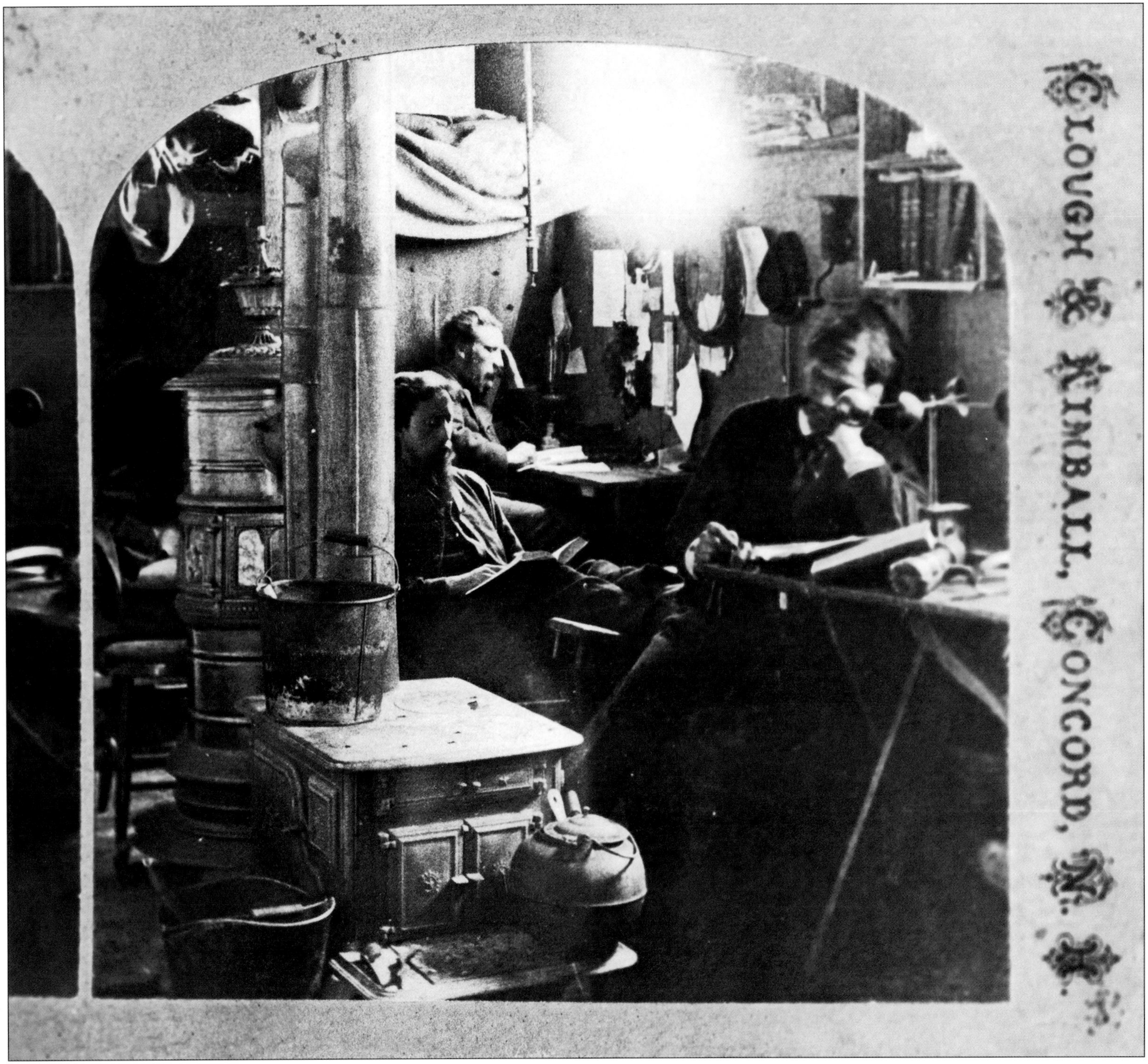

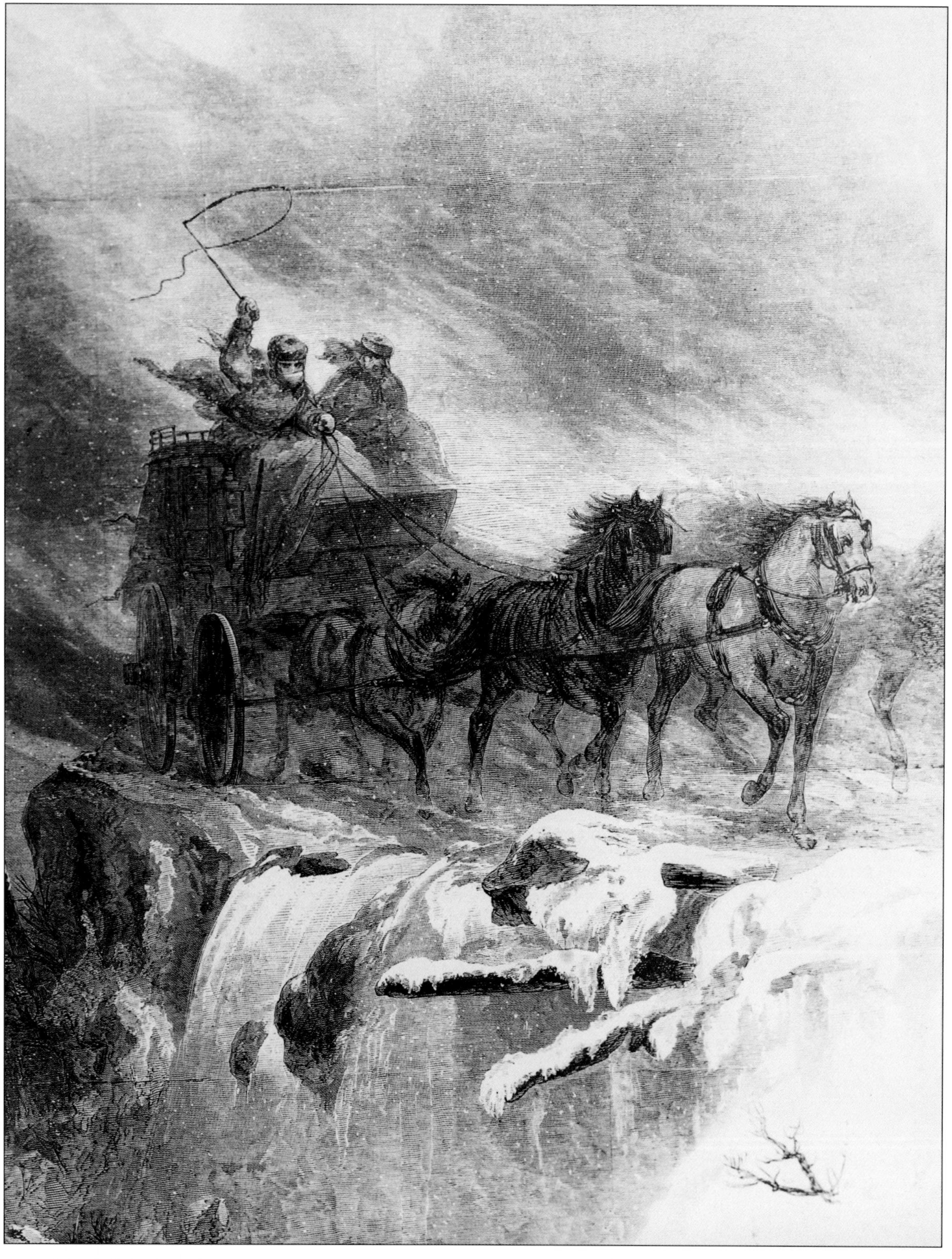

In the middle of a blizzard an artist depicts the hazard and danger of driving a U.S. Mail stagecoach near a slippery edge at an area called Guy's Gulch. Made for *Harpers* weekly, by Theodore R. Davis

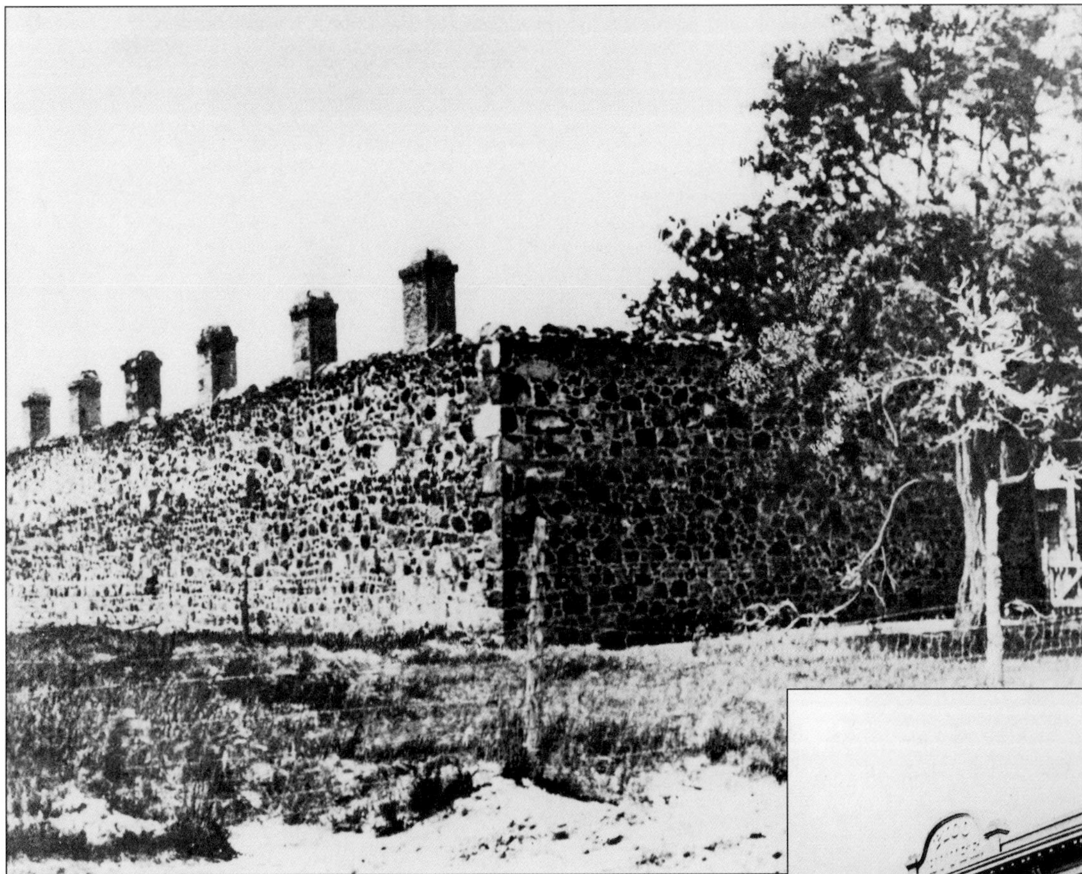

This fort in Utah was constructed as a traveler's way station and refuge from the Indians. Brigham Young directed the construction, which was paid for from church funds. Completed in 1867, inside there was a deep well that provided water. Used as a station for the Overland Stage route, the fort held many sacks of gold bullion. "The Cove Fort," as it was called, had a telegraph room among its twelve rooms.

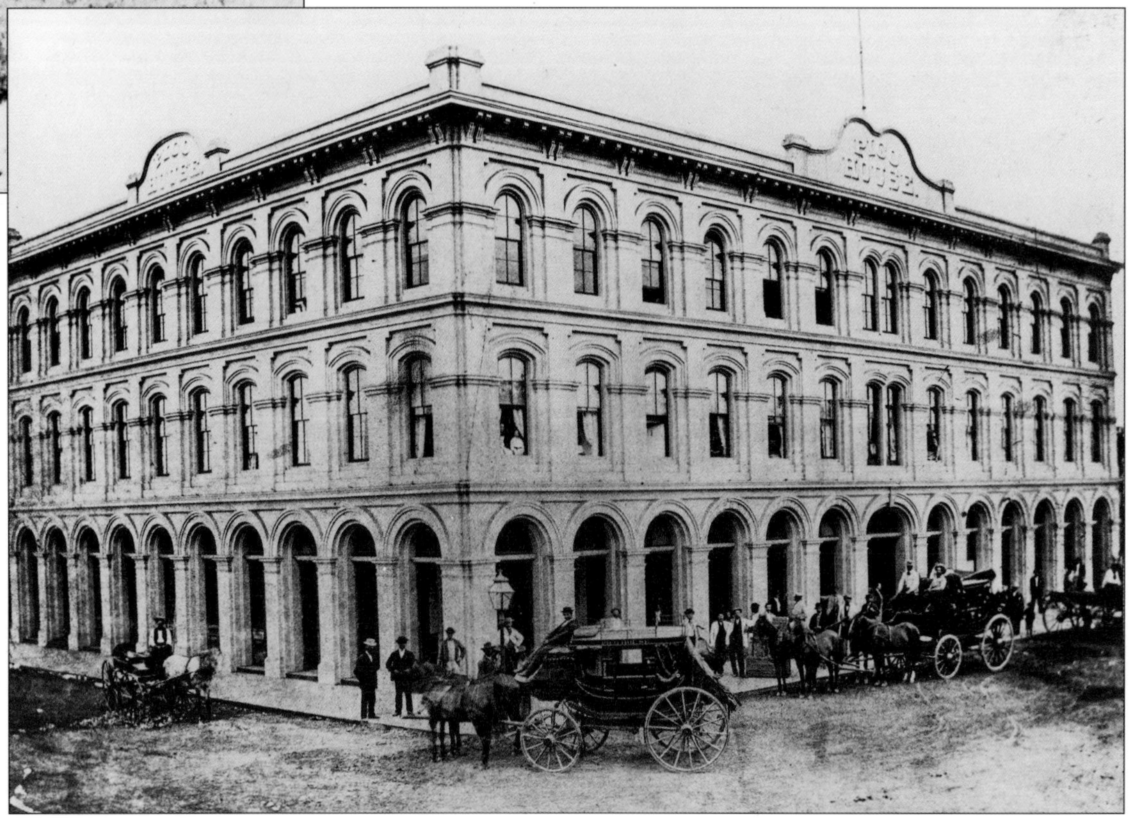

Although the first hotel built in Los Angeles was the Lafayette, the Pico House was where most of the society centered for years. Built in 1869, it had gaslights, several bathtubs, and direct stagecoach exits. Built by Governor Pio Pico himself.

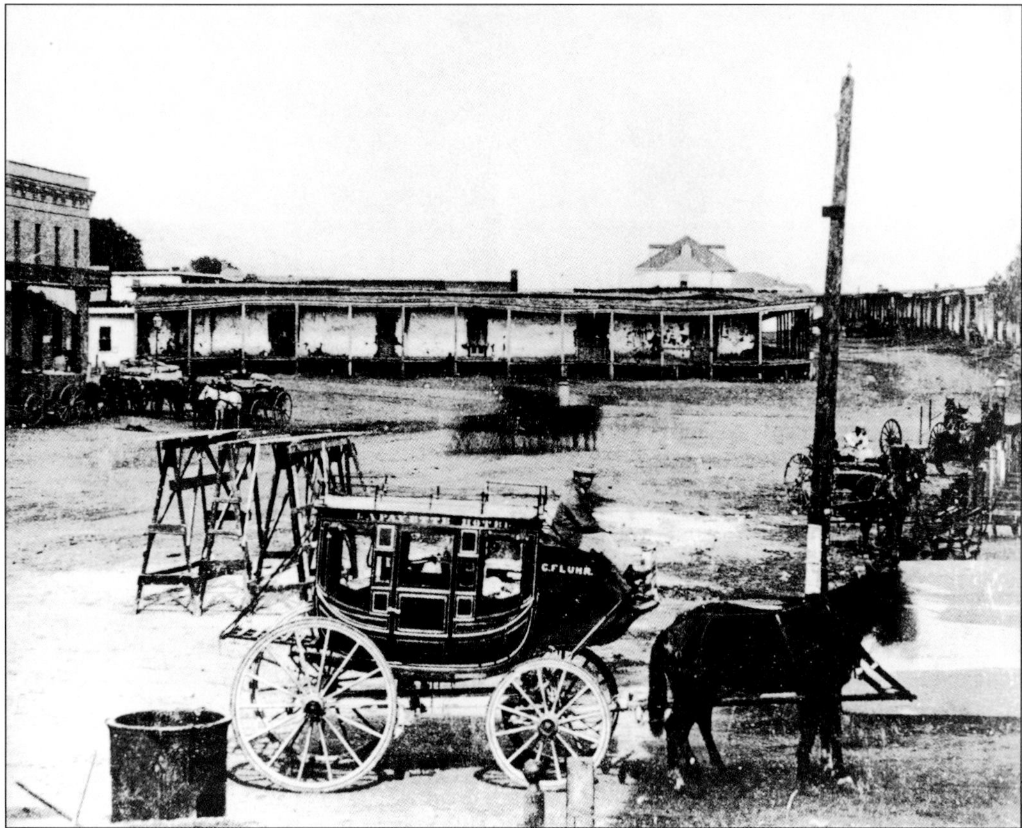

The scene of the Chinese riots in Los Angeles. This began when a member of a one faction kidnapped a woman froma rival faction, which, they declared, had been stealing from them. The first faction swore out an arrest warrant, and the police, catching up to them in their own fast stage, arrested her and brought her back to Los Angeles.

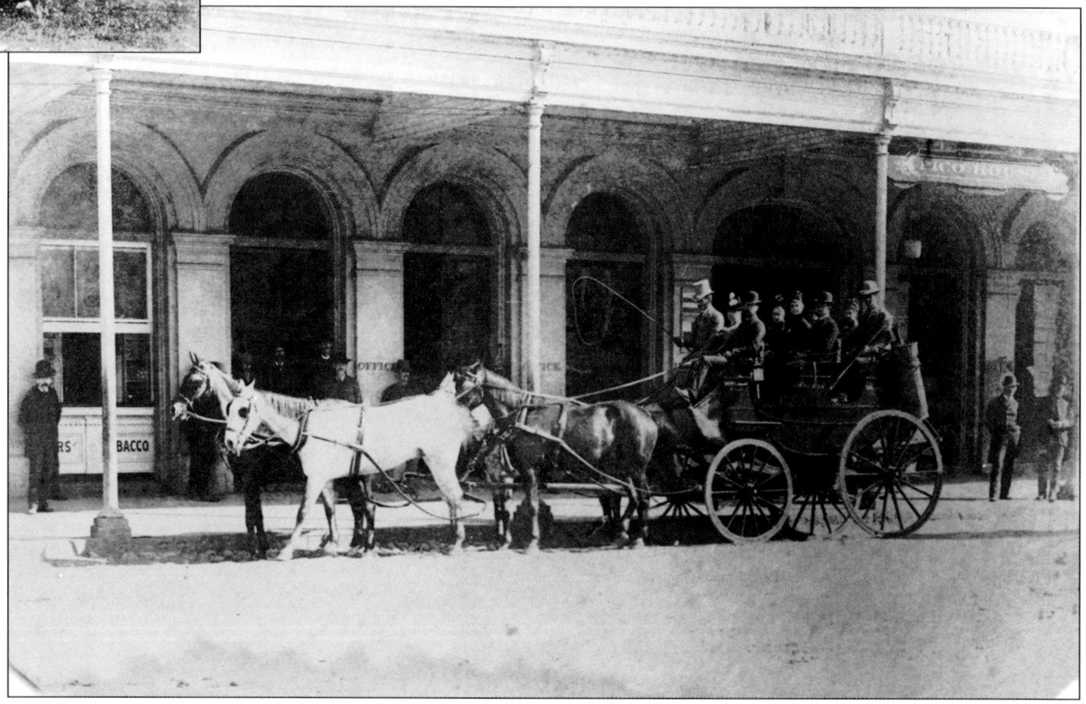

This rare Albumen photo shows a full stagecoach ready to leave from the Pico House.

This early photo of Fort Union, North Dakota, was taken by a member of the Fisk Expedition to Idaho and Montana in 1866. There was another Fort Union built in Montana in 1826. This fort, built in 1829, had troops stationed until 1865. It was only 50 yards from the Montana border.

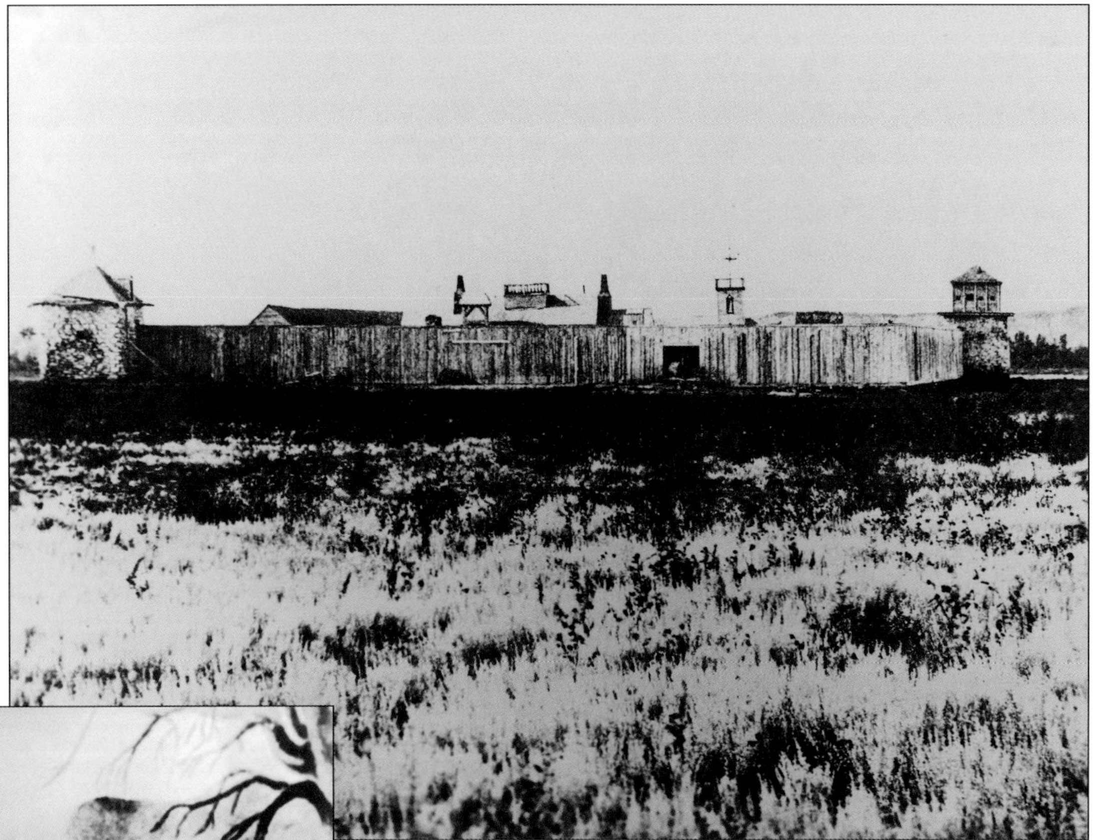

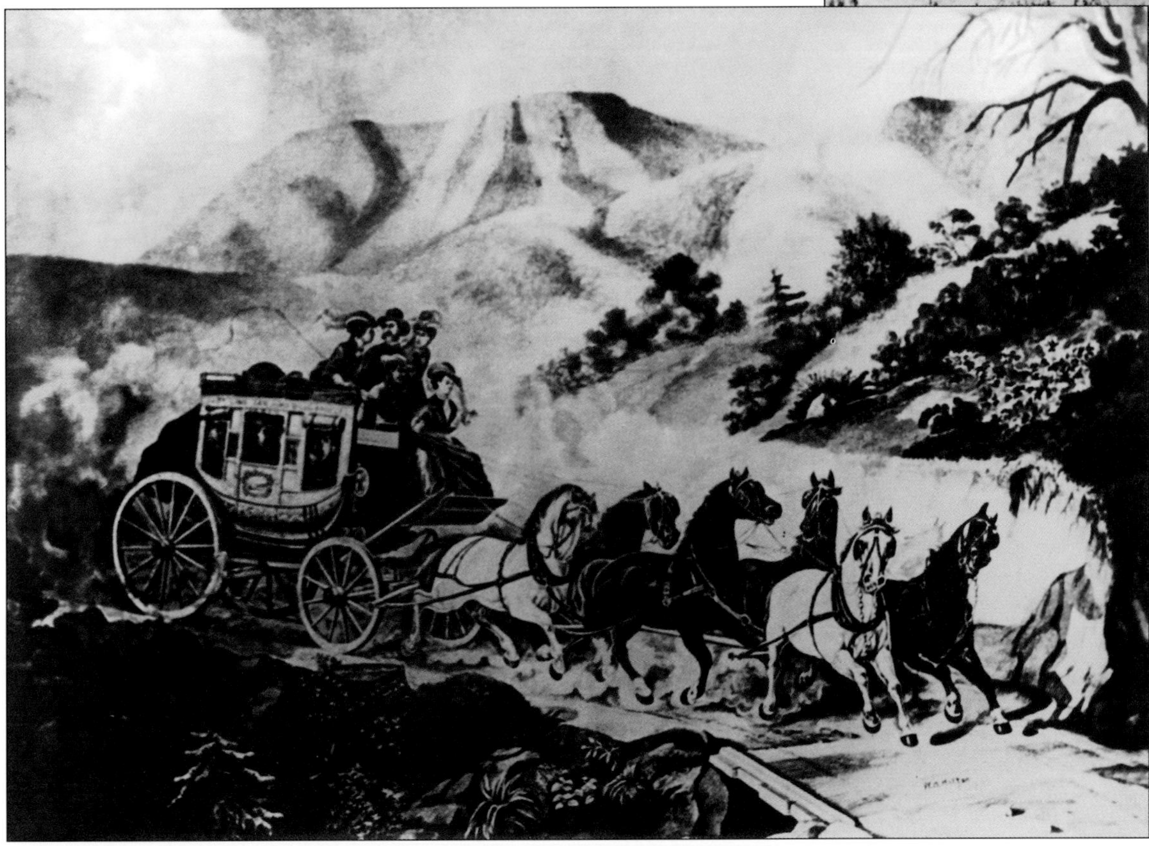

A crayon drawing in a salon at San Luis Obispo, California. From Ben Powers.

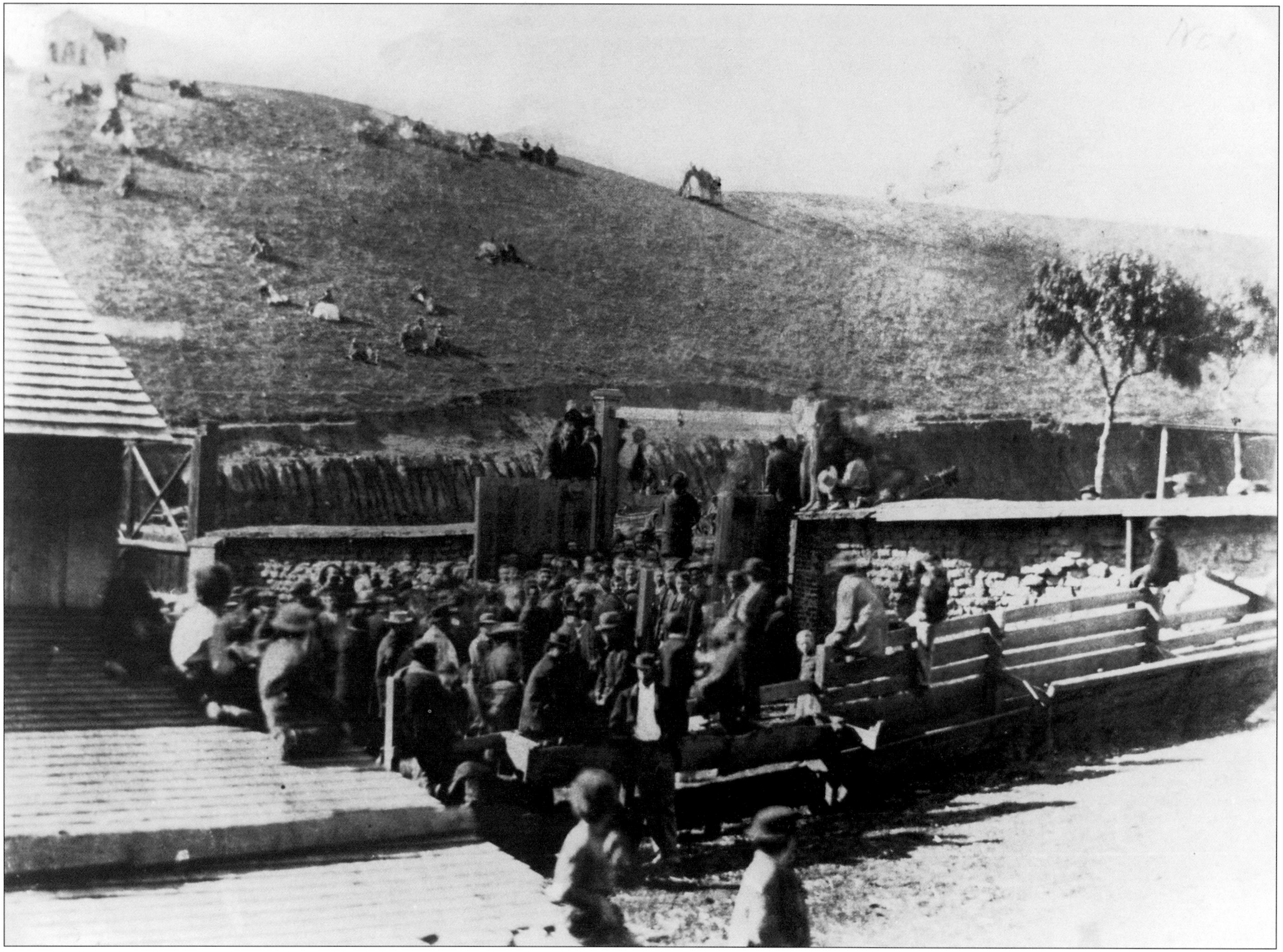

In early Los Angeles, justice was meted out by vigilantes who took to hanging a man for murder. In this case the condemned man was Mr. Tachenairs, a Frenchman. He died by the rope in 1870 and was seen by one and all at the corner of Temple and New High Streets. The hill in the background was called Pound Cake Hill and is now the sight of the red sandstone Court House.

Chapter 3

1861-1871

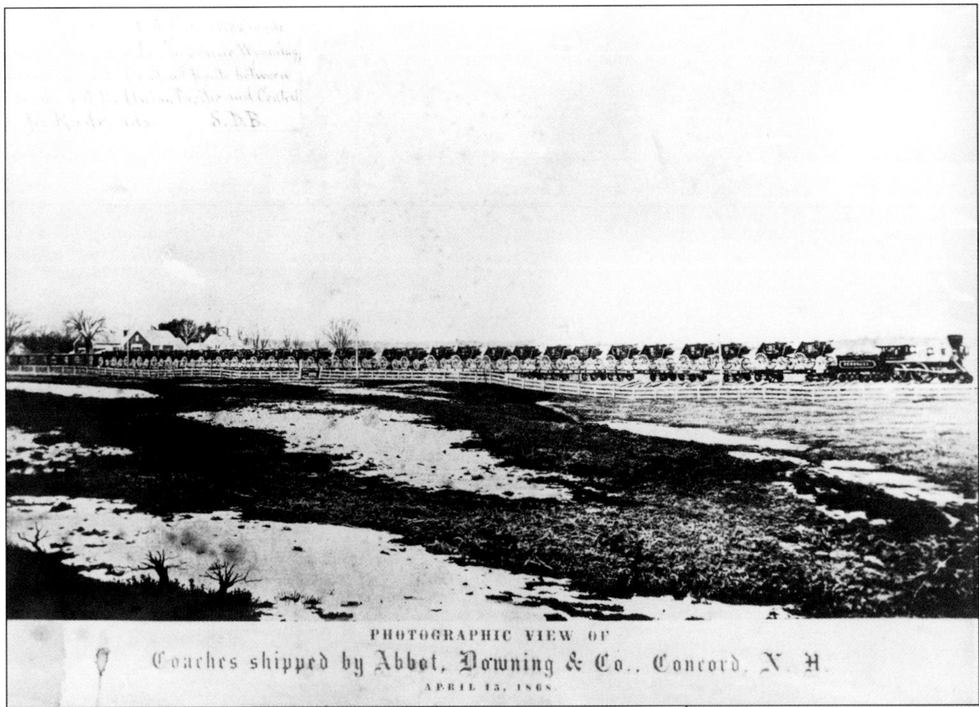

In April of 1868 the Albert Downing Company shipped this long trainload of stagecoaches out of Concord, New Hampshire, bound for Cheyenne, Wyoming. They were to be used on the Overland Route between the terminals of the Union Pacific and Central Pacific railroads.

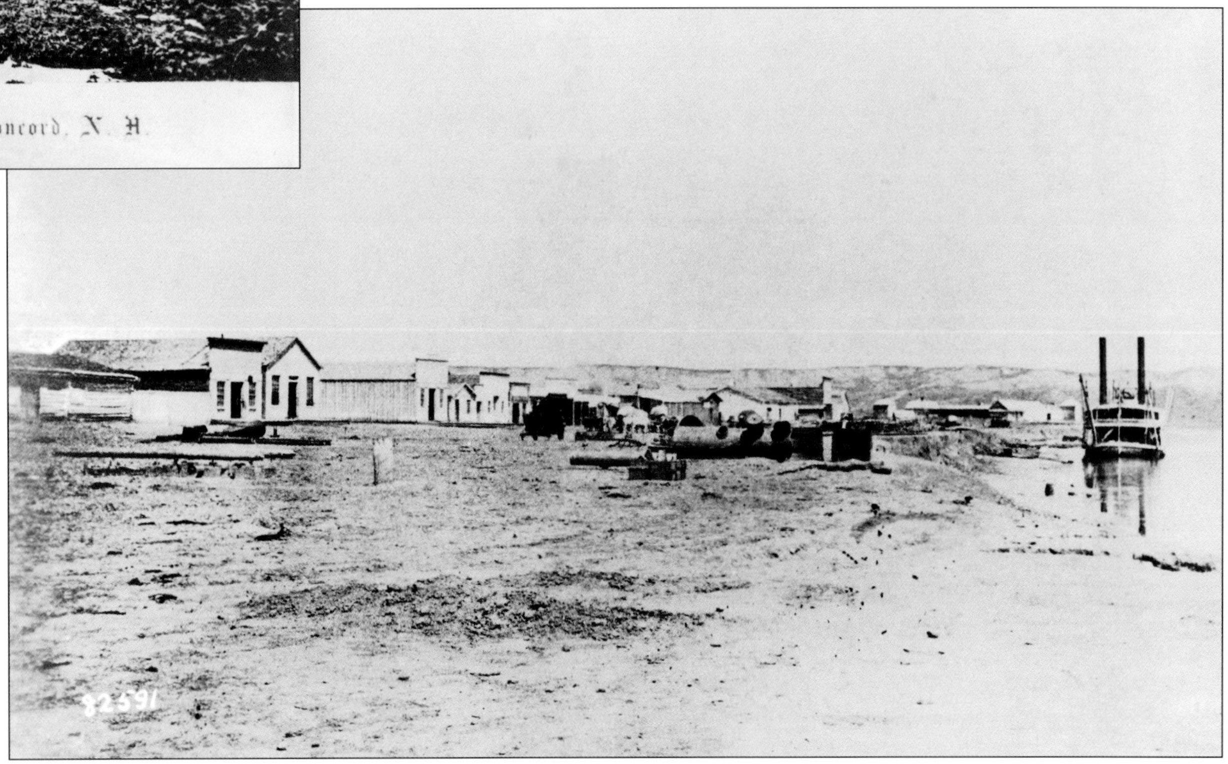

This photo of Fort Benton, Montana, was a trading post as well as a Overland Stage stop. It was around 1867, when this photo was taken looking east.

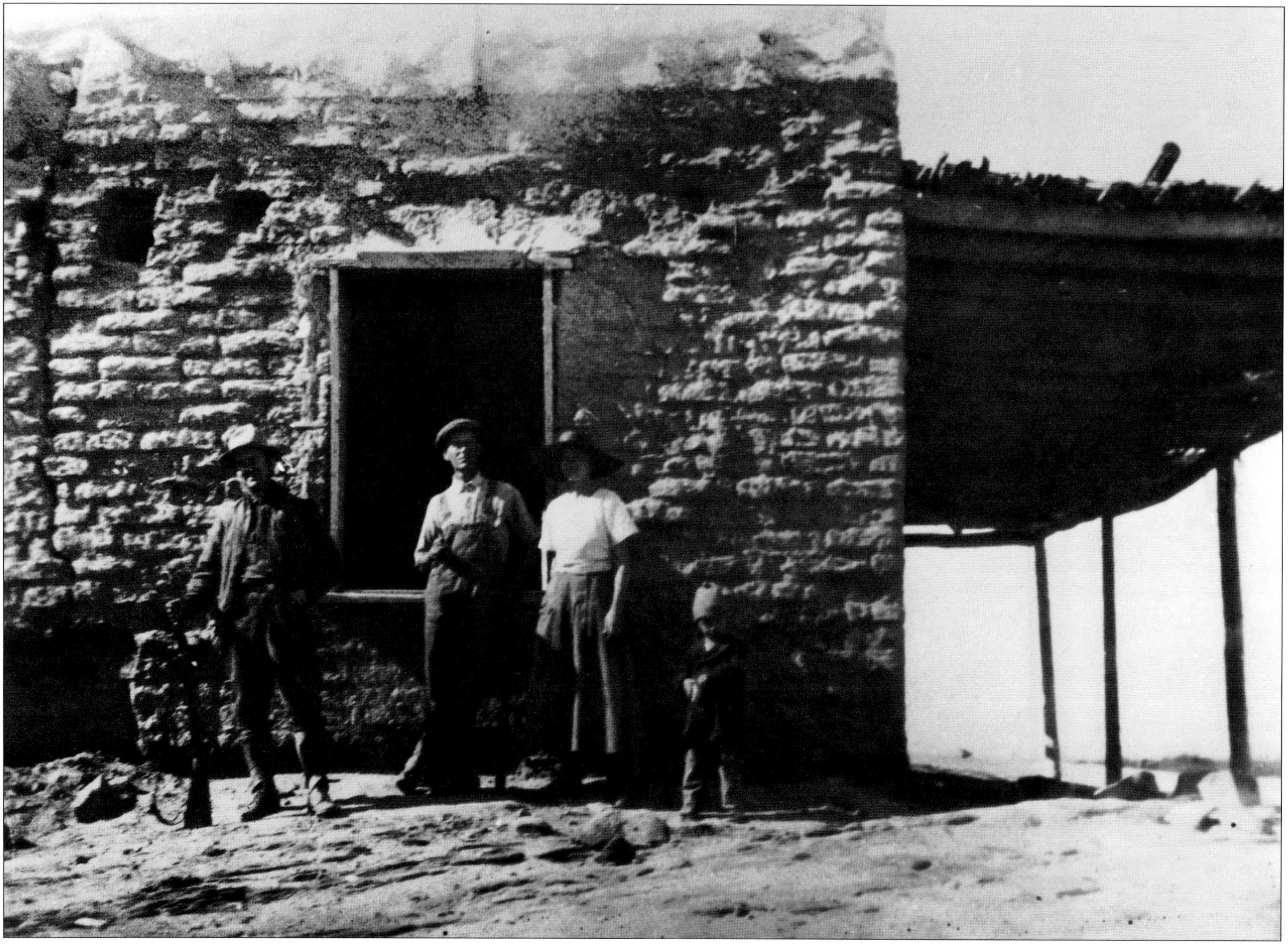

The Butterfield Stage Station at Gila River taken by an unknown photographer. It was 48 miles east of Yuma and was built in 1856. The armed station crew and a youngster pose for their portrait.

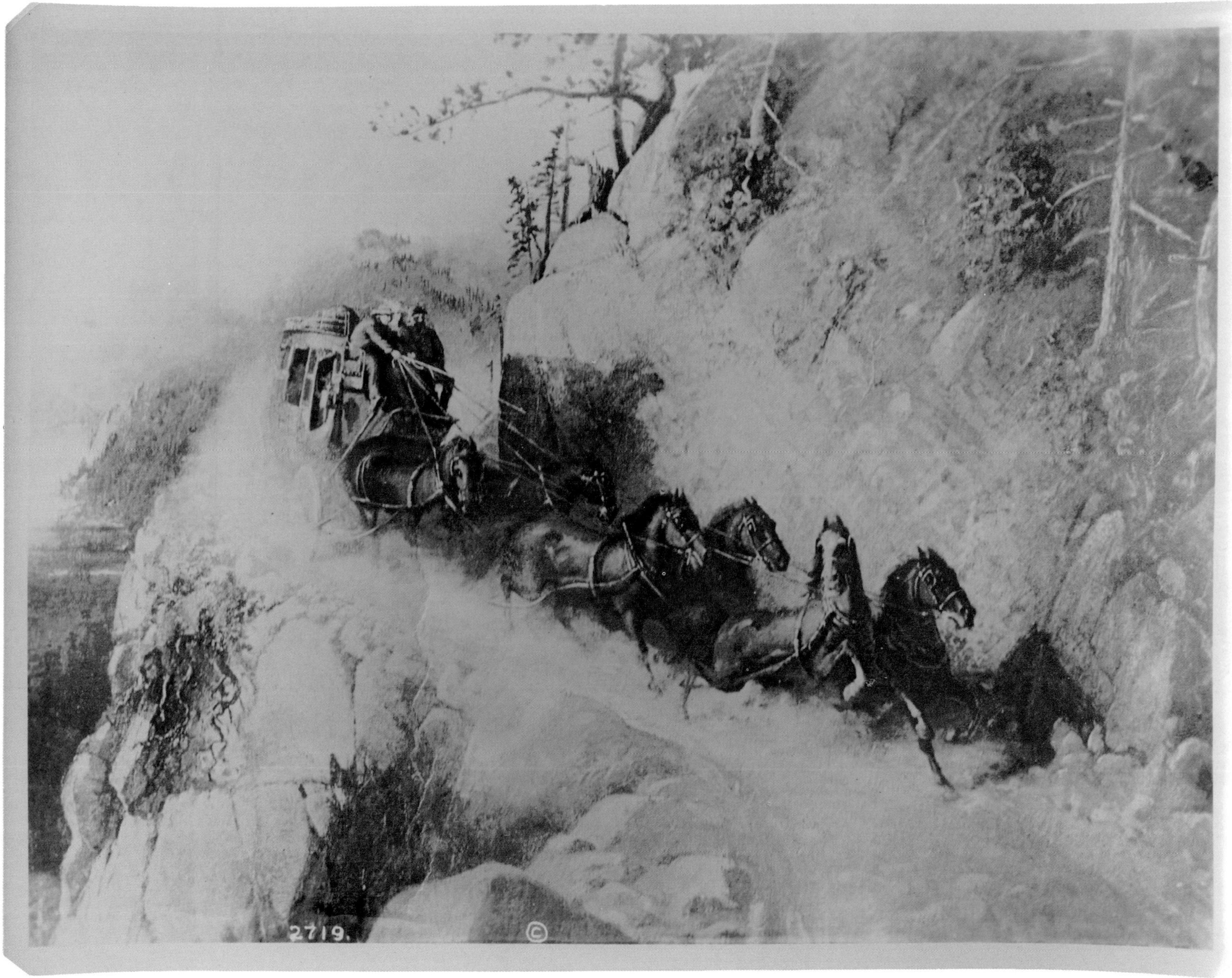

A fine painting by artist Gustav Boughain of a stage crossing the Sierras Nevada.

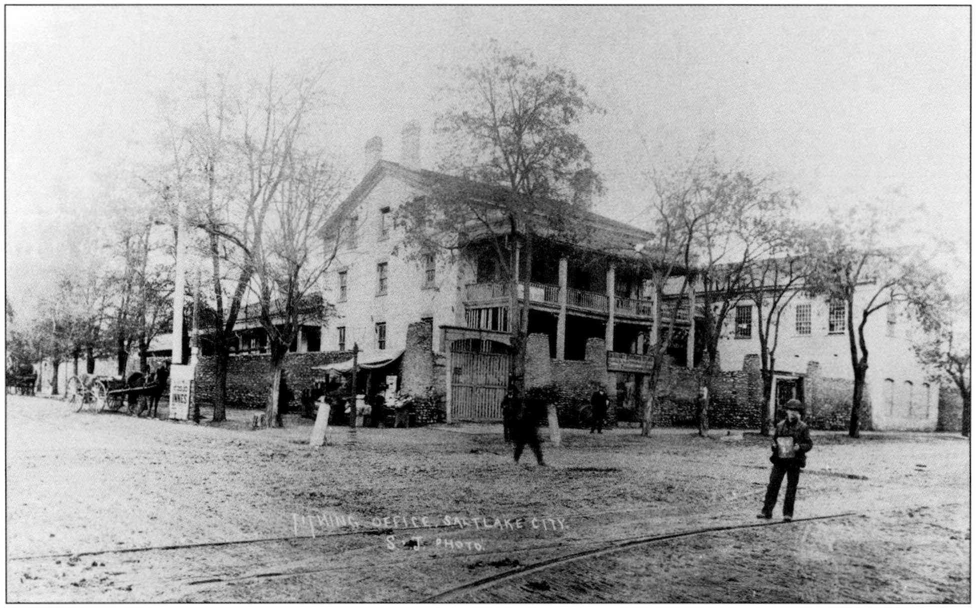

An early photo of Salt Lake, Utah, showing the Tithing office, where exchanges were made between gold dust and silver dollars. This photo is credited to Sainsbury and Johnson.

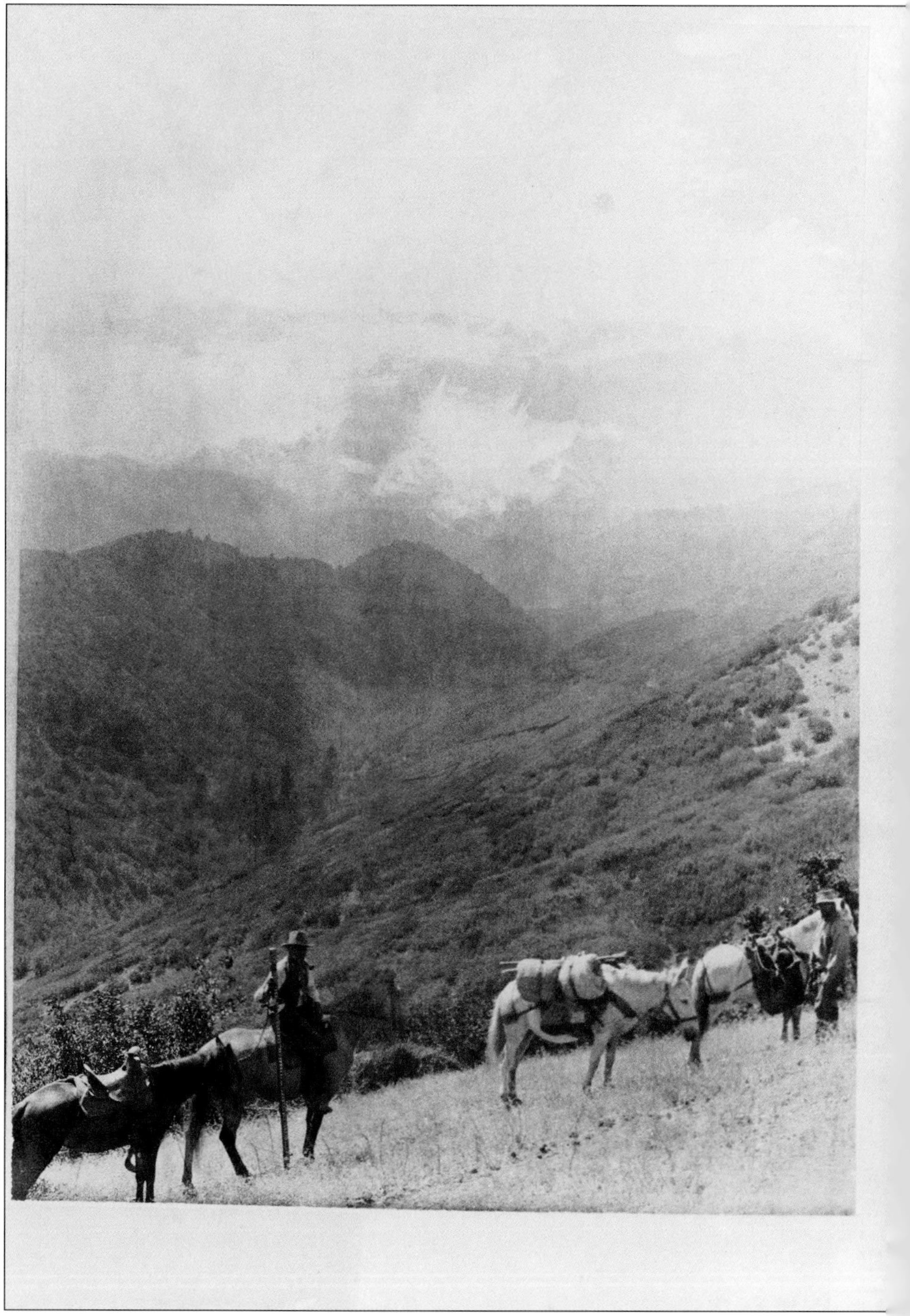

A early day surveyor stops for his photo near Fort Tejon, California.

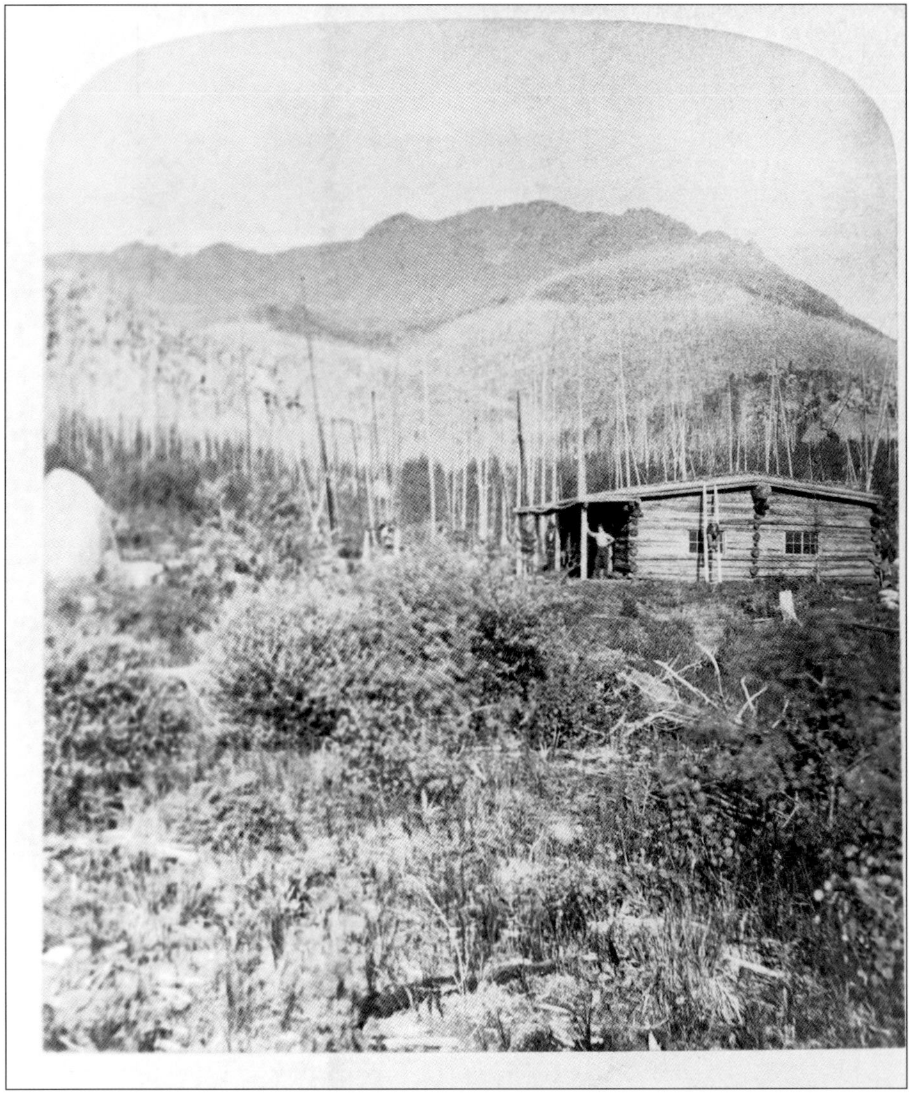

This photo of the Pike's Peak halfway house and stage stop is from an early stereo card. It was taken by Gurney.

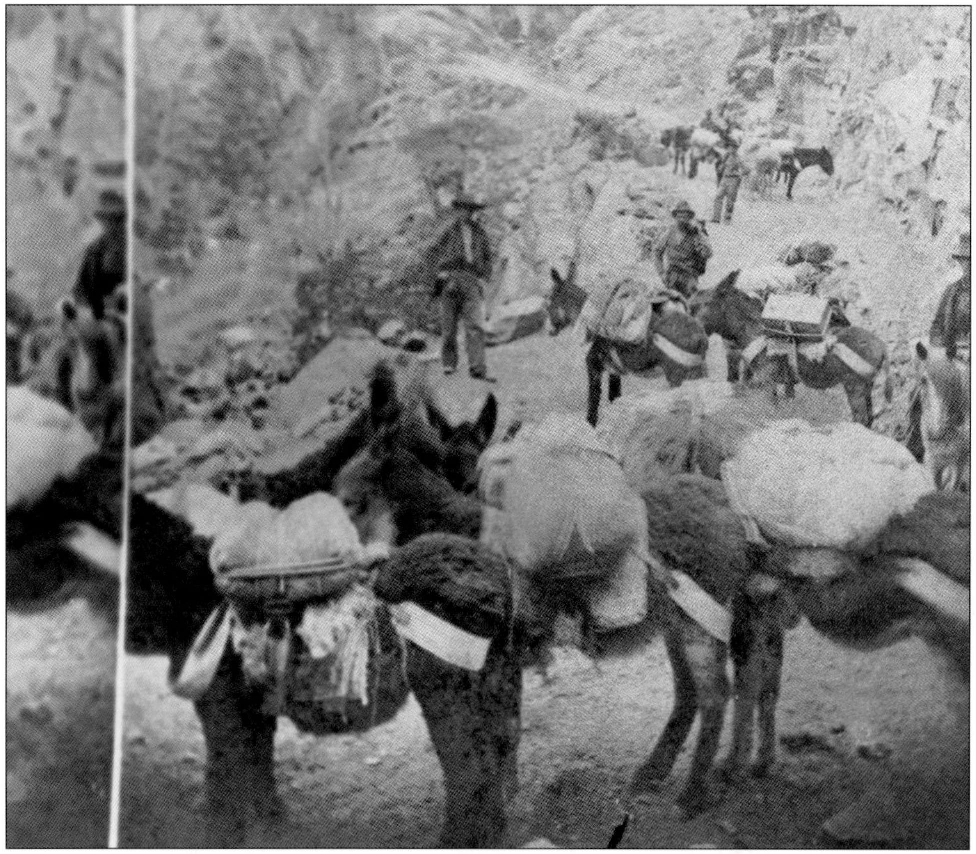

A stereo photo card image by W.G. Chamberlin of Colorado, showing the Ute Pass by which leads travelers to the Indian Agency and the South Park.

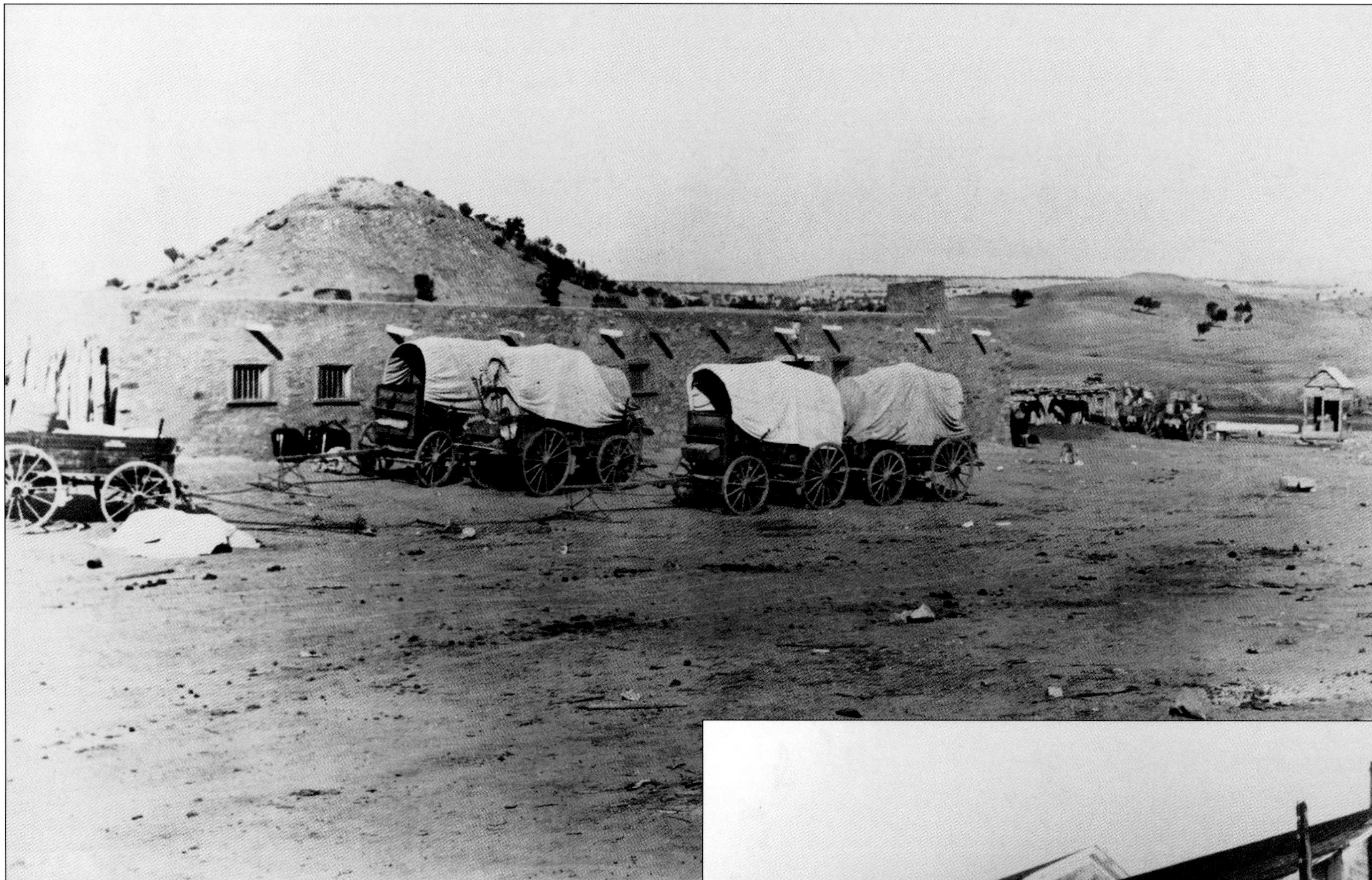

The Lorenzo Hubbell Trading Post, showing prairie schooners at the Indian agency at Ganado, Arizona. The photo is stamped by Ben Powers.

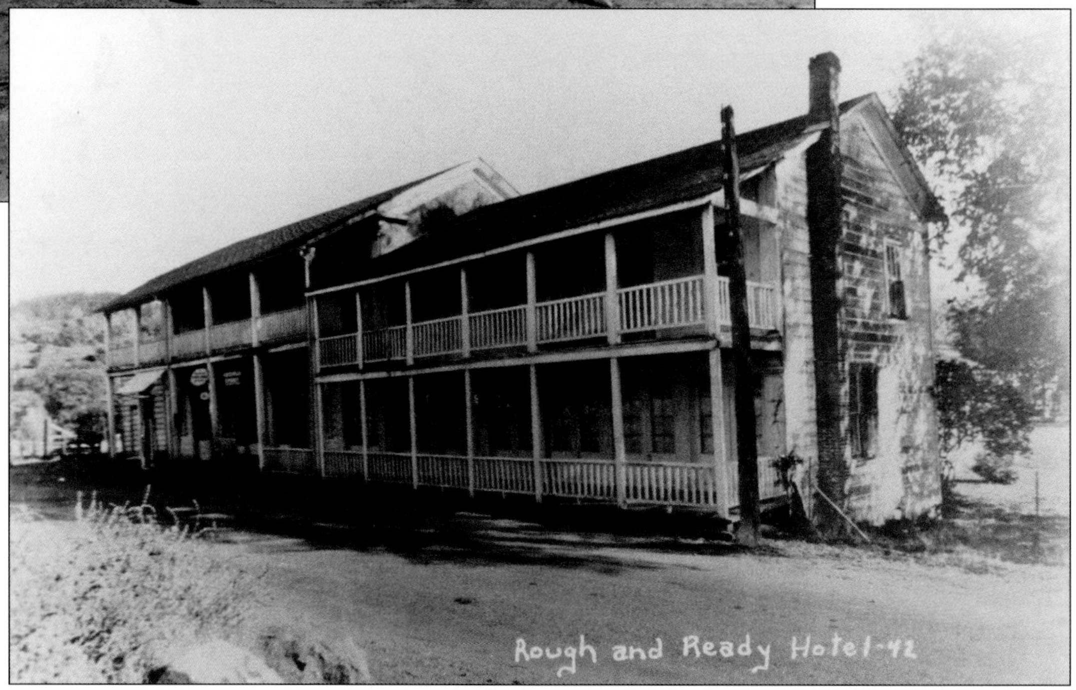

The "Rough and Ready Hotel" started as a barracks for troops stationed there in the early days of California gold rush.

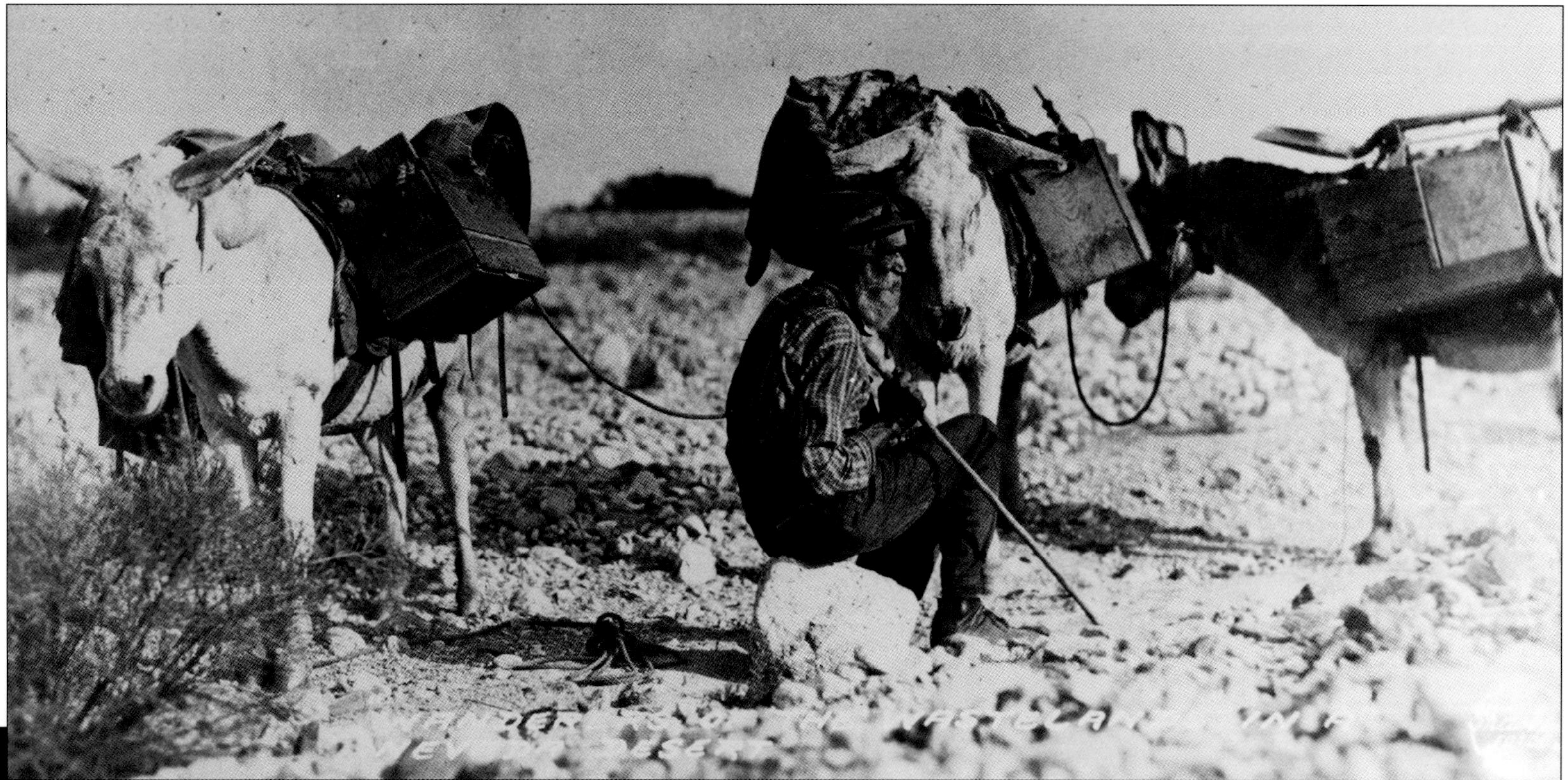

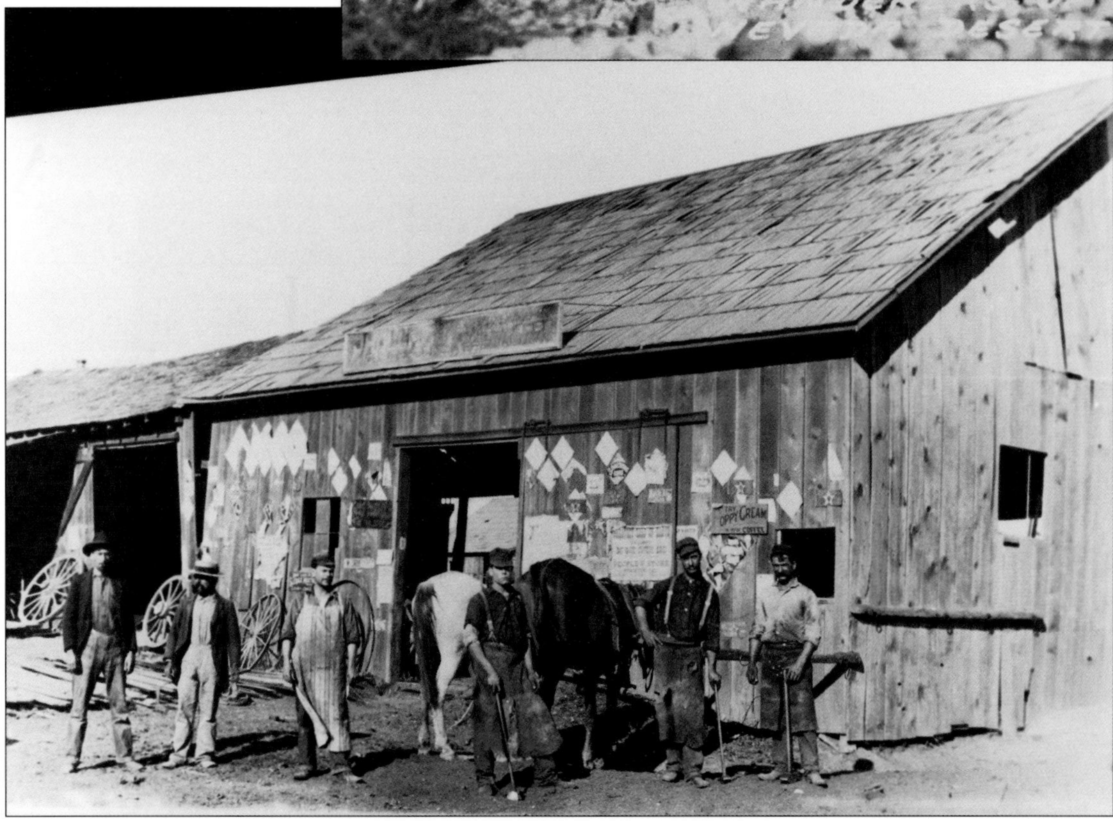

A prospector still looking for the gold dust at the end of the trail, somewhere in the Nevada desert.

These much needed blacksmiths pose for their portrait before shoeing some horses.

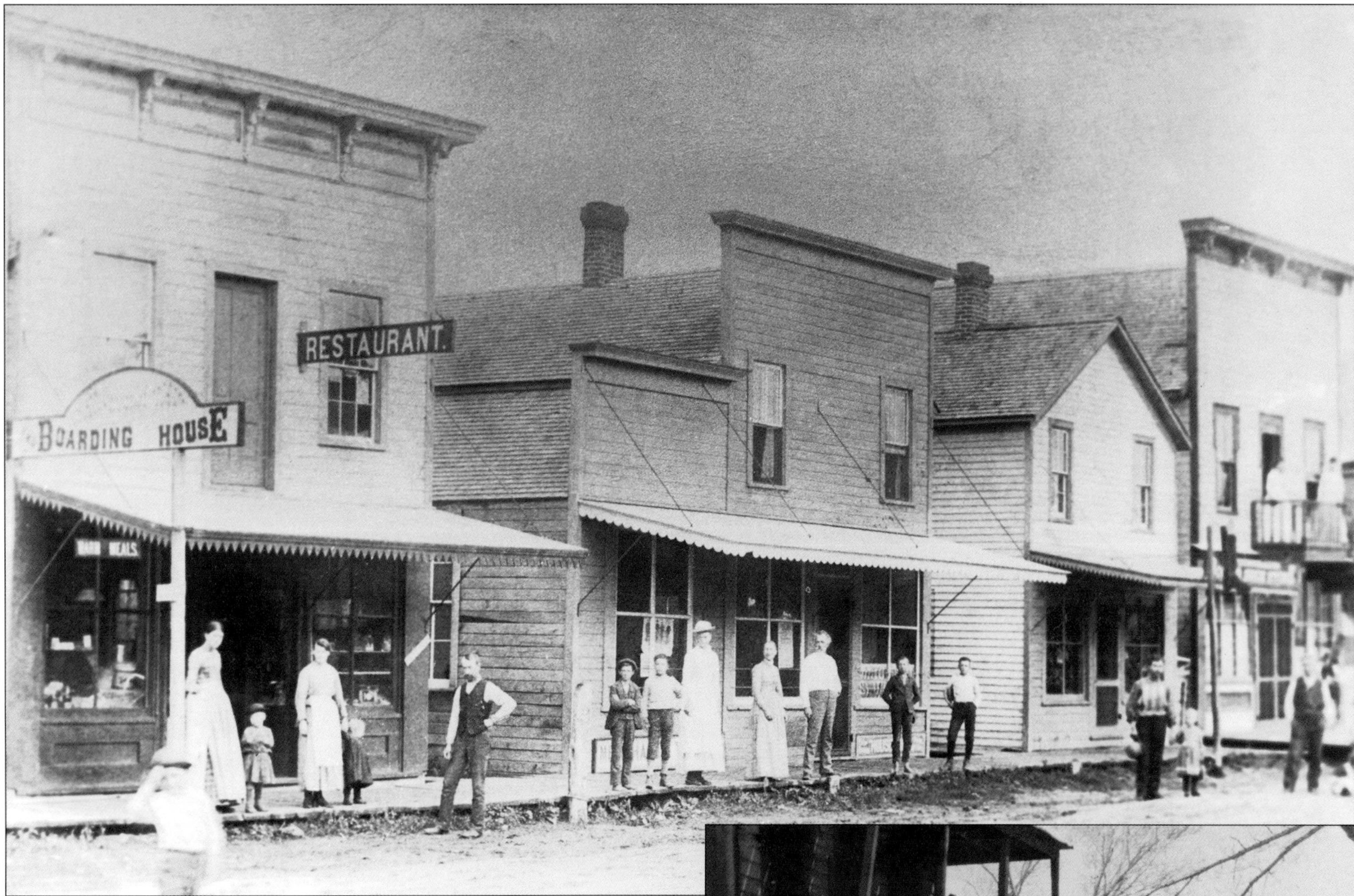

A typical western town photographed with the entire population posing for their portrait. The business section consisted of a boarding house, a fine restaurant, a merchandise and clothing store. Standing alongside a little girl is a fireman in uniform.

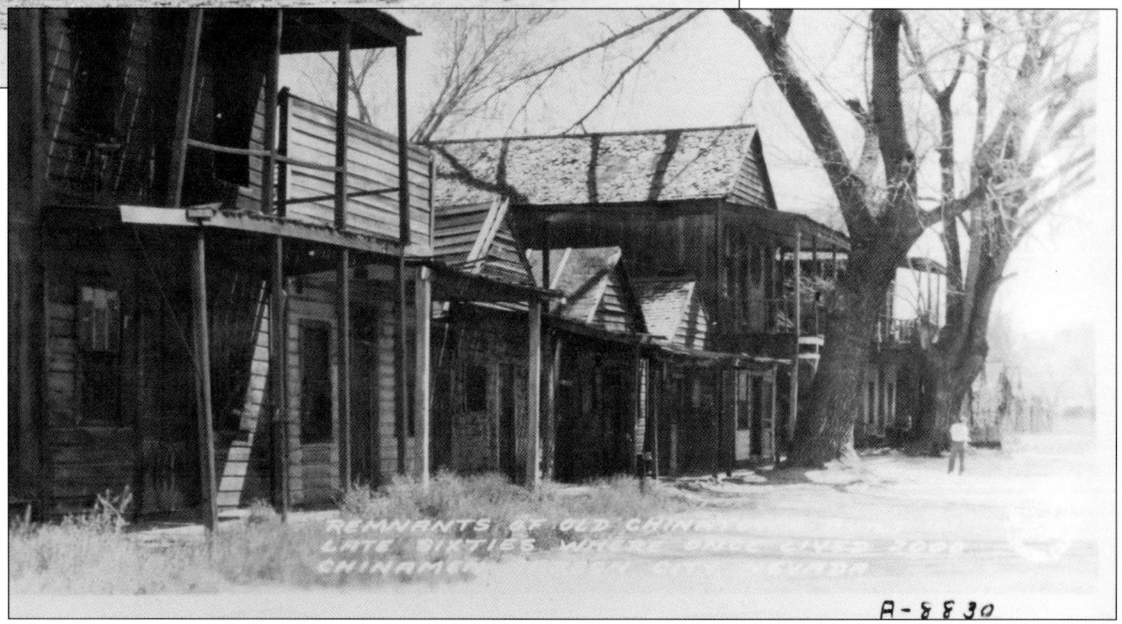

The remnants of old Chinatown which would have been very busy during the eighteen sixties. The sight is in Carson City, Nevada. Photographed by B. Frasher.

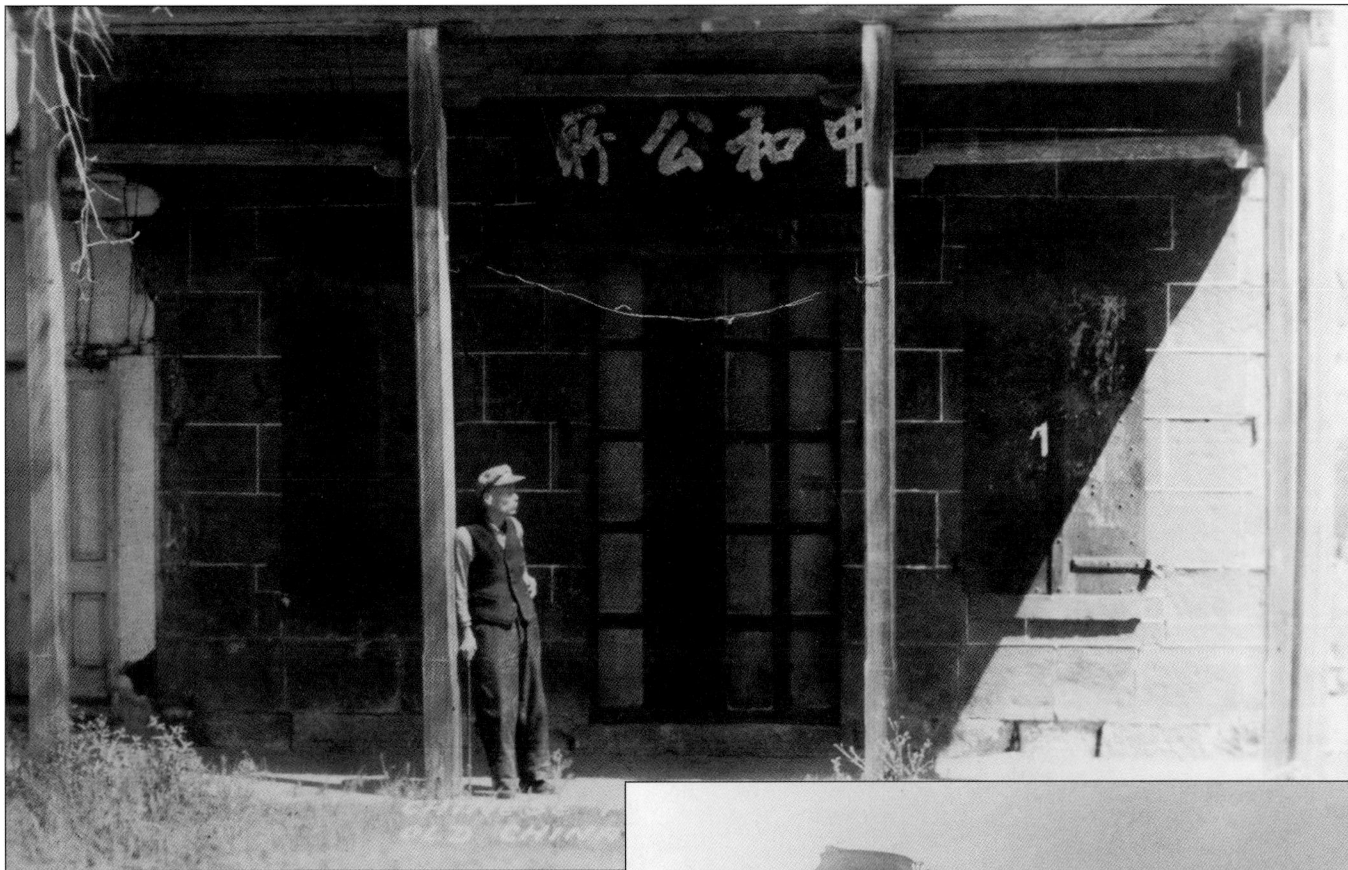

Burton Frasher turned his camera on the Chinese Free Mason Hall, in the Carson City, Nevada, Chinatown.

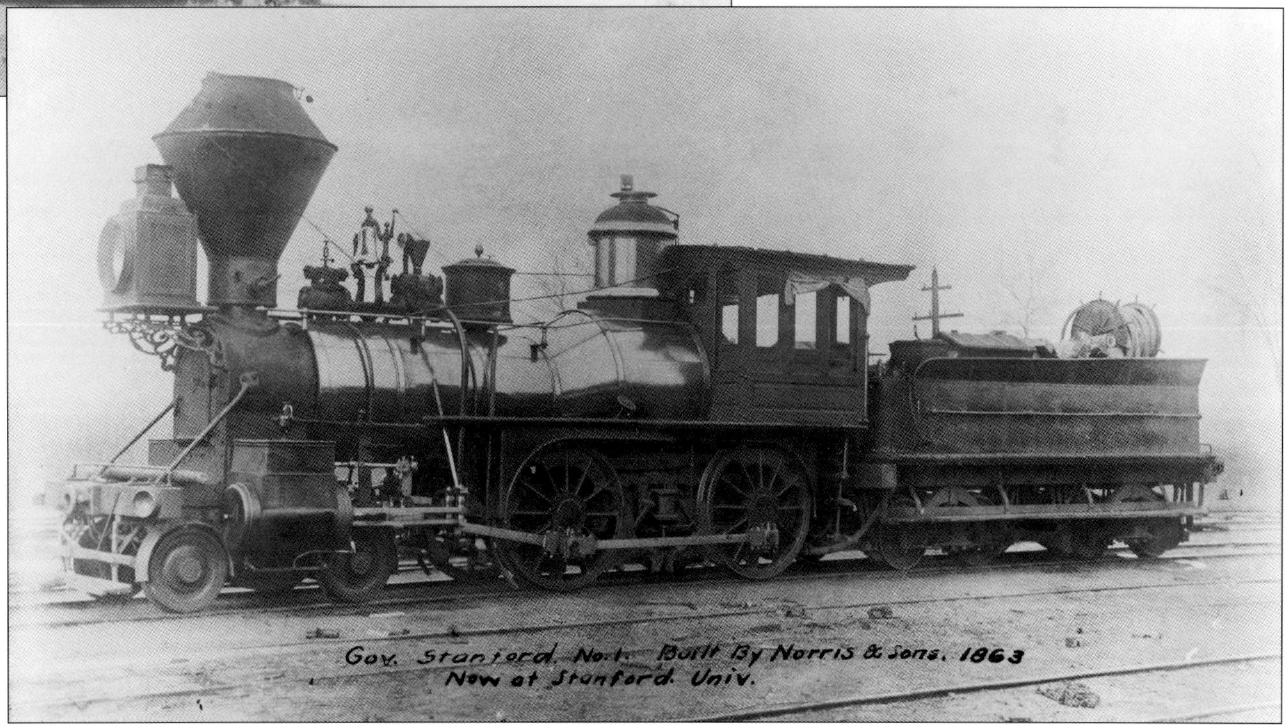

One of the first engines to travel west. It was built by Norris and Sons and was named the "Governor Stanford" in 1863.

A stagecoach is about to leave the depot at Harlem, Montana. The photo is from an original glass plate negative.

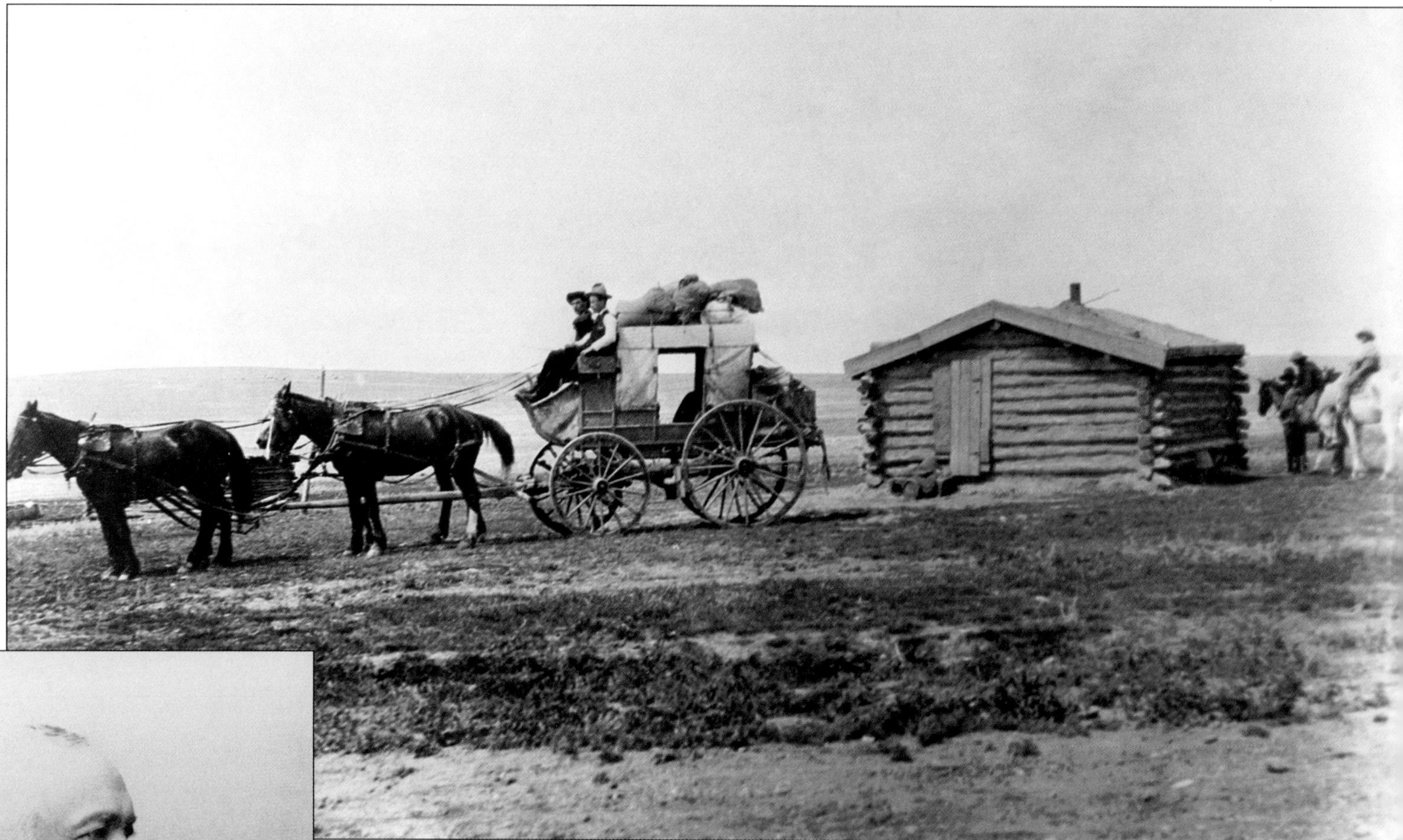

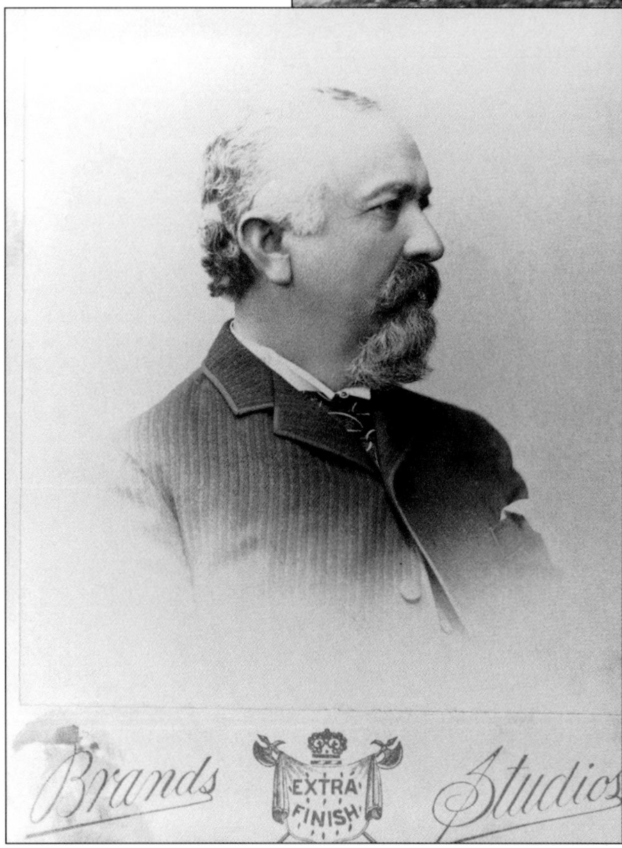

A portrait of W.W. Palmer of the Grand Hotel in Pueblo, Colorado. The photographer, Brand, had his studio in Chicago, where the famous "Palmer House" was named for Mr. Palmer.

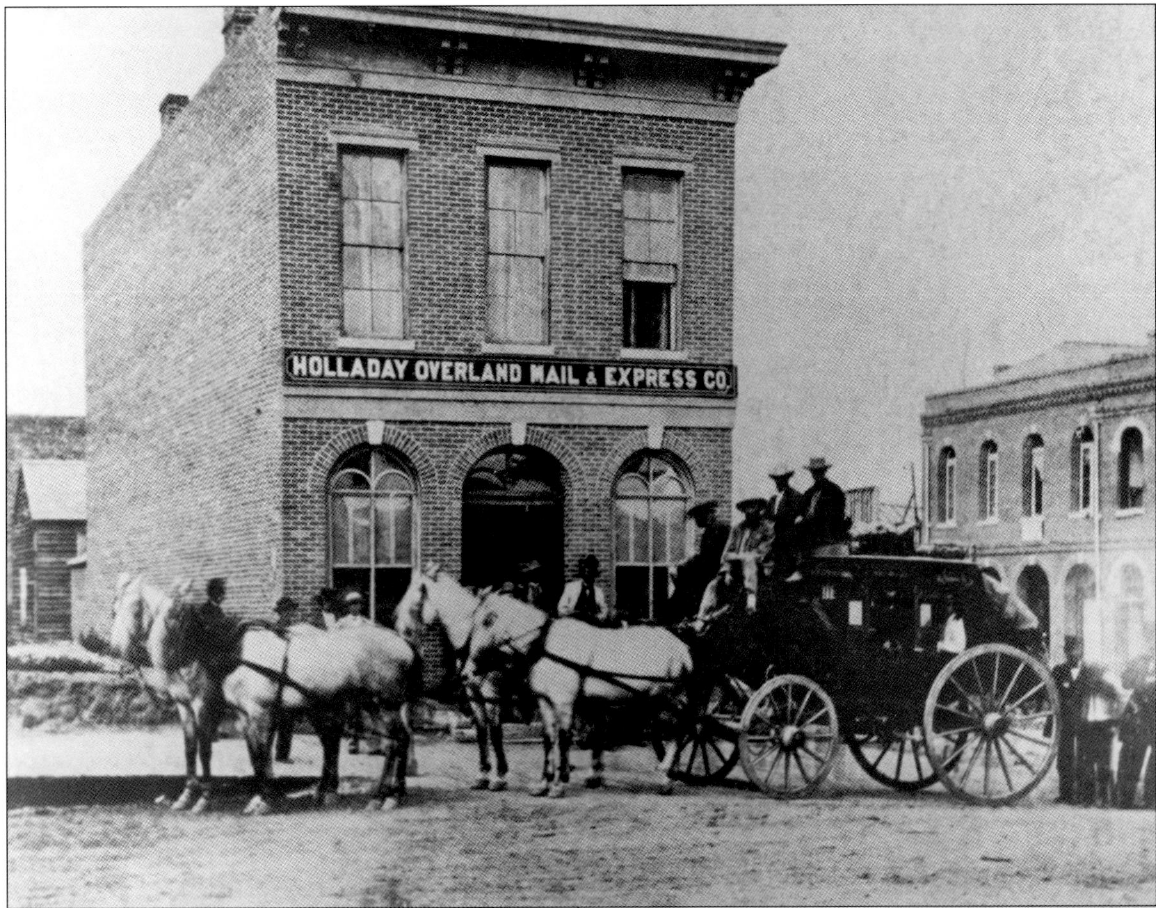

The Holladay Overland Mail & Express office is the scene of this fine portrait with a full load of cargo and passengers.

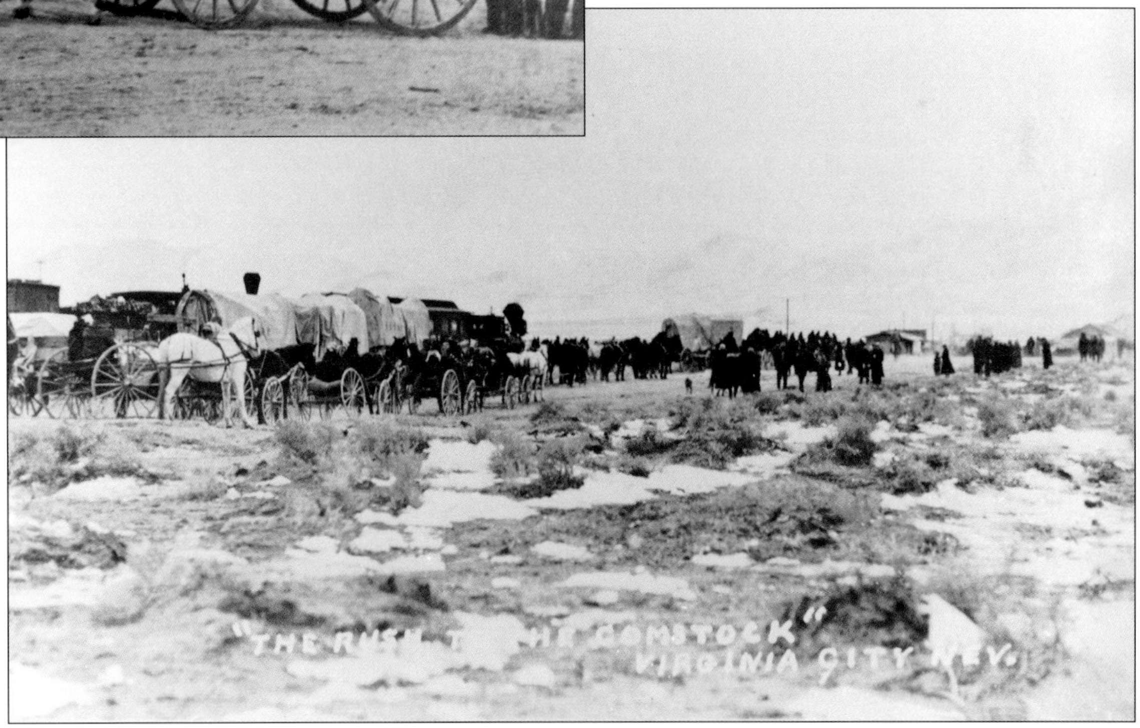

"The Rush to the Comstock," Virginia City, Nevada. By railroad, covered wagon, and foot, gold seekers all made their way through the desert.

A fast moving stage on its run to Goldfield, Nevada, in the desert.

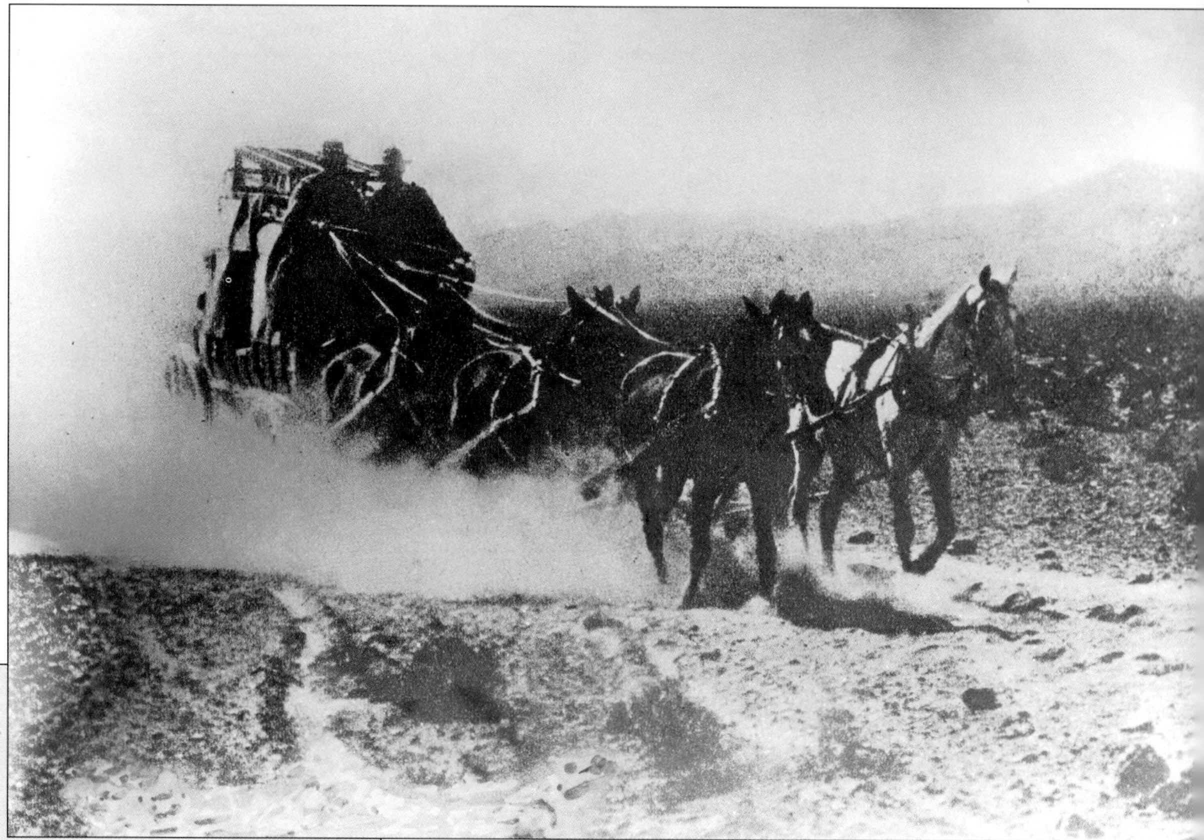

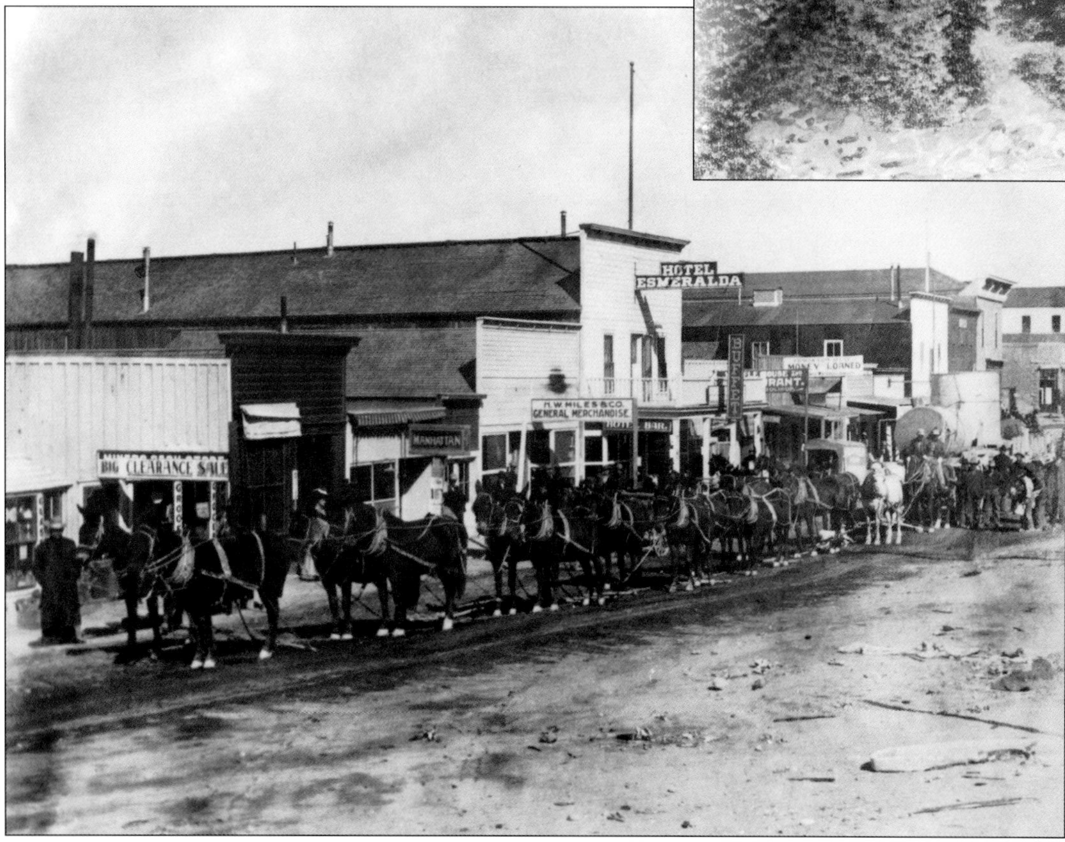

To haul a large boiler into the town of Goldfield, Nevada it took eighteen mules and horses. They are seen here marching down the main street as onlookers wonder what is next.

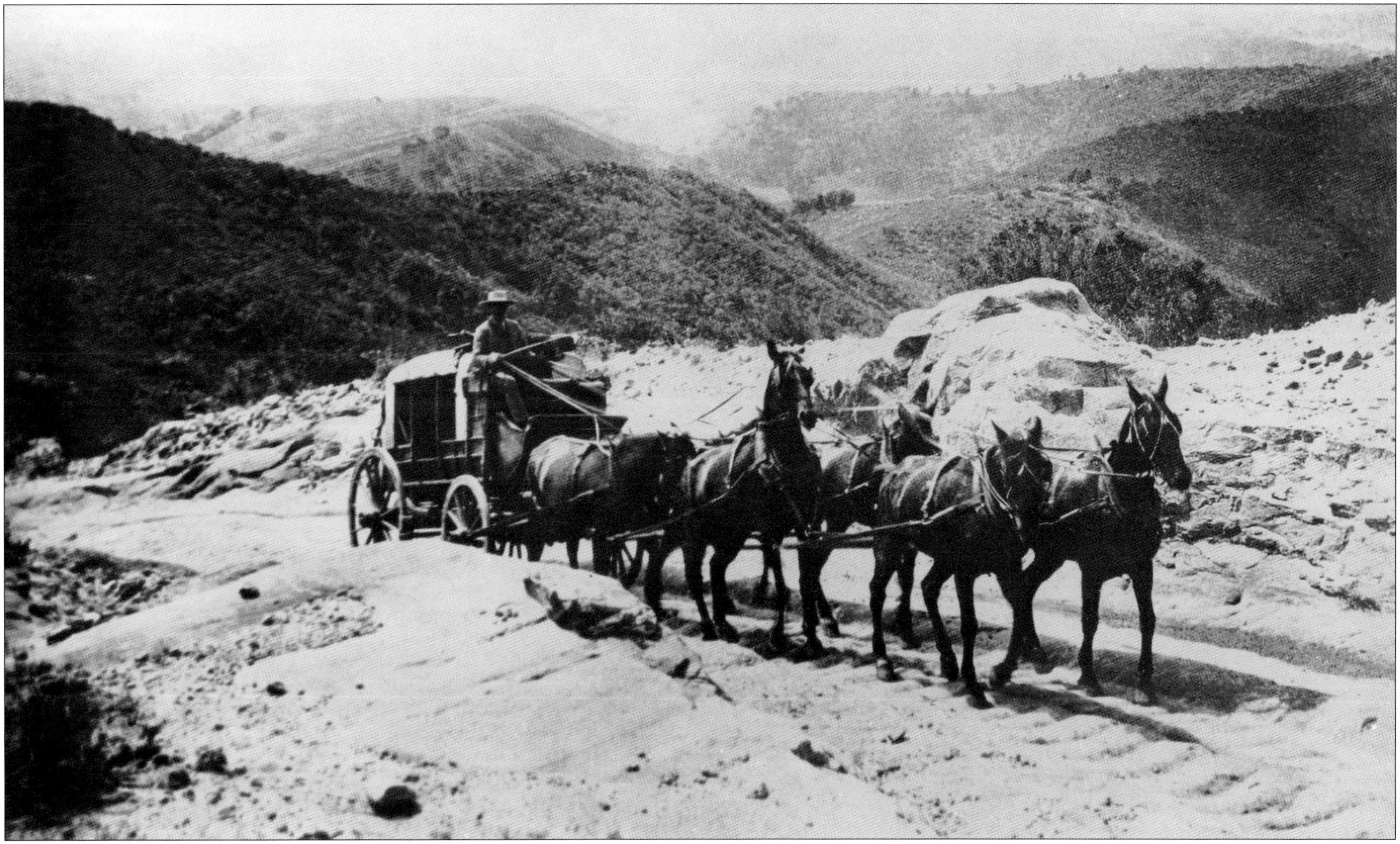

On the road of San Marcos Pass, these six mules find rough going on the sandy road. Photographed by W.H. Jackson.

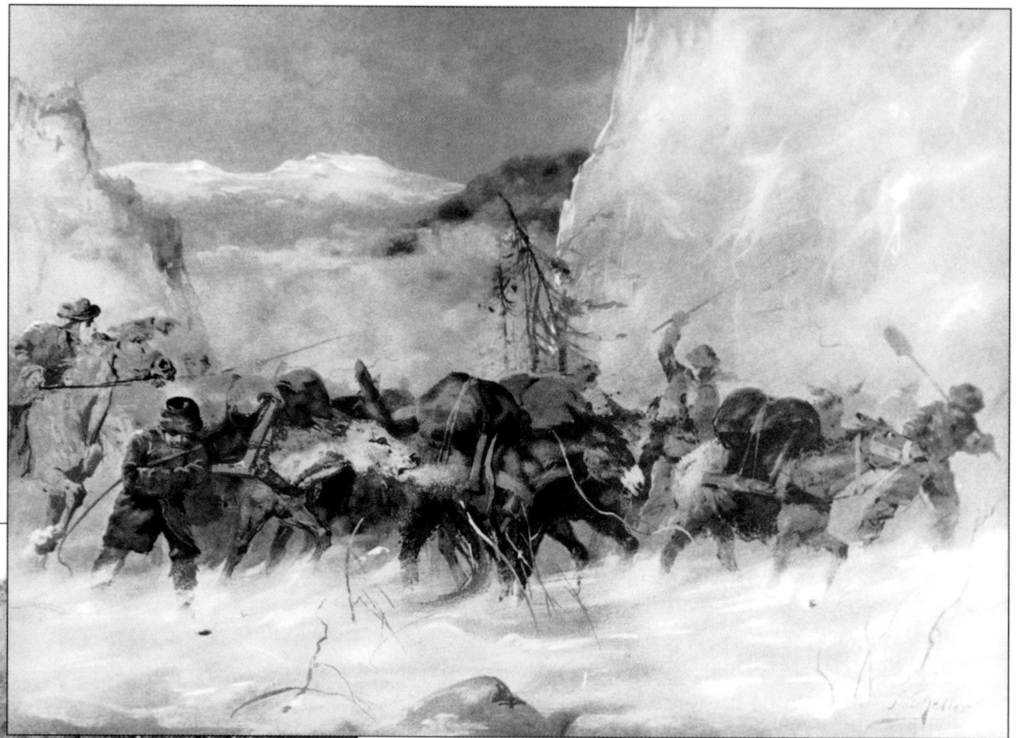

An artist's rendering of miners with their pack mules fighting through a winter blizzard on the way to the mines.

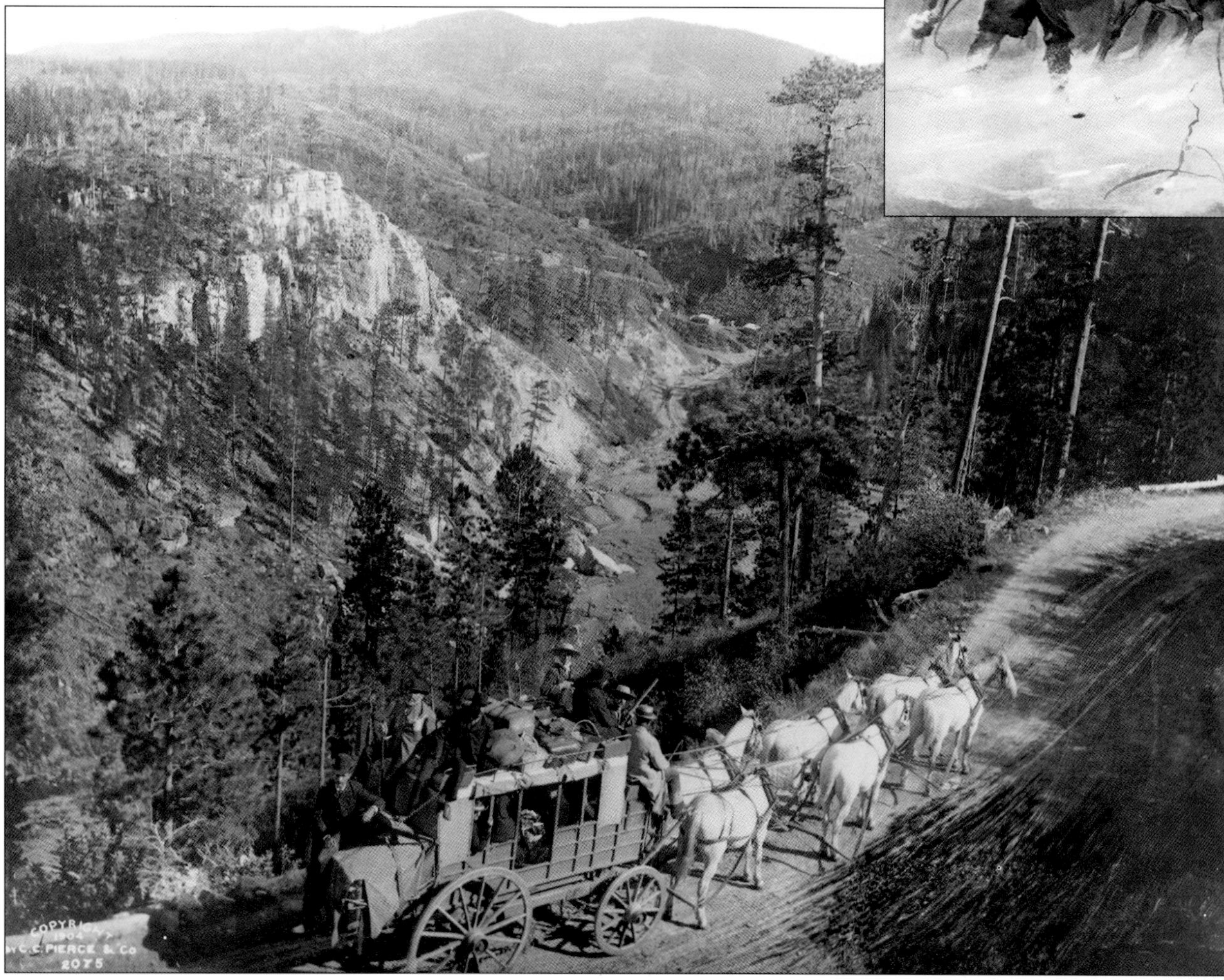

"On the way to the mines" armed with a shotgun and a full load of passengers, including one who has two hooks for hands. The view is by W.H. Jackson, although it seemed that C.C. Pierce & Co. had at some point taken out a copyright on the photo. Pierce was a well-known photo catalog house dealing with photographs from the West. They seemed to have stamped their name on many well-known photographs not taken by them.

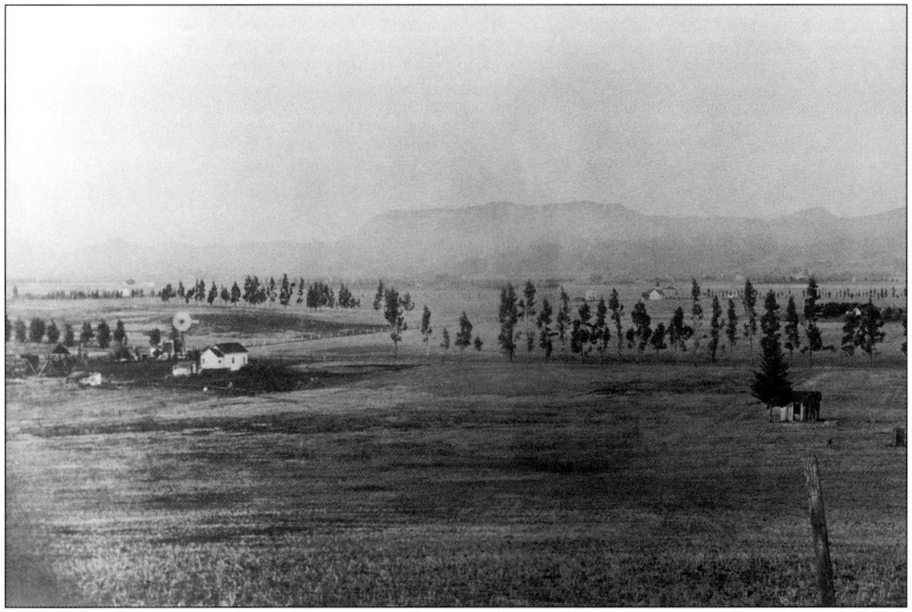

A very early view of the San Fernando Valley, California. Present day Hollywood would be just past the line of trees. Even in this early photo we see the clouds of soot and smoke trapped by the mountains in the rear.

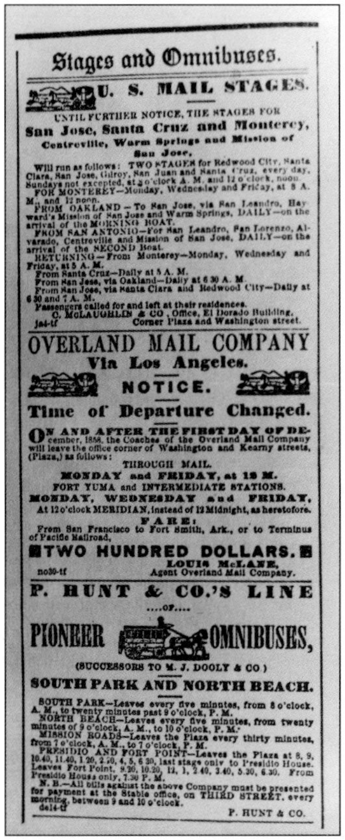

Stages and Omnibuses.

U. S. MAIL STAGES.

UNTIL FURTHER NOTICE, THE STAGES FOR

San Jose, Santa Cruz and Monterey, Centreville, Warm Springs and Mission of San Jose,

Will run as follows: TWO STAGES for Redwood City, Santa Clara, San Jose, Gilroy, San Juan and Santa Cruz, every day, Sundays not excepted, at 9 o'clock A. M. and 12 o'clock, noon.

FOR MONTEREY—Monday, Wednesday and Friday, at 8 A. M., and 12 noon.

FROM OAKLAND—To San Jose, via San Leandro, Hayward's Mission of San Jose and Warm Springs, DAILY—on the arrival of the MORNING BOAT.

FROM SAN ANTONIO—For San Leandro, San Lorenzo, Alvarado, Centreville and Mission of San Jose, DAILY—on the arrival of the SECOND Boat.

RETURNING—From Monterey—Monday, Wednesday and Friday, at 5 A. M.

From Santa Cruz—Daily at 5 A. M.

From San Jose, via Oakland—Daily at 6 30 A. M.

From San Jose, via Santa Clara and Redwood City—Daily at 6 30 and 7 A. M.

Passengers called for and left at their residences.

C. McLAUGHLIN & CO., Office, El Dorado Building, Corner Plaza and Washington street.

ja4-tf

OVERLAND MAIL COMPANY

Via Los Angeles.

NOTICE.

Time of Departure Changed.

ON AND AFTER THE FIRST DAY OF DEcember, 1858, the Coaches of the Overland Mail Company will leave the office corner of Washington and Kearny streets, (Plaza,) as follows:

THROUGH MAIL.

MONDAY and FRIDAY, at 12 M.

FORT YUMA and INTERMEDIATE STATIONS.

MONDAY, WEDNESDAY and FRIDAY,

At 12 o'clock MERIDIAN, instead of 12 Midnight, as heretofore.

FARE:

From San Francisco to Fort Smith, Ark., or to Terminus of Pacific Railroad,

TWO HUNDRED DOLLARS.

LOUIS McLANE, Agent Overland Mail Company.

no30-tf

P. HUNT & CO.'S LINE

....OF....

PIONEER OMNIBUSES,

(SUCCESSORS TO M. J. DOOLY & CO.)

SOUTH PARK AND NORTH BEACH.

SOUTH PARK—Leaves every five minutes, from 8 o'clock, A. M., to twenty minutes past 9 o'clock, P. M.

NORTH BEACH—Leaves every five minutes, from twenty minutes of 9 o'clock, A. M., to 10 o'clock, P. M.

MISSION ROADS—Leaves the Plaza every thirty minutes, from 7 o'clock, A. M., to 7 o'clock, P. M.

PRESIDIO AND FORT POINT—Leaves the Plaza at 8, 9, 10.40, 11.40, 1 20, 2 20, 4, 5, 6 30, last stage only to Presidio House. Leaves Fort Point, 9.20, 10.20, 12, 1, 2 40, 3.40, 5.30, 6.30. From Presidio House only, 7.30 P. M.

N. B.—All bills against the above Company must be presented for payment at the Stable office, on THIRD STREET, every morning, between 9 and 10 o'clock.

de14-tf

P. HUNT & CO.

A newspaper clipping of advertisements for "Stages and Omnibuses" to California and U.S. Mail stages for places such as San Jose, Santa Cruz, and Monterey, with stops at Oakland, and onward to San Antonio.

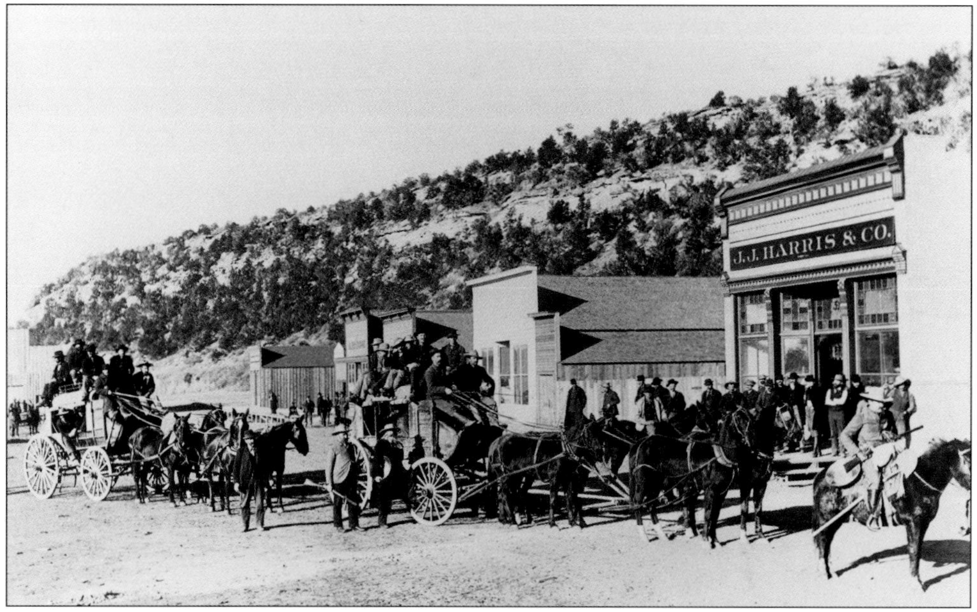

This great photograph by William H. Jackson shows stagecoaches lining up in Dolores for the trip to San Juan. This photo has been named several ways, among them, "Leaving for the Fort" and "Going to Telerdo and Ouray Colorado." In addition, an edition by Detroit. Publishing, printed as a post card, took out the last stagecoach, and retouched it to make the horse's head at the right complete.

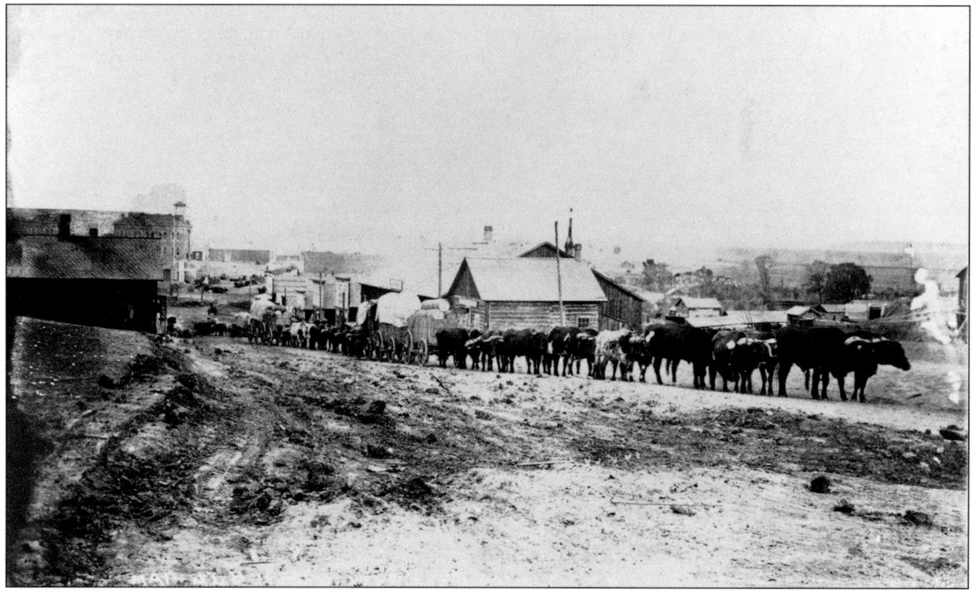

On the main road out of Buffalo, Wyoming Territory, bull whackers lead their oxen loaded with supplies for the railroad. The photo was taken by Dalgleish of Sterling Colorado.

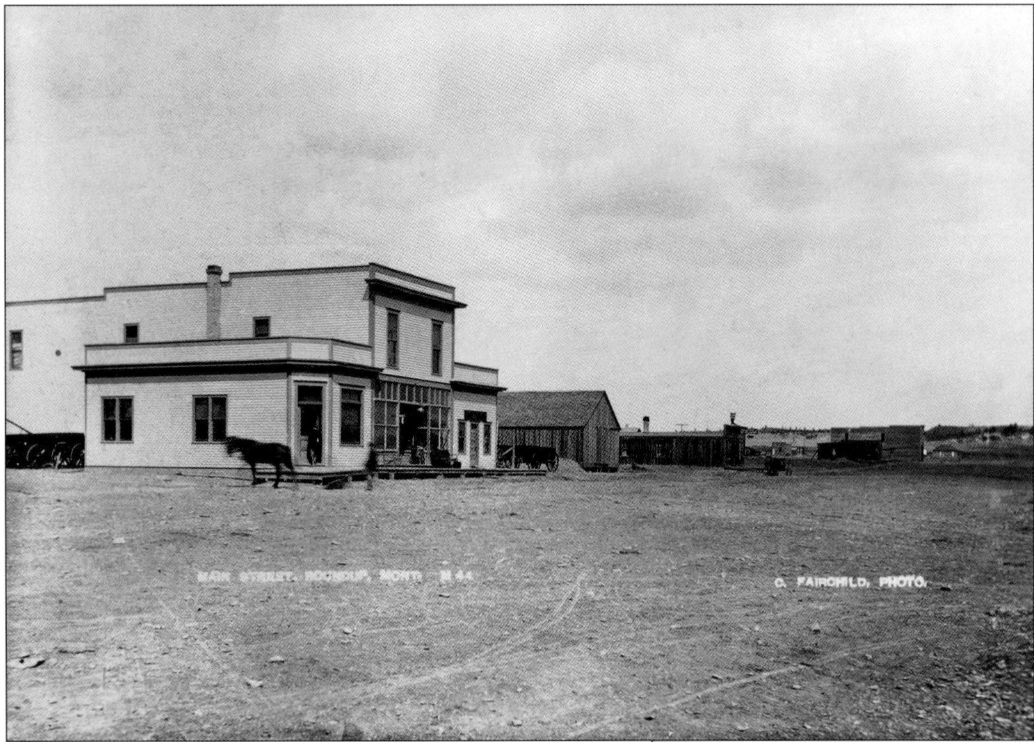

A simple photograph of the main street of Roundup, Montana. Photographed by C. Fairchild of the same town.

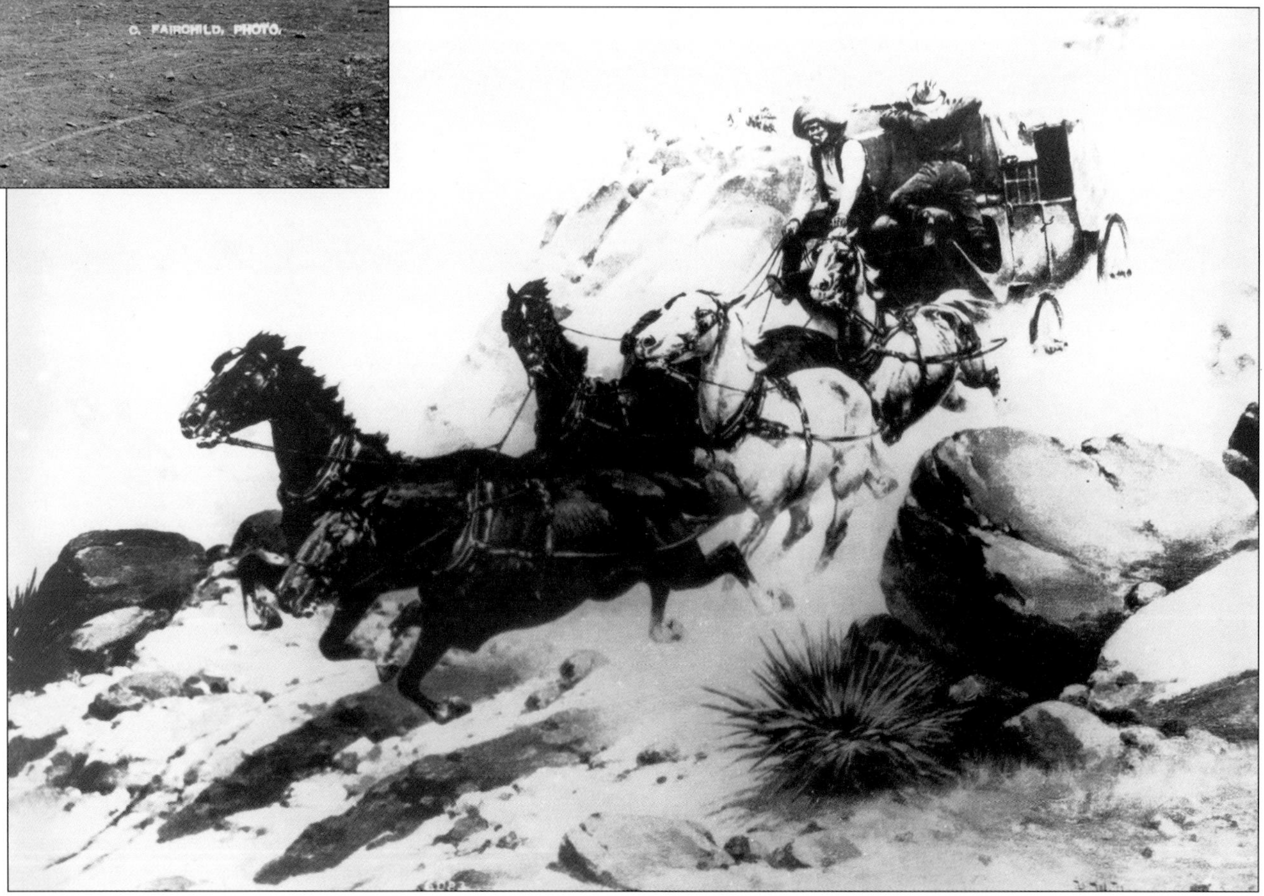

This fine painting by R.W. Hanson, gives the idea that this is a runaway stage, with its horses leaping down the road. But after careful study we see that the rifleman on board is aiming his gun at some would-be robbers.

Standing outside their hotel, stagecoach travelers wait for the coach to arrive. Some of the men are armed, but don't mind having their photograph taken.

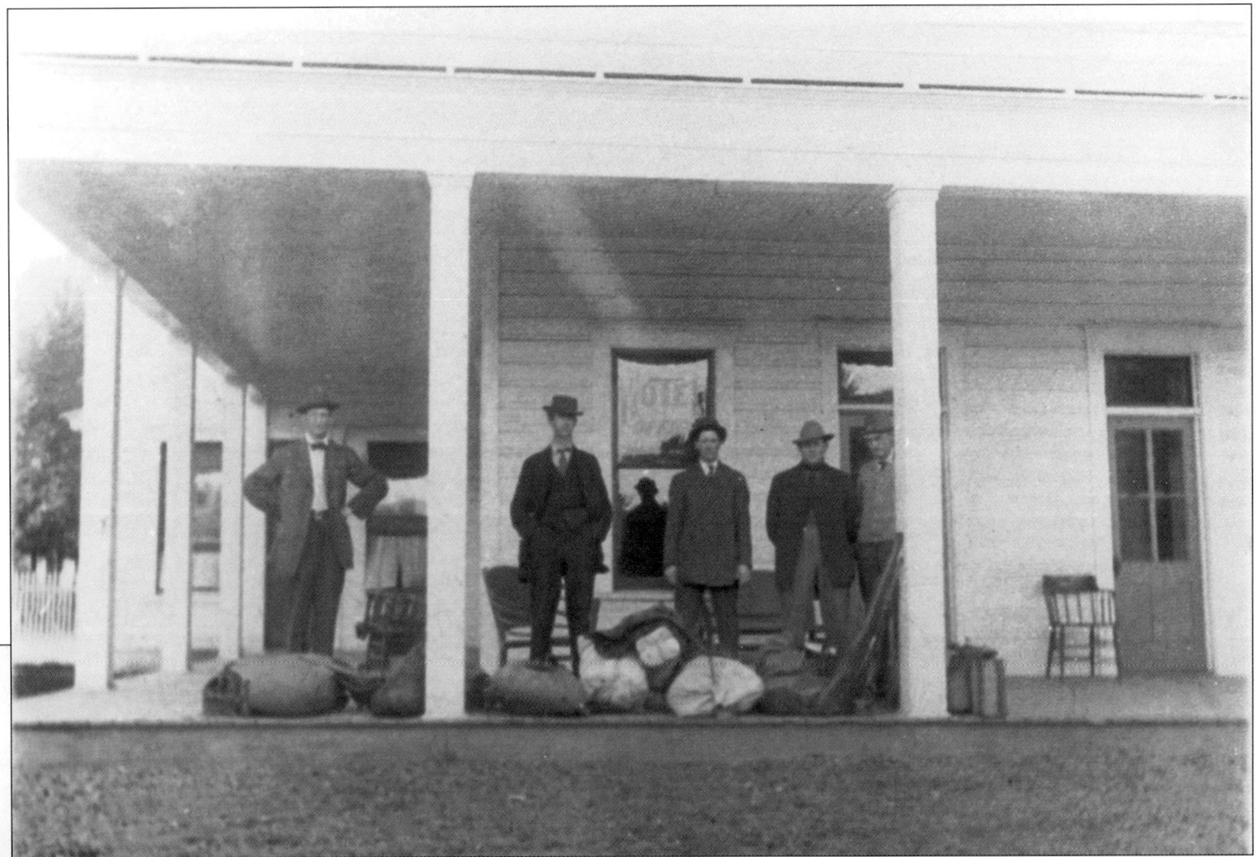

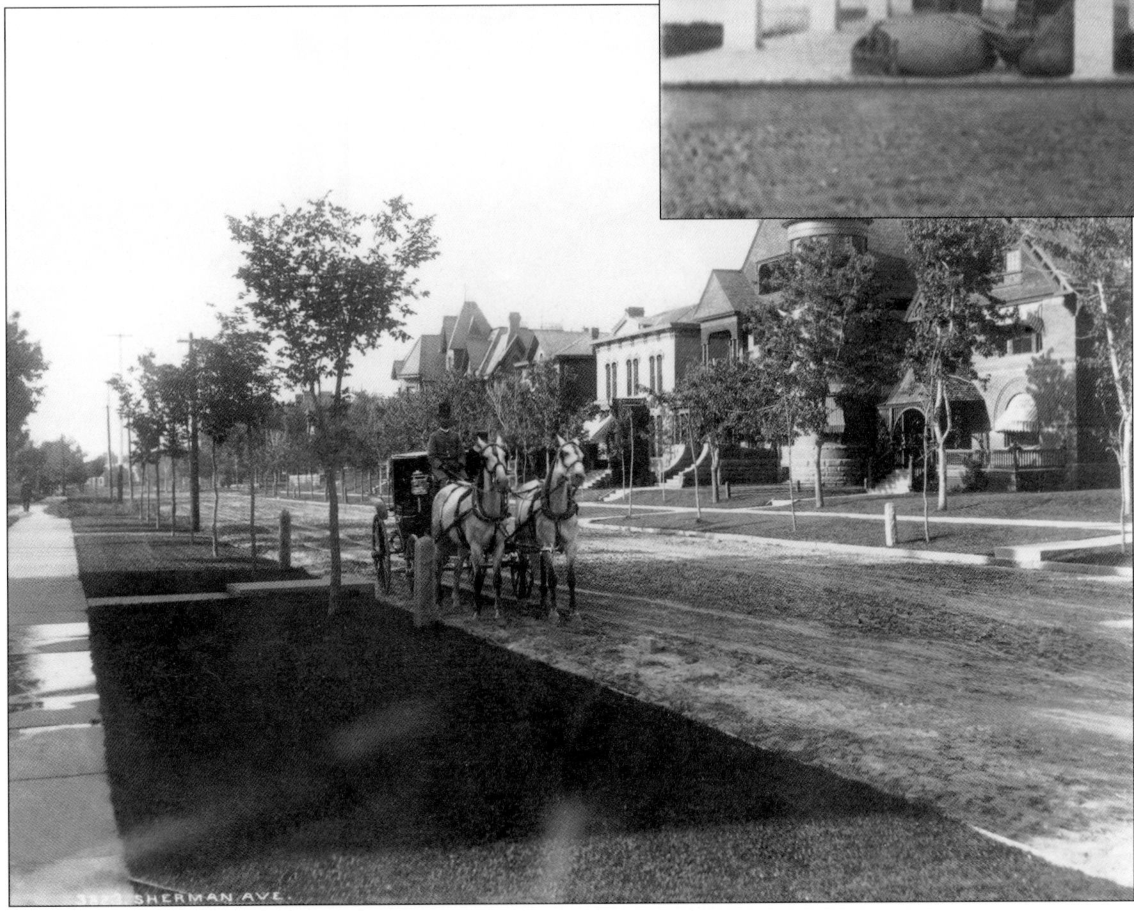

The fine eye of W.H. Jackson is evident in this photograph taken by him along Sherman Avenue, the mansion row of Denver, Colorado, with a fine two-horse stage parked outside a large home.

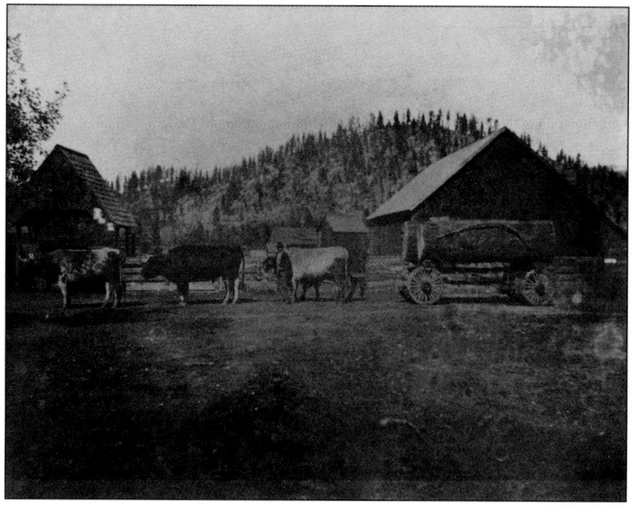

A logging cart with heavy wood wheels, pulled by teams of oxen makes an interesting comparison to the fast moving stagecoaches that traveled over the western countryside. This photo was taken near Placerville, California.

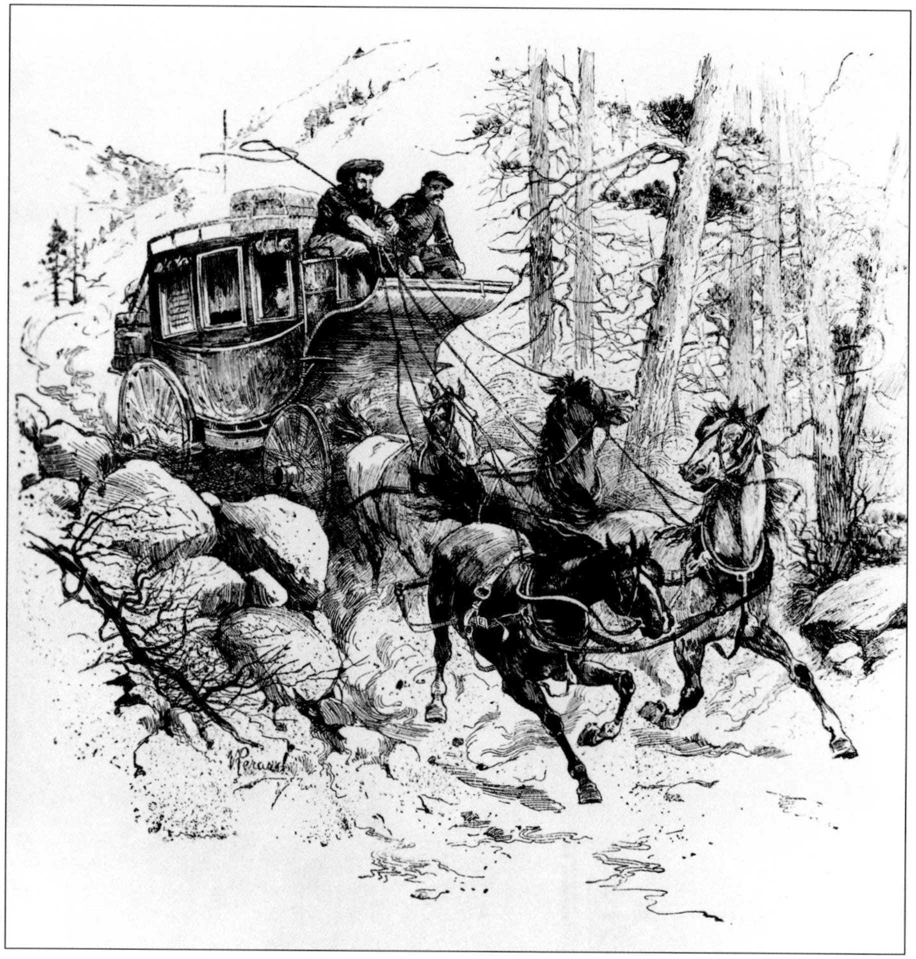

A fine pen and ink drawing by Perasch showing a stage on its way through the redwood forest.

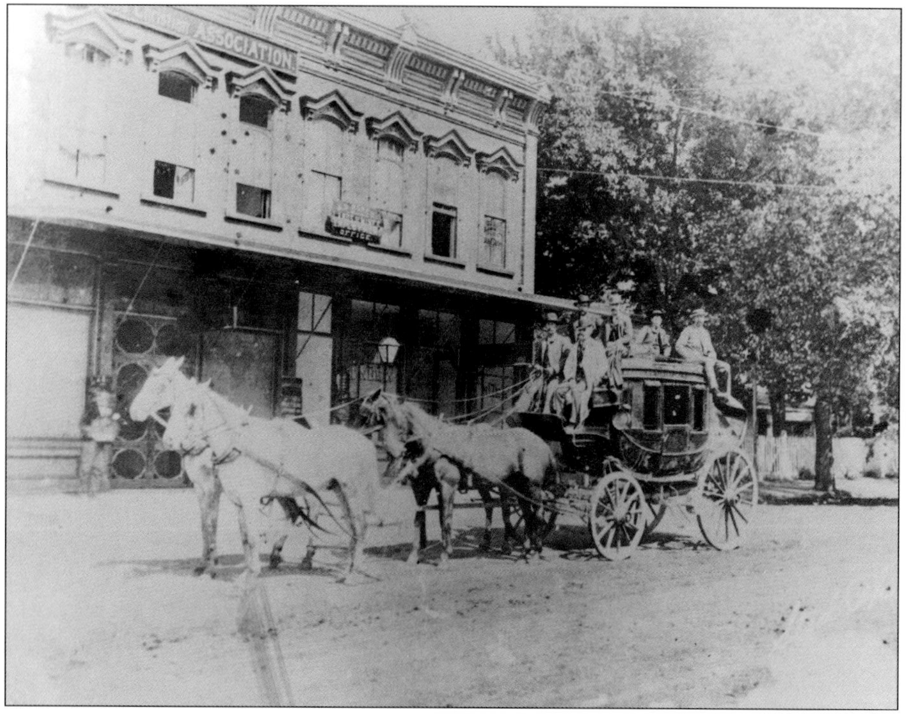

The stage entering San Bernardino, California, after a long ride from the desert. A Steele photograph, from the same town.

A very early photograph of Williams, Arizona. The town was just beginning, judging by the rows of wooden buildings and even some tent structures. The photograph is credited to Ben Wittick.

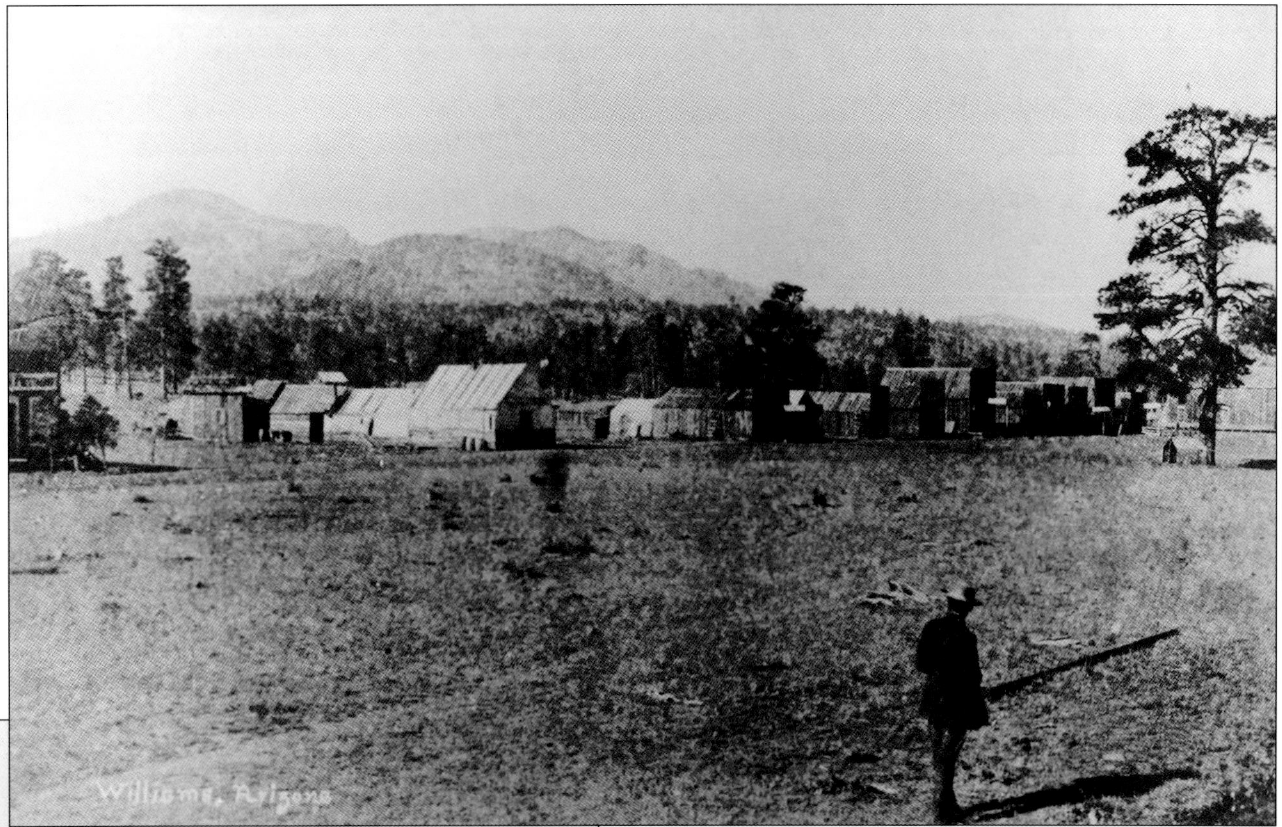

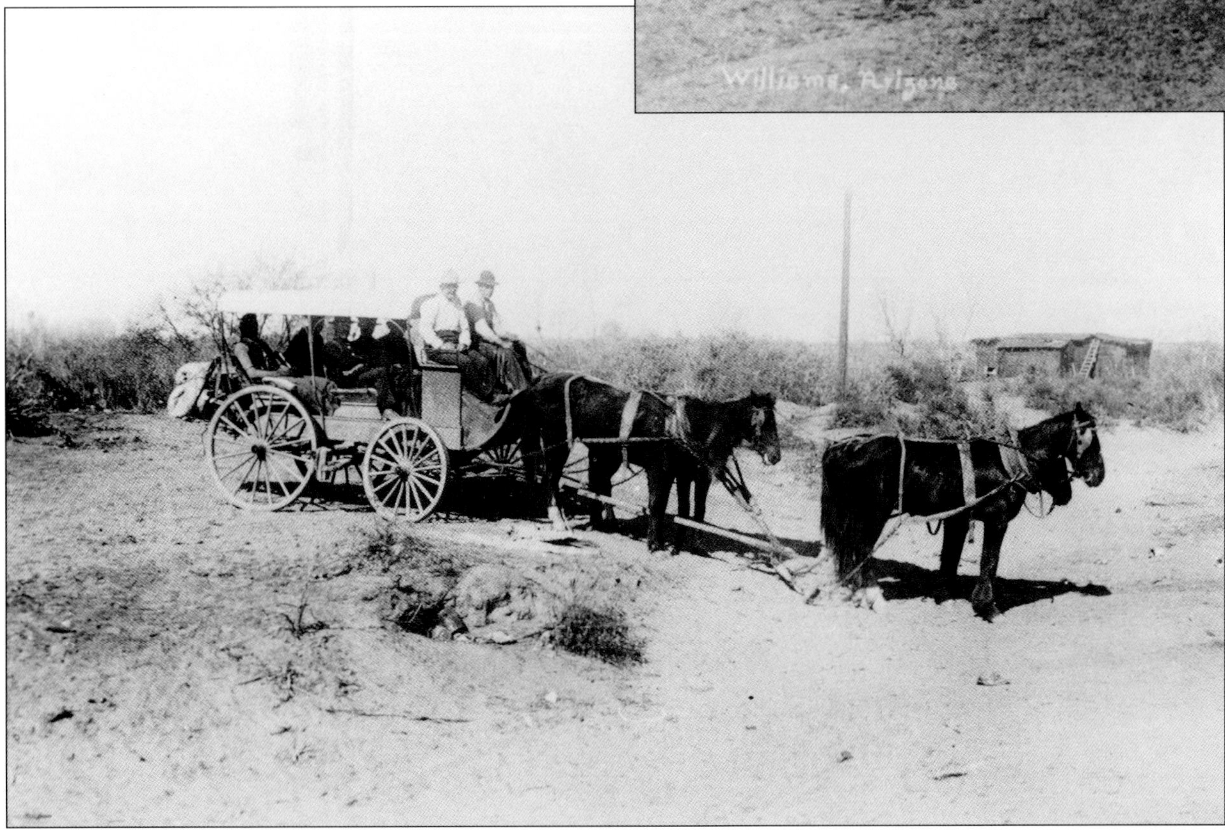

Stopping for a photograph, the stage is on the road to Yuma, Arizona, with several passengers including an Indian and a soldier.

Chapter 4

1872-1881

One of the first steam engines to travel west was the T.B. Judah, named after one of the founders of the railroad.

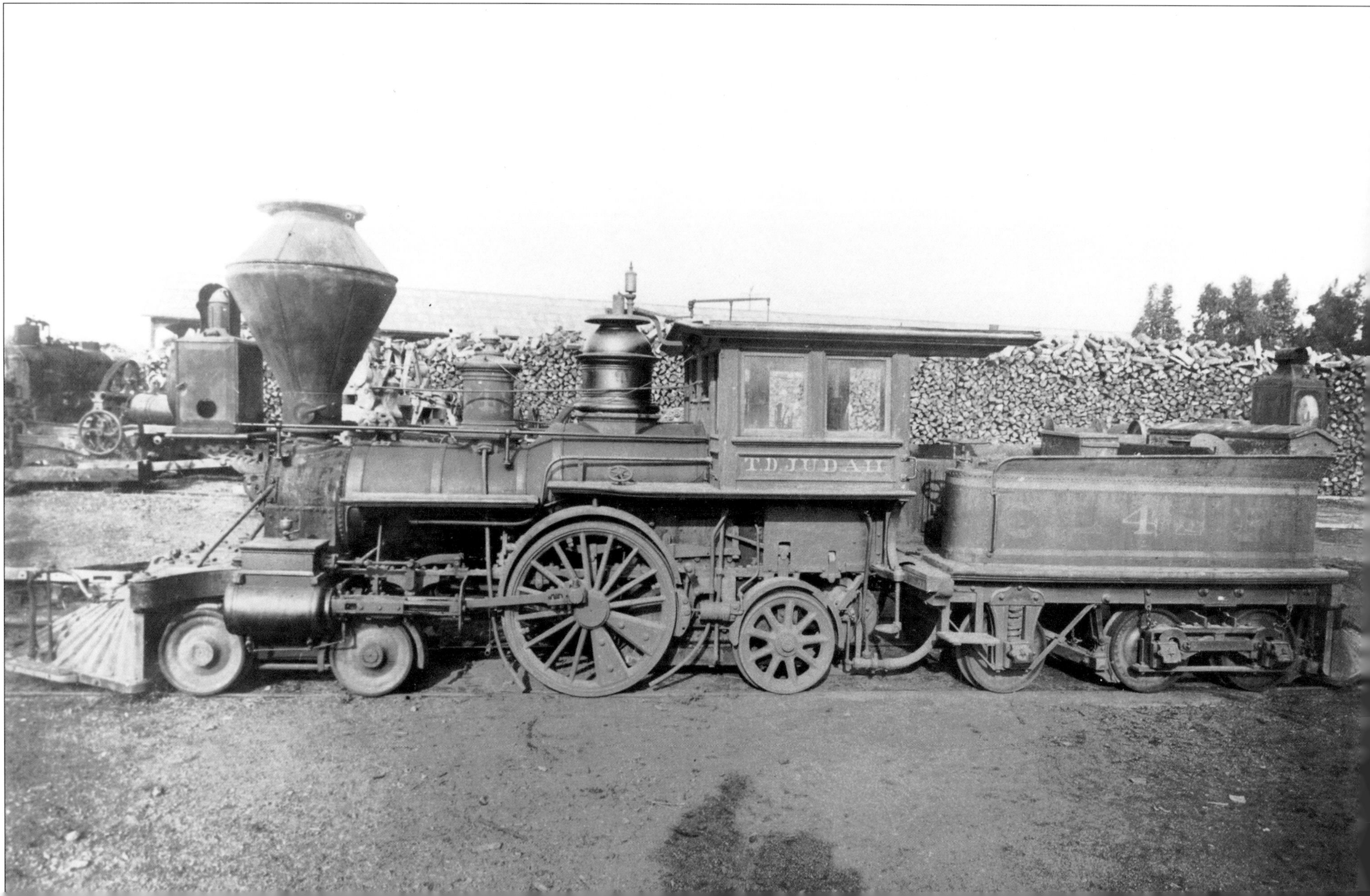

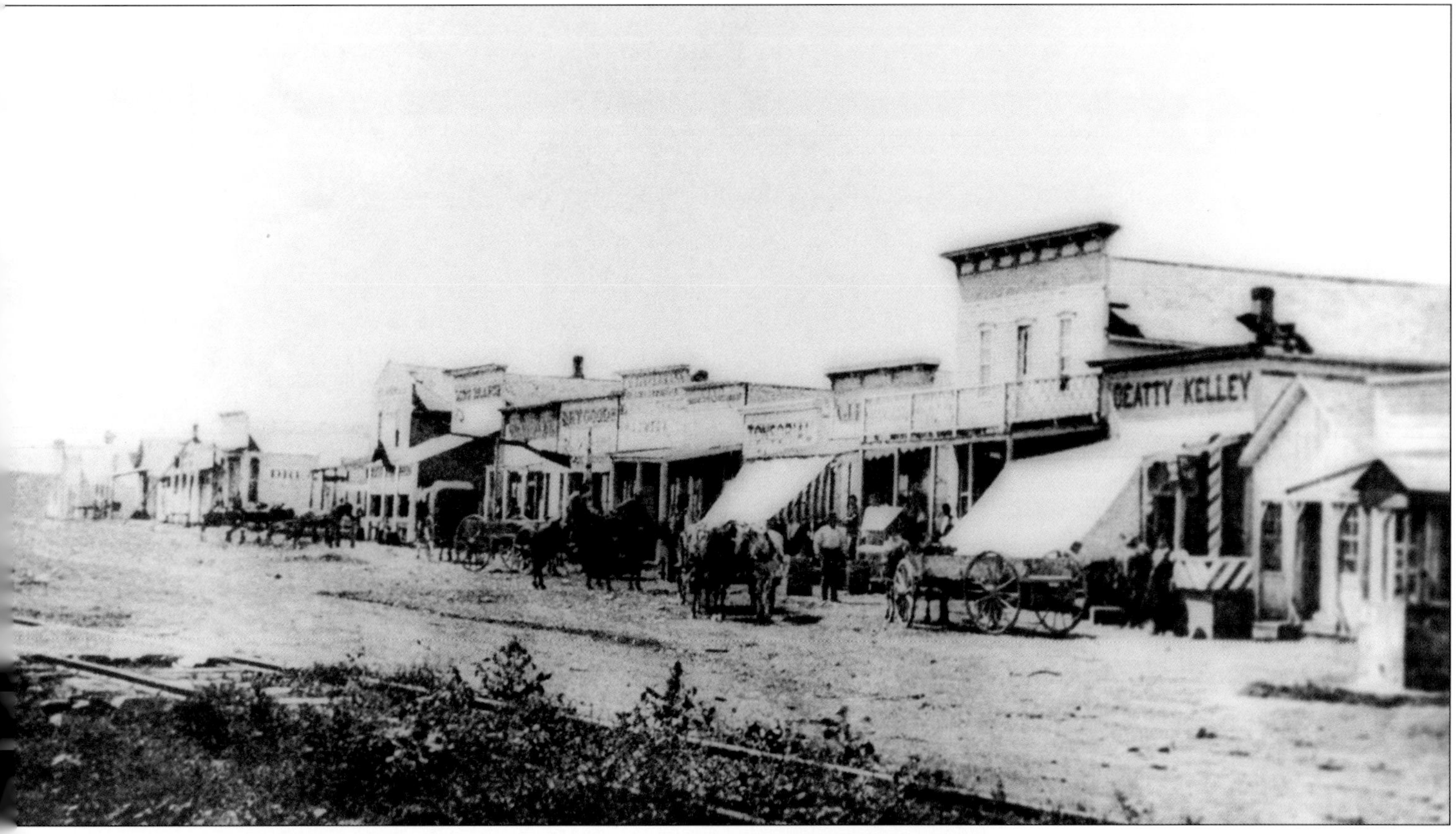

Dodge City in 1878, along the railroad tracks and main street.

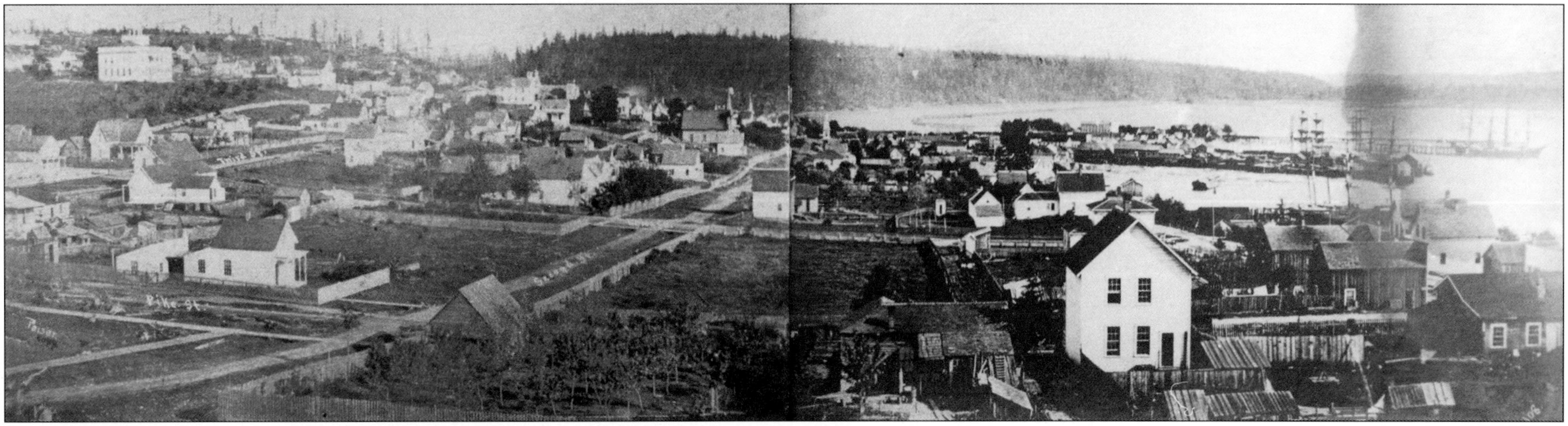

A panoramic photograph of Seattle, Washington, in 1878, using two prints together to form the long view of the city. We can see the harbor with three- and four-masted ships anchored off shore.

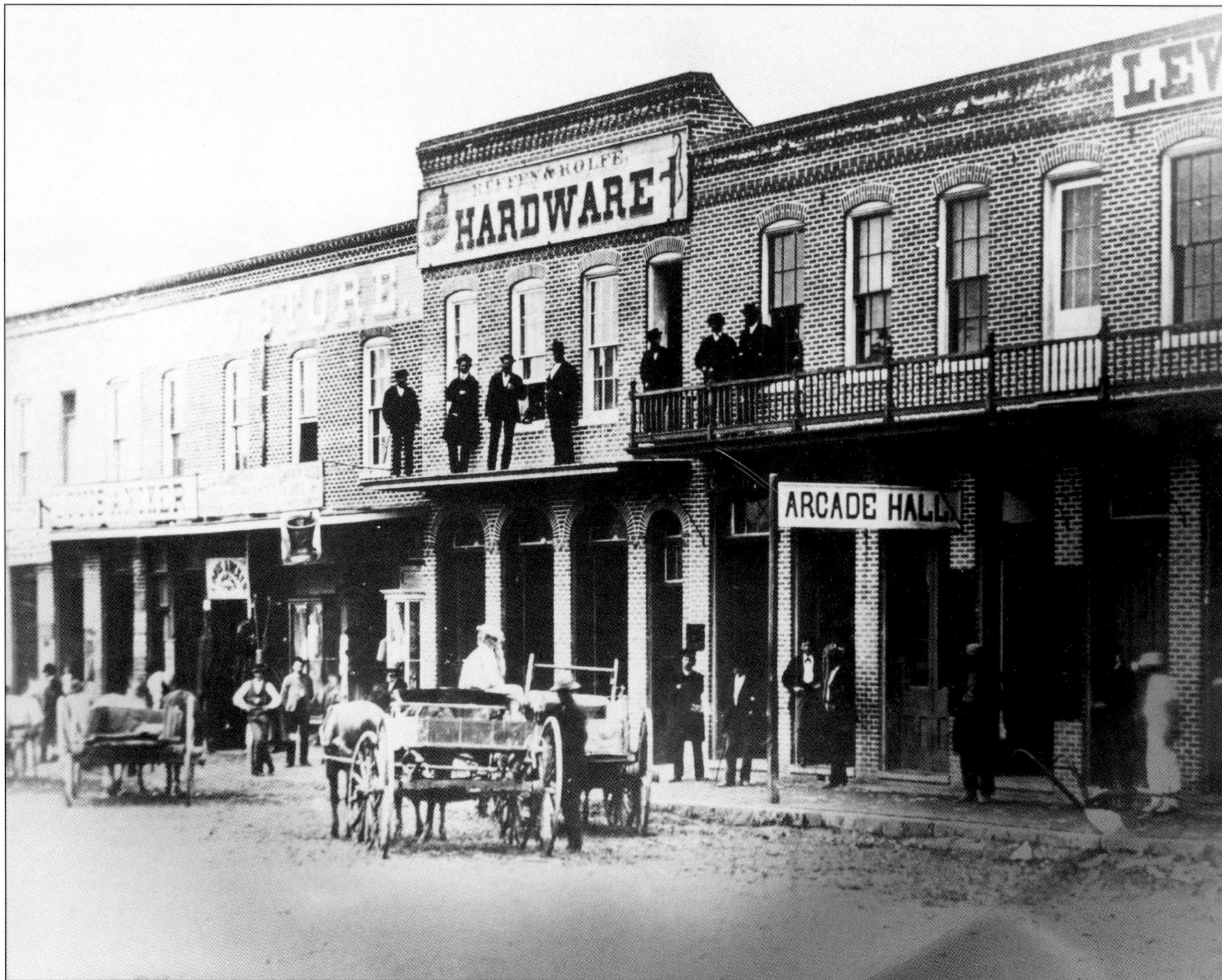

A 1875 photograph of main street San Bernardino showing the Ruffin and Rolfe Hardware store. Along with the drug store and arcade this building contained other stores and saloons.

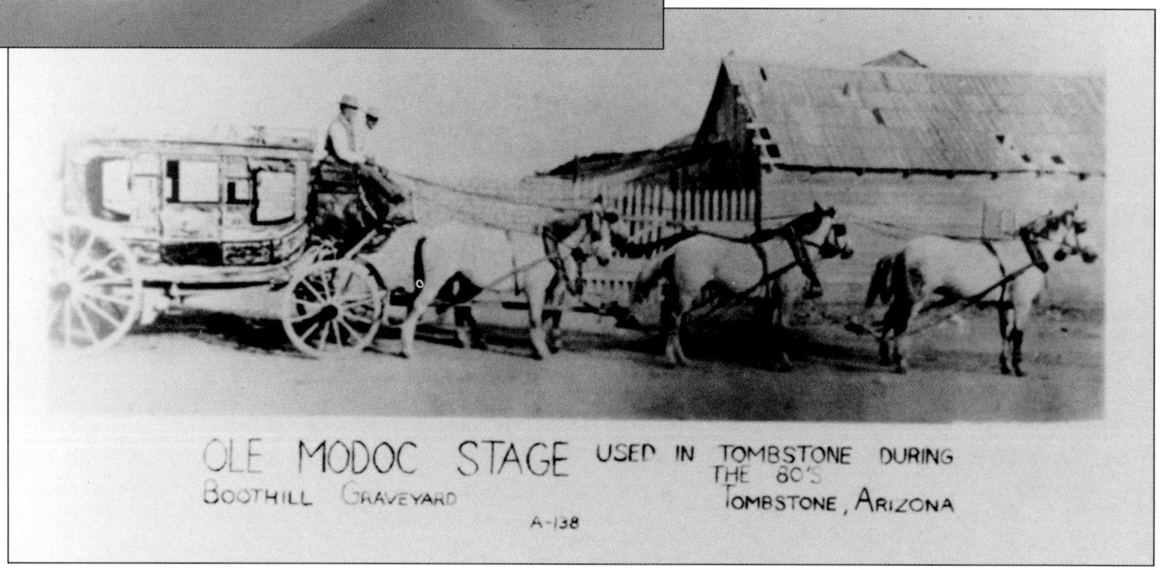

The Old Modoc Stagecoach used around Tombstone, Arizona, in the 1880s.

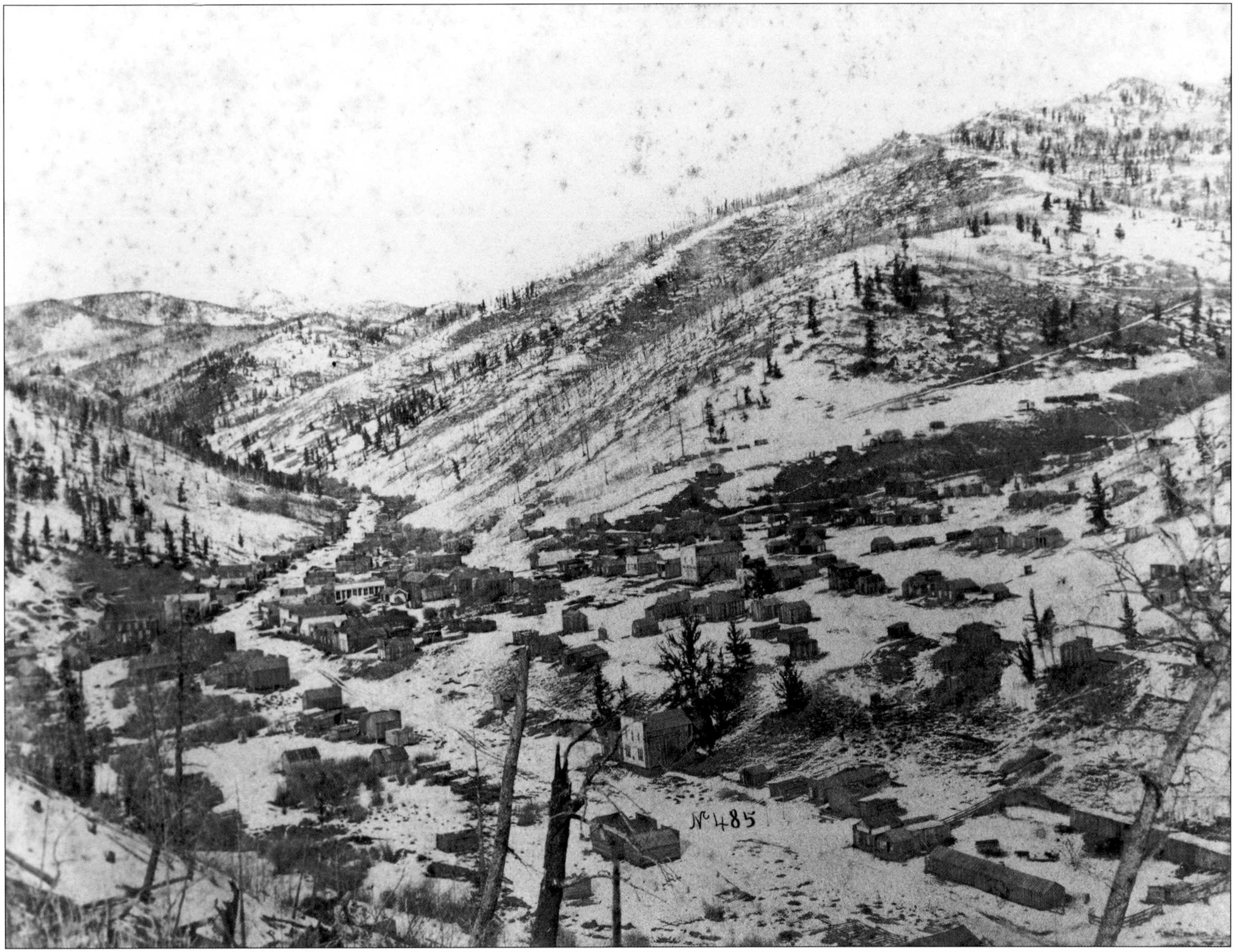

A very rare over all photograph of Bonanza, Colorado. Although this photo print had a lot of foxing (brownish spots and stains) the image still contains all the details. In the middle of winter the stream, known as Kerber Creek, that runs through town is frozen over. When rich ore was found in the surrounding hills, more than five thousand people flooded into the area. Bonanza swelled to twenty thousand before the gold and silver played out. In 1937 a fire destroyed the entire business district. No one is mining there anymore and people have moved on. The photograph was taken by Frank Kuykendall, whose large stamp is on the back of the mount.

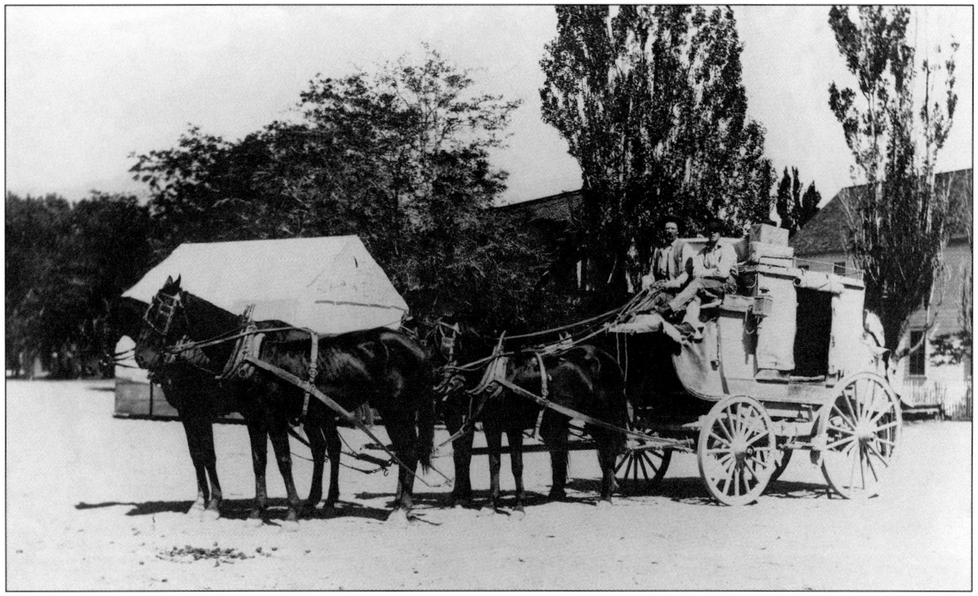

Arriving in Auburn, California with the U.S. Mail, the stage stops for its portrait. One can only imagine how little light was given off from those small oil lamps on either side of the coach. The photograph is from a glass negative.

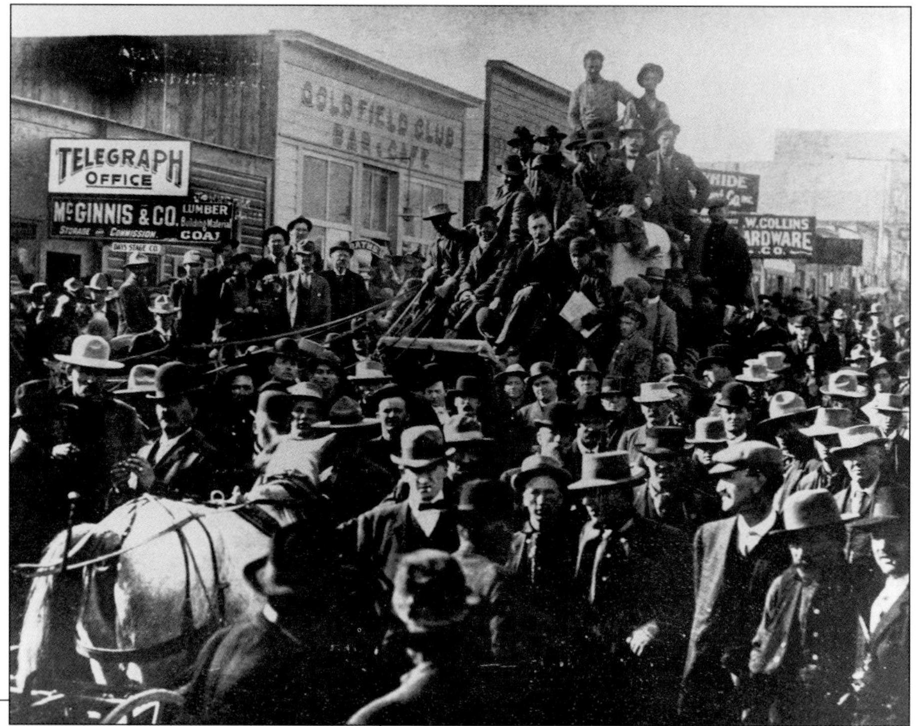

It looks like the entire town of Goldfield, Nevada, has turned out to pose for the photographer who stood along the main street.

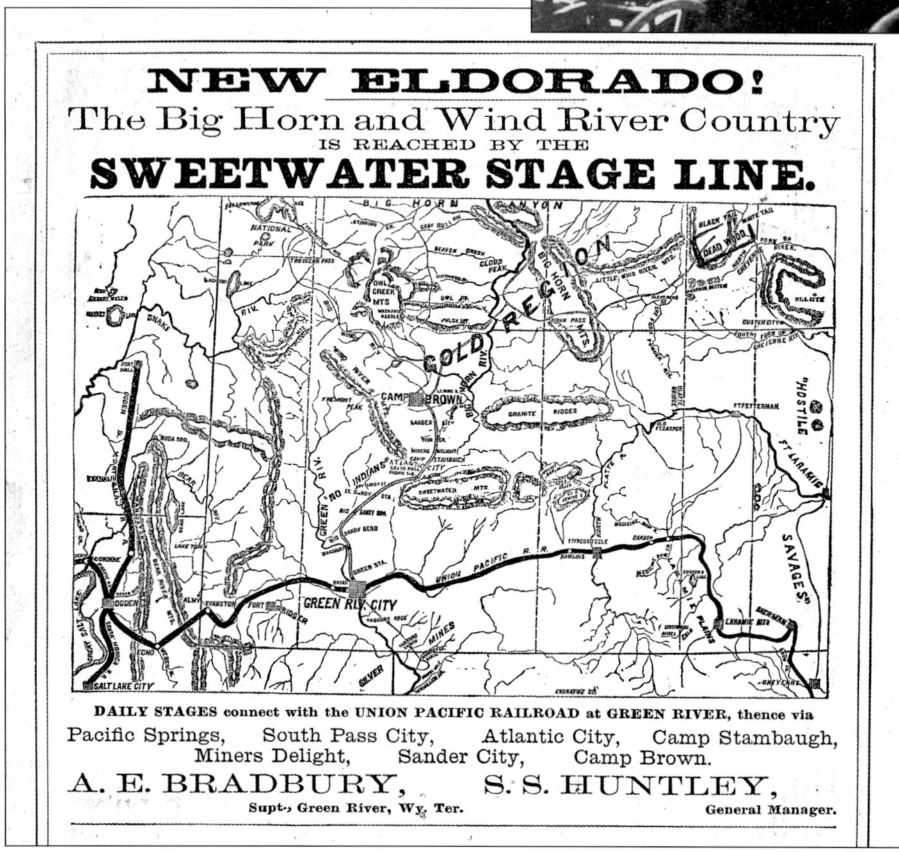

The Sweetwater Stage Line map of the Big Horn and Wind River country.

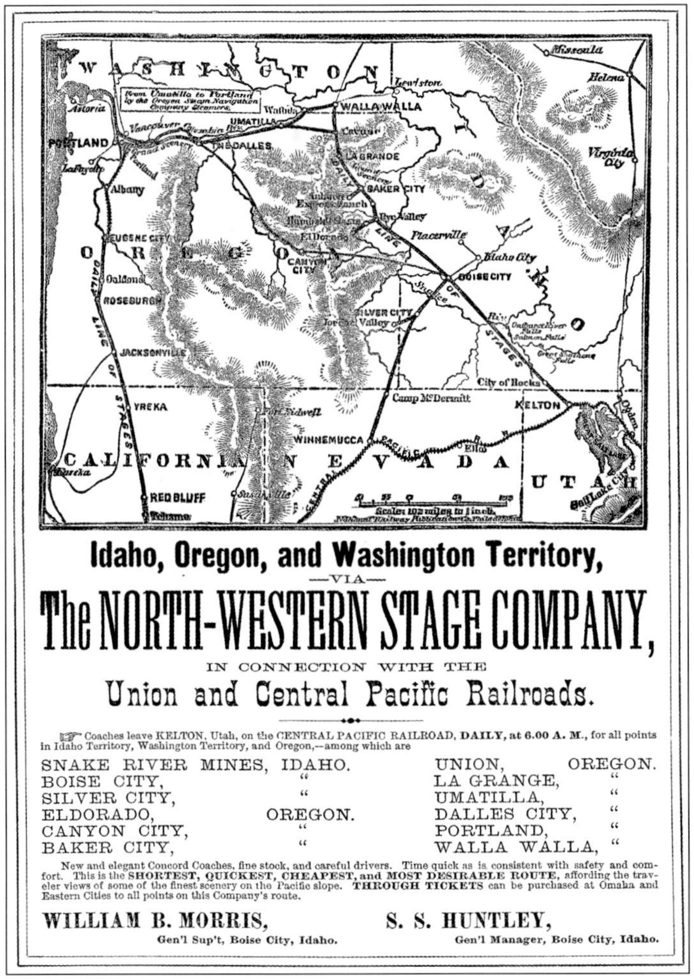

The North-Western Stage Company map through Idaho, Oregon, and Washington Territory.

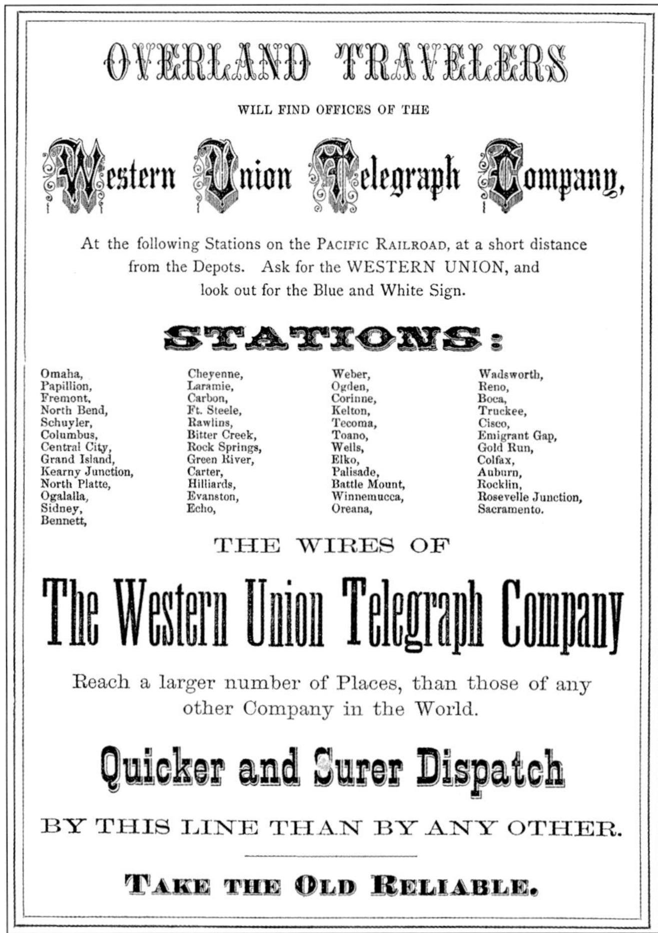

An advertisement in the 1878 Williams Overland Travelers book informs the reader of all the Western Union Telegraph stations that it serves in the West.

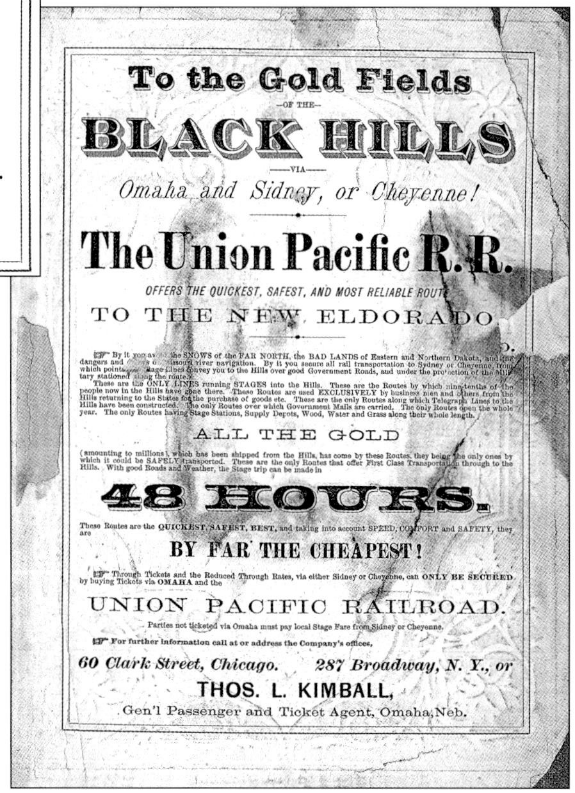

The Union Pacific Railroads advertisement for people wanting to find gold in the Black Hills. The flyer states that it takes you just so far, then you get to go by stagecoach over good government roads. Plus! There is military stationed along the way. These are the only lines running stages into the hills, and the only route that has stage stations, supply depots, wood, water, and grass along the whole way.

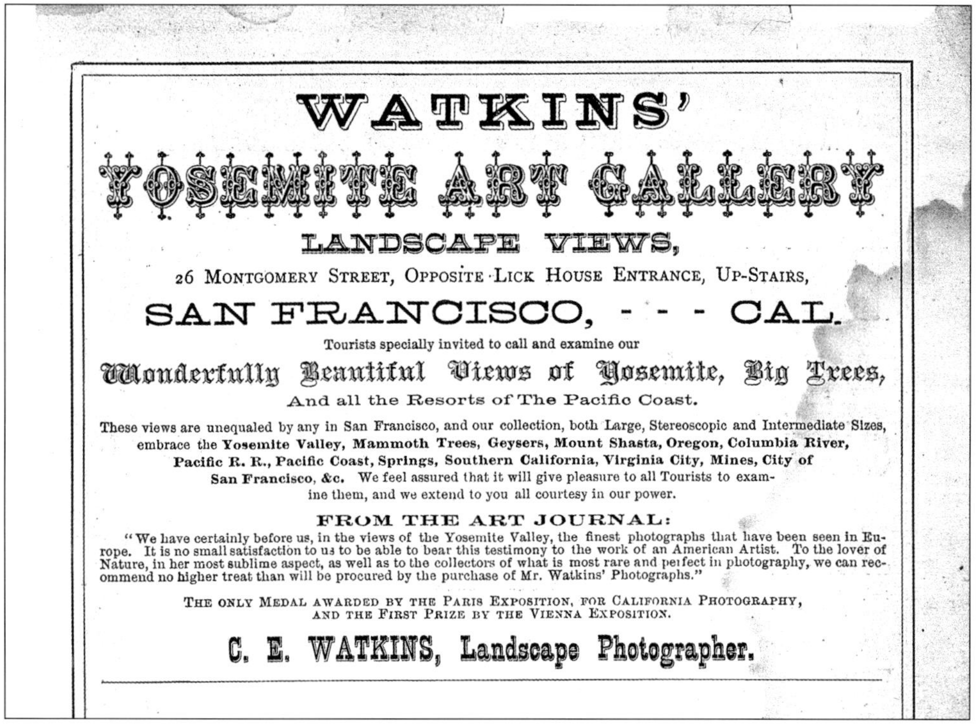

Photographer Carlton Watkins was already a master photographer when he placed this advertisement in Williams 1878 Travel Book.

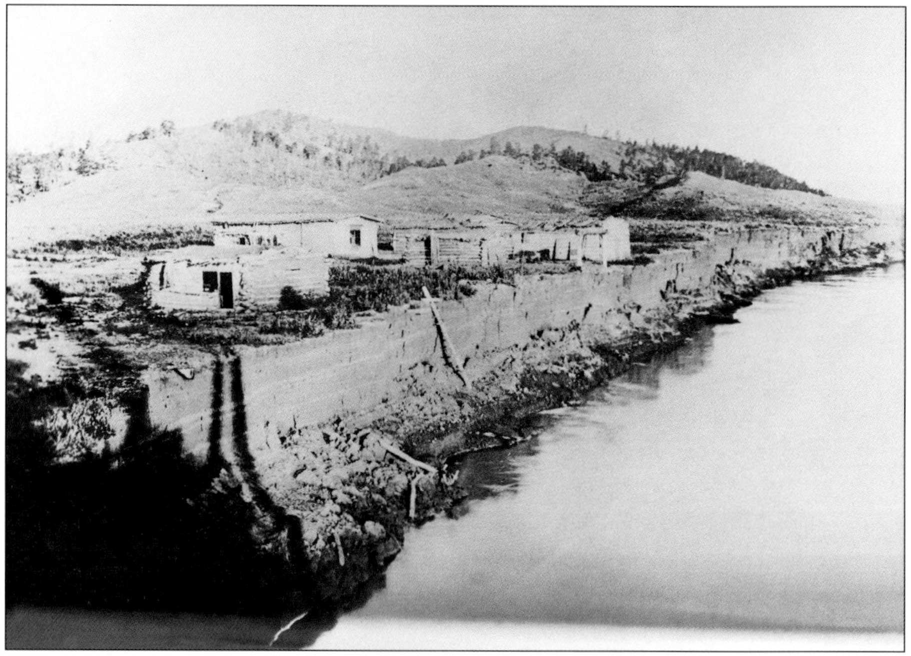

F.J. Haynes took this photograph of Carroll, Montana, in 1881. In case of an Indian attack the inhabitants had the escape ladder near by.

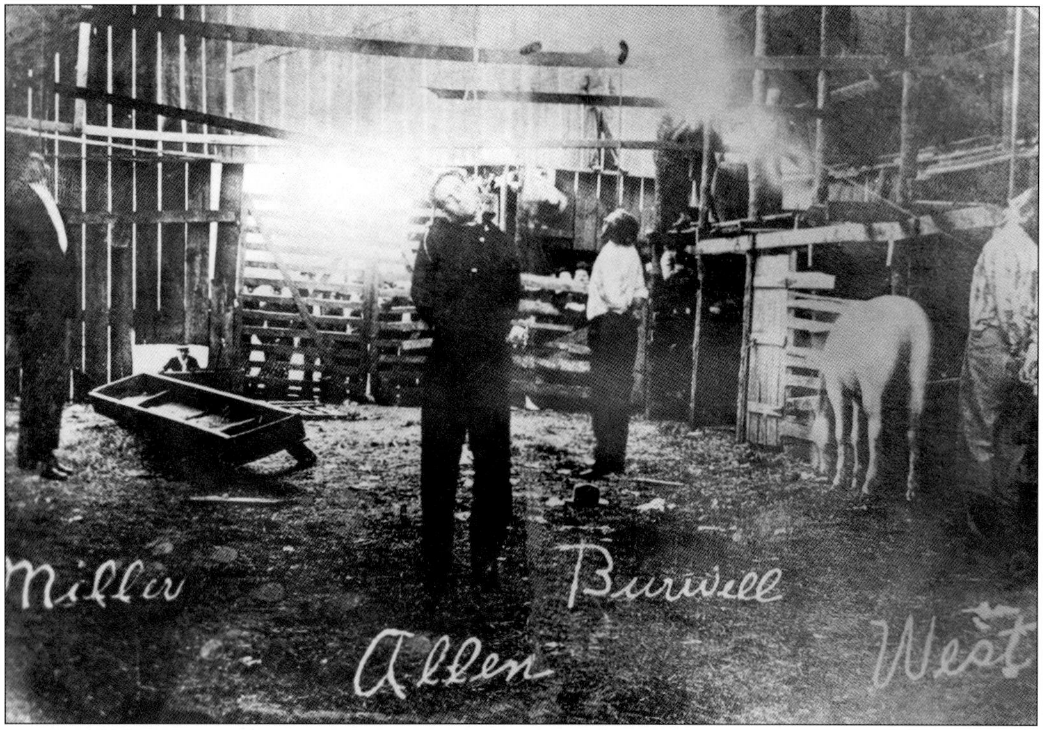

These four bank robbers and murderers got their just deserts and where hung in a barn. The four, named Miller, Allen, Burwell, and West, made Western history by hanging together.

The Oklahoma town of Kildare, is celebrating either statehood or the 4th of July. As late as 1990 there were still ninety people living in the town. The stagecoach pulled by a team of eight horses with The Board of Trade banner hung on its side. This fantastic photograph from a cracked glass plate even has a band hanging on the back of the stage and a man holding the flag. All are posing for an unknown photographer.

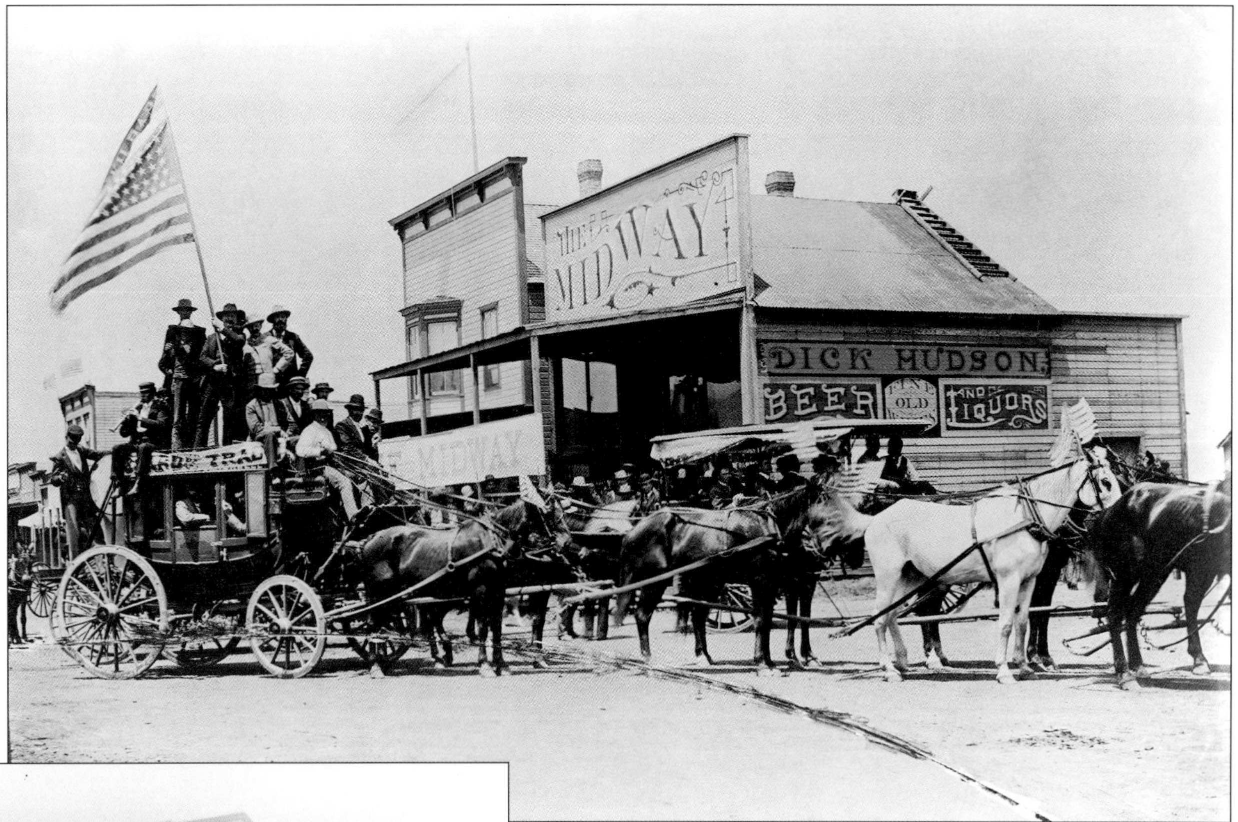

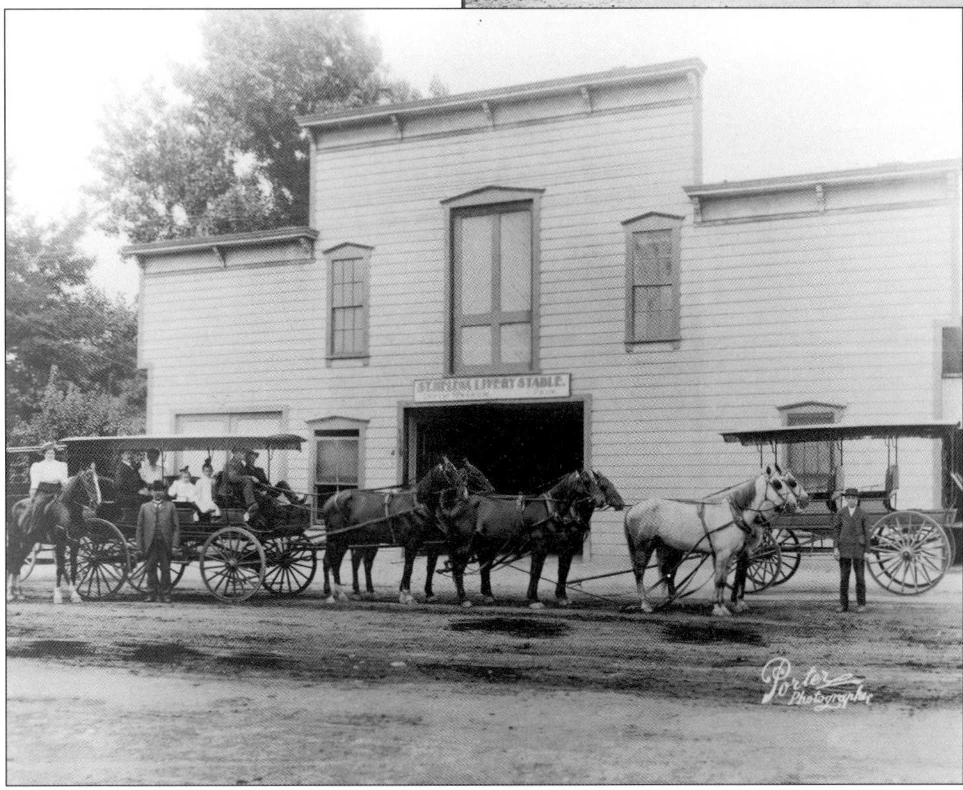

A fine photograph taken by Porter of St. Helens, Minnesota, showing the St. Helens Livery Stable. Out in front are some of the stages they had to ferry people around in.

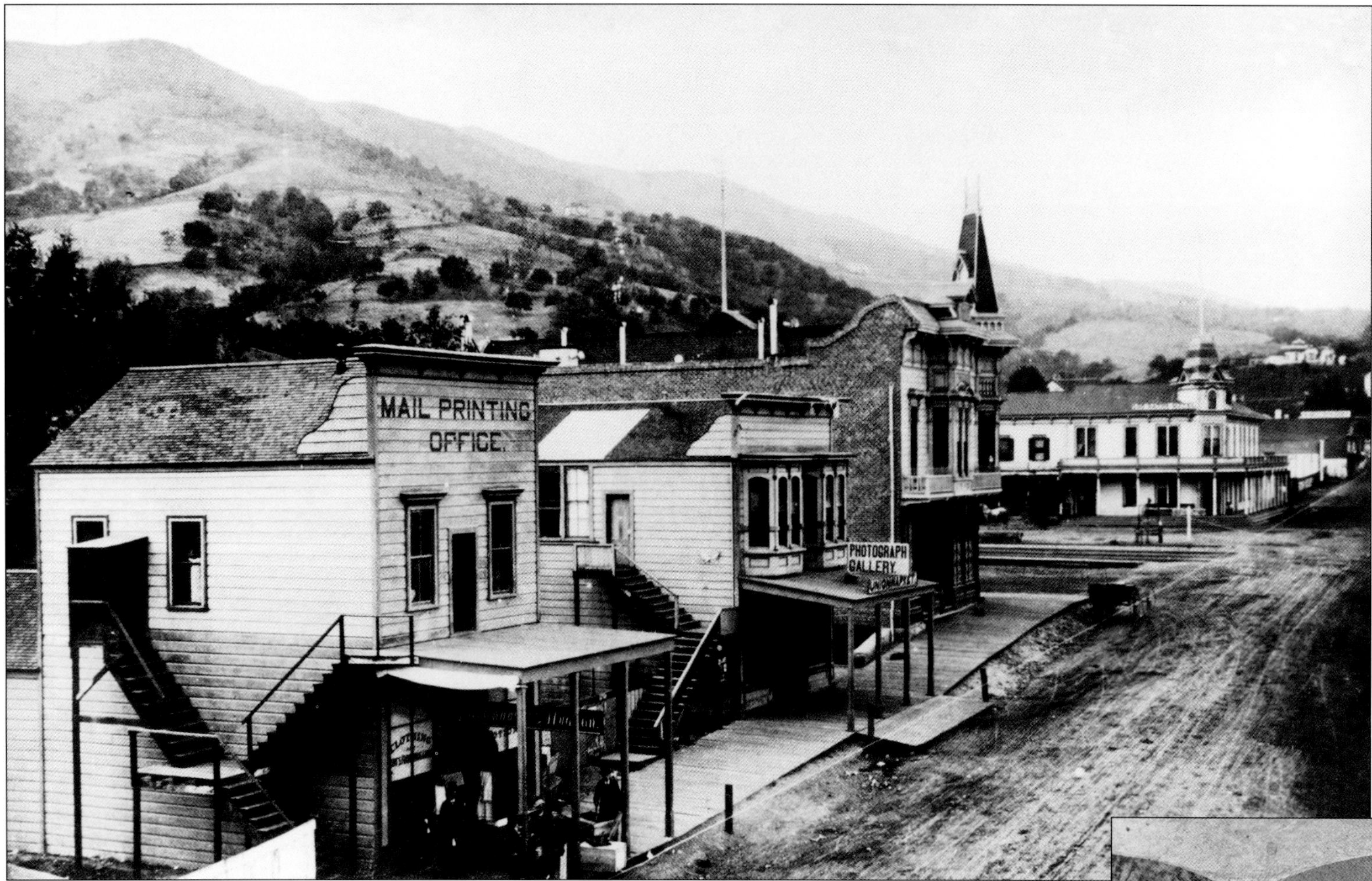

The town of Los Gatos, California, was a jumping off point for many who would go east from here into the gold fields of California. The photograph was made from the original glass plate.

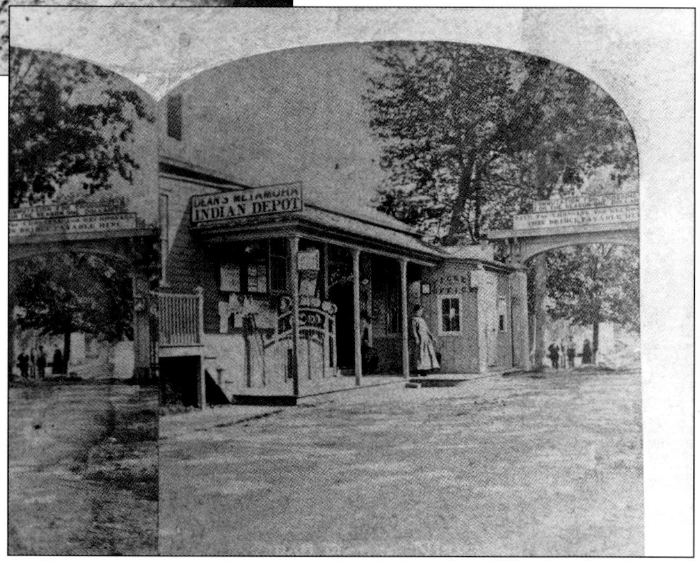

The photo from a fading stereo card shows the Indian Depot outside of Yellowstone Park. The signs are for fees to enter the area.

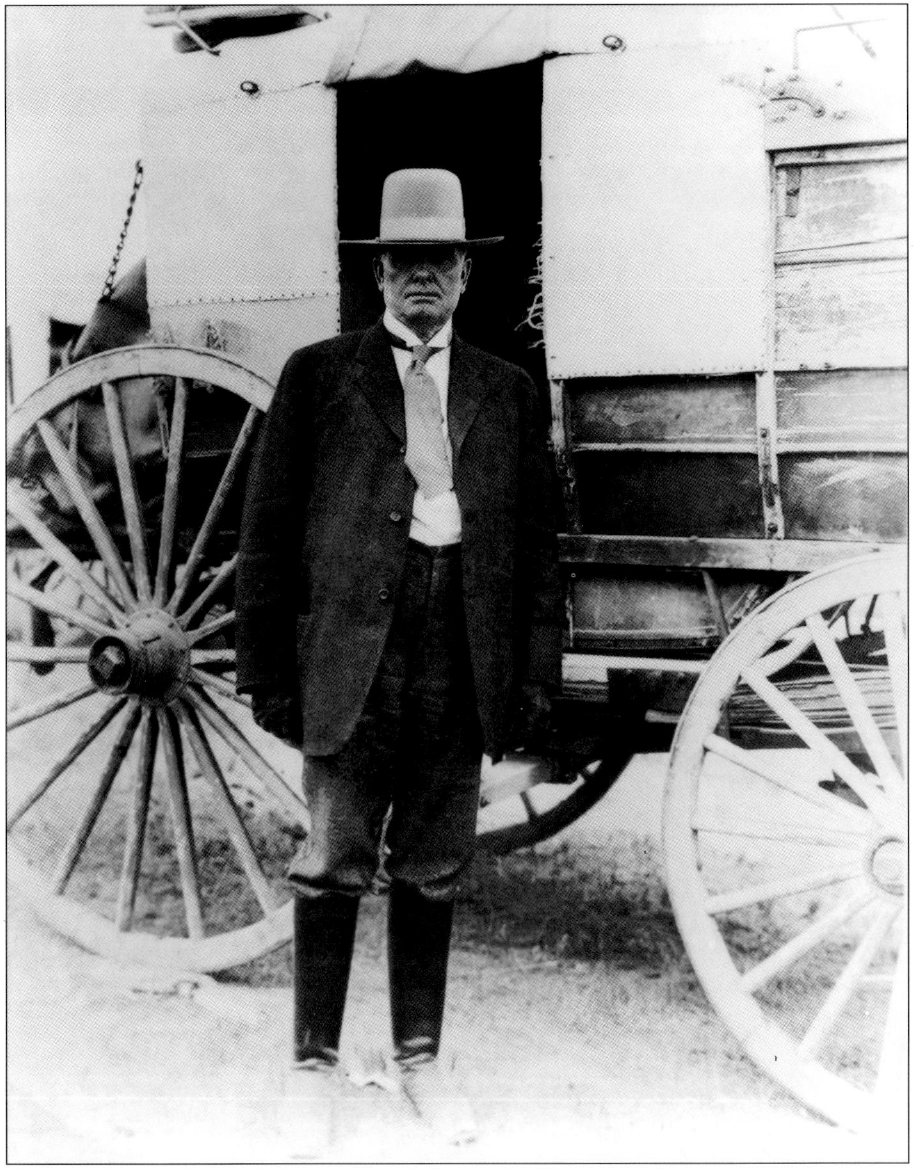

A hard looking stage driver poses for his portrait in front of his mud wagon coach.

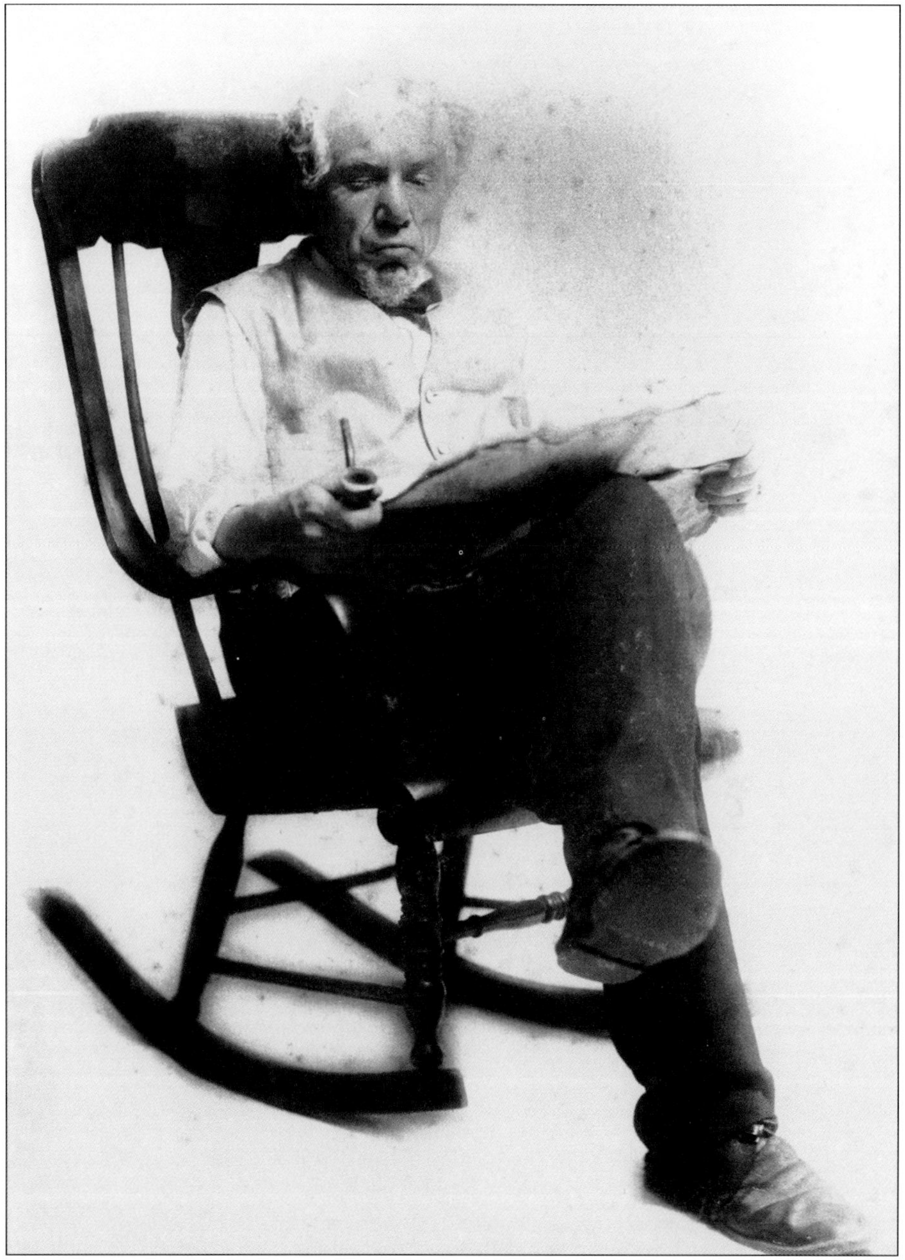

Phil Ott, a champion stage driver, is seen here in his rocking chair.
The photographer, Davies, is from Portland, Oregon.

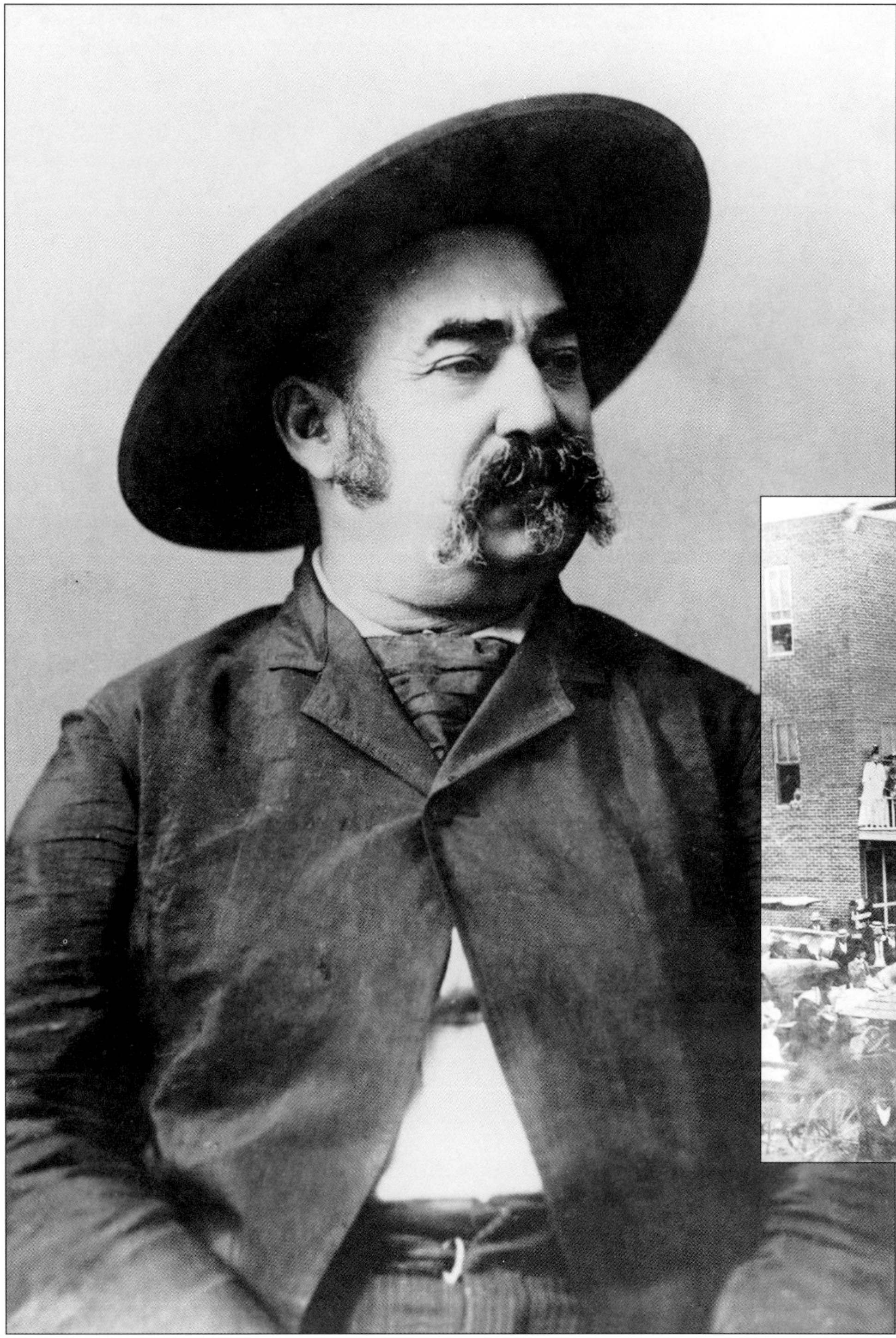

A rare photograph of the famous sure shot John X Biedler. He killed more outlaws and Indians in fair fights than any other man, while working for Wells Fargo and traveling in Montana, Salt Lake, and other western areas. This original photo was presented in 1889 to photographer D.F. Barry by C. Kinsh of Helena, Montana.

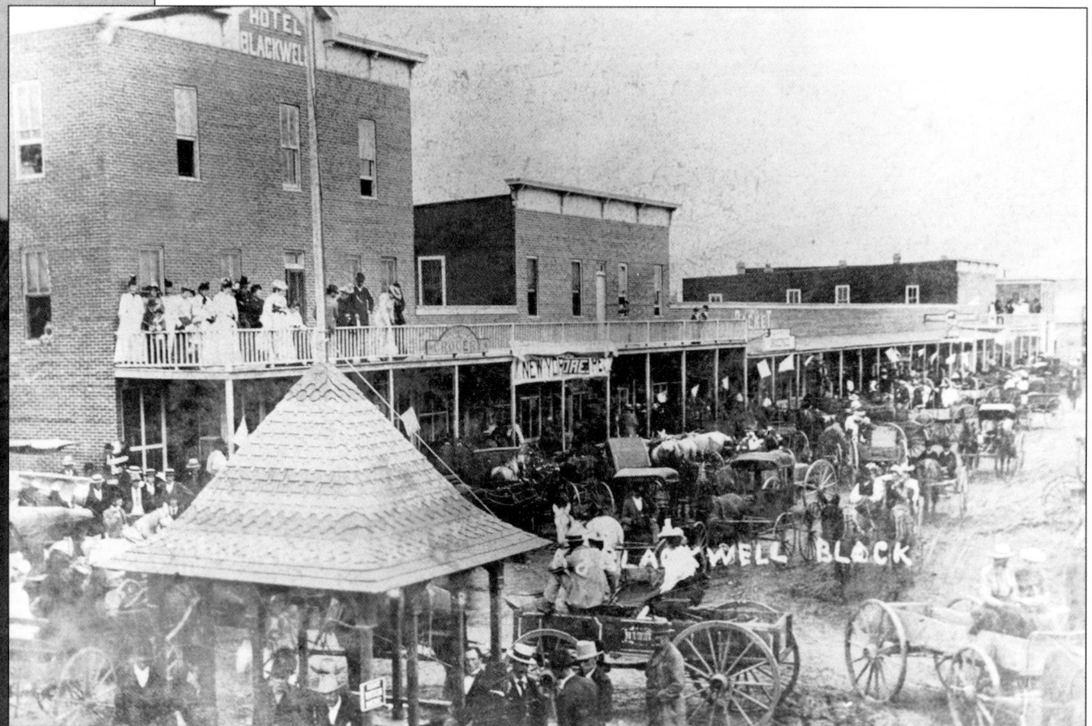

The A.J. Blackwell Block in Oklahoma celebrating of the arrival of the first railroad.

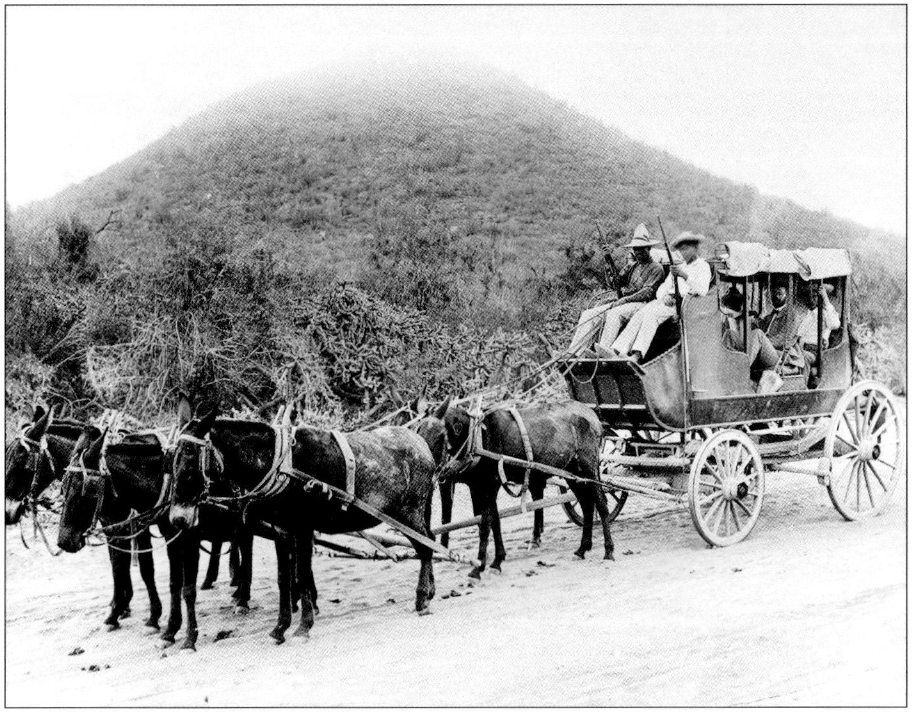

The stage to Rio Yaque, Mexico. This Mexican mud wagon has six mules. Both the driver and the assistant have rifles on the ready. It is said that this was the same type of stagecoach that took Billy The Kid in, when he was captured.

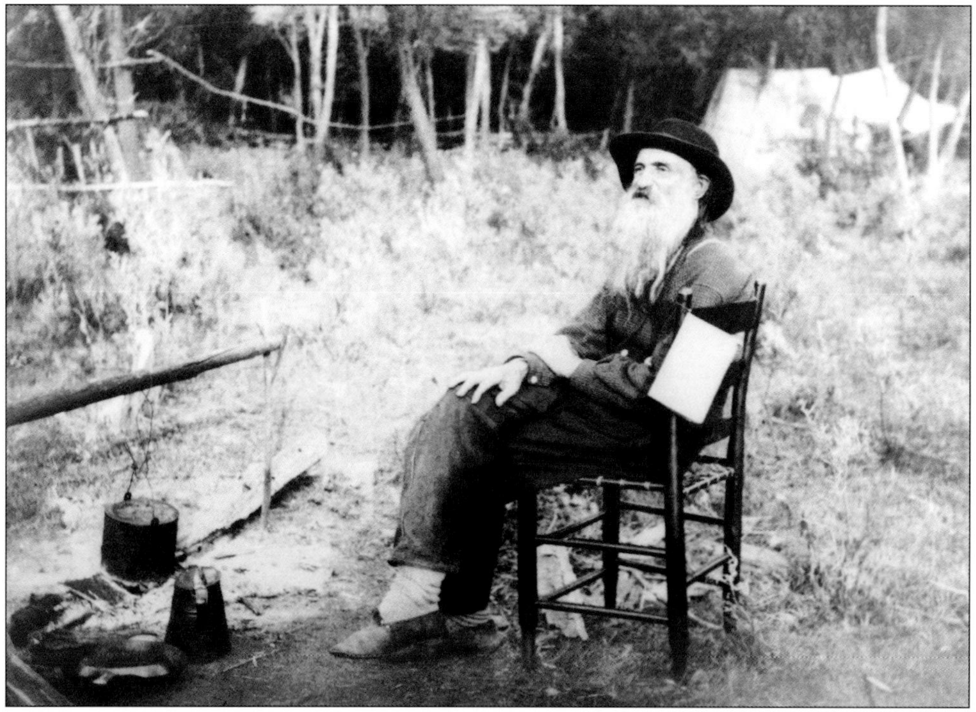

This is S.H. Meek, a stagecoach driver. He is the brother of Steven H. Meek a hunter and trapper in the year 1833. This photograph was given to Ben Powers by Mr. Britt, the son of the early day photographer of Jacksonville, Oregon.

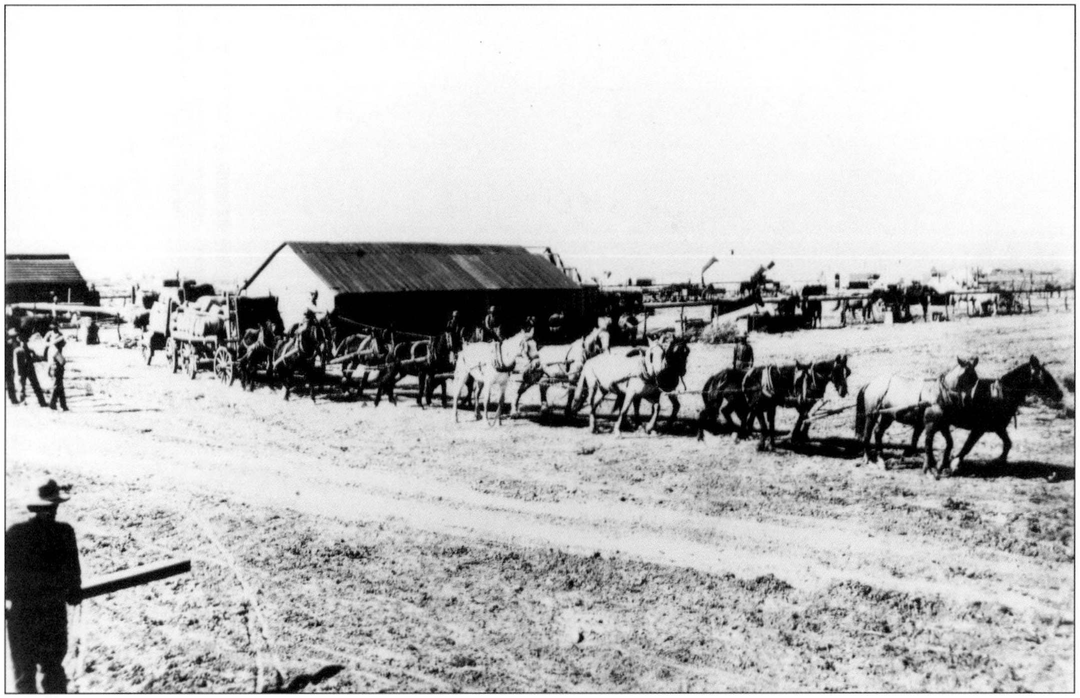

Tugging with all their might this team of mules and horses is moving some machinery and supplies to Winnemucca, Nevada, from a nearby depot.

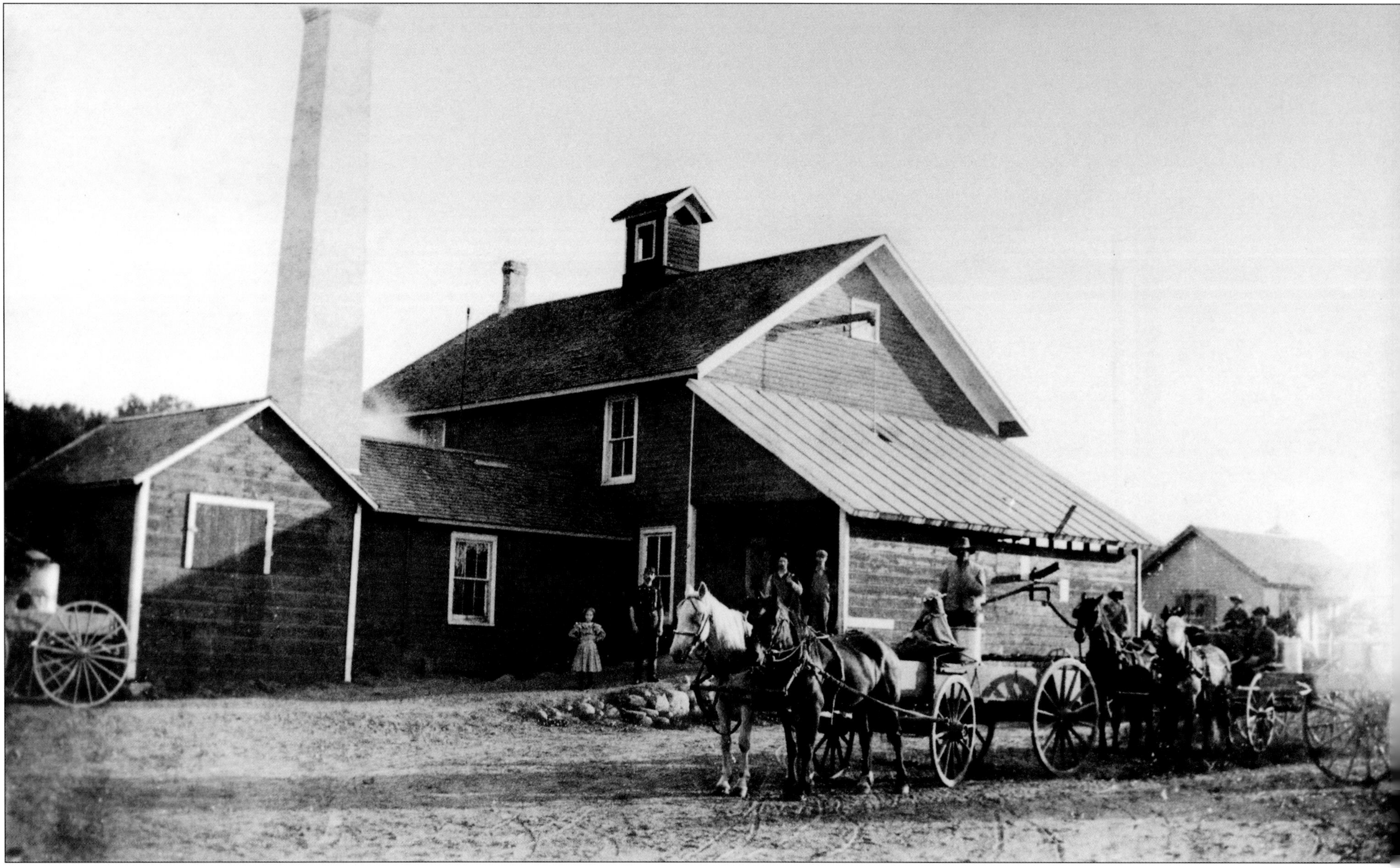

A marvelous photo taken of a brewery showing the horse-drawn wagons filling up for delivery.

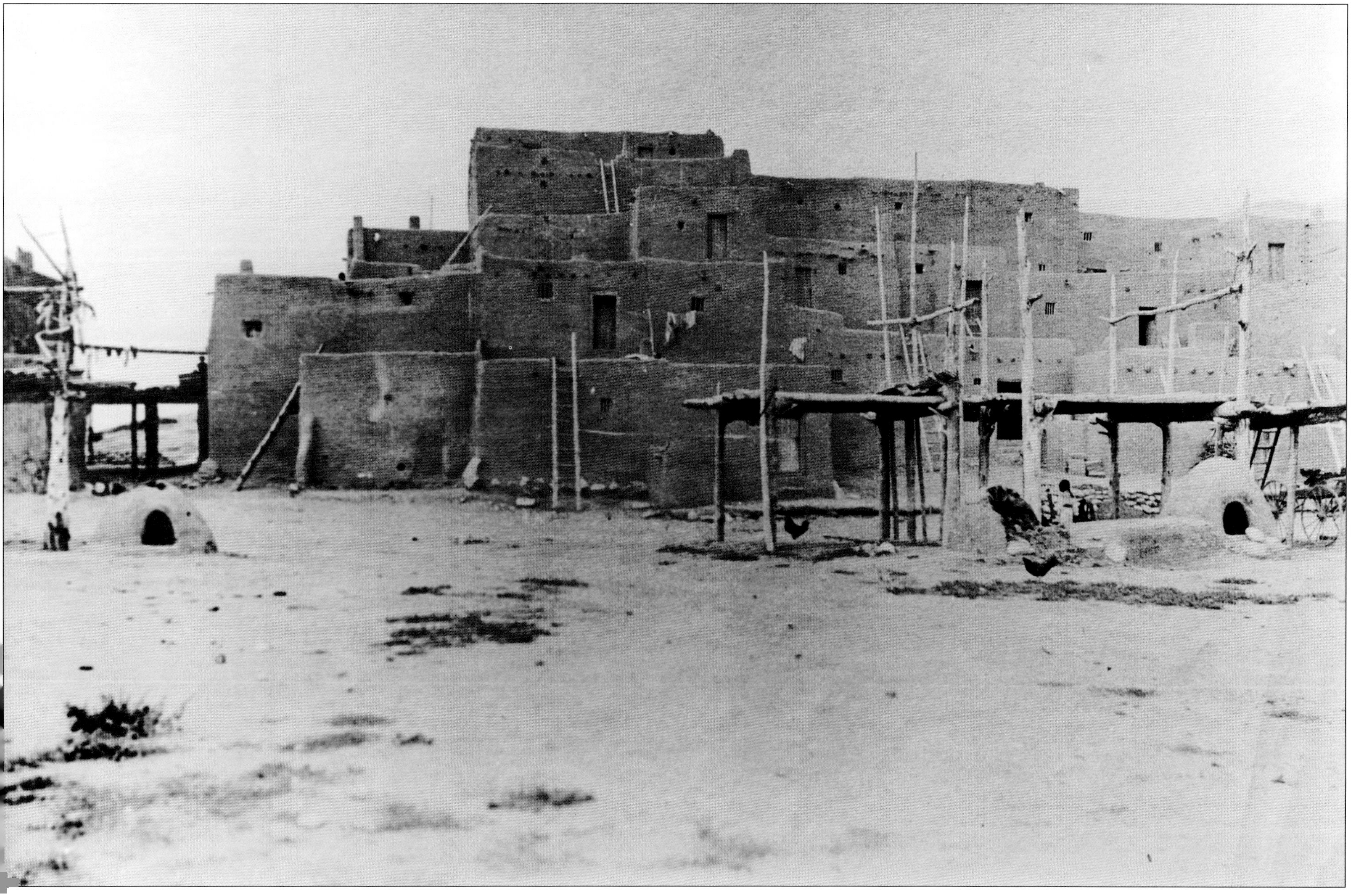

Several old New Mexico Indian pueblos almost look abandoned.

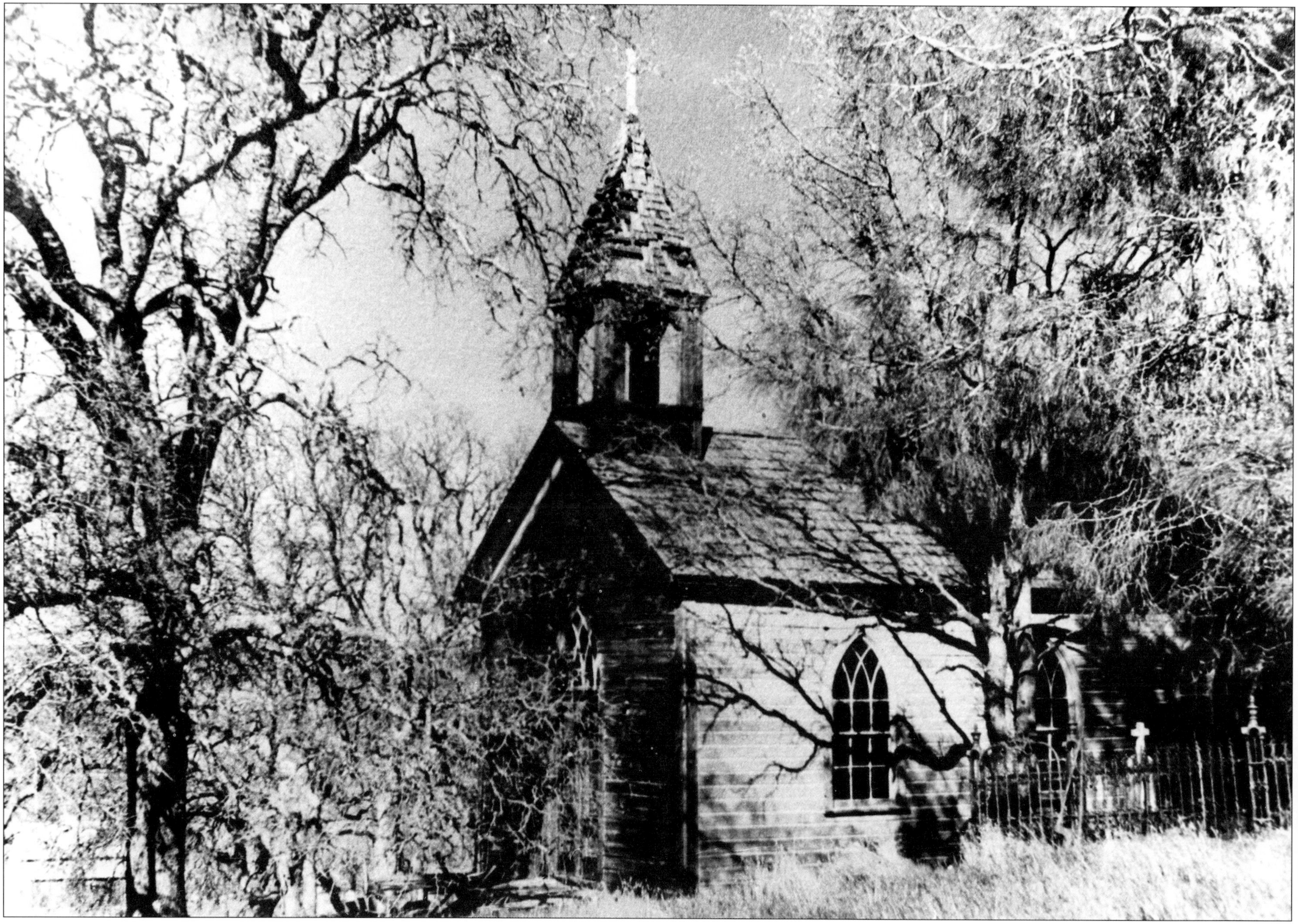

This Catholic church stood In the Chinese camp in the gold region of northern California.

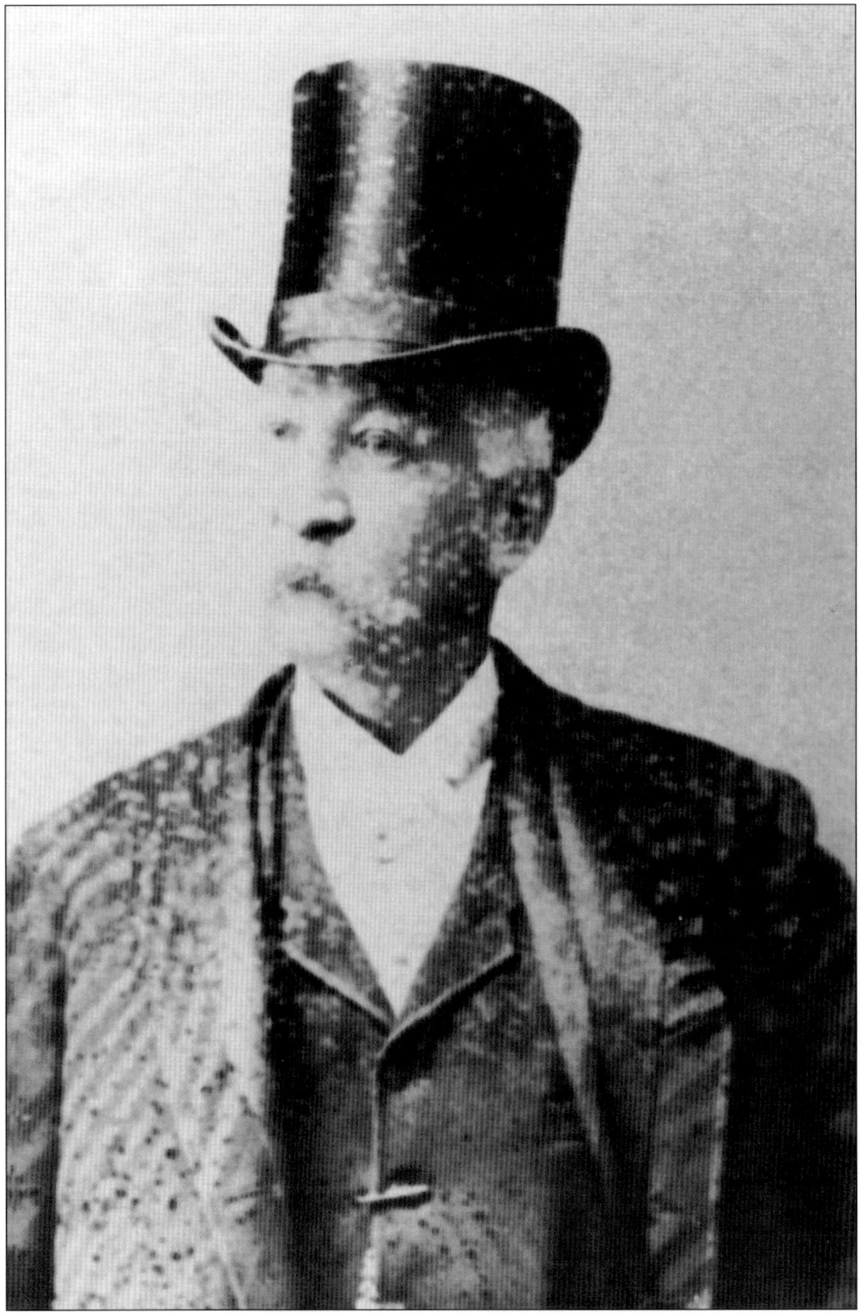

Charles C. Bolton, wearing a fine tall hat, was photographed by Tabor of San Francisco. Who would think of him as a the terrible stage robber named "Black Bart?" This CDV card is even signed by him. He supposedly stole twenty-three Wells Fargo boxes of treasure.

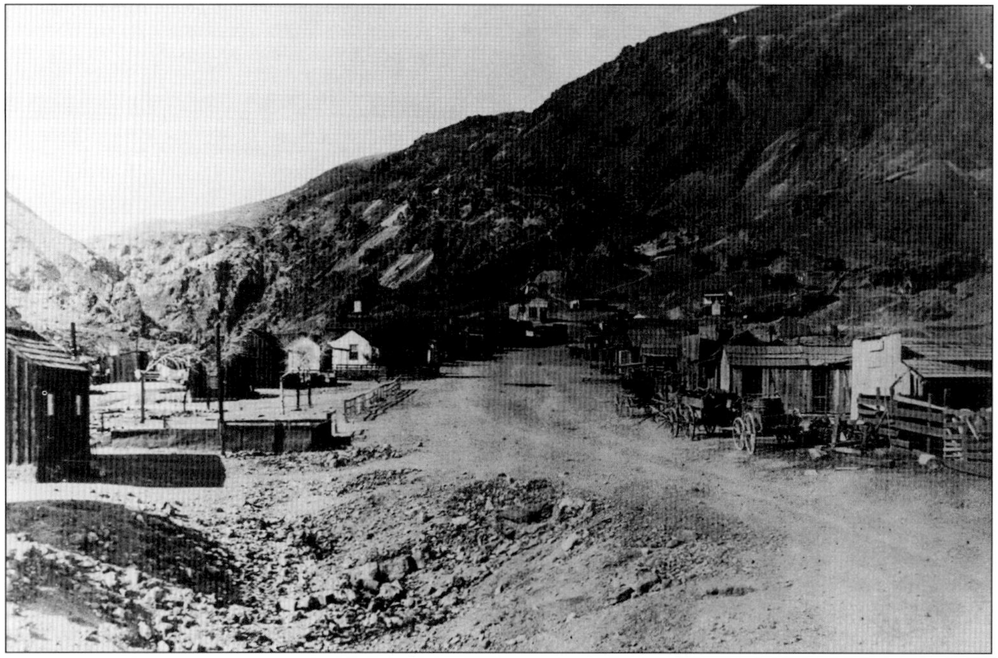

Looking down the main road of Calico, California, the mine was way up into the tall hills. We can make out the tailings from the mine, but the structure is not visible.

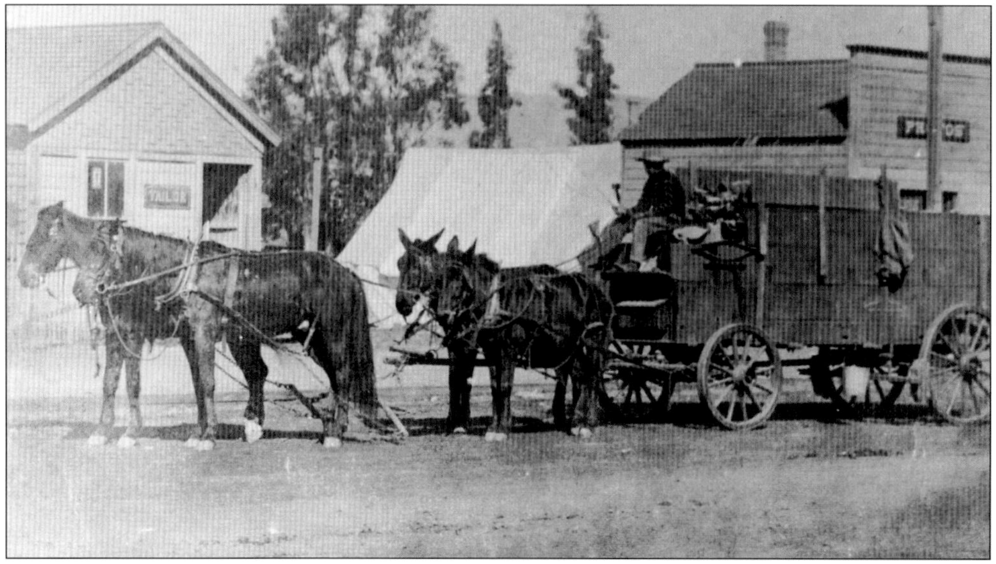

A photograph of a freighter hauled by two horses and two mules. Behind the pole is a photo studio, possibly of the person who took this photograph.

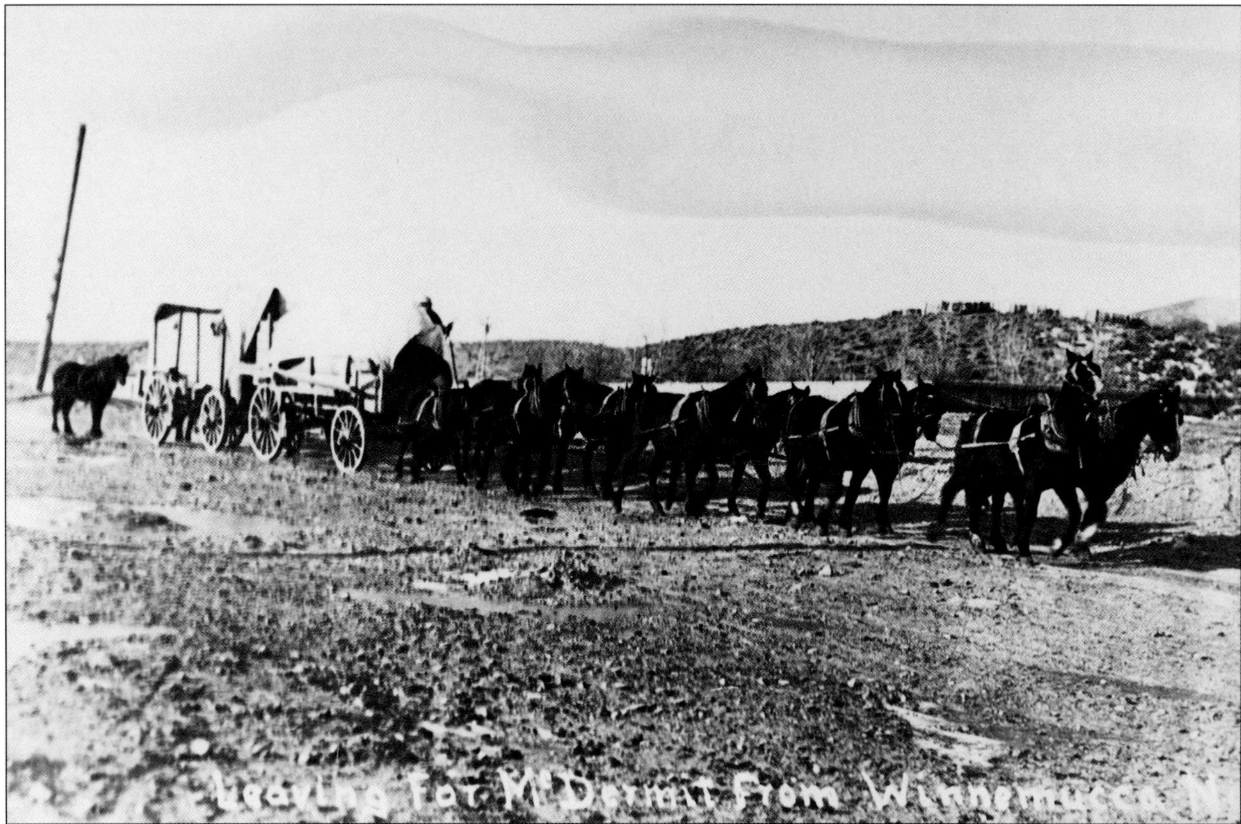

A load of supplies from Winnemucca, Nevada, begins its trip to McDermitt.

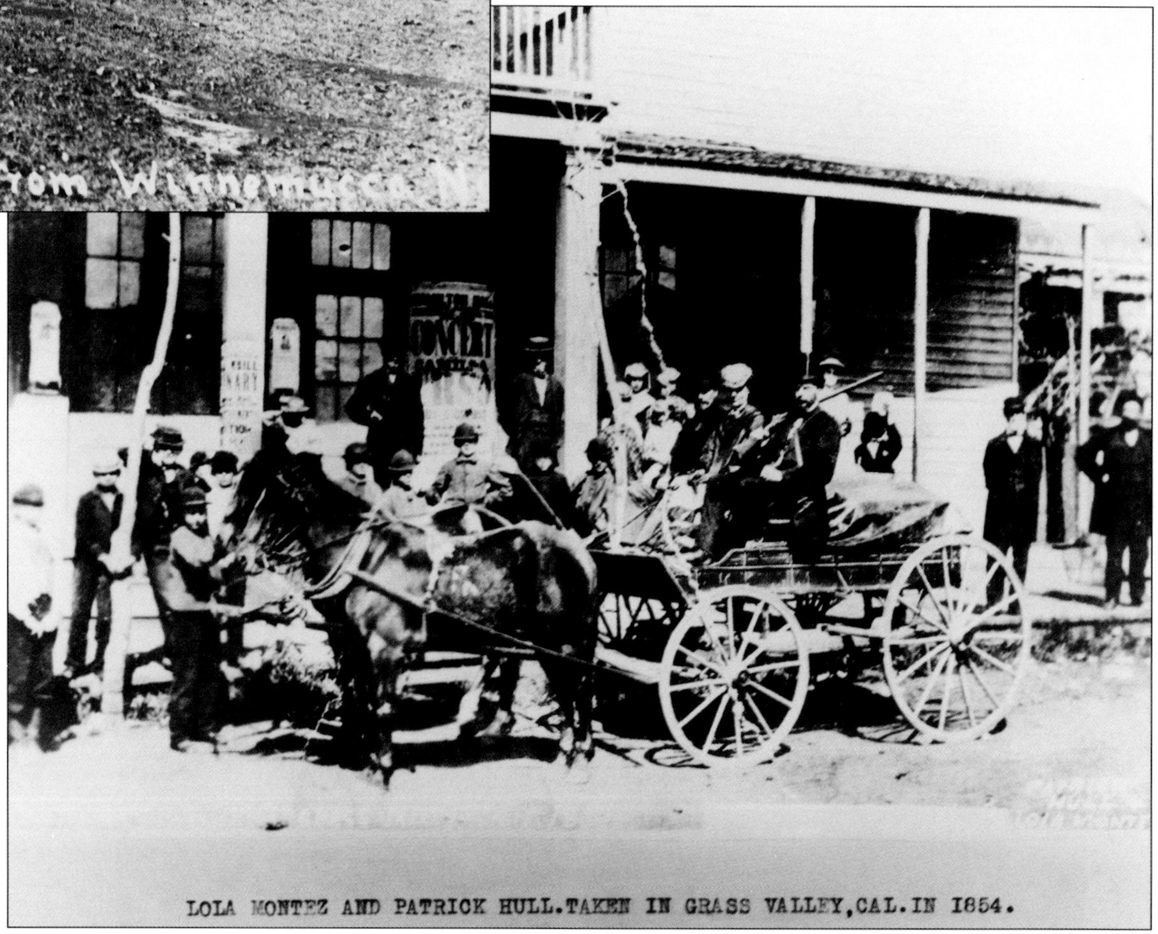

Parked outside the hotel where she will perform is Lola Montez. With her, riding shot gun, is Patrick Hull. The photograph was taken in Grass Valley, California.

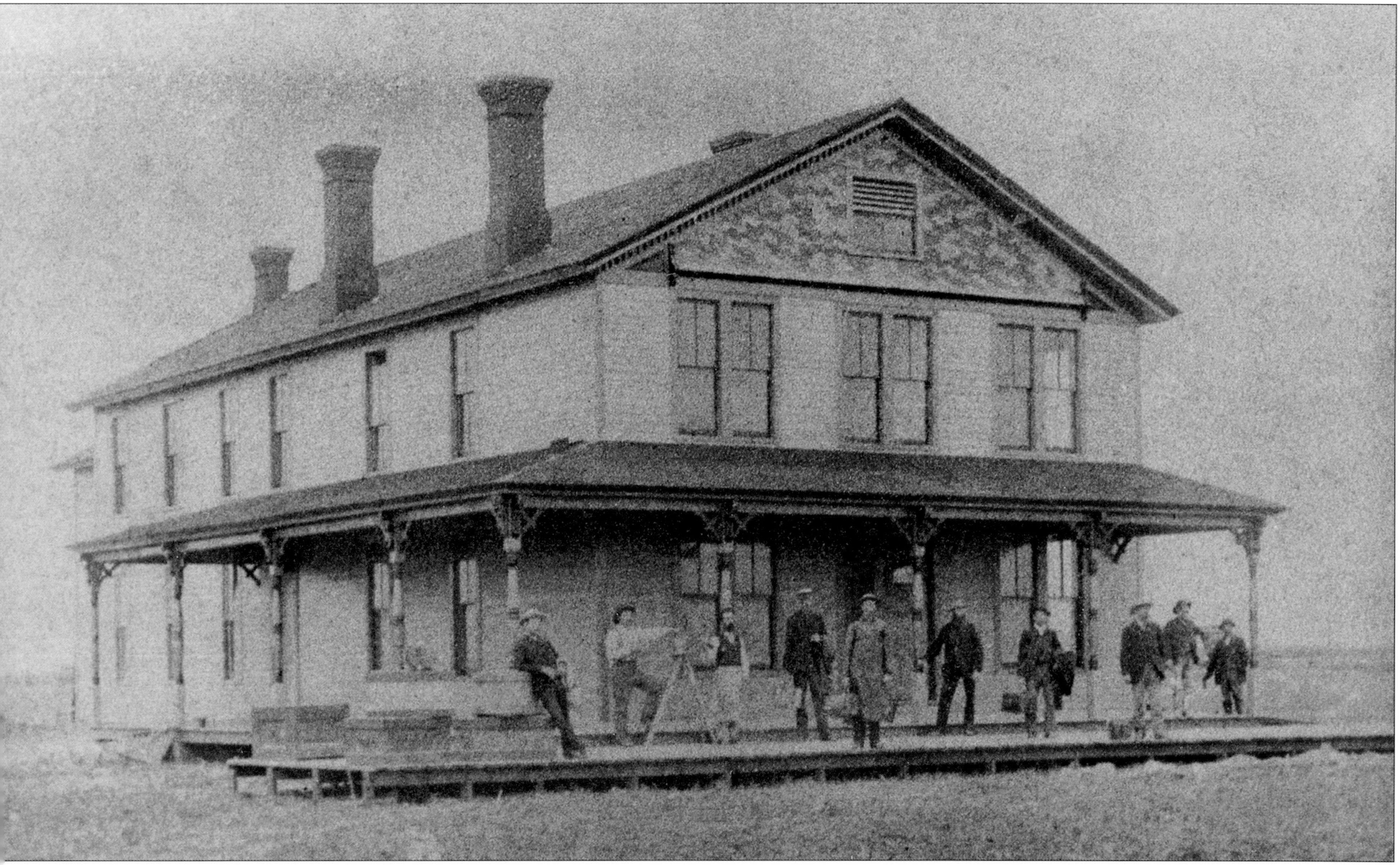

The Wells Fargo Station at Abilene, Kansas in the 1800s. The men are waiting for the stage to make connections.

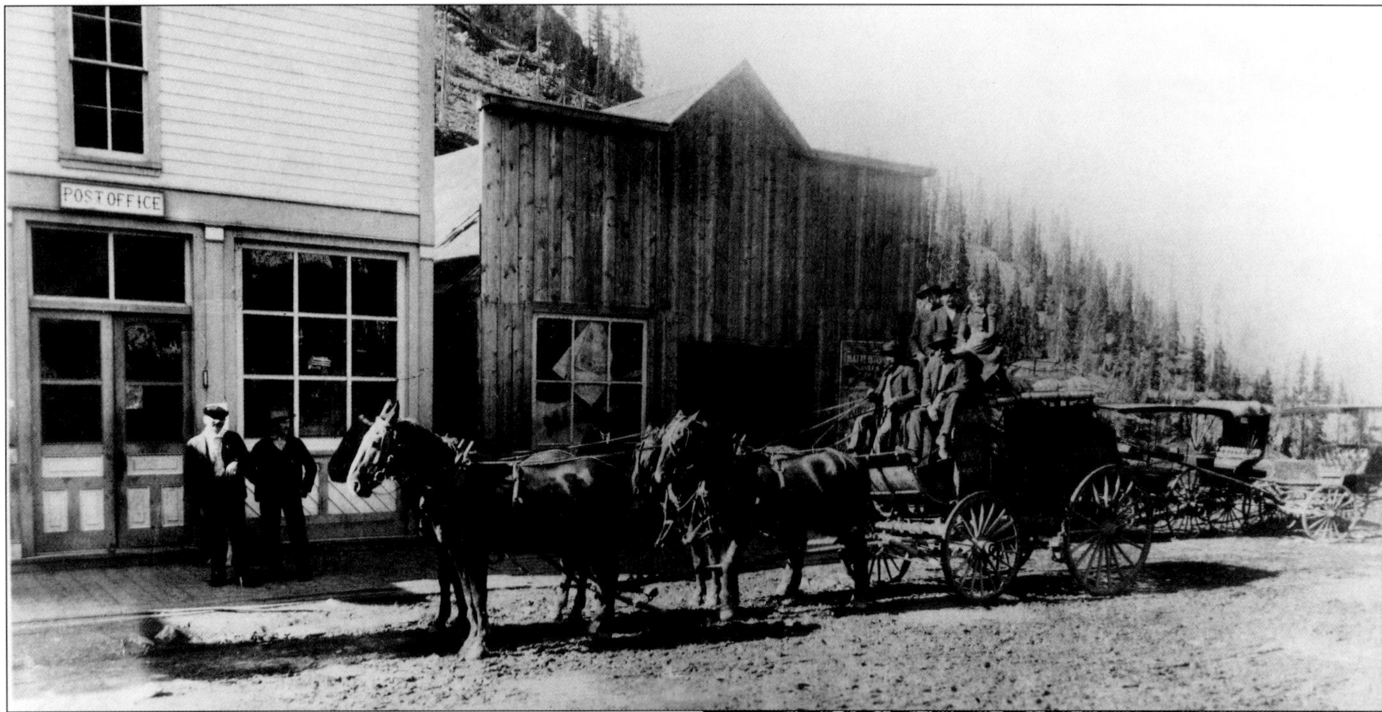

A photo taken at Red Mountain, Colorado, next to the post office. It is said to be at the highest elevation of any post office in the United States, at 11,300 feet above sea level. The stage looks to be fully loaded with passengers and the U.S. Mail.

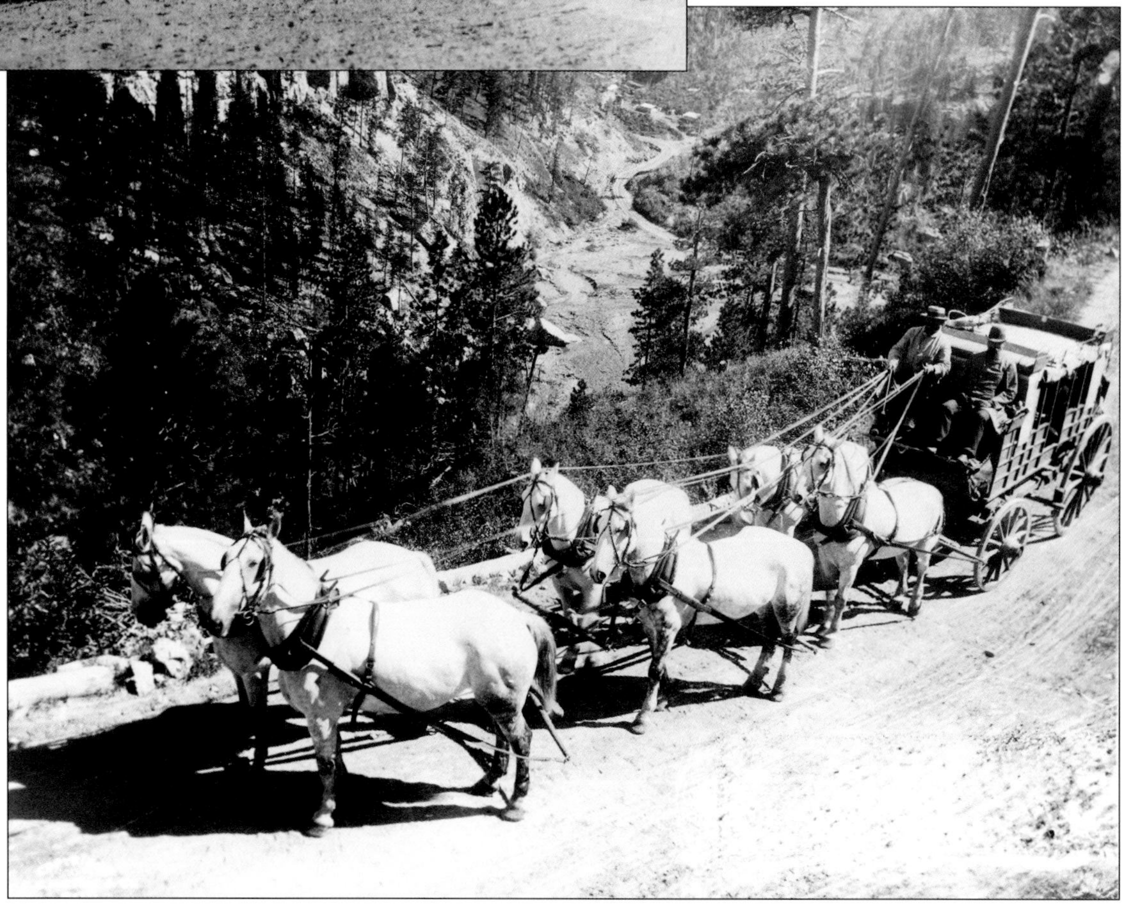

The team of white horses returning from carrying passengers to the mines along the Old Stage Road. Photographed by W.H. Jackson.

Chapter 5

1882-1895

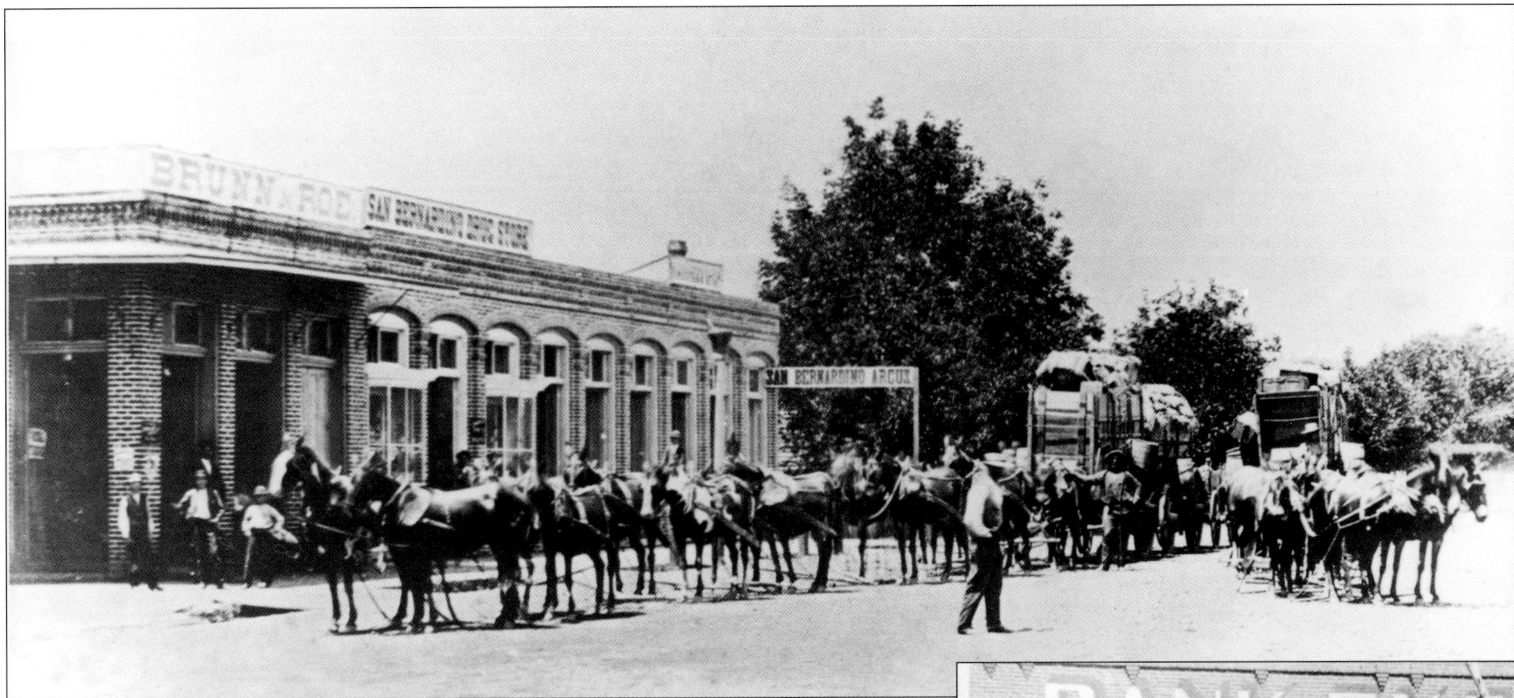

Steele's photo service took this early photo in 1800 of San Bernardino, California showing several long freight haulers arriving in town.

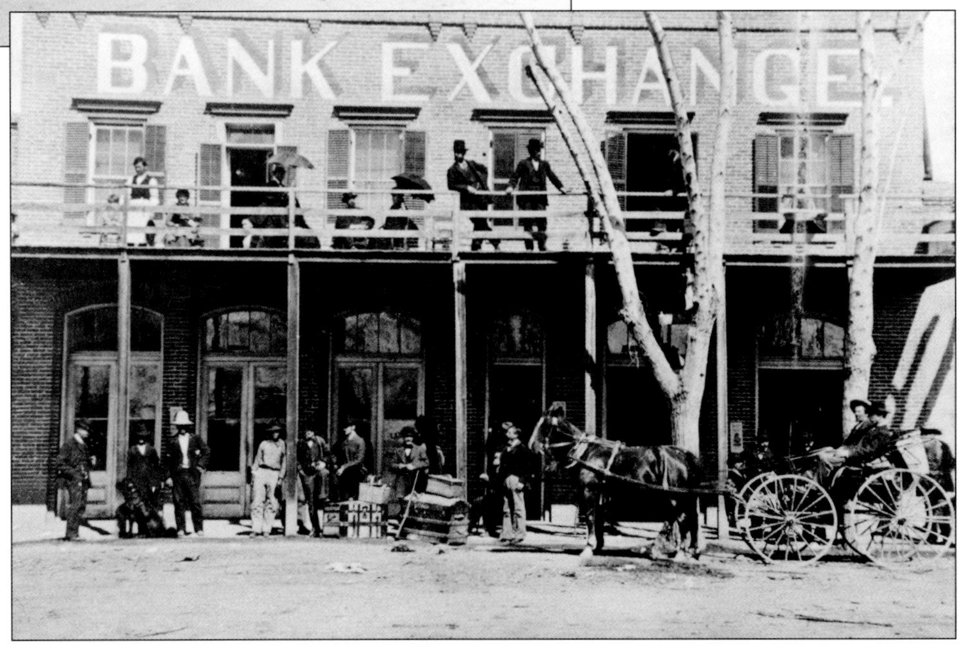

The Bank Exchange building in San Mateo, California, shows a Concord buggy loaded with passengers and their full chests. Some weary travelers, including an armed gentleman with a rifle, are waiting for the local stage to arrive.

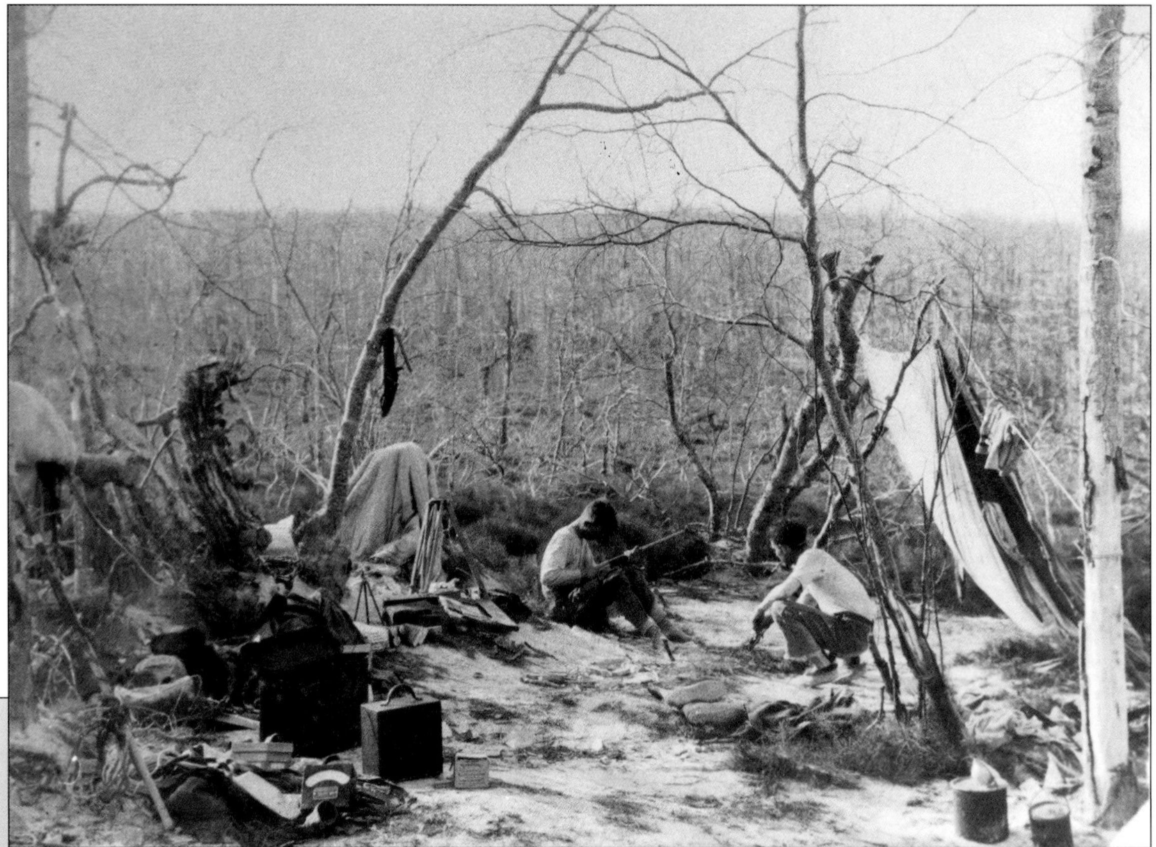

Two photographers out in the west, sitting among their equipment. One is cleaning his carbine rifle, while a holstered six-shooter hangs from a tree limb, just in case. With careful study you can see several sizes of tripods, camera cases, two cans of chemicals, and survey equipment. On the left foreground are Sterling crayons and several boxes of glass plate negatives in front of a large camera case. A camera is under the blanket in the rear. The instrument is a Conrad Hubbert rheostat, for darkroom use. While their boots are sitting in the camp, they wear Indian moccasins. A large pick ax and other tools lean against the brush. The third party who took this very interesting photograph is unknown.

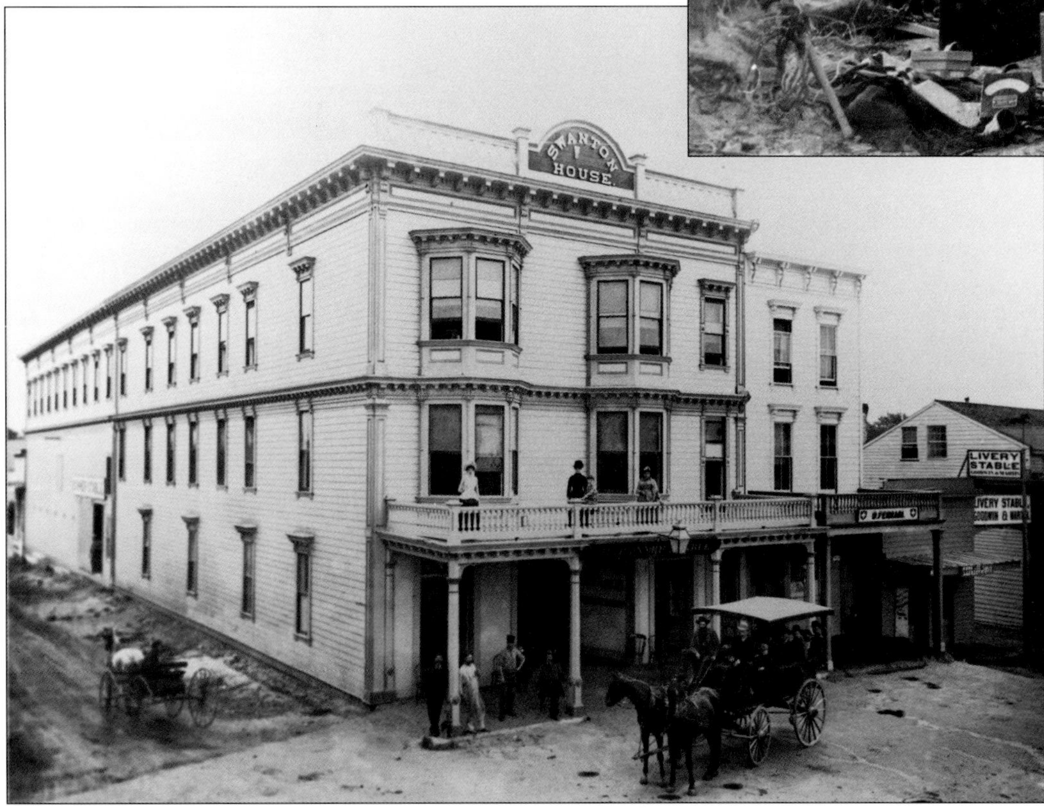

In 1889, the Swanton Hotel was one of the finest in Monterey, California. The photo is from the original glass plate.

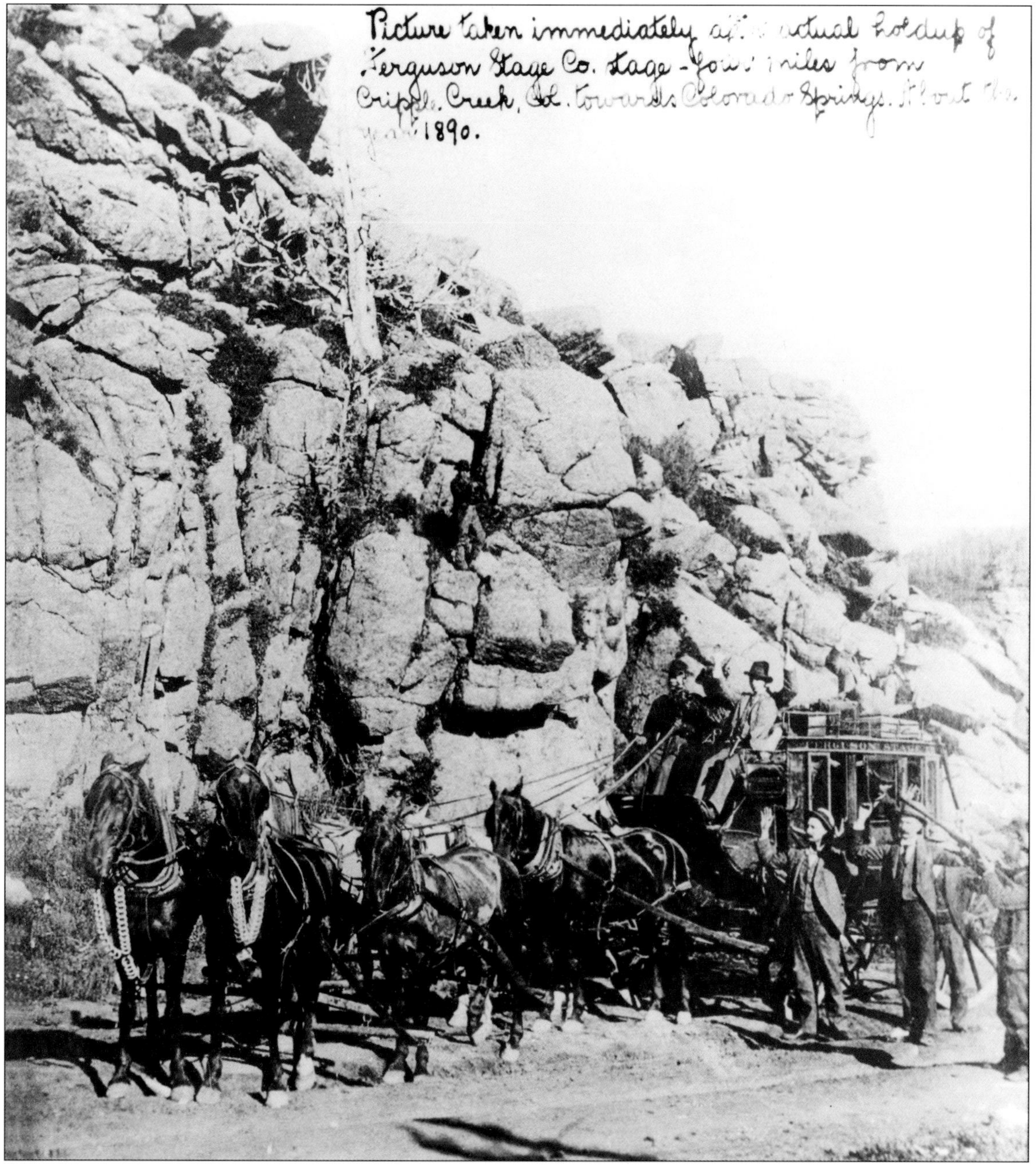

In this rare photo the crew reenacts a stage robbery that just happened. The Ferguson Stage was only four miles from Cripple Creek when it was set upon by the robbers. In the photo one outlaw, to the far right, held the stage driver at bay, while up on the rock in the center the other robber stands.

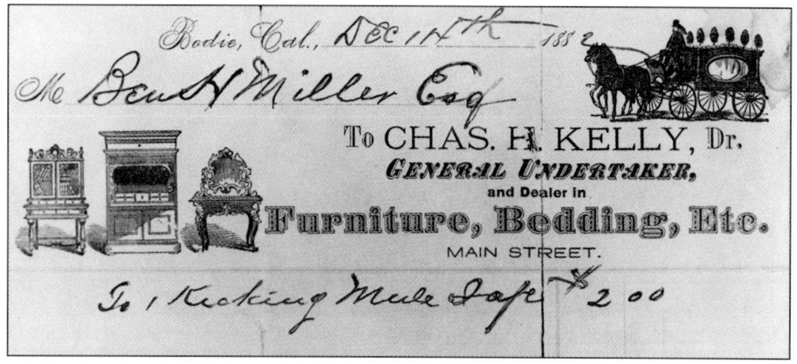
Bodie, Cal., Dec 14th 1882

Mr Ben H Miller Esq

To CHAS. H. KELLY, Dr.
GENERAL UNDERTAKER,
and Dealer in
Furniture, Bedding, Etc.
MAIN STREET.

To 1 Kicking Mule Cafe $2 00

A receipt for $2.00 made out to "Kicking Mule Cafe." Charles H. Kelly was Bodie's undertaker, and dealer in furniture and other fine products.

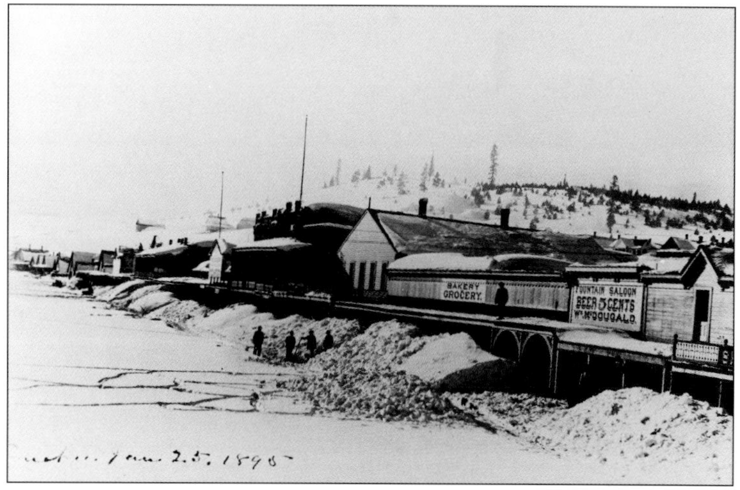

Truckee, California, in the grips of a winter snow storm that piled fifteen feet of snow in some places.

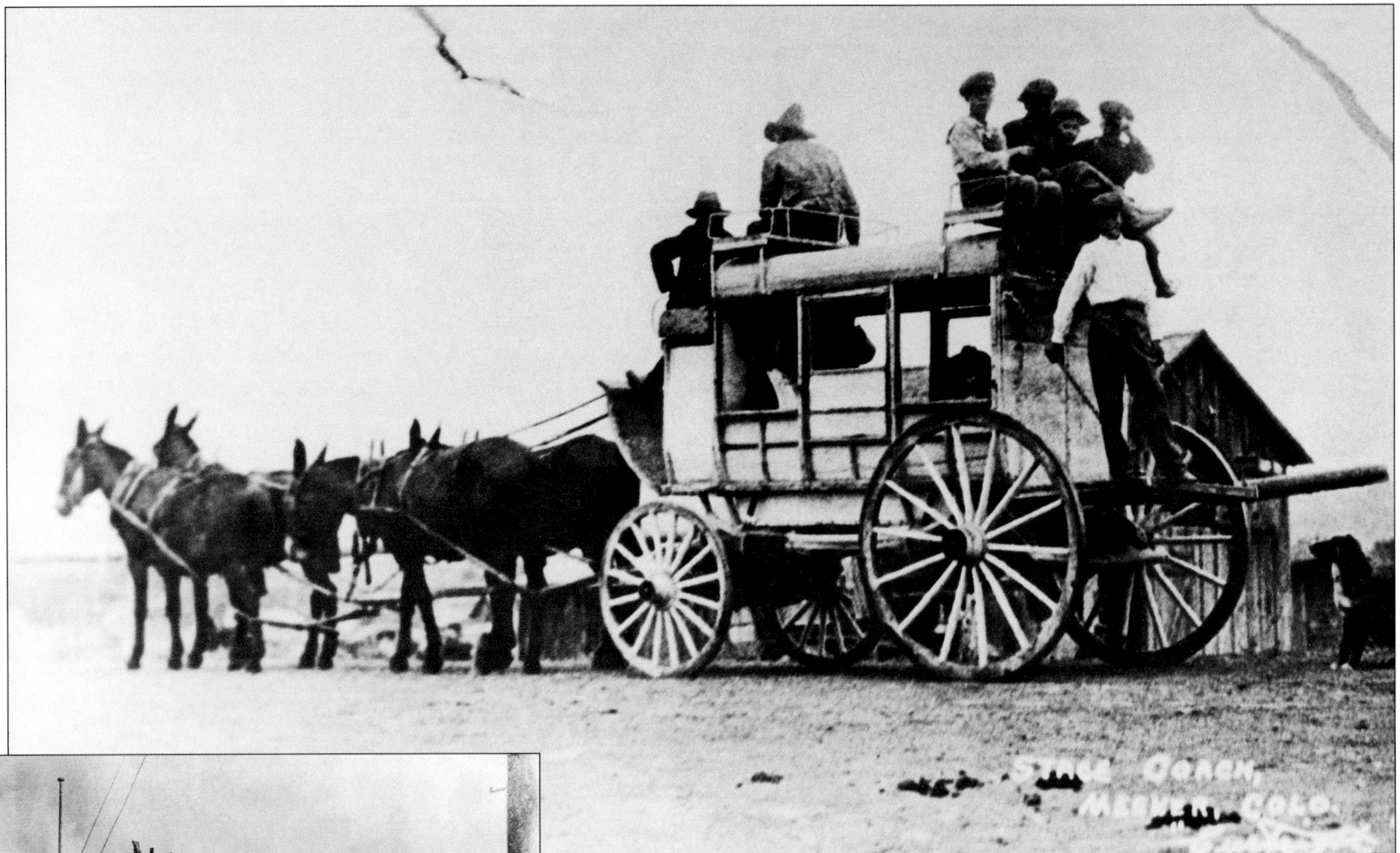

This ripped photo still has an interesting history, as it shows the Meeker, Colorado, stage hitched to four mules and waiting to load up.

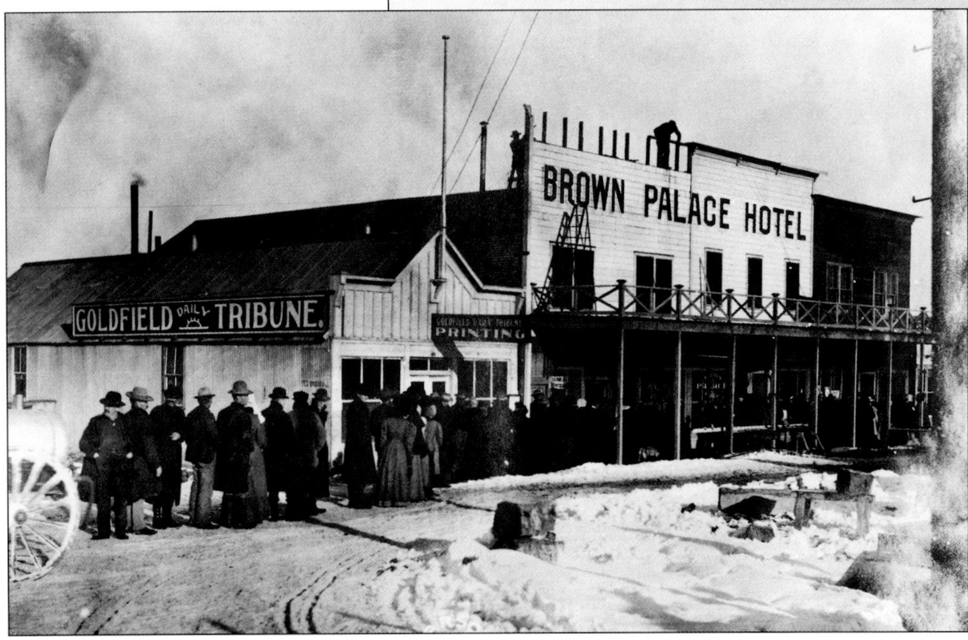

Winter in Goldfield, Nevada, sent the miners and town folks to line up for coal to keep warm. A monopoly demanded $95.00 per ton in cash. There were over 7500 applicants for the coal the first day.

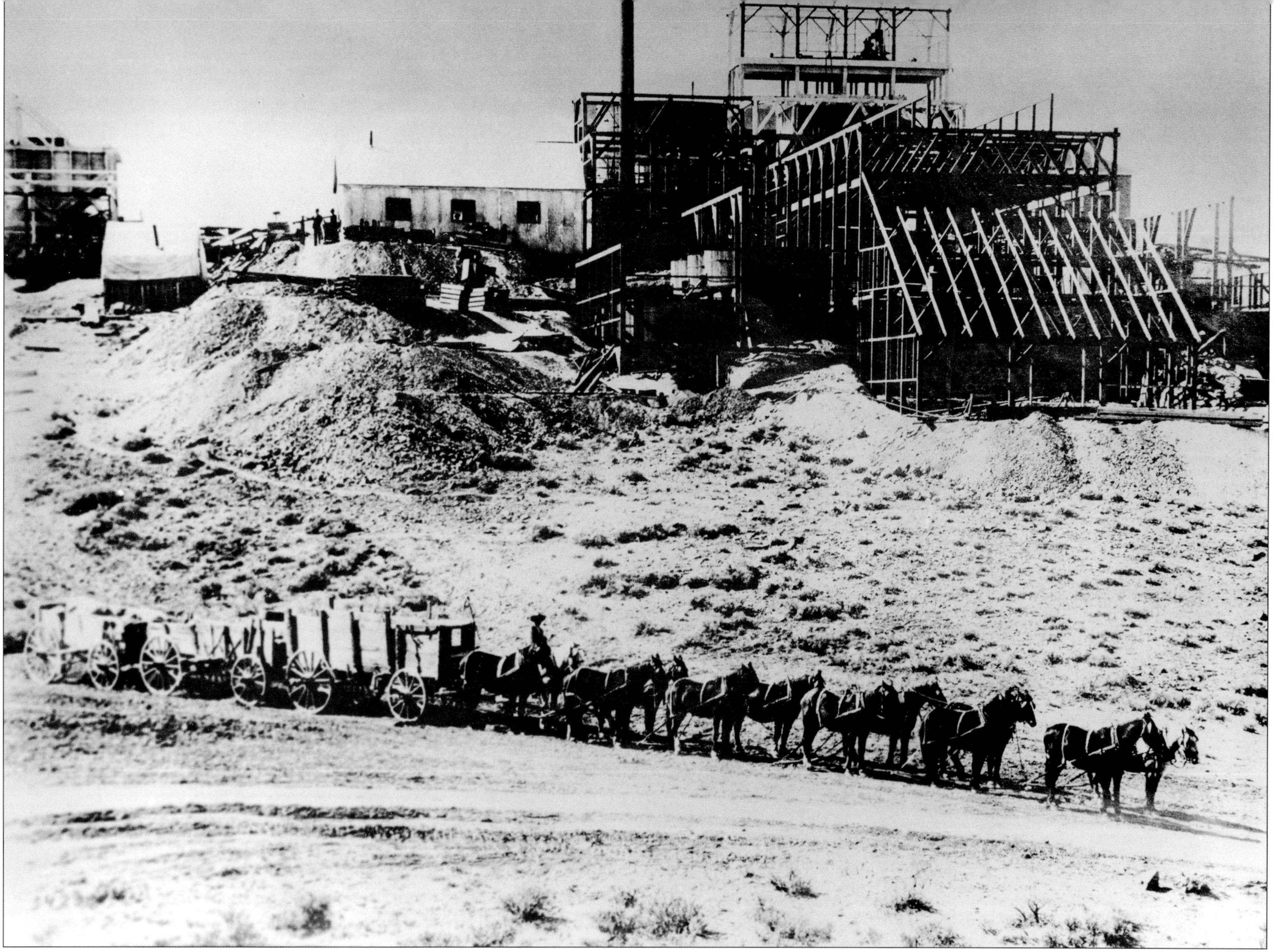

The large mine being built in Goldfield, Nevada, sits atop a hill where there are already mining pilings from the previous small structure. Bringing in supplies is a team of horses and mules.

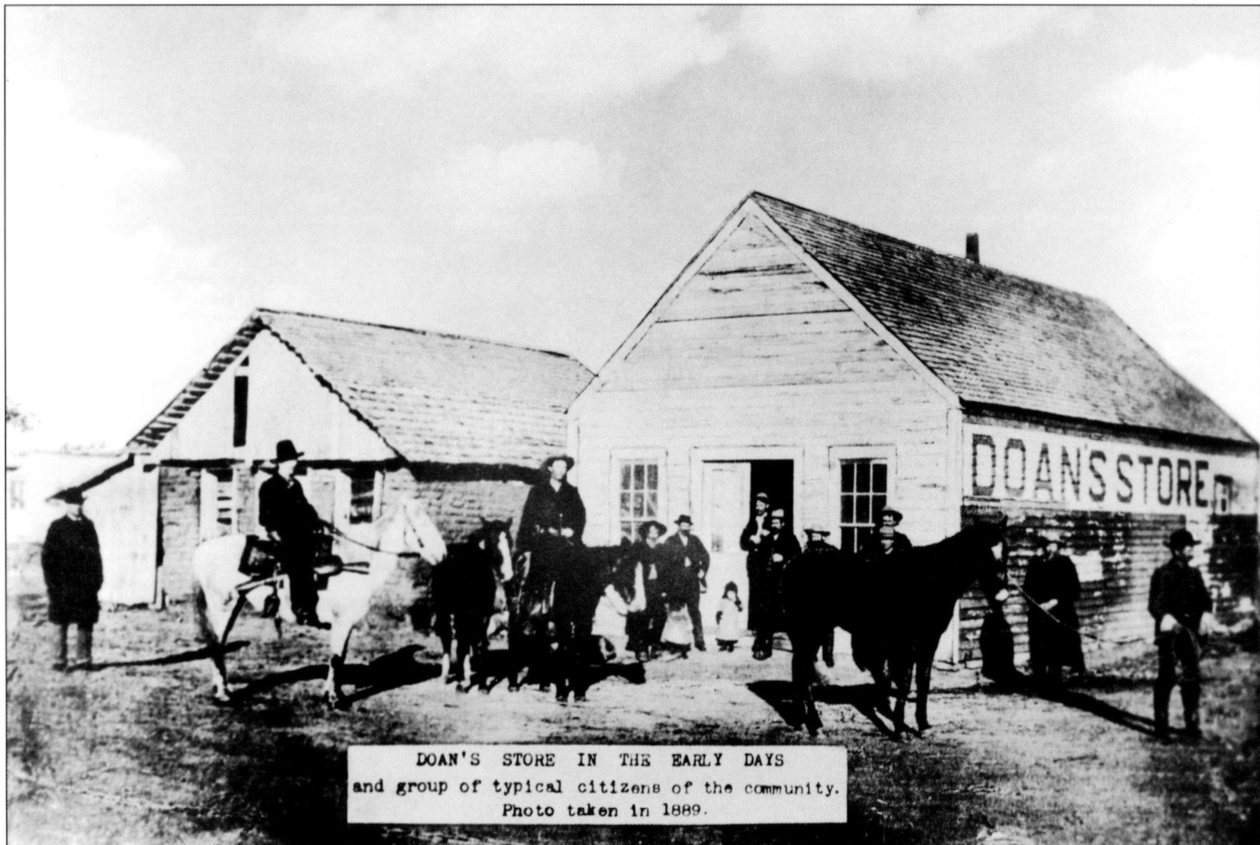

The famous Doan's Store, which was originally owned by two brothers. They began by trading and then supplying citizens as well as Indians.

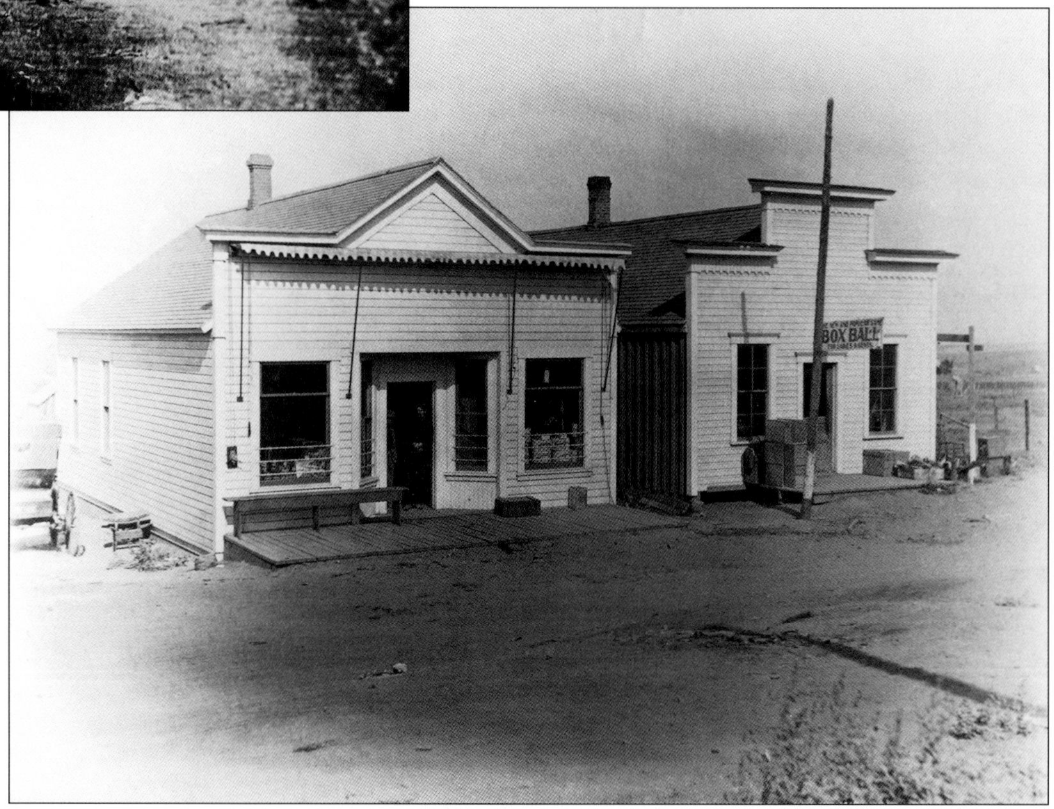

Two stores in Tonopah, Nevada, were both owned by "Grandpa." One was a grocery store and the other a gaming store that featured the NEW Box Ball, for ladies and gentleman.

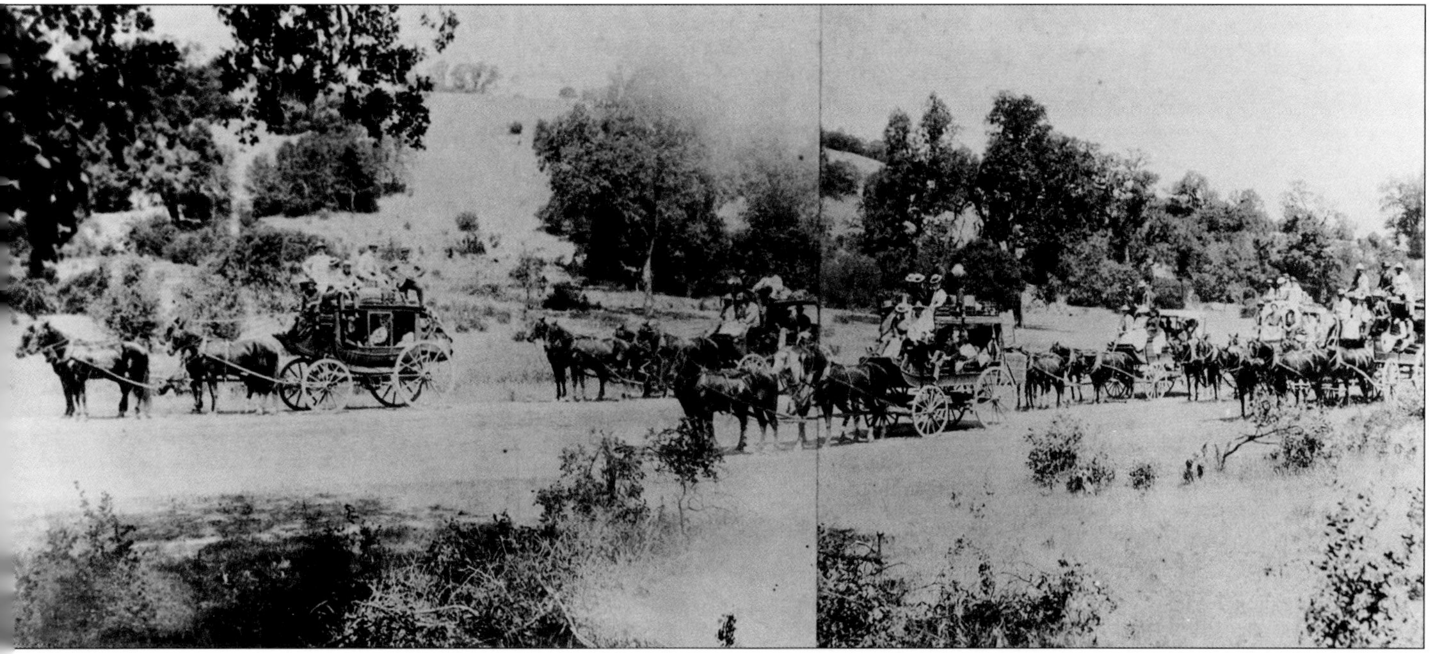

Using two photos joined together, the W.H. Miller Stage Lines advertised that it took travelers to places such as Blue Lakes, Saratoga Springs, Witter Springs, Potter Valley, and all resorts in Mendocino and Lake County resorts.

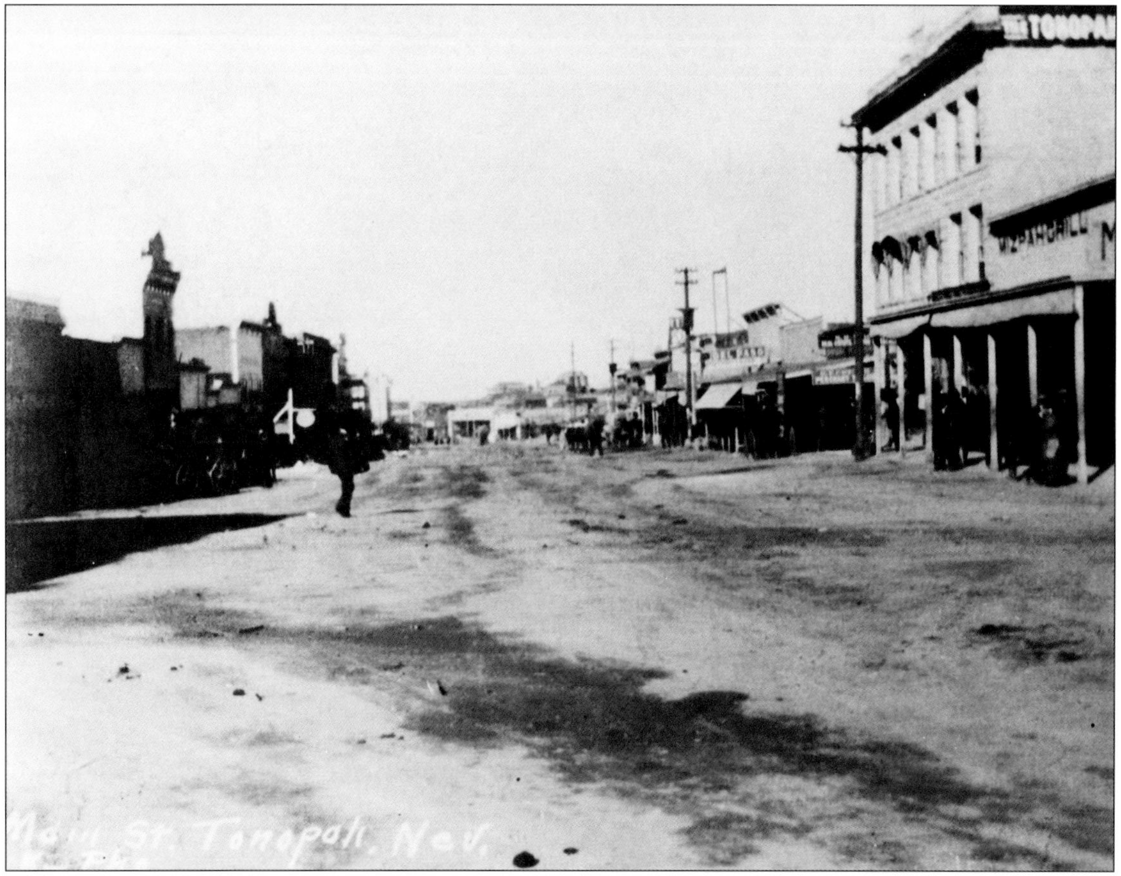

The main street of Tonopah, Nevada, looks almost deserted. Perhaps this photograph was taken after the mines had played out.

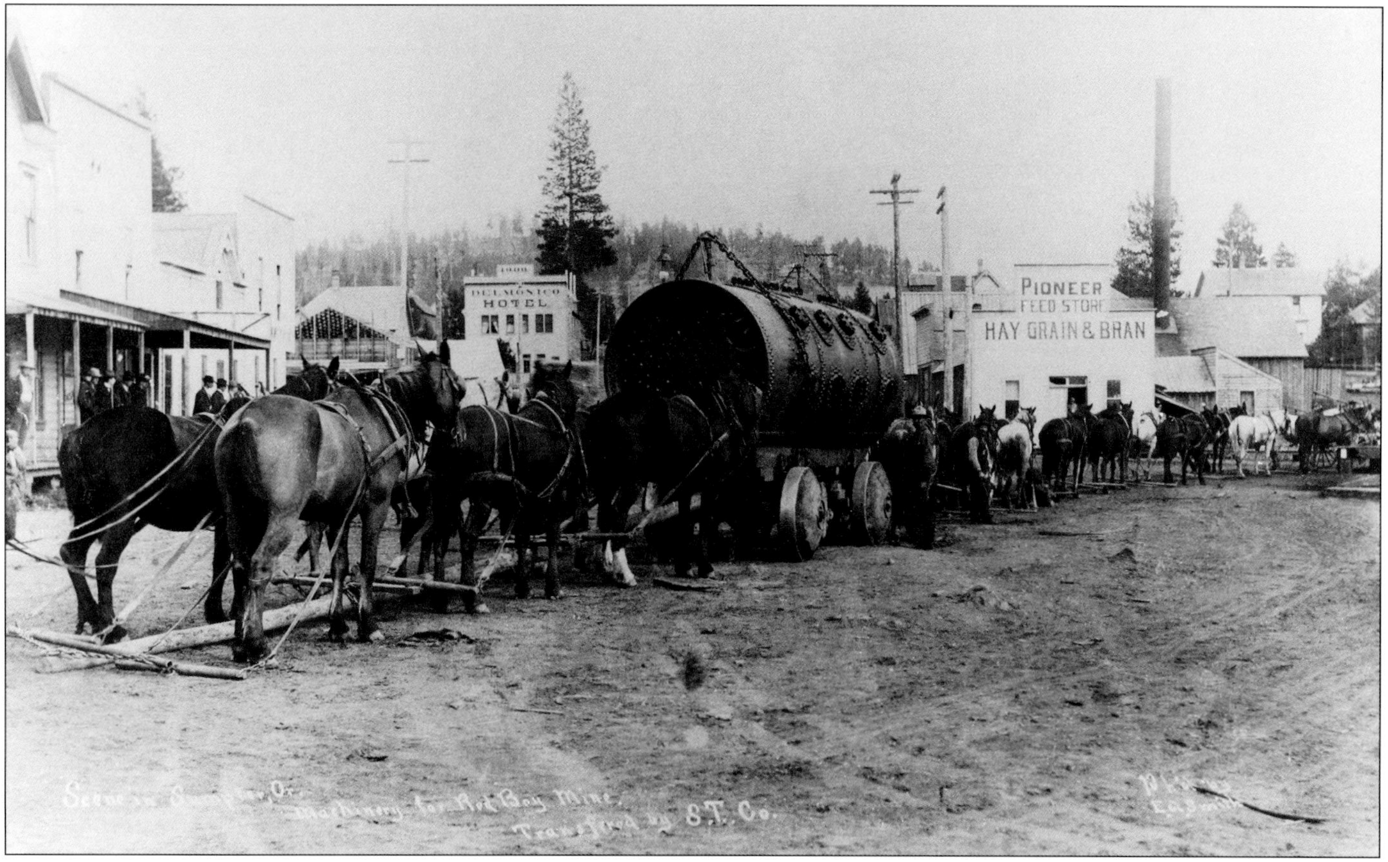

The street scene in Sumpter Oregon, when the huge piece of machinery for the Red Bay Mine went through town. Teams of mules and horses, fore and aft, were necessary to move the heavy weight.

Charles McCoy's team hauling 15 tons of barley up hill to Simi Valley, California. The mules are really straining to make the steep grade. The photo is credited to the Garden City Foto Company.

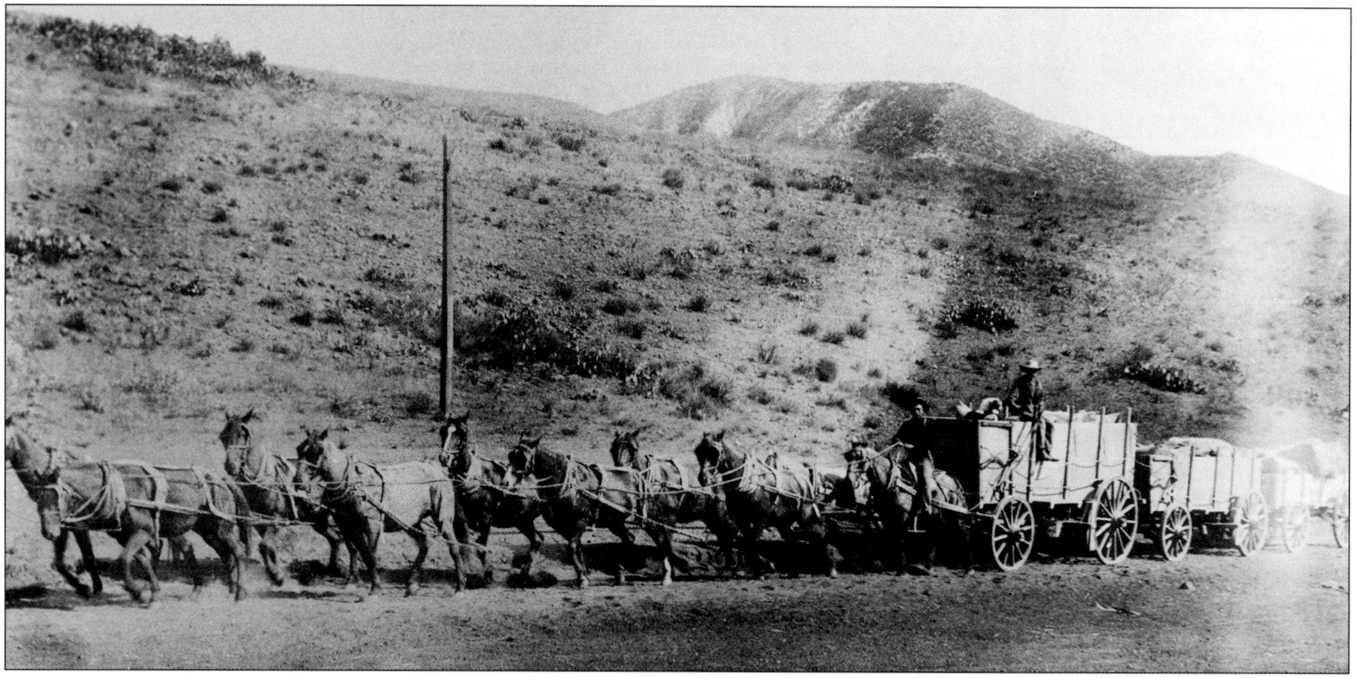

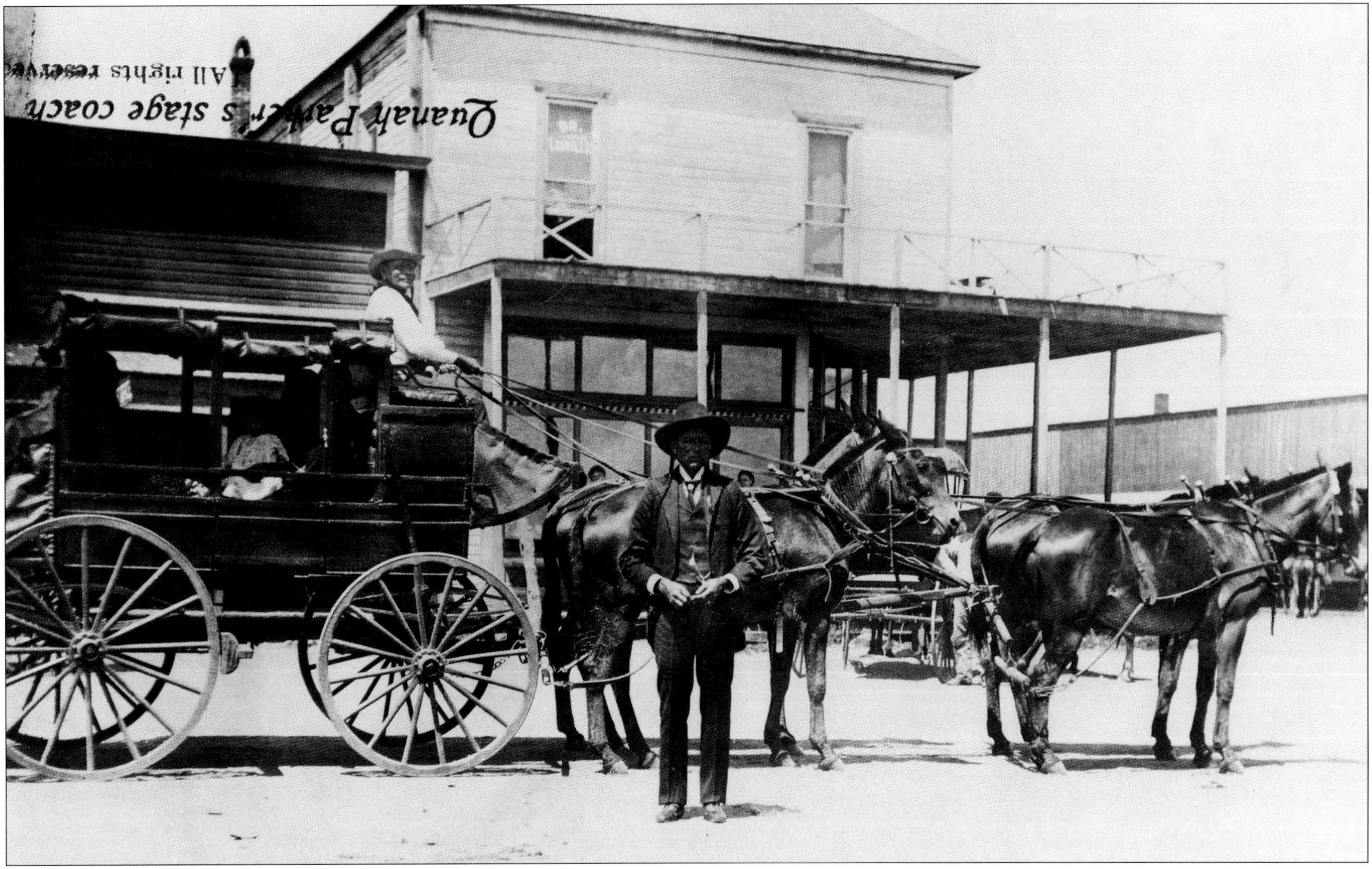

The U.S. government made peace with Comanche Chief Quanah Parker and presented him with a fine stagecoach to begin business. Parker stands proudly in front of it for his portrait.

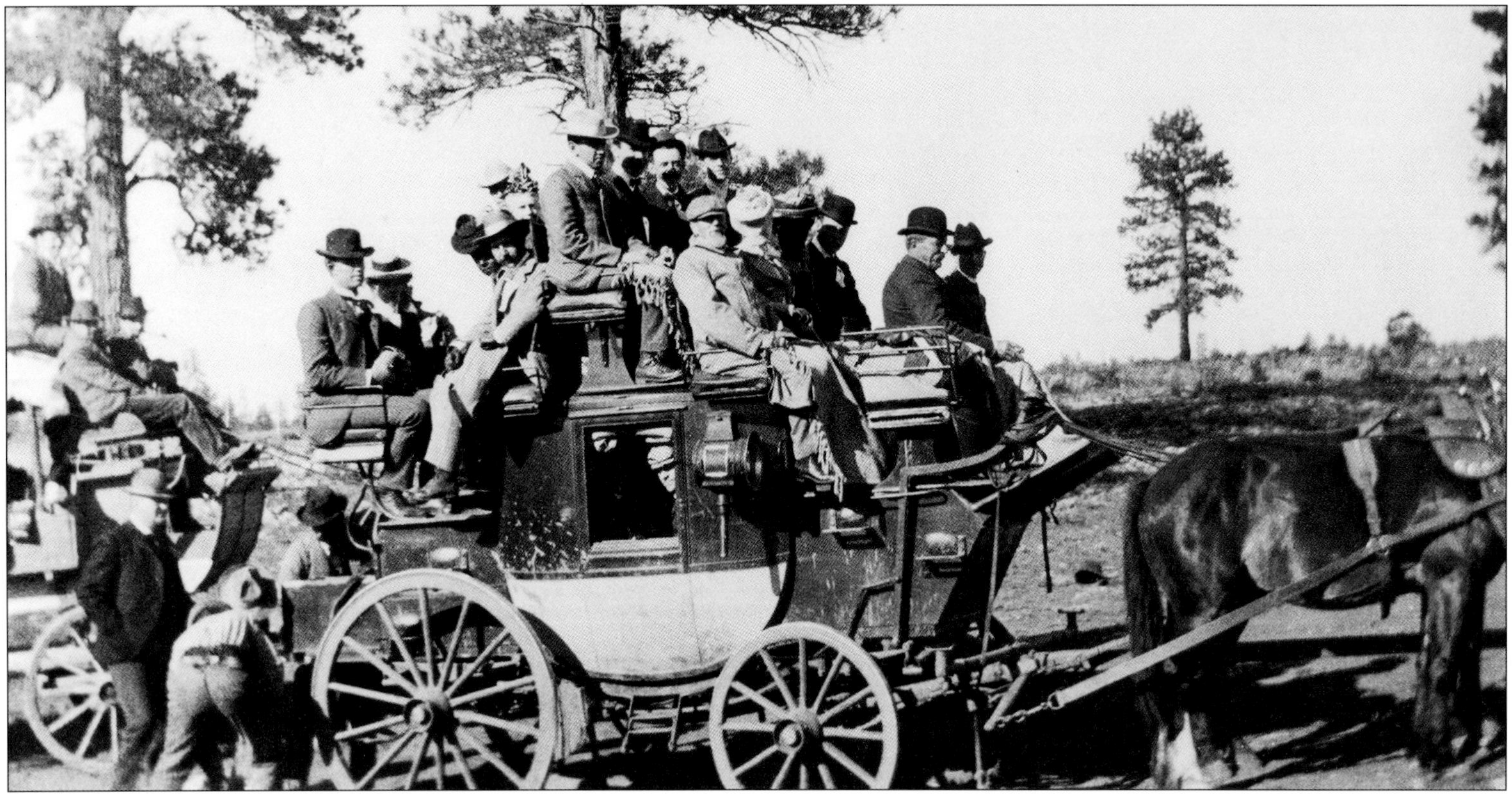

These early tourists were just leaving to view the Grand Canyon in Arizona by way of stagecoach.

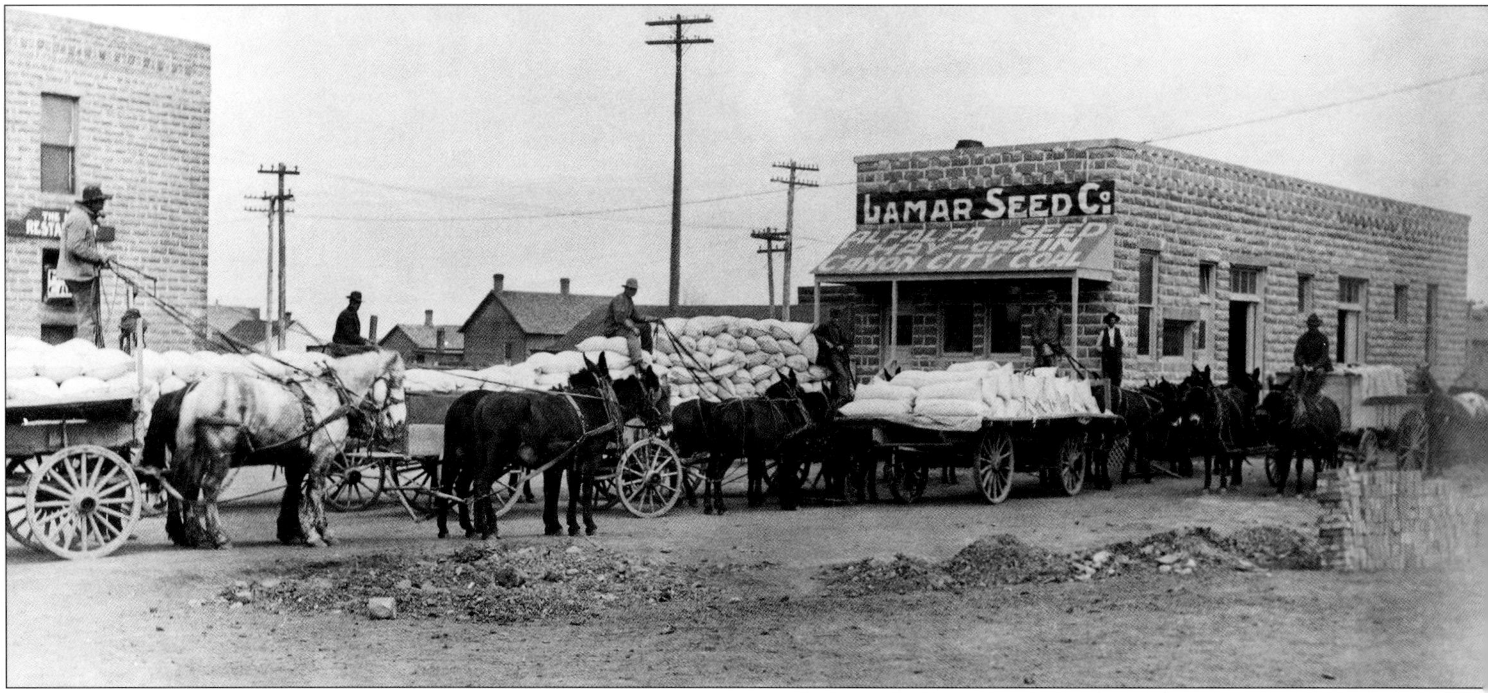

Lamar, Colorado's Lamar Seed Company is taking on large shipments of supplies for local farmers, judging by the many bags of seeds and other supplies.

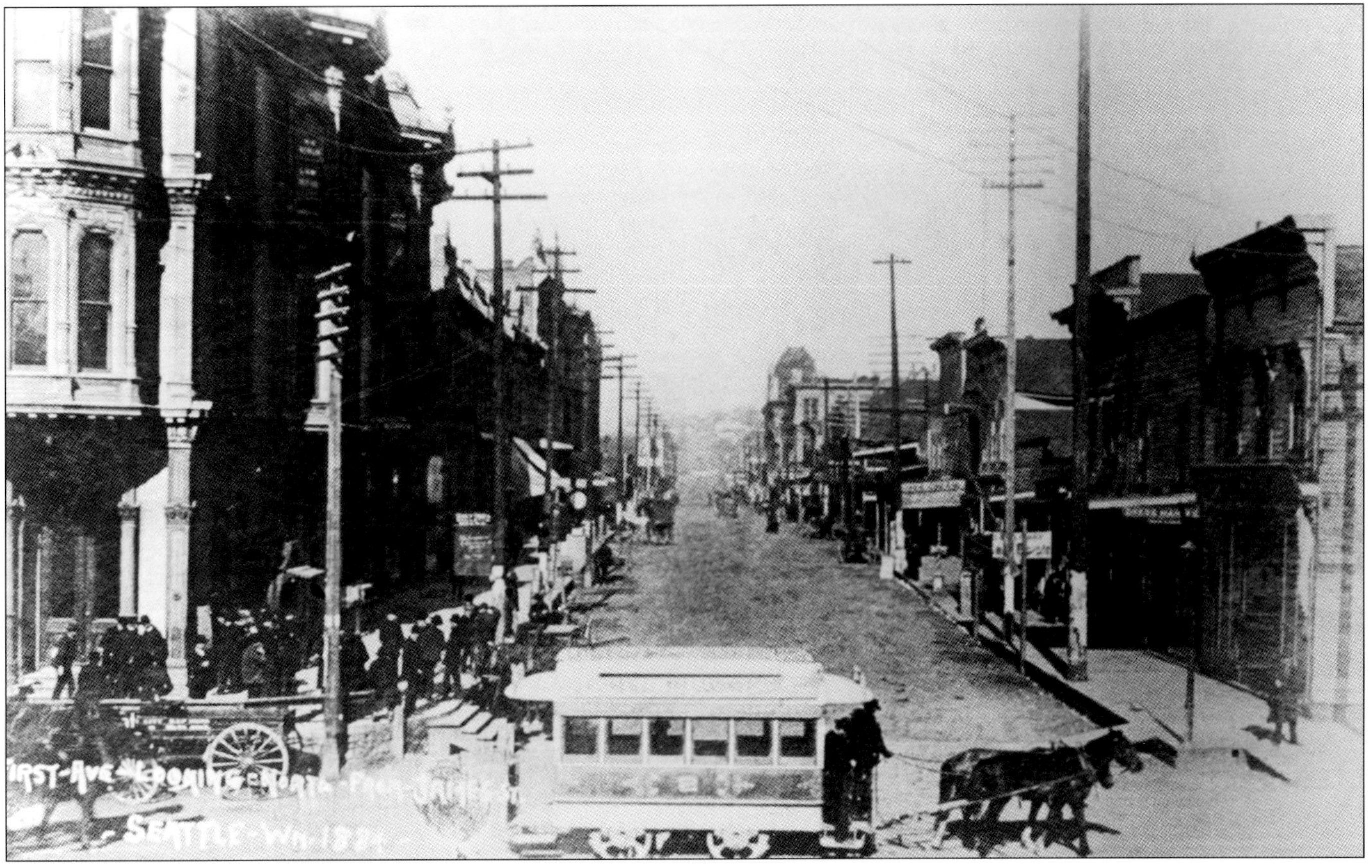

First Avenue in Seattle, Washington, 1884. The horse-drawn street car and wagons lined the streets.

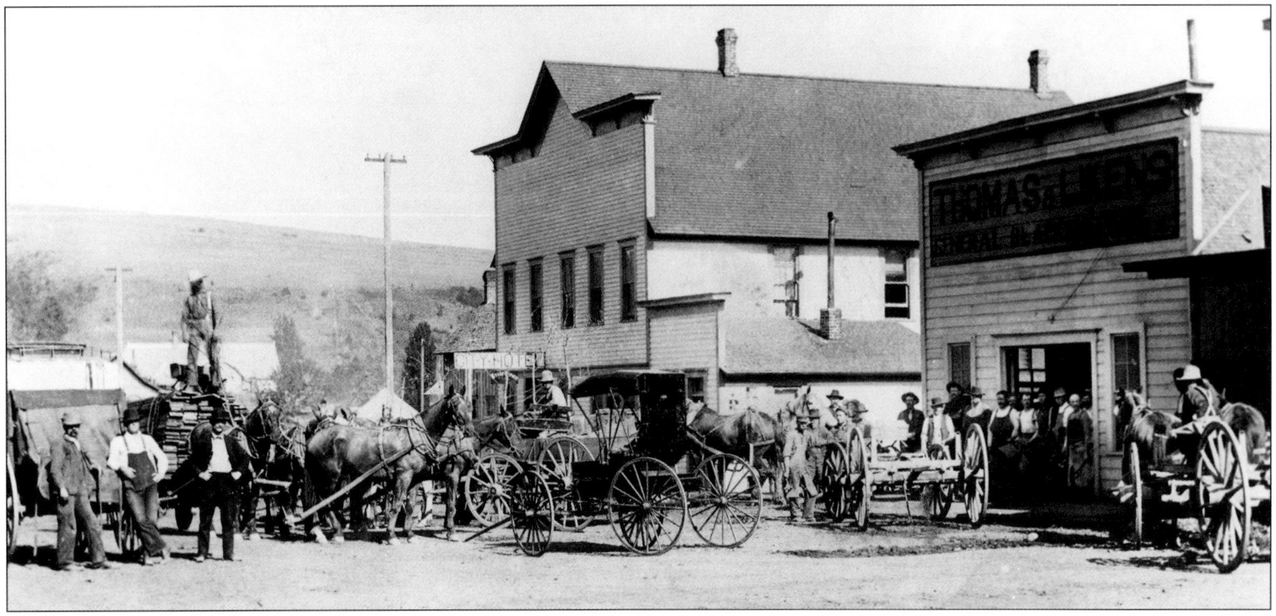

A very busy work day at the Thomas & Likens blacksmith shop. Among all the horse-drawn coaches and carts sits a stagecoach, viewed from the back at the far left of the photograph.

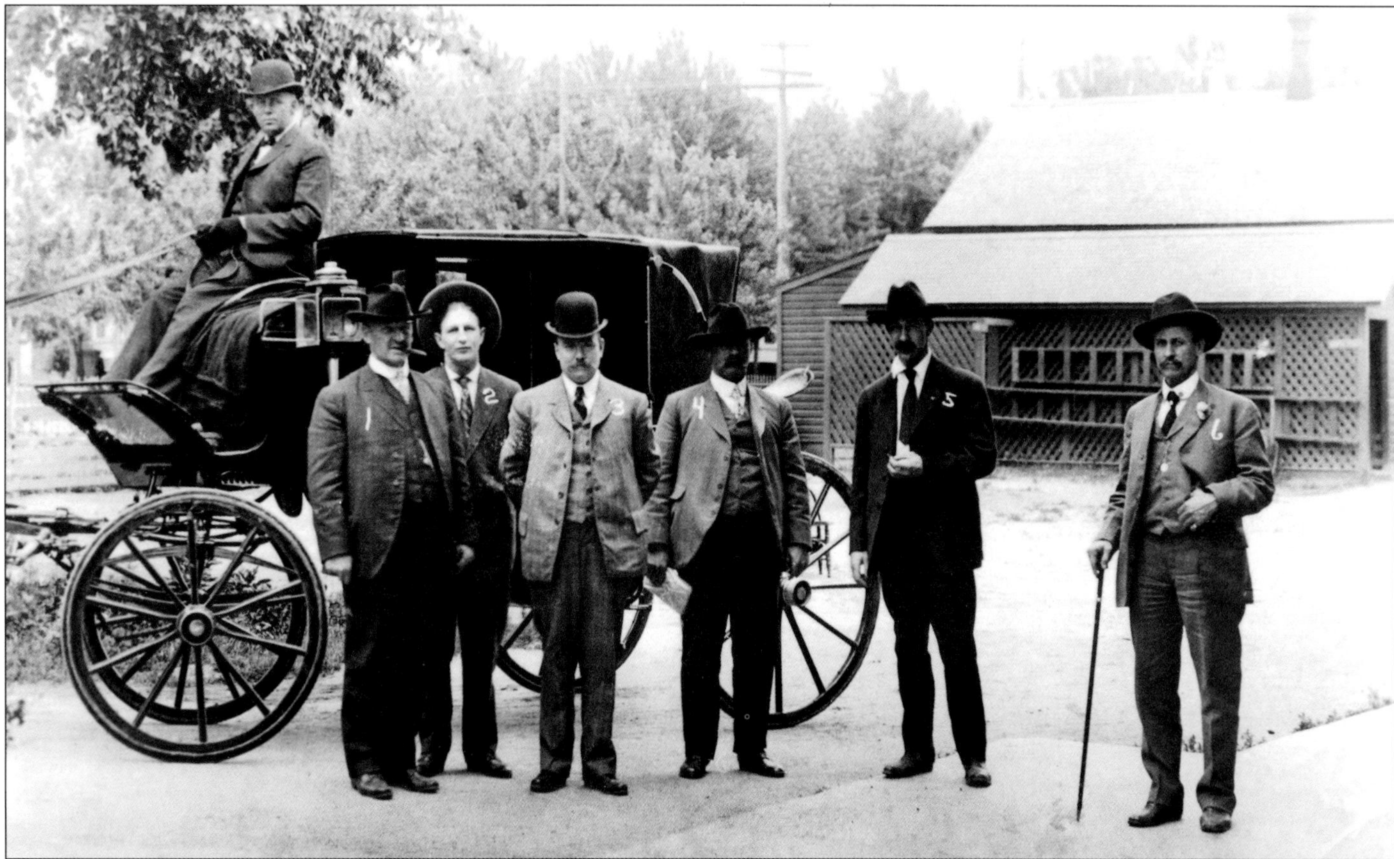

Charles Siringo of Pinkerton's Agency stands by on the right after he captured the "Mad Bomber," Alber Horsley, alias Harry Orchard. He stands with his hands in cuffs behind him looking very dapper in his bowler. Acting on orders of the miners union, this man bombed the train station as the scab workers were on the train ready to go to work. Those listed in the photo are (left to right): Eugene Whitney, warden of the penitentiary; R. Barthel; Alber Horsley; Dan W. Ackley, guard; Edgar Hawley, associated with State's attorneys; and Charles Siringo. This photograph was given to Ben Powers by Charles Siringo.

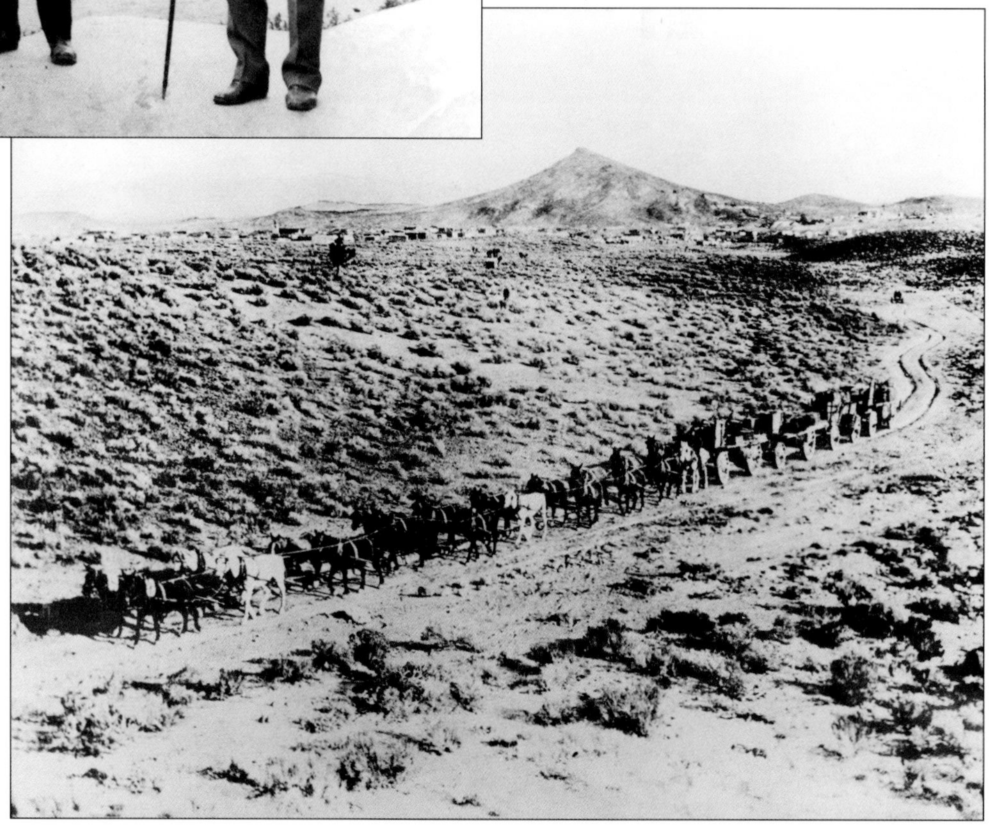

A twenty mule team leaving Goldfield, Nevada, follows a much traveled cut in the road. In the background we see the huge mountain that has been the vein of the miners seeking their fortunes.

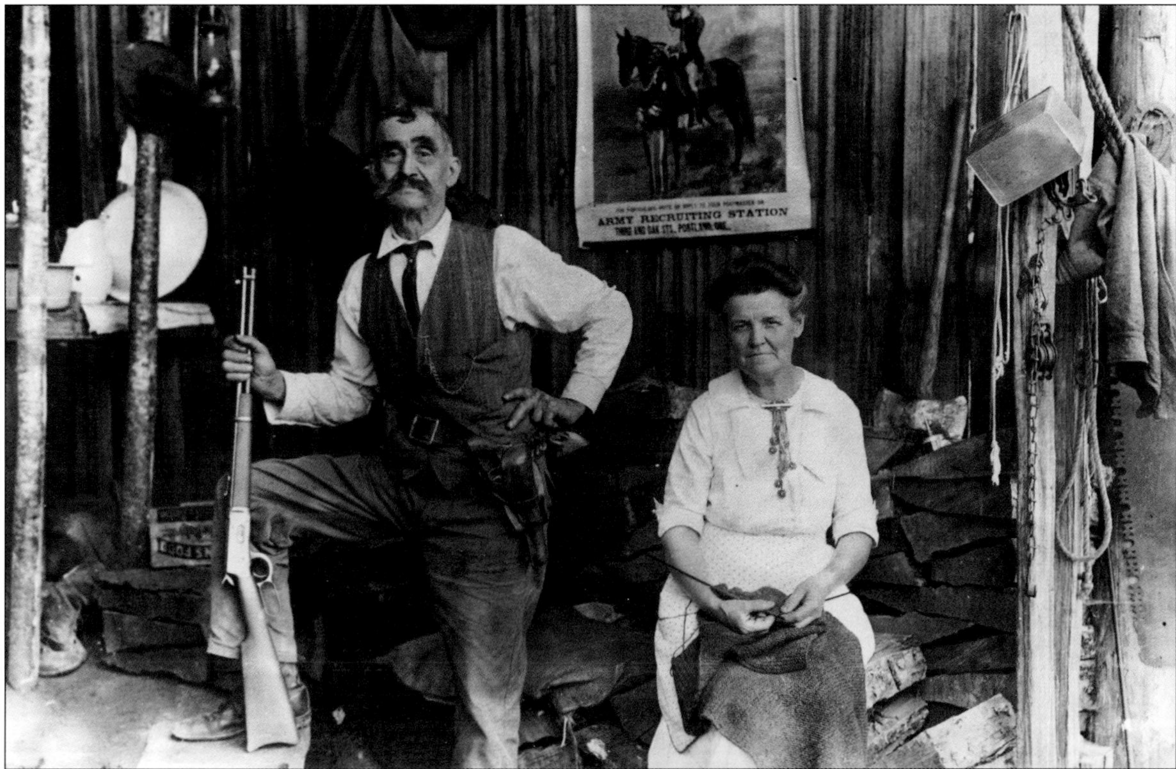

In northern California's gold country, men and women had to arm themselves from outlaws, Indians and runaways. This couple seems to be armed for any event.

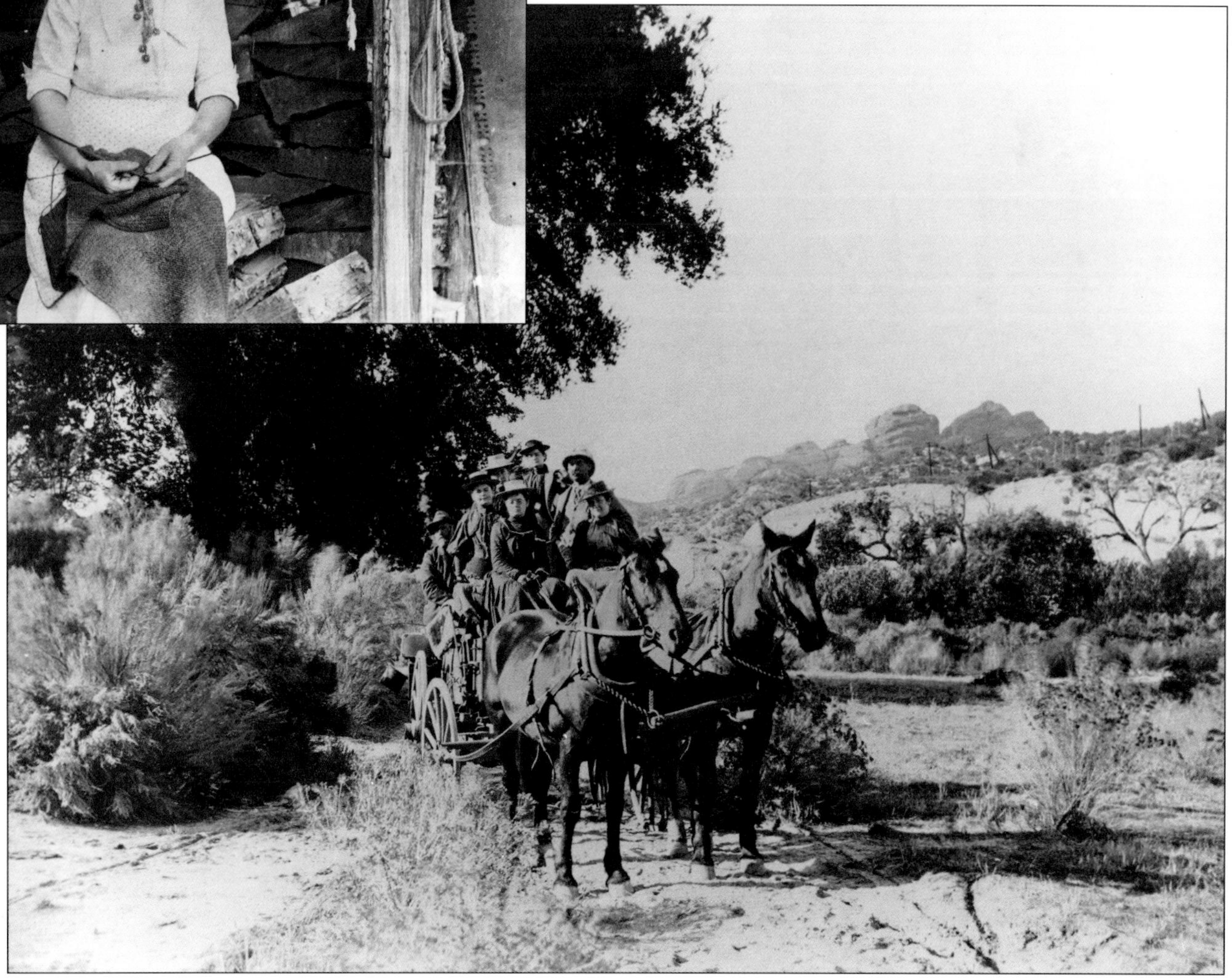

A women driver and passengers stiffen for their photograph on the road from San Bernardino. Along for the ride is a Englishman who may by sight-seeing.

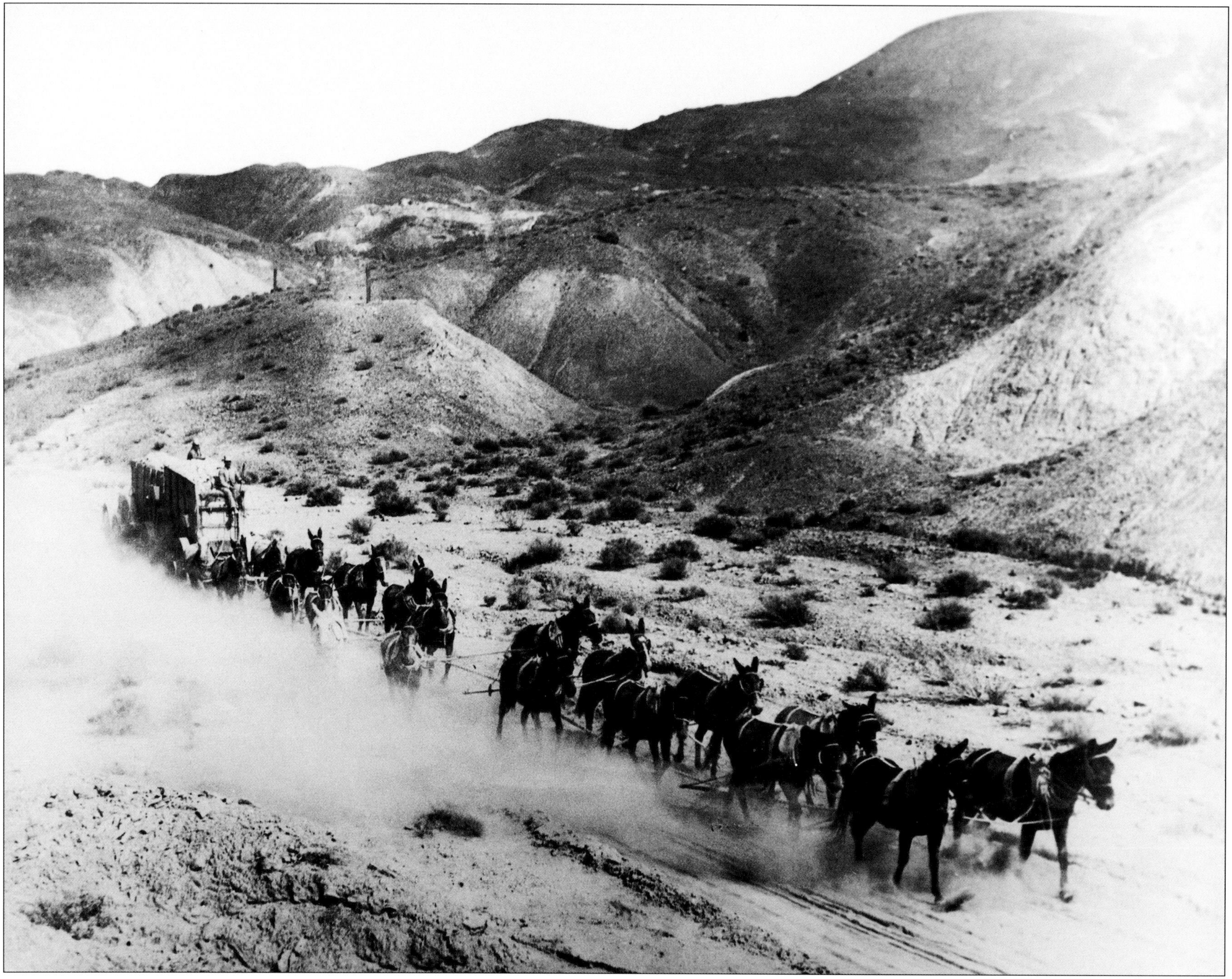

A fast moving twenty-mule team on the way to the borax mines in the hot desert. Photo by W.H. Jackson.

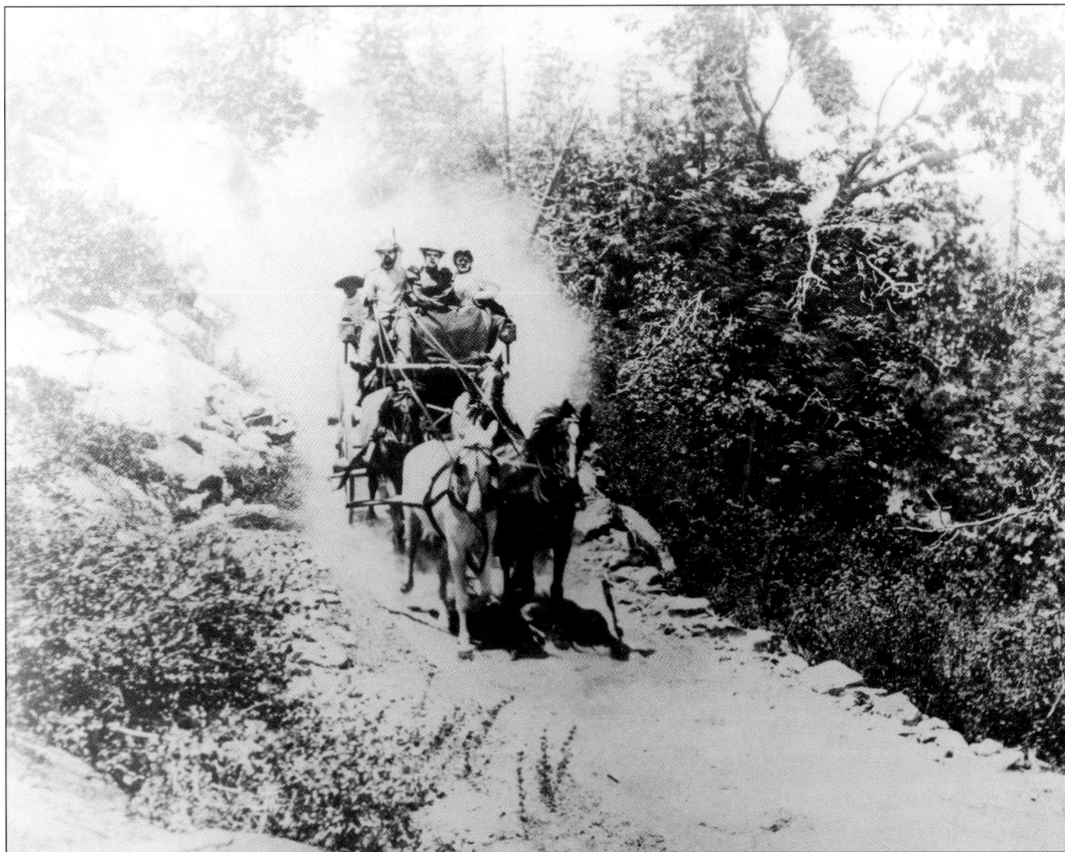

This photograph of a fast moving stagecoach, taken in California, is entitled, "Staging Days."

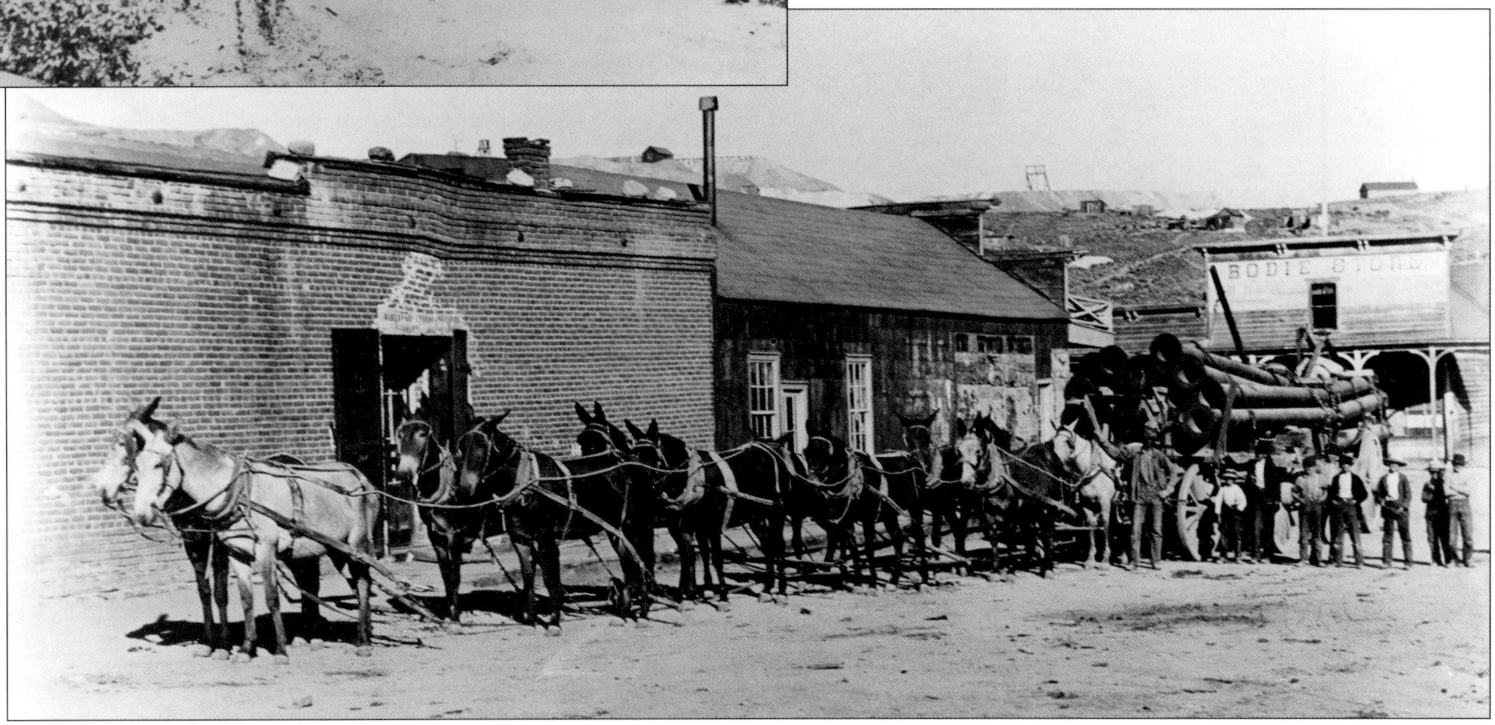

When Bodie, California, was in full swing, scenes like this were common. A huge stack of piping is being transported to the mines by a long line of mules.

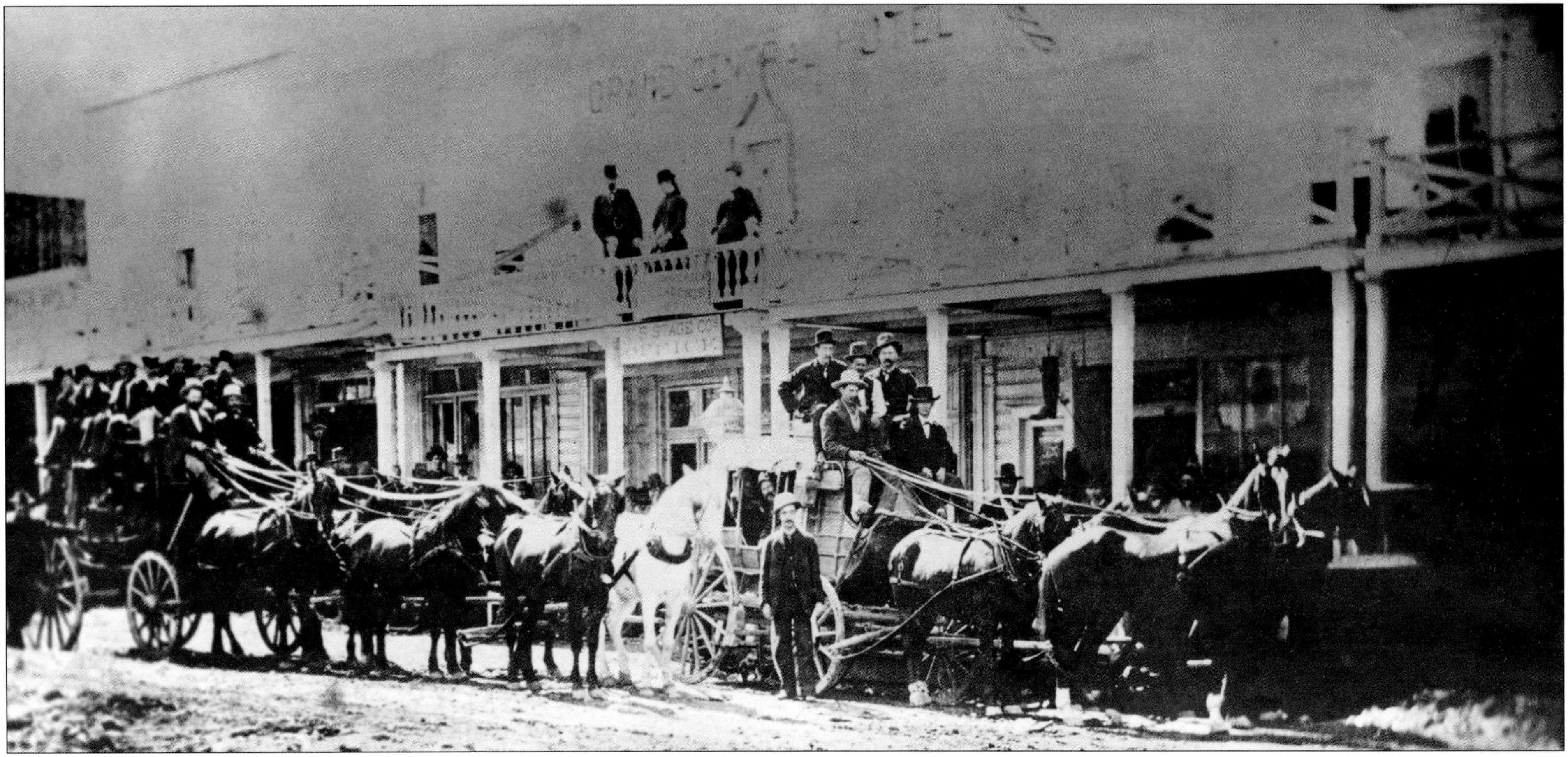

Parked in front of the Grand Central Hotel in Bodie, California, are several stagecoaches filled to capacity. The U.S. Stage Company's sign hangs above the door.

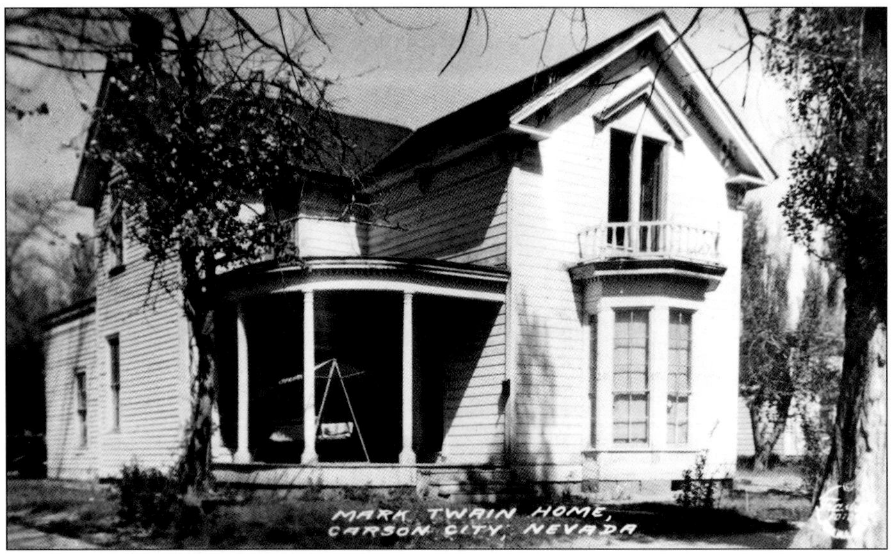

Mark Twain's home while he lived in Carson City, Nevada. Photo by B. Frashers.

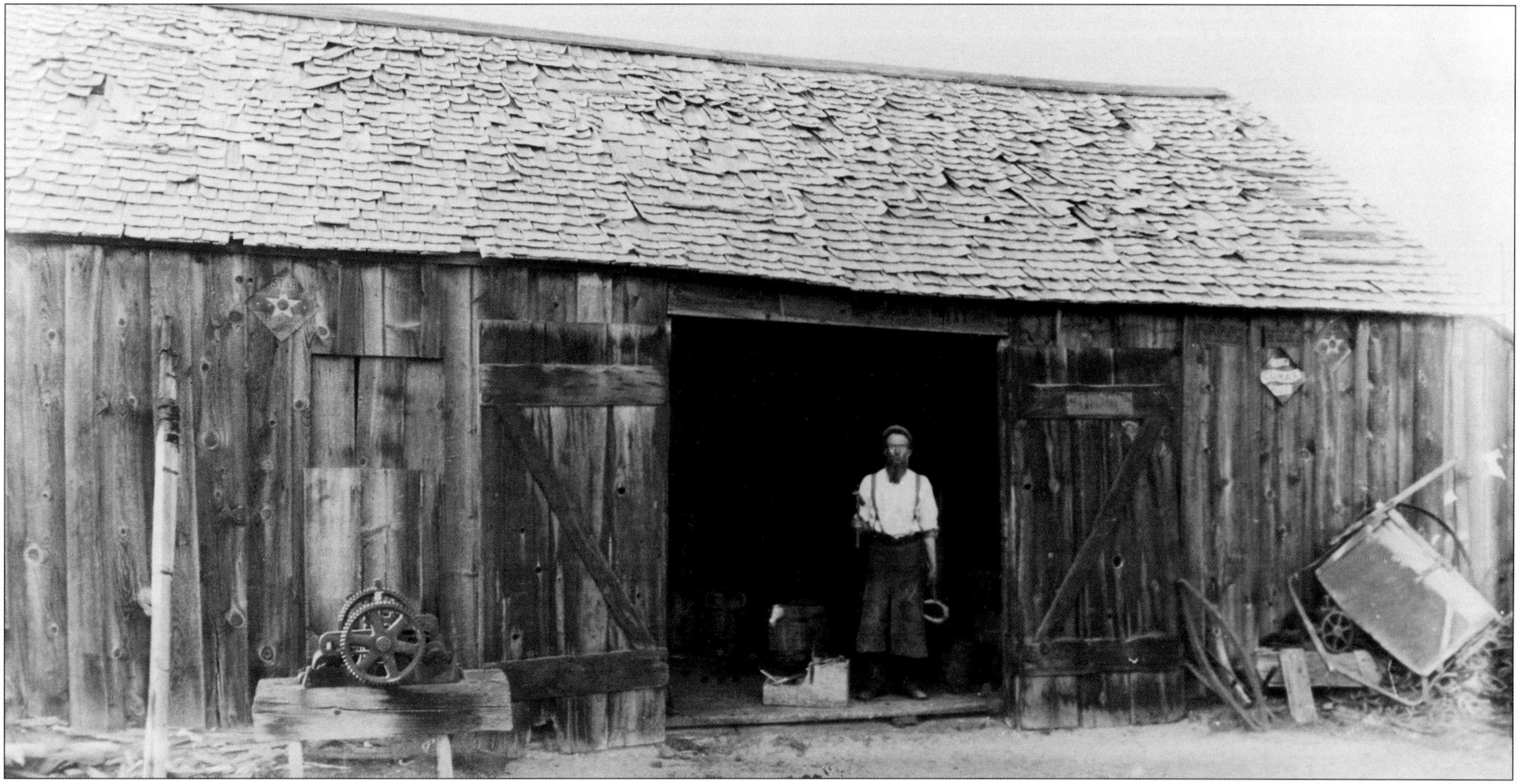

One of the many blacksmiths in Bodie stops his work to pose for the photographer.

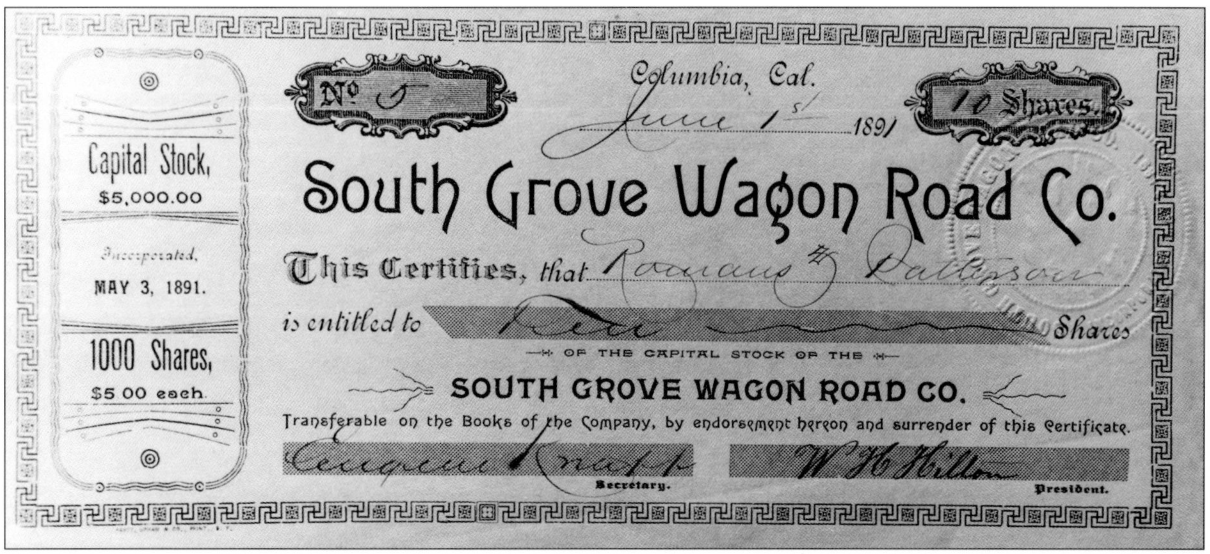

Capital Stock,
$5,000.00
Incorporated,
MAY 3, 1891.
1000 Shares,
$5.00 each.

Nº 5

Columbia, Cal.
June 1st 1891

10 Shares.

South Grove Wagon Road Co.

This Certifies, that Romans F. Patterson is entitled to Ten Shares

OF THE CAPITAL STOCK OF THE

SOUTH GROVE WAGON ROAD CO.

Transferable on the Books of the Company, by endorsement hereon and surrender of this Certificate.

Secretary. President.

A capital stock certificate from the South Grove Wagon Road Company. The site was at Columbia, California, one of the richest mining areas in northern California.

In Steamboat Springs, Colorado, the stages are lined up in front of the Steamboat Cabin Hotel for the day's passengers.

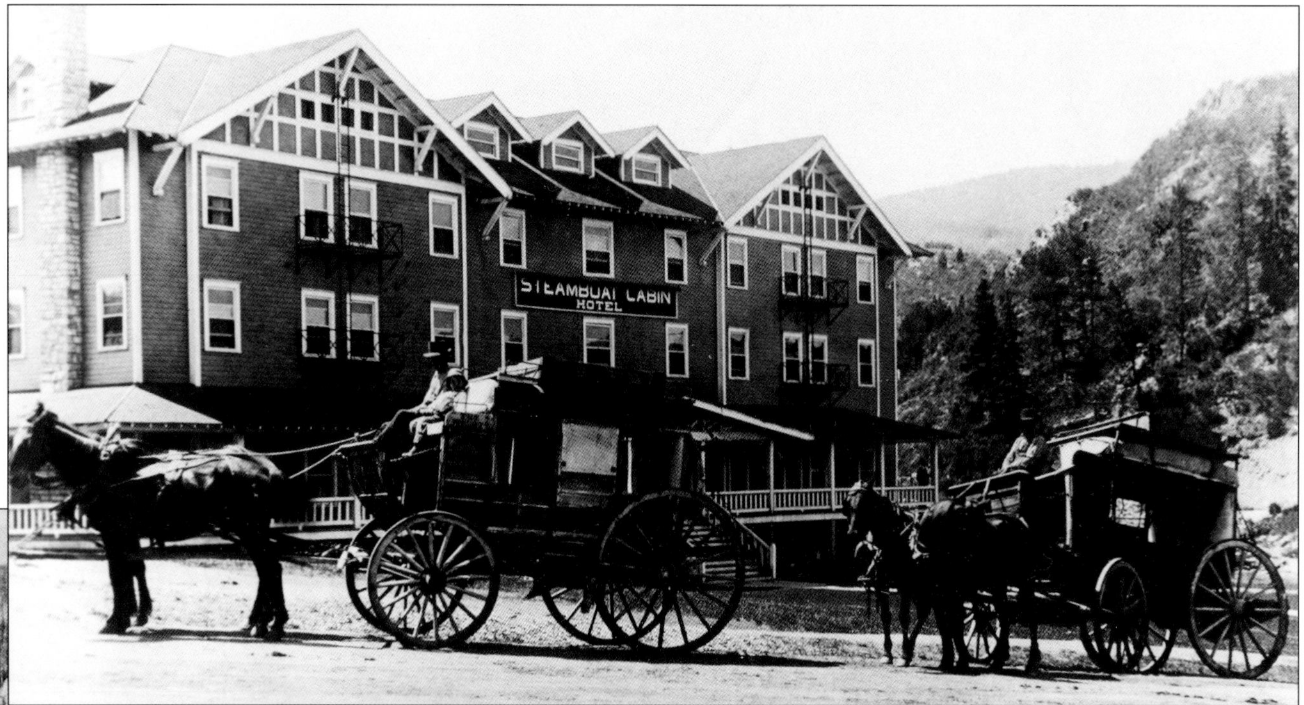

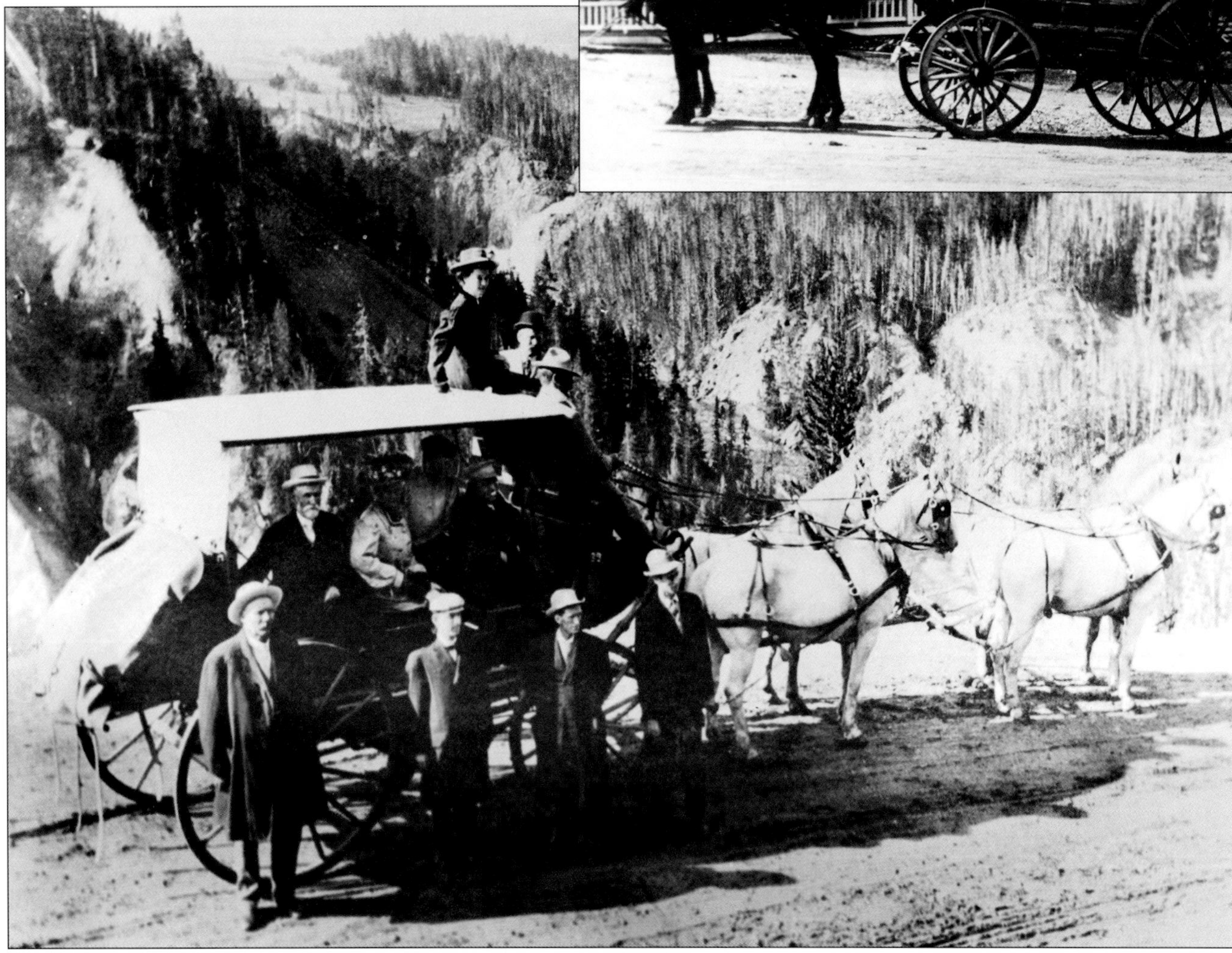

Tourists pose by the stagecoach they are riding, as they travel around Yellowstone Park.

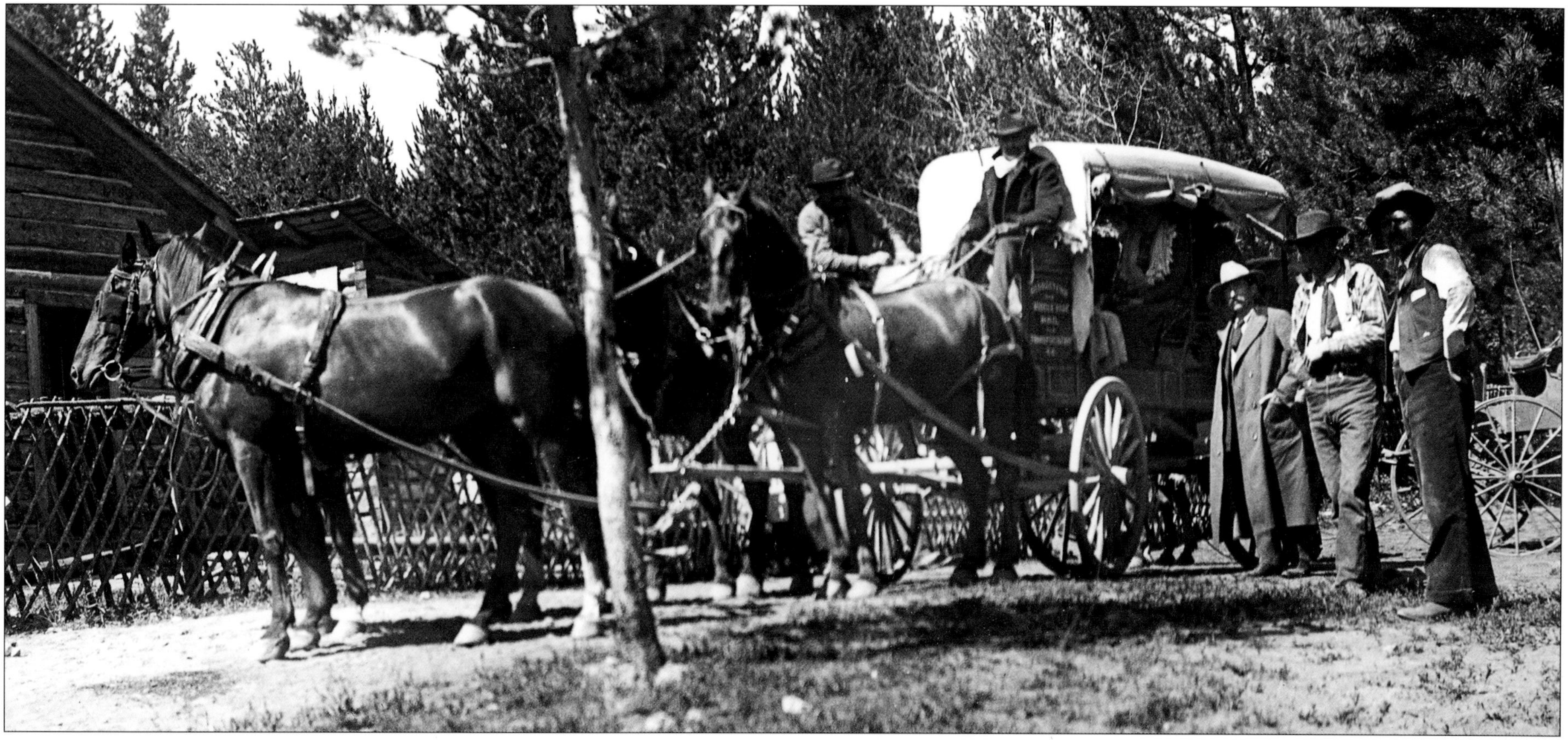

The Georgetown & Middle Park U.S. Mail stagecoach waits for its passengers. Pinkerton agent Charles Siringo stands nearest the coach, his hand in his pocket. Beside him, with his arm in a sling, is an outlaw he is transporting, and to the right is an unknown deputy. This photograph is from an original glass plate.

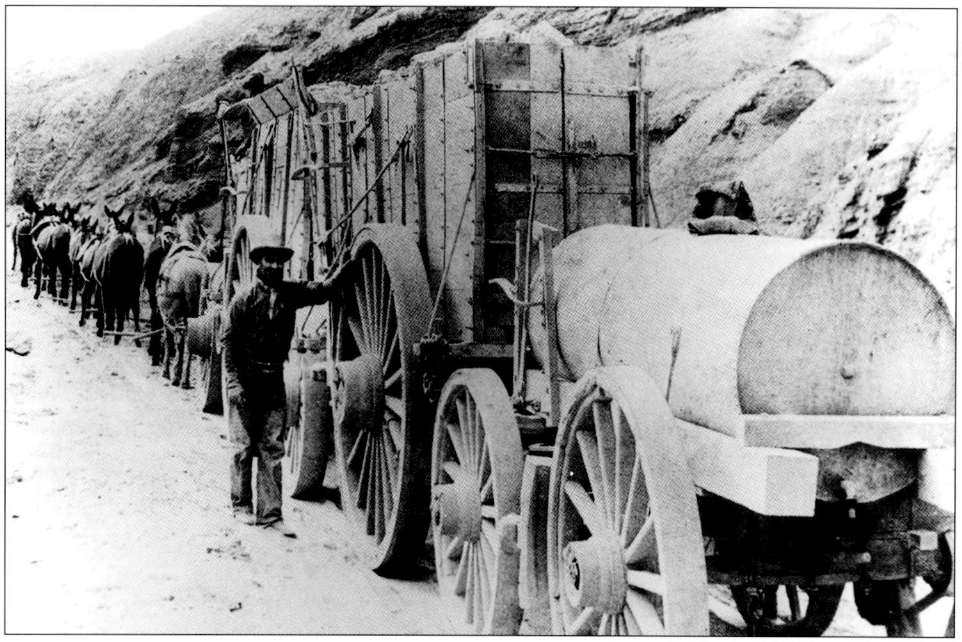

Outside of Doggett, California, a driver stops for his photograph, before resuming the transportation of the mined hunks of borax. Notice he is also hauling a large tank of water for himself as well as the mules.

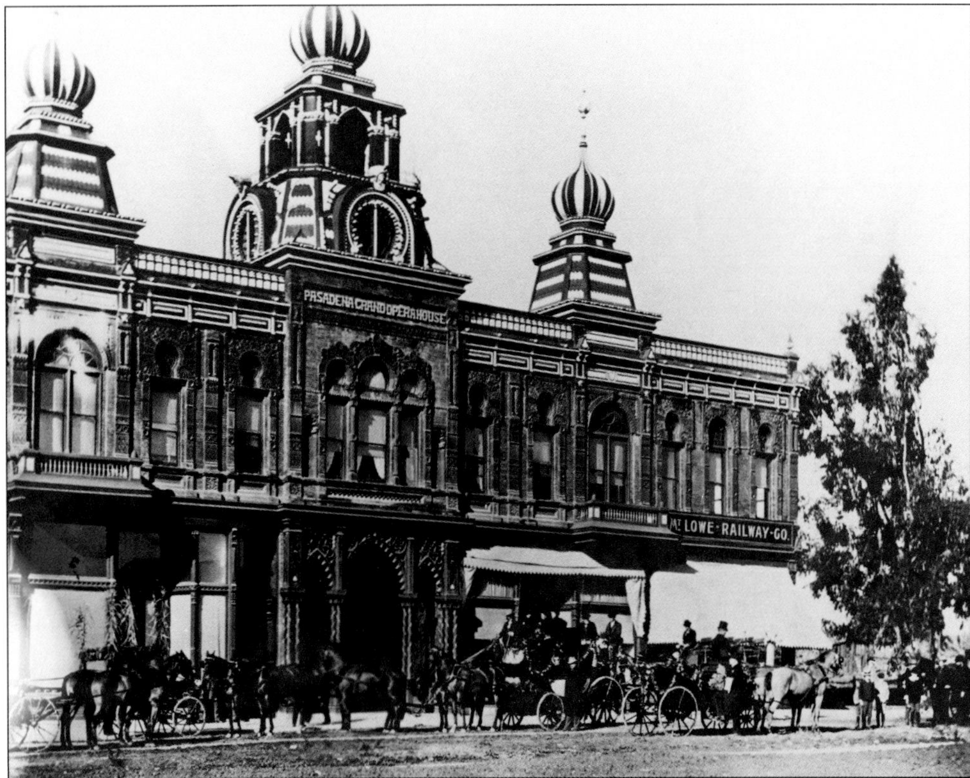

In Pasadena, California, the Mount Lowe Railway's main office was just completed when this photograph was taken. In front are the many stages to carry passengers to the Mount Lowe site.

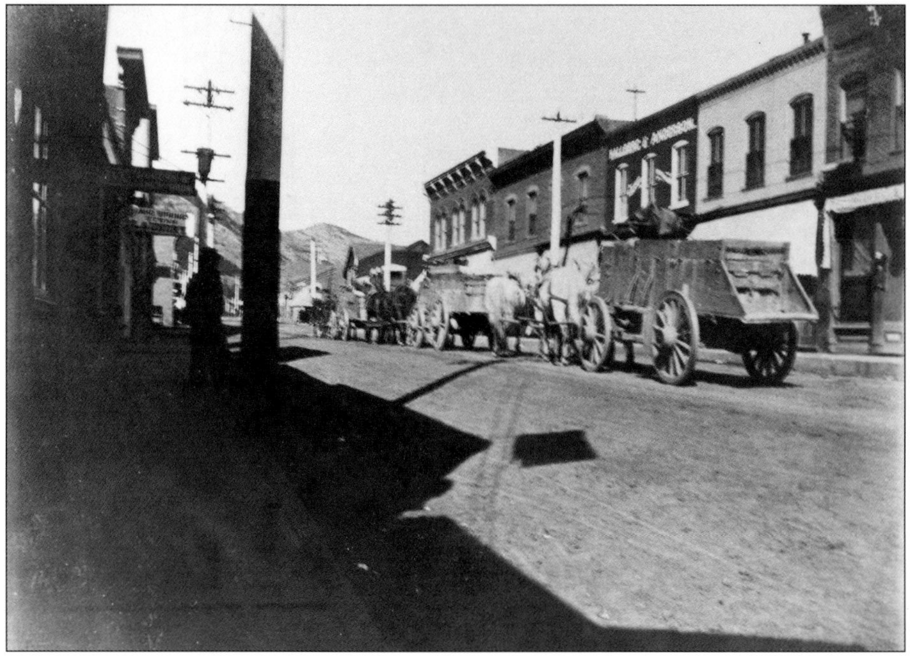

A lonely freight slowly makes its way through Idaho Springs, Idaho.

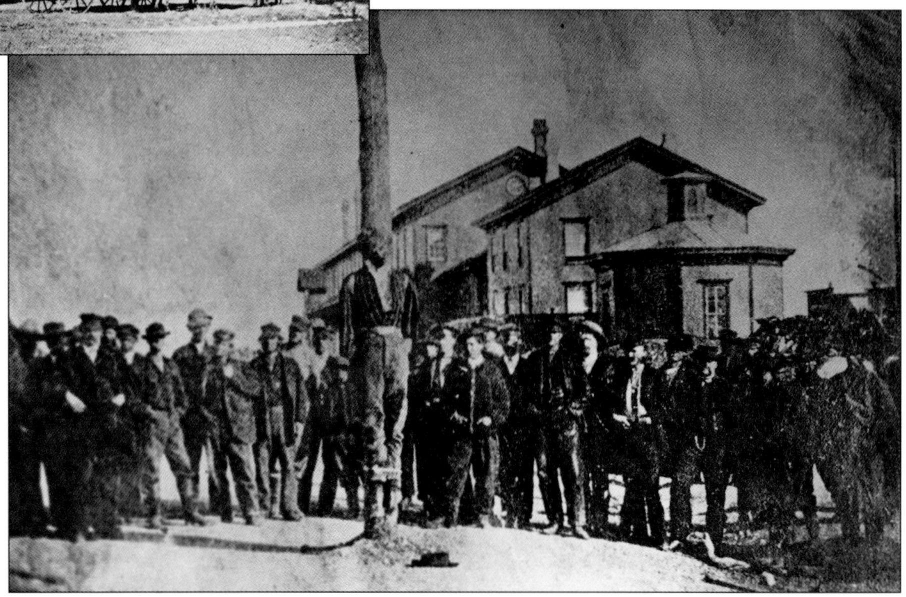

A hanging is a hanging and these town folks got their man. Tied and bound and hanging from a telegraph pole, this man may have robbed and killed for the last time.

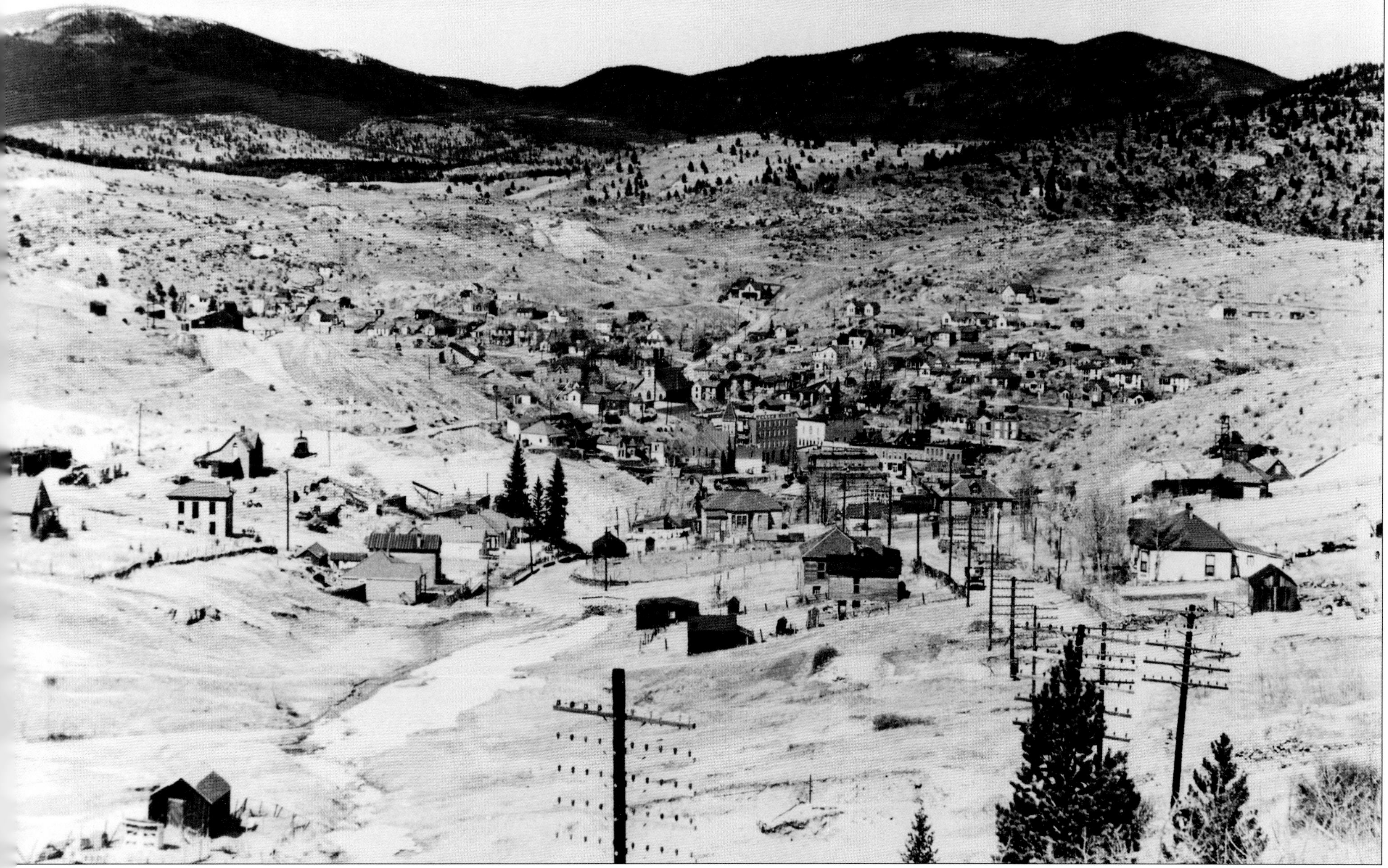

A bird's-eye view of Central City, Colorado. We can see the mining piles on the left and to the rear, which made this town site important. The photo was taken by H. I. Standley, of the town.

Chapter 6
1896-1915

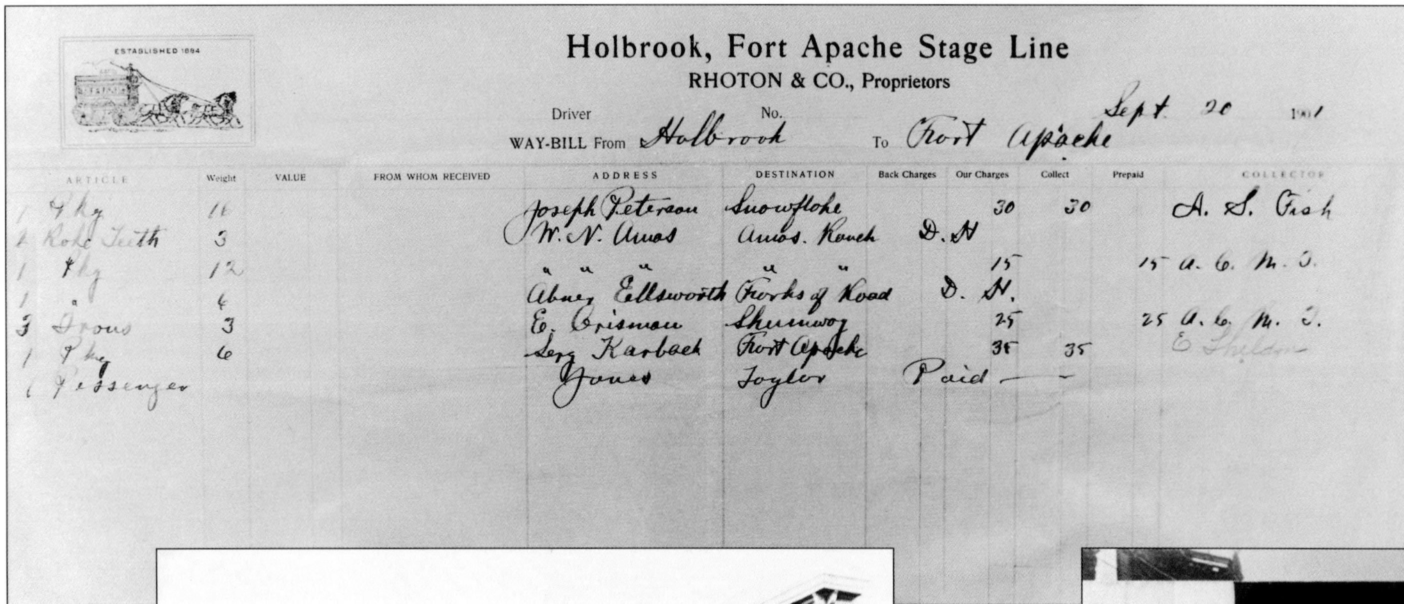

ESTABLISHED 1894

Holbrook, Fort Apache Stage Line
RHOTON & CO., Proprietors

Driver No. Sept. 20 1901
WAY-BILL From Holbrook To Fort Apache

ARTICLE	Weight	VALUE	FROM WHOM RECEIVED	ADDRESS	DESTINATION	Back Charges	Our Charges	Collect	Prepaid	COLLECTOR
1 Pkg	16			Joseph Peterson	Snowflake		30	30		A. S. Fish
1 Roll Teeth	3			W. N. Amos	Amos Ranch	D. H				
1 Pkg	12			" "			15		15	A. C. M. I.
1 "	6			Abner Ellsworth	Forks of Road	D. H.				
3 Irons	3			E. Crisman	Shumway		25		25	A. C. M. I.
1 Pkg	6			Serg Karback	Fort Apache		35	35		E. Sheldon
1 Passenger				Jones	Taylor	Paid				

The waybill for the Holbrook, Fort Apache Stage Line looked like this in 1901. A interesting entry was of a person whose destination was "The Forks of Road." The line went from Holbrook to Fort Apache.

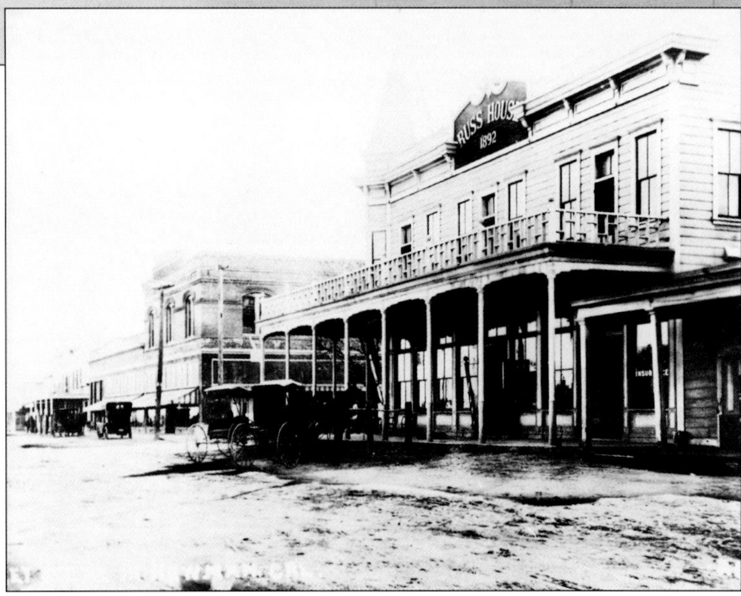

Coaches parked in front of the Russ House in the town of Newman, California.

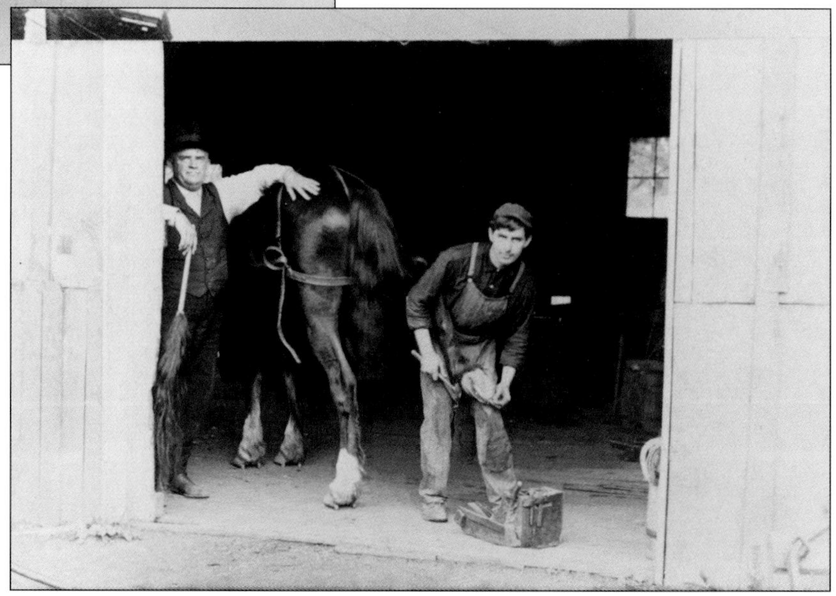

Blacksmith William Spencer mends a horse shoe for a customer in 1911.

A fine example of a blacksmith and harness shop belonged to Grandpa Woodruff and Uncle Bill Lawrence. It was called "The Old Harness Shop," and was located in Lawless, Iowa. The photo was taken in 1913.

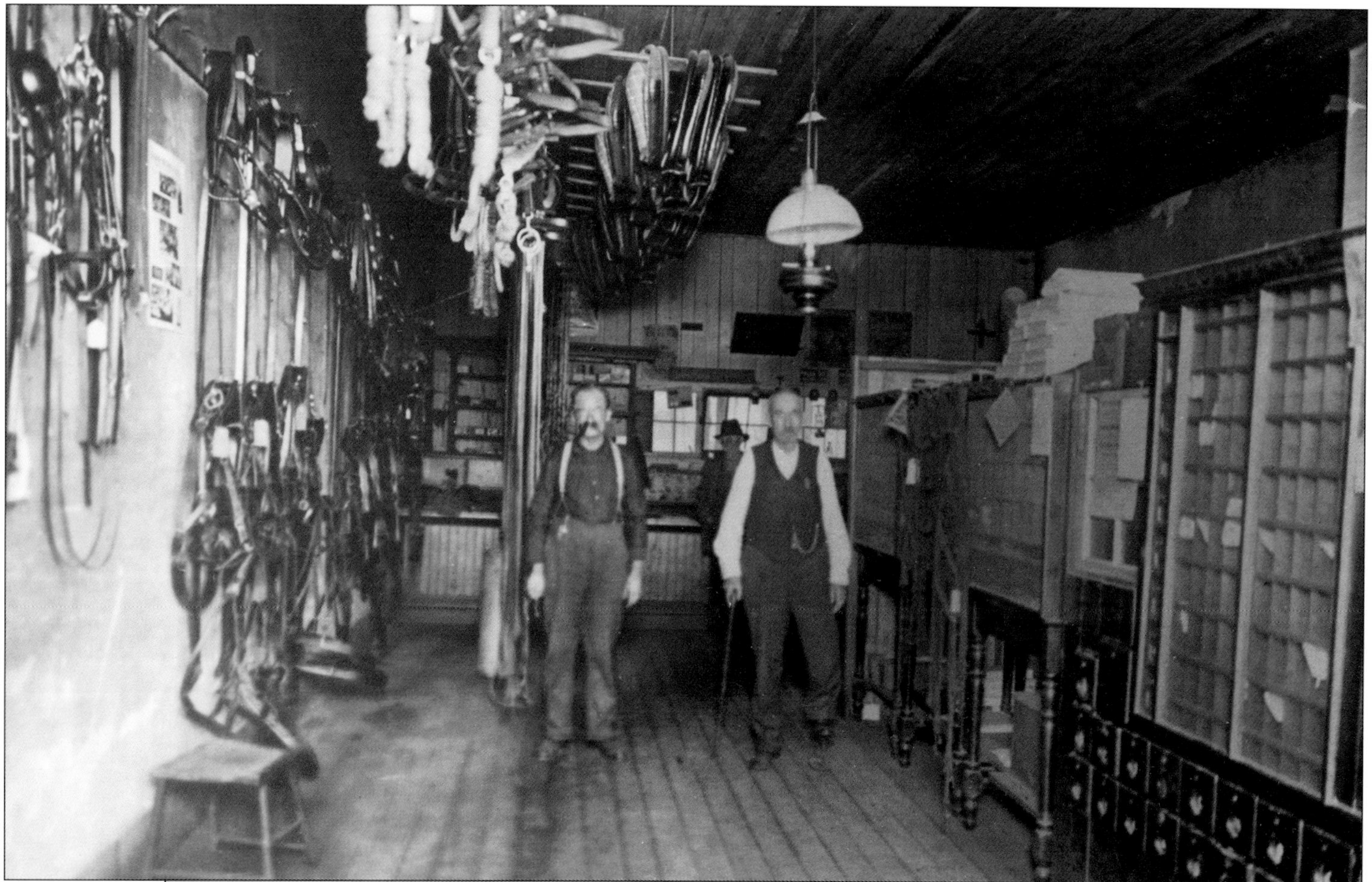

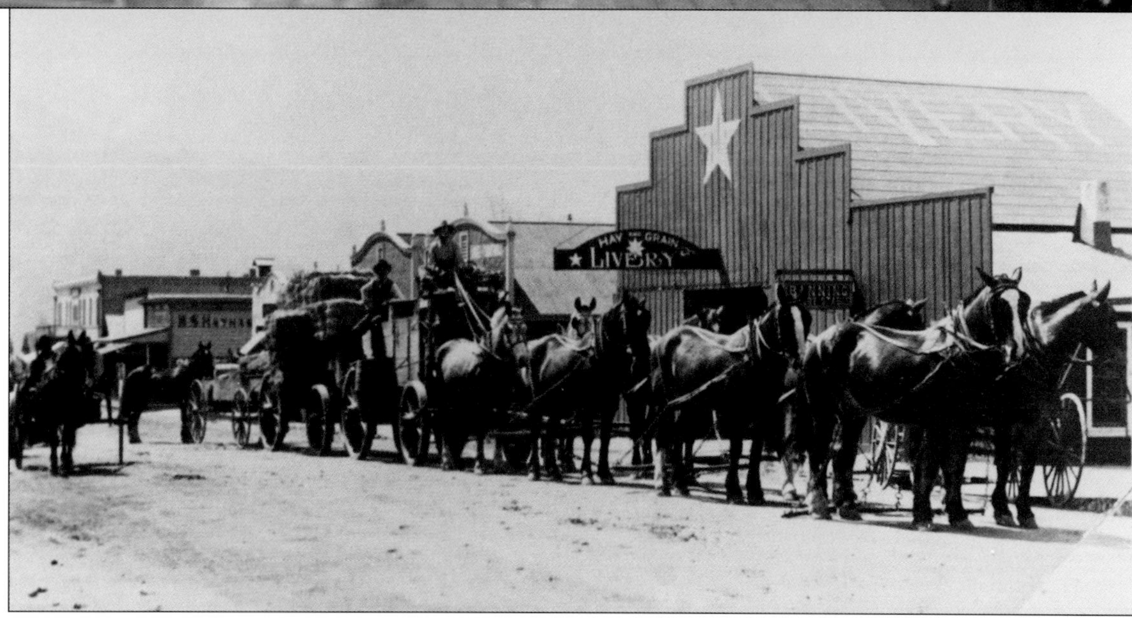

Banning, California in 1910 was the scene of these teams driving down main street, past the towns Livery Stables. They are off to the desert, carrying feed, water, and supplies.

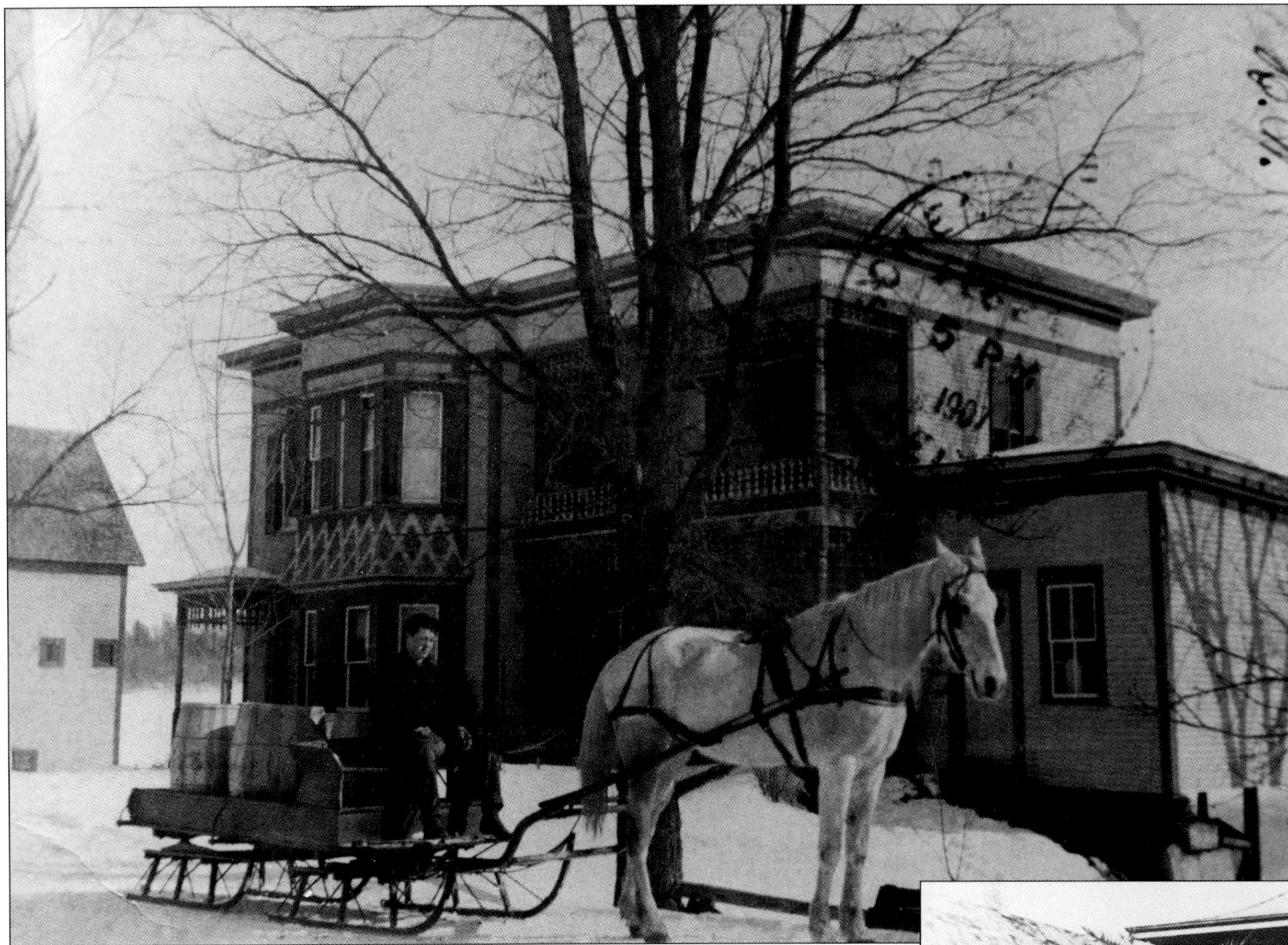

The time is 1907 and the delivery of food and supplies must get through no matter what kind of weather. Riding on two-seated pung, or sleigh, the driver will meet his schedule.

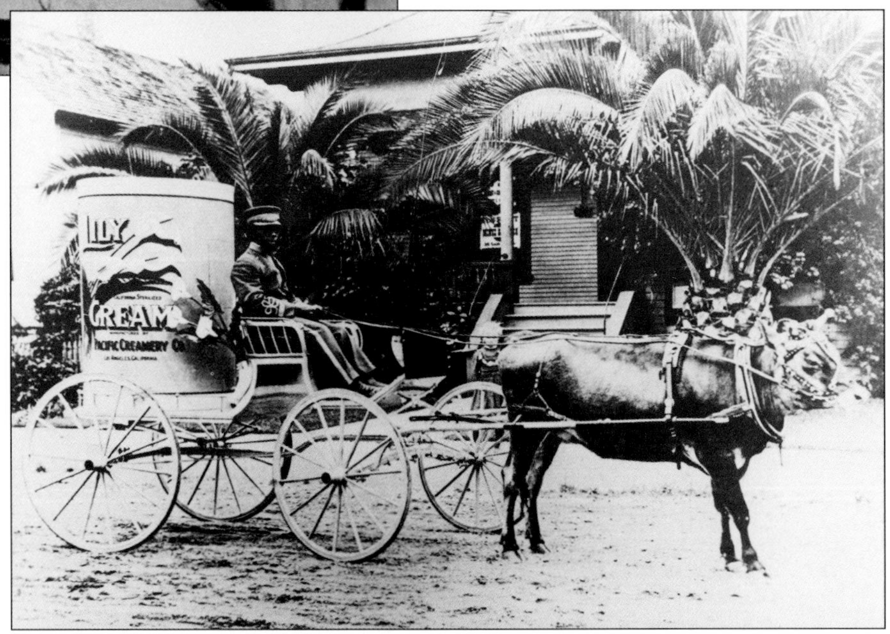

The Lily Creamery deliver wagon in Anaheim, California. A lone ox is pulling the load.

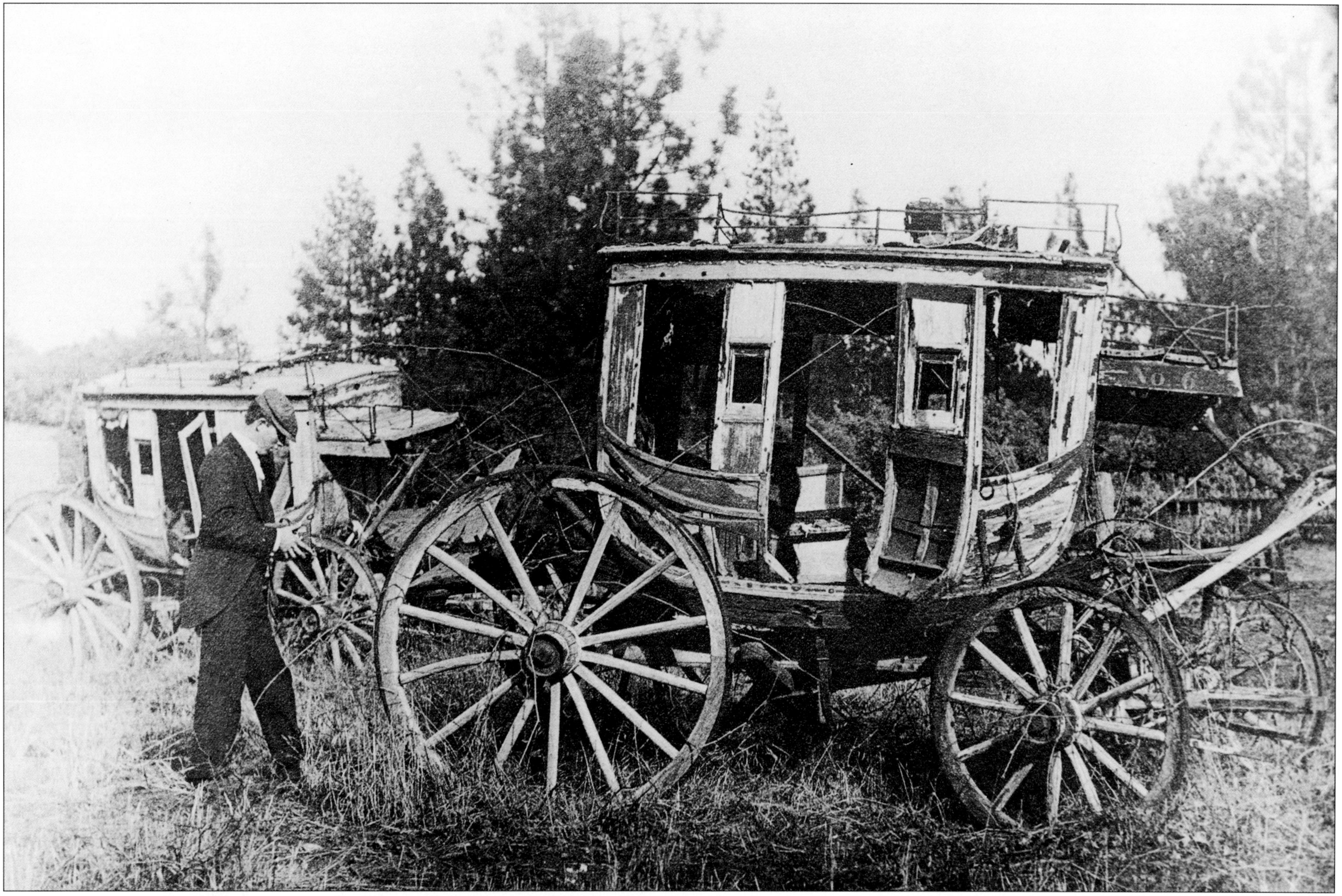

A man taking a picture of an old Concord stagecoach, using a box camera. Both of the stages lie abandoned near Colfax, California. This photo was taken by O. Bradford of San Francisco in 1912.

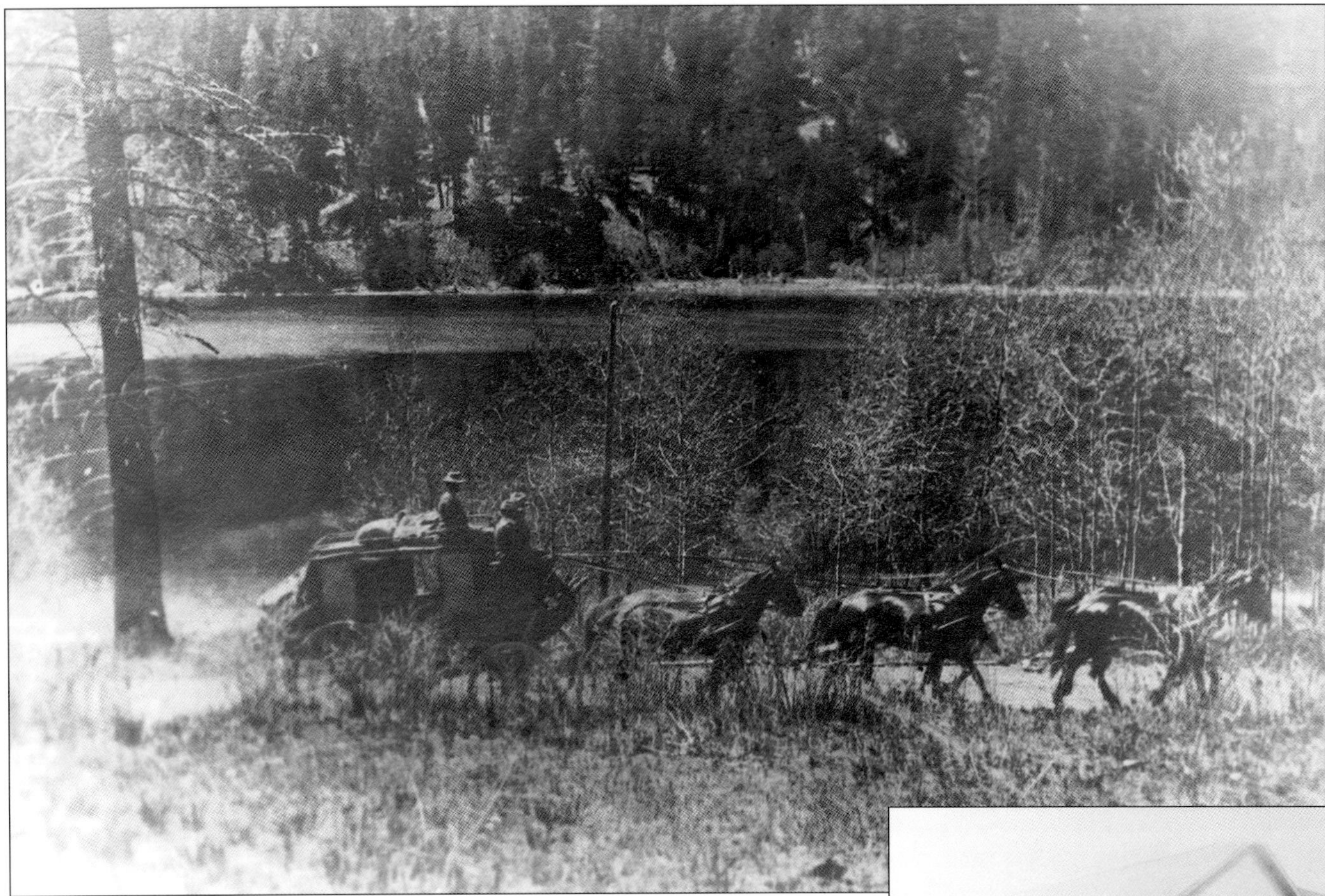

Emile La Forest, later the street equipment superintendent of the Wells Fargo Company in San Francisco, was the driver of this fast moving stage on "The Caribou Road," in British Columbia.

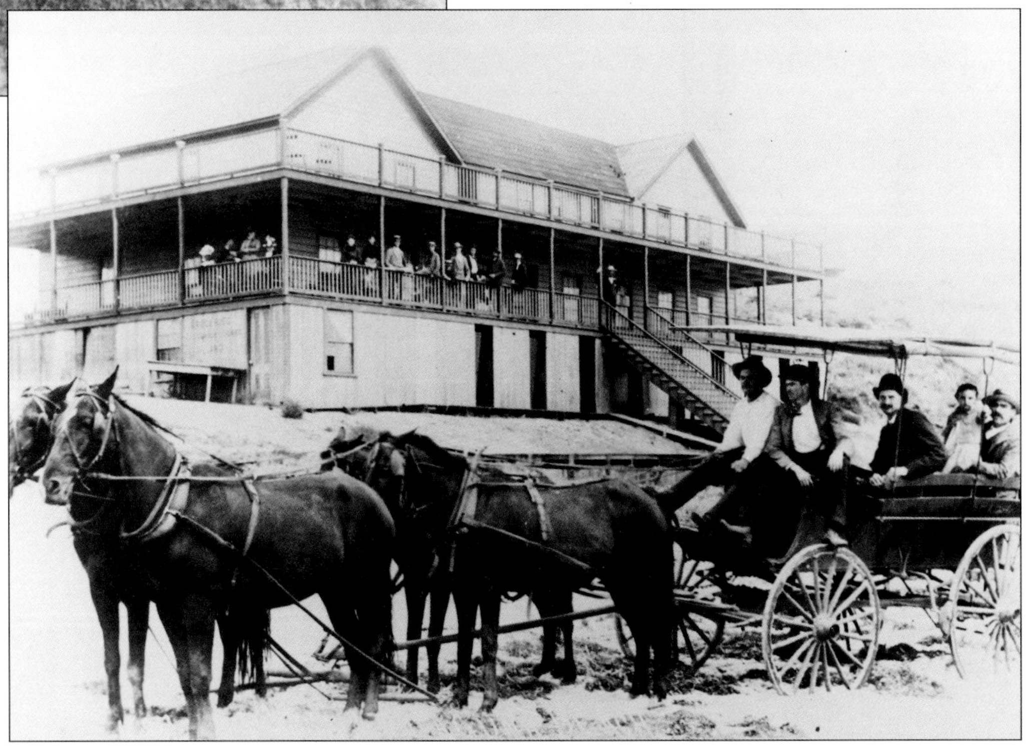

A surrey with a fringe on top, photographed in front of the early Laguna Hotel, and early Laguna Beach, California, establishment.

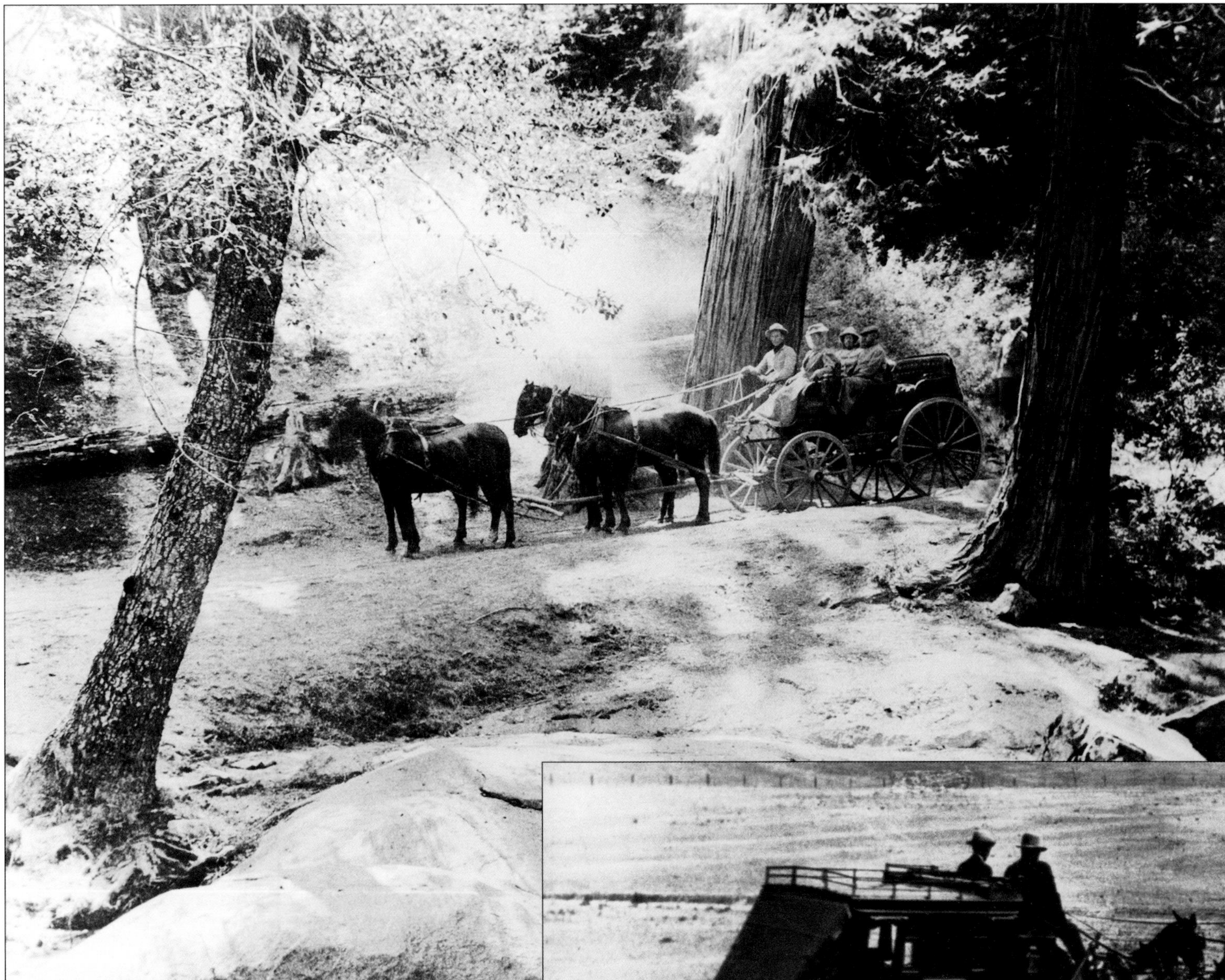

A beautiful scene in the Yosemite Park as photographed by one of the passengers.

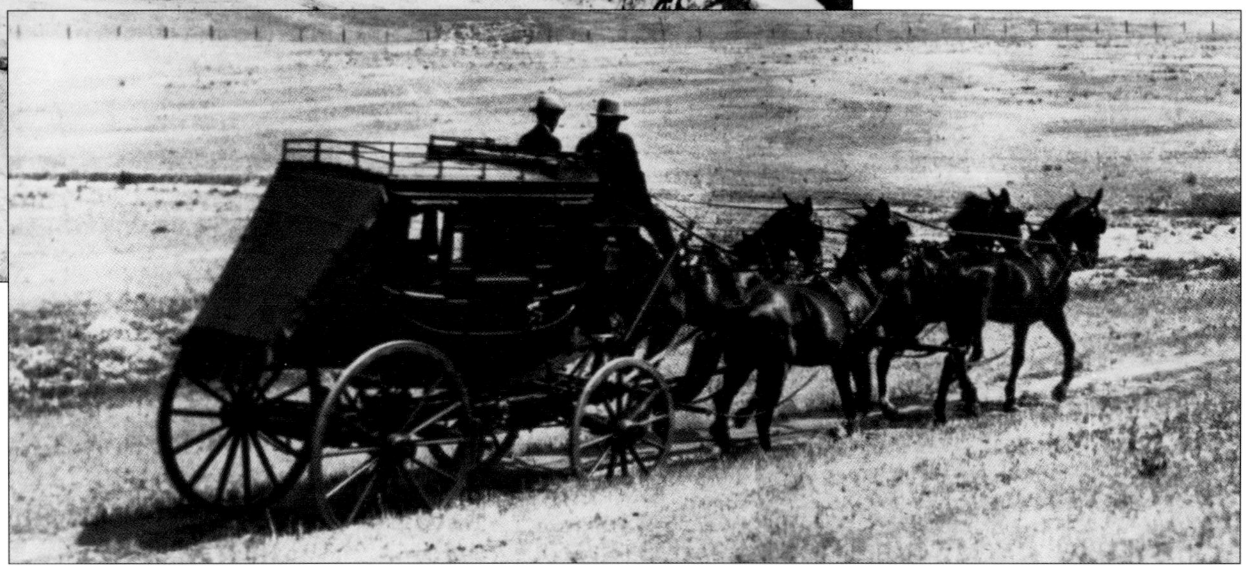

A stage on the way to Virginia City, Nevada, doesn't wait for the photographer. In this case it is B. Frashers.

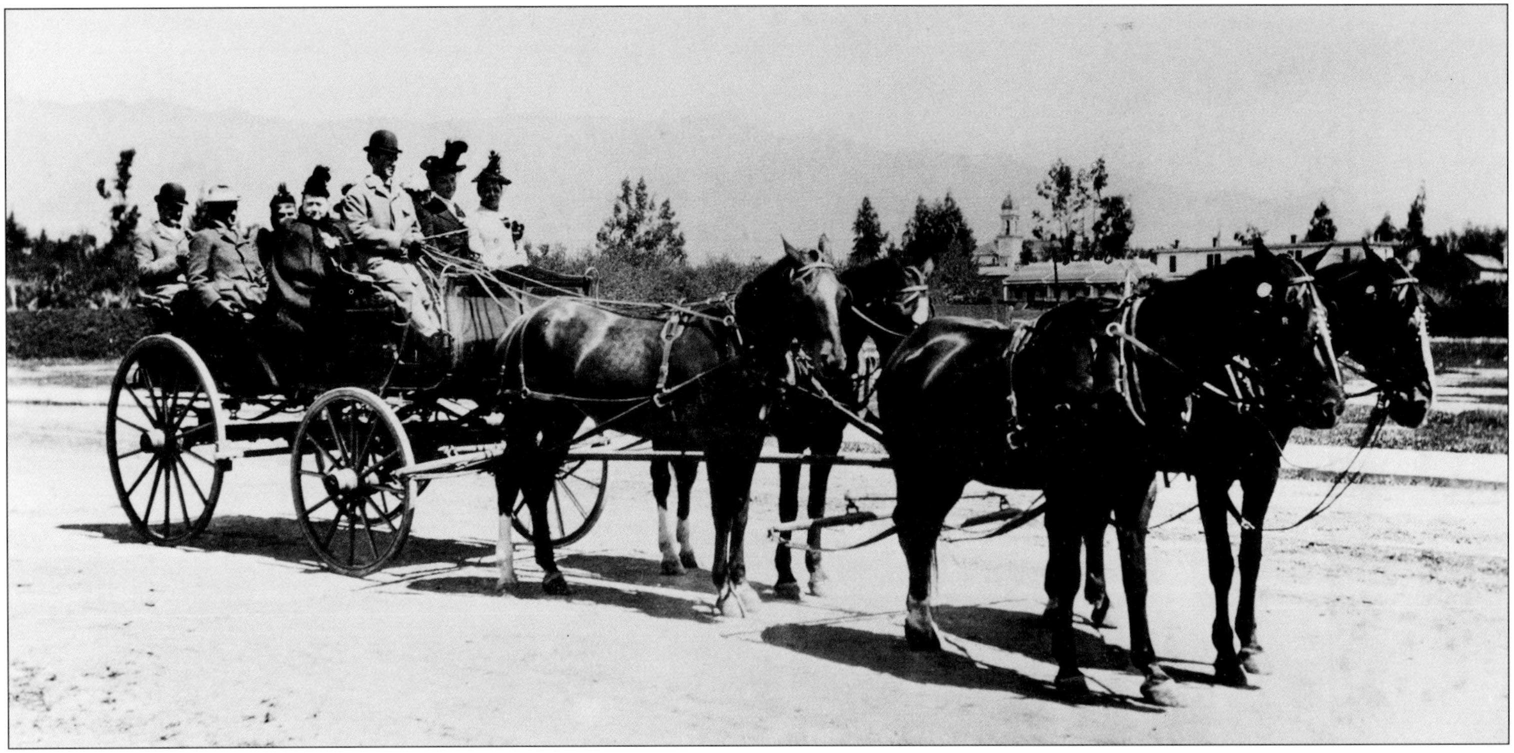

This four-horse runabout was driven by Professor Lowe in Pasadena, California.

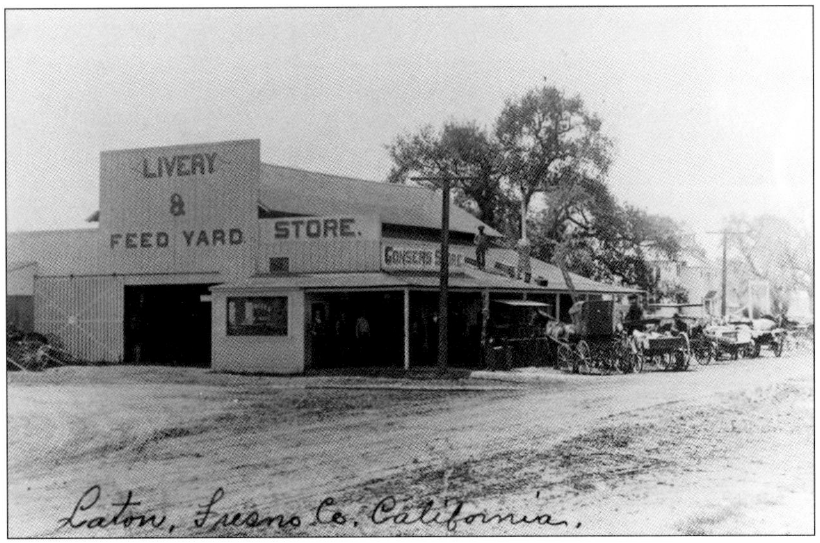

Laton, in Fresno County, California, had a livery and feed store that was the center of business.

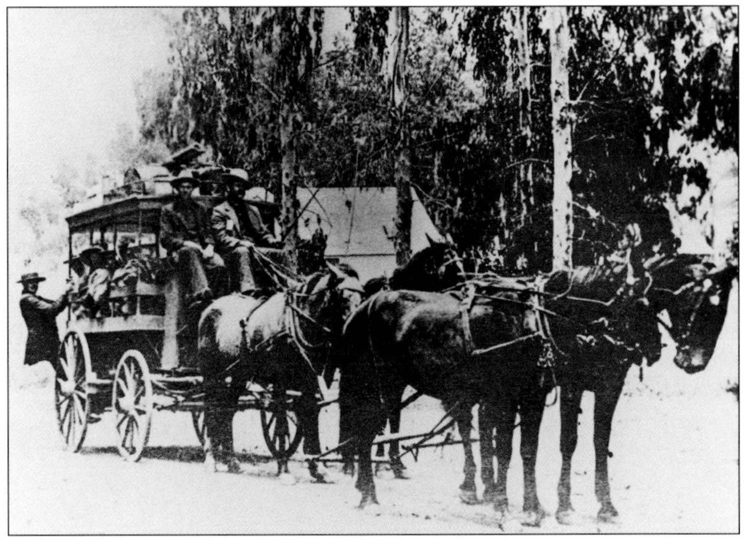

The stagecoach at Laguna, California, is leaving for El Toro with a coach full of passengers.

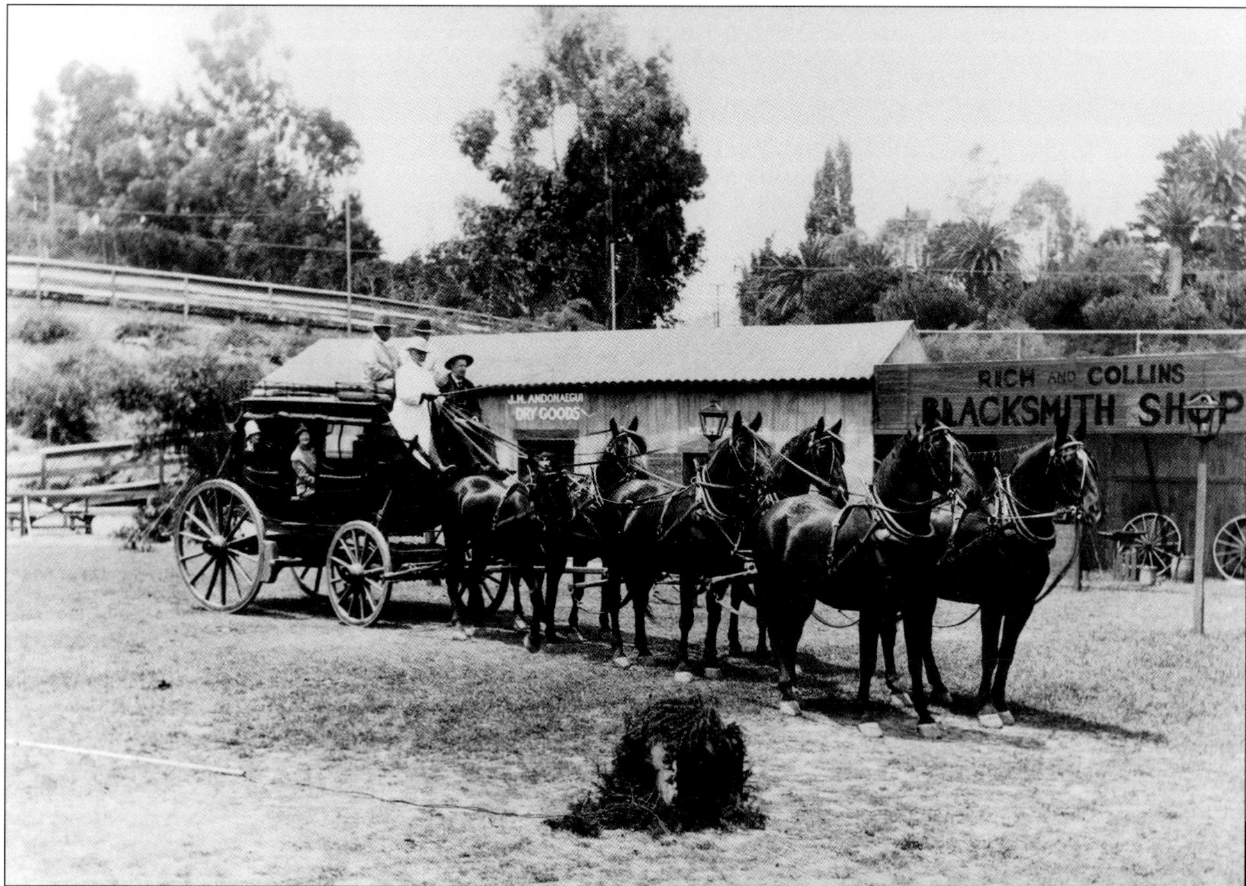

A Wells Fargo stage at a stop by the blacksmith shop in Santa Barbara, California.

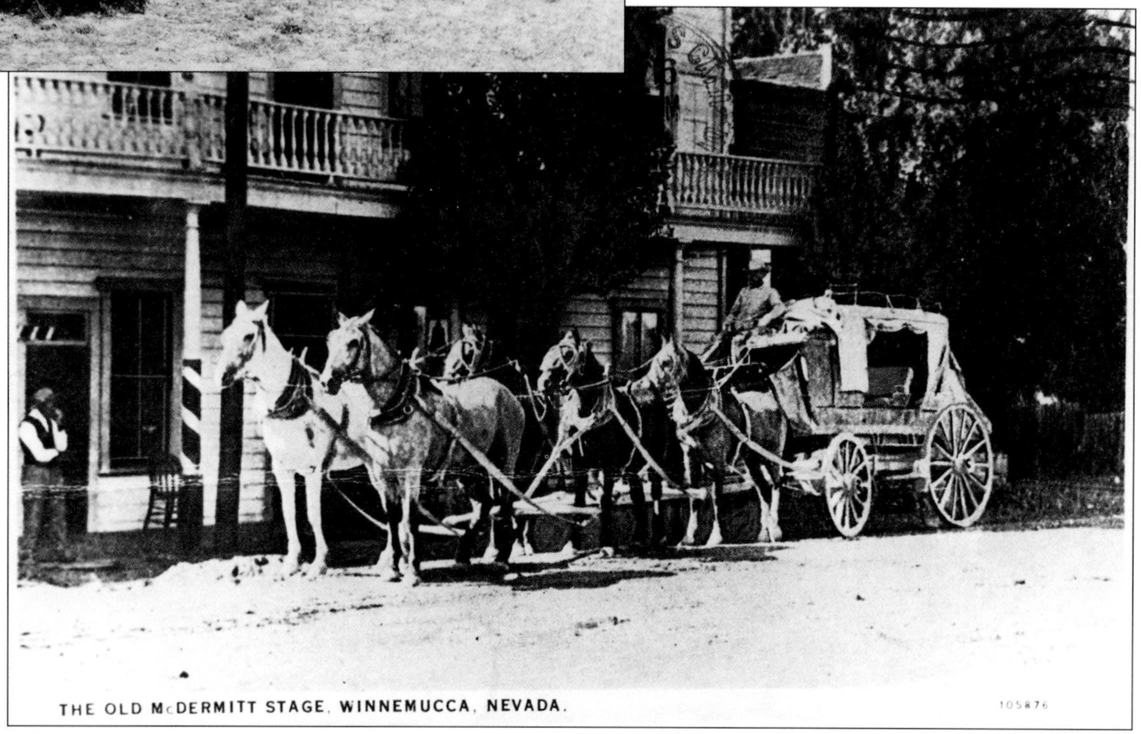

The McDermitt Stagecoach waits for passengers at a hotel in Winnemucca, Nevada.

The main street of Ely, Nevada, looked like this in the early 1900s. In this very rare photo there were even some puffing automobiles on the dirt streets, as well as some women dressed in white and watching the camera man.

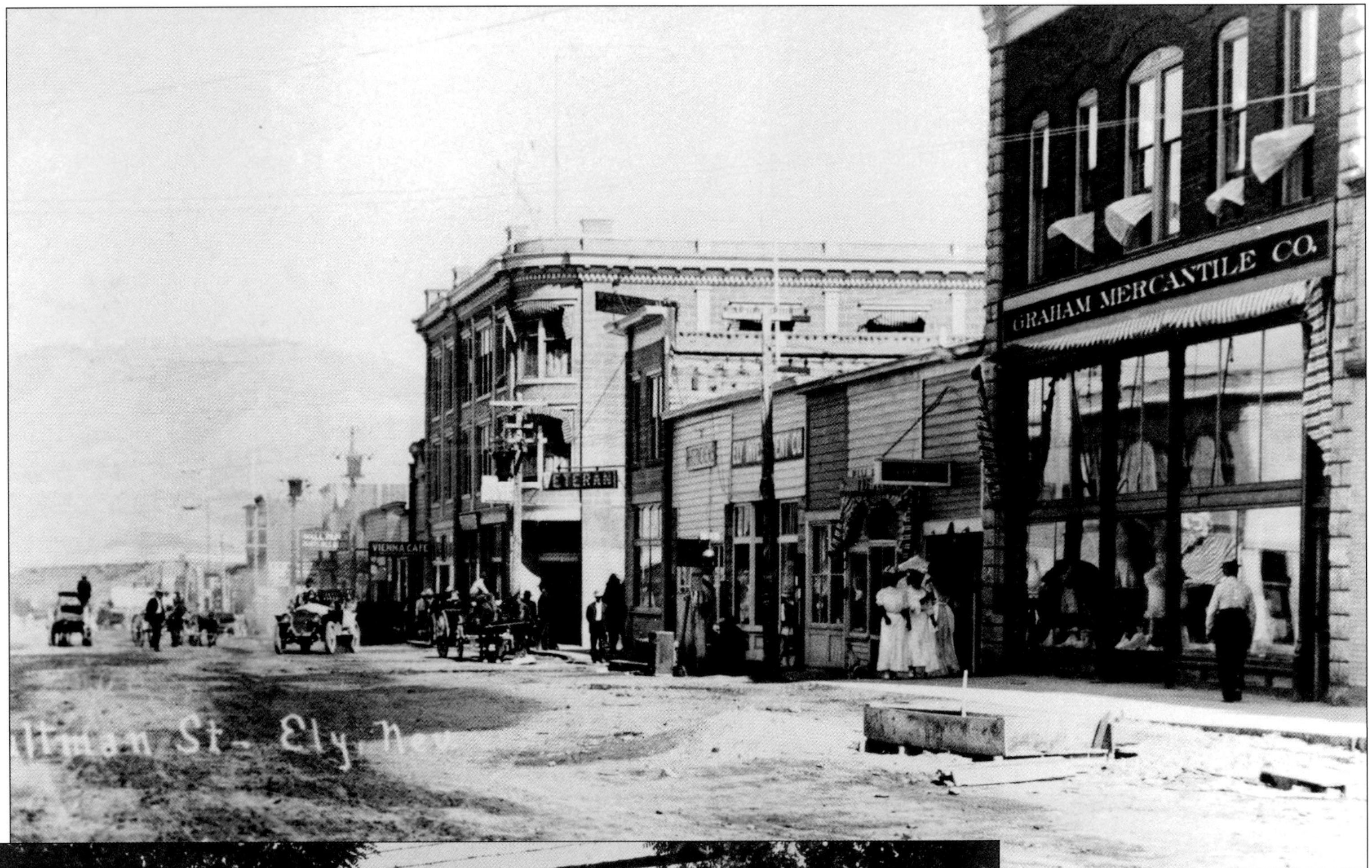

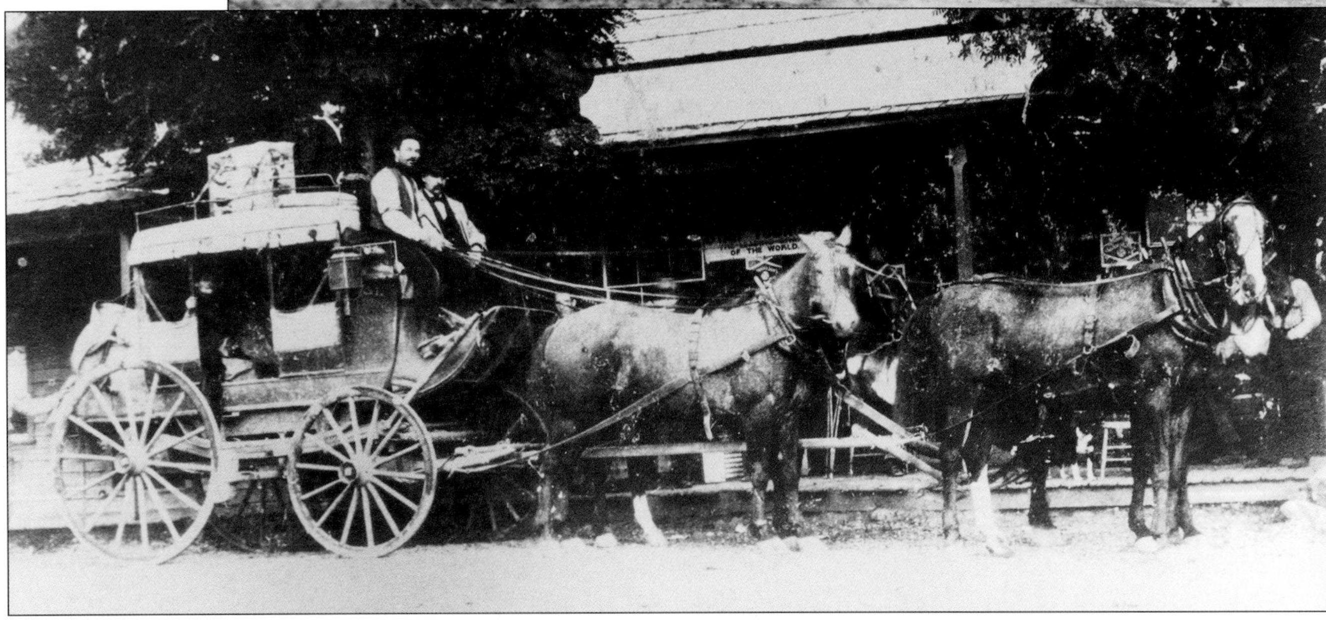

This rare stagecoach photo was taken in Lewiston, Trinity, Colorado in 1894. The stage driver is N.H. Hampton. Shackled behind him is three-time murderer, Blackjack Hugh. This stage was held up by the Ruggles Brothers in 1896. They were captured and both hanged in Redding, California. In the hold up, John Ruggles shot and killed Buck Montgomery. Charles shot the driver, Boyce, and a passenger.

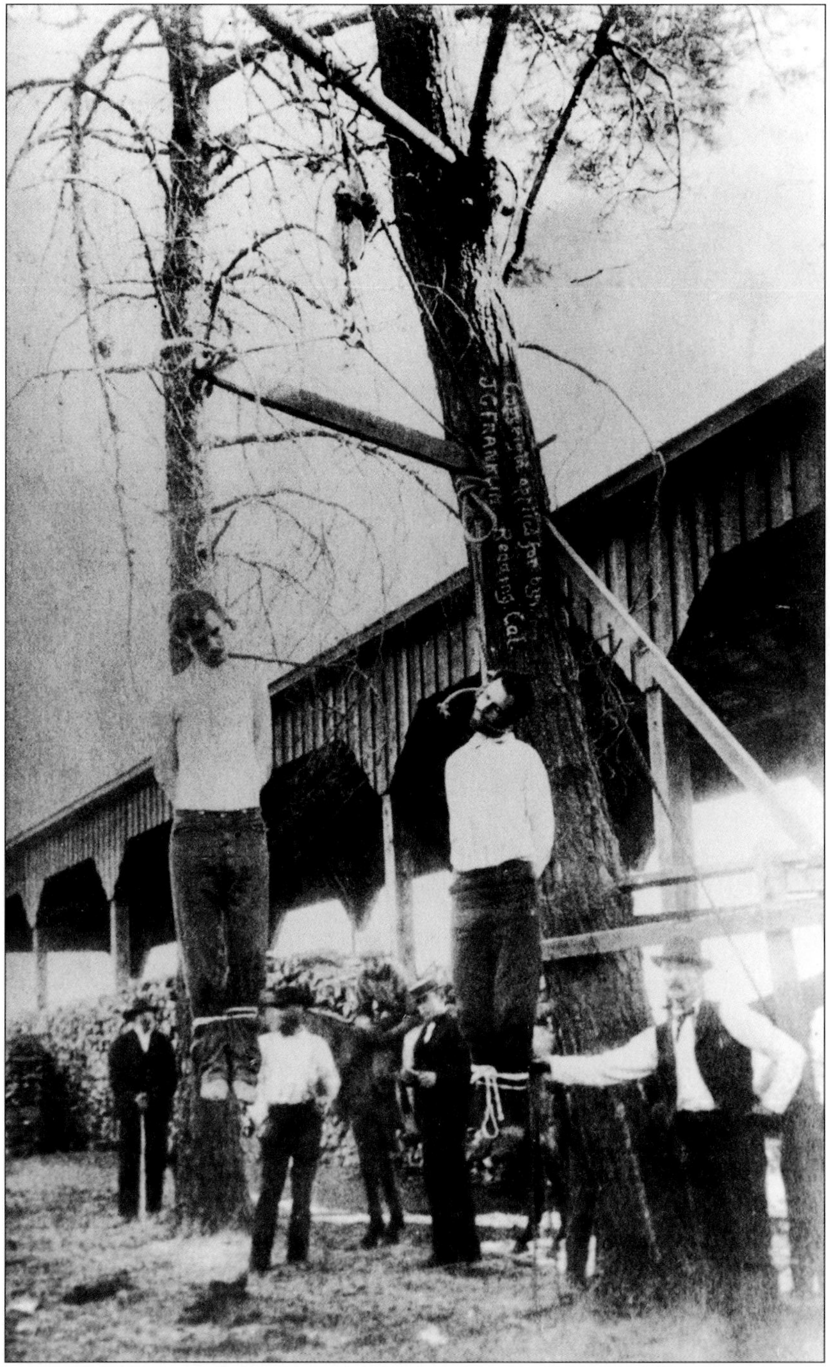

This photograph is of the hanging of the Ruggles brothers Redding. California, for the shooting of Boyce, a passenger, and Buck Montgomery during a hold up.

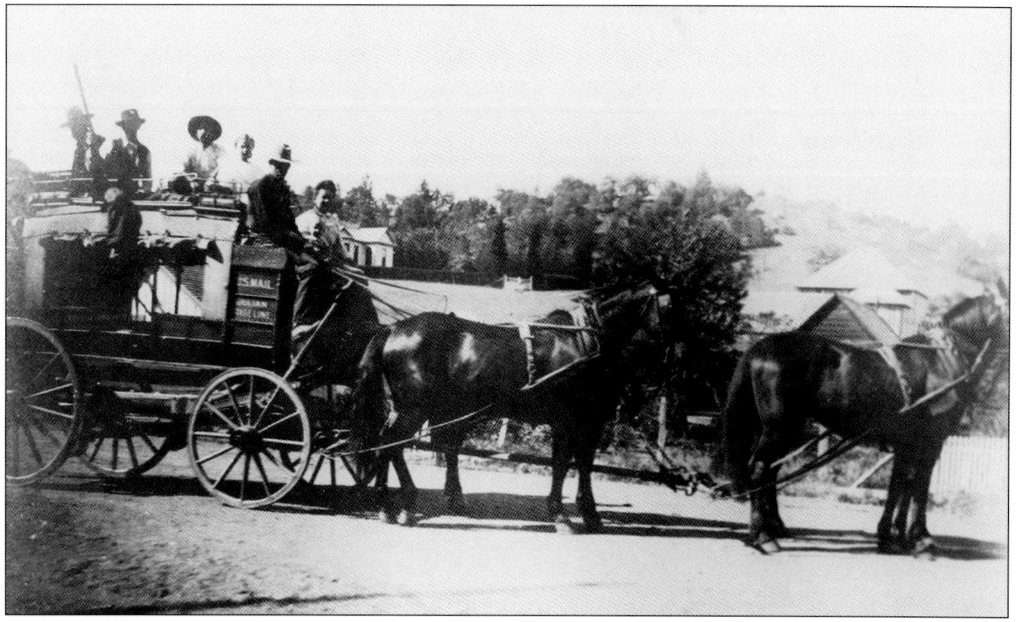

The U.S. Mail stage from Julian, California, a gold-producing town not far from San Diego.

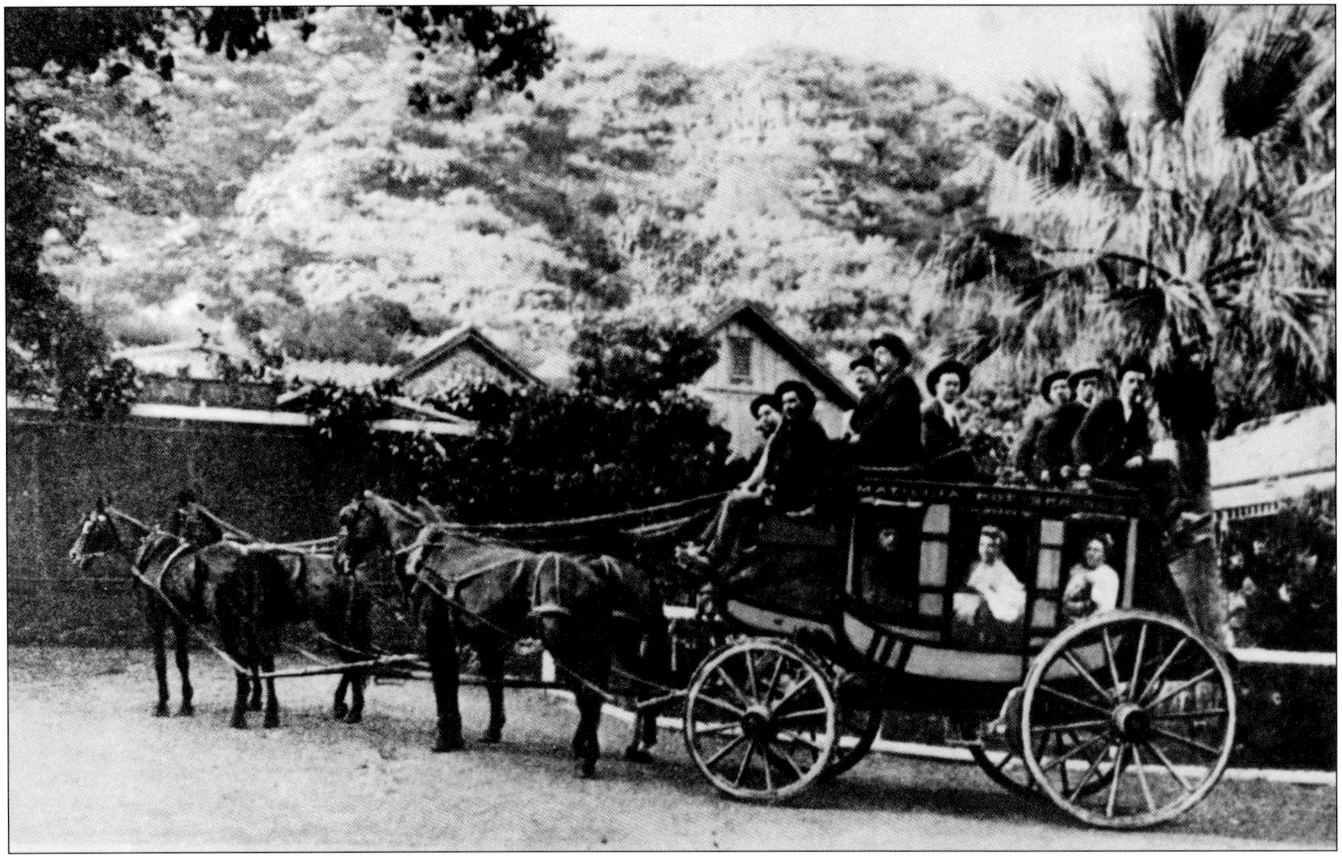

The Matilija Stagecoach from Ventura County, California.

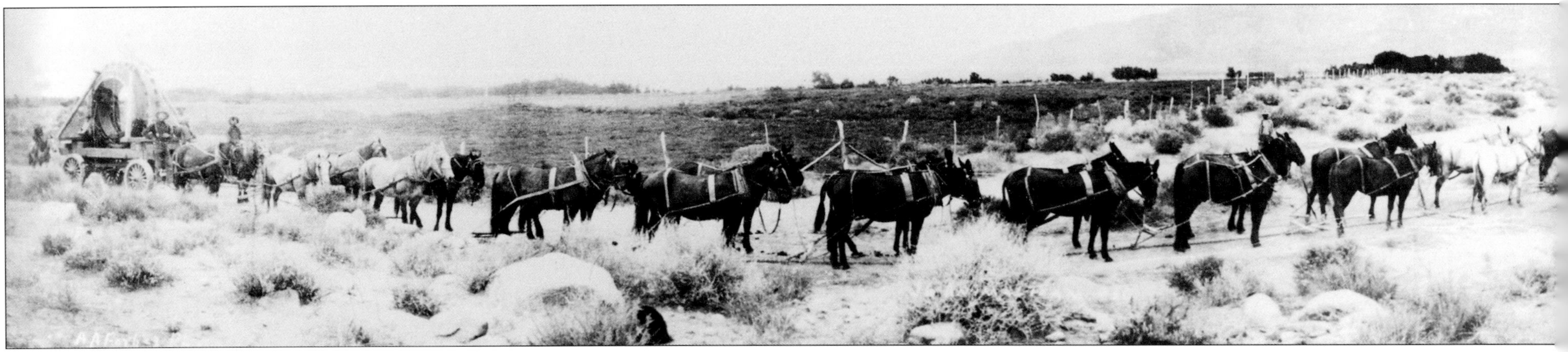

Photographer Forbes took this panoramic photograph of a long train of mules pulling some mining equipment through the desert toward Bodie, California.

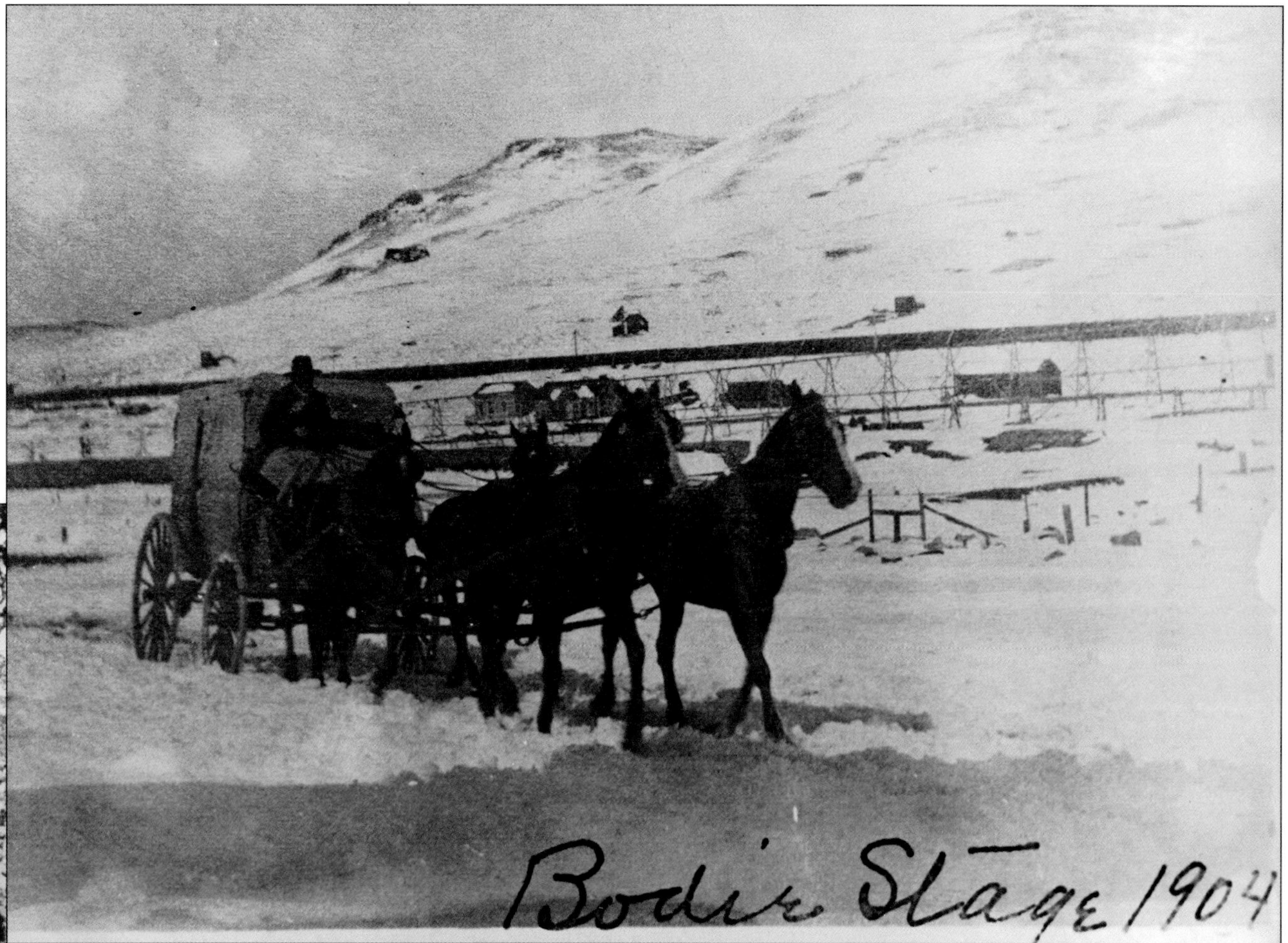

In the cold of winter, the Bodie Stage leaves town with the U.S. Mail. In 1904 Bodie's mining operations were winding down and many people had left.

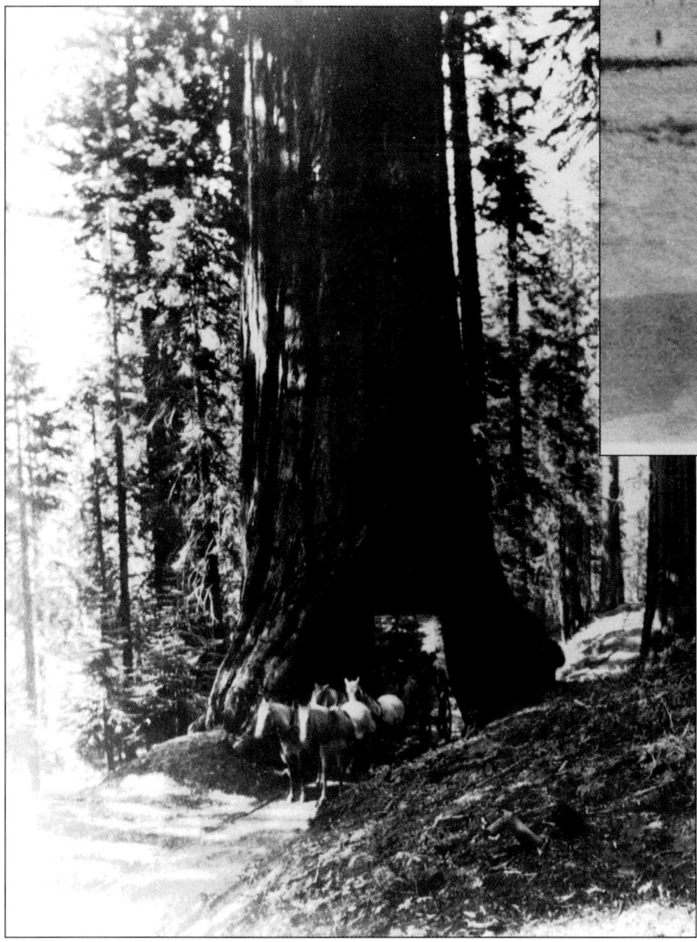

In the Maraposo Grove of Big Trees, California. A spring wagon is taking passengers on a trip through the center of a giant red wood. Photographer Grant Jackson has his small stamp on the edge of the mount.

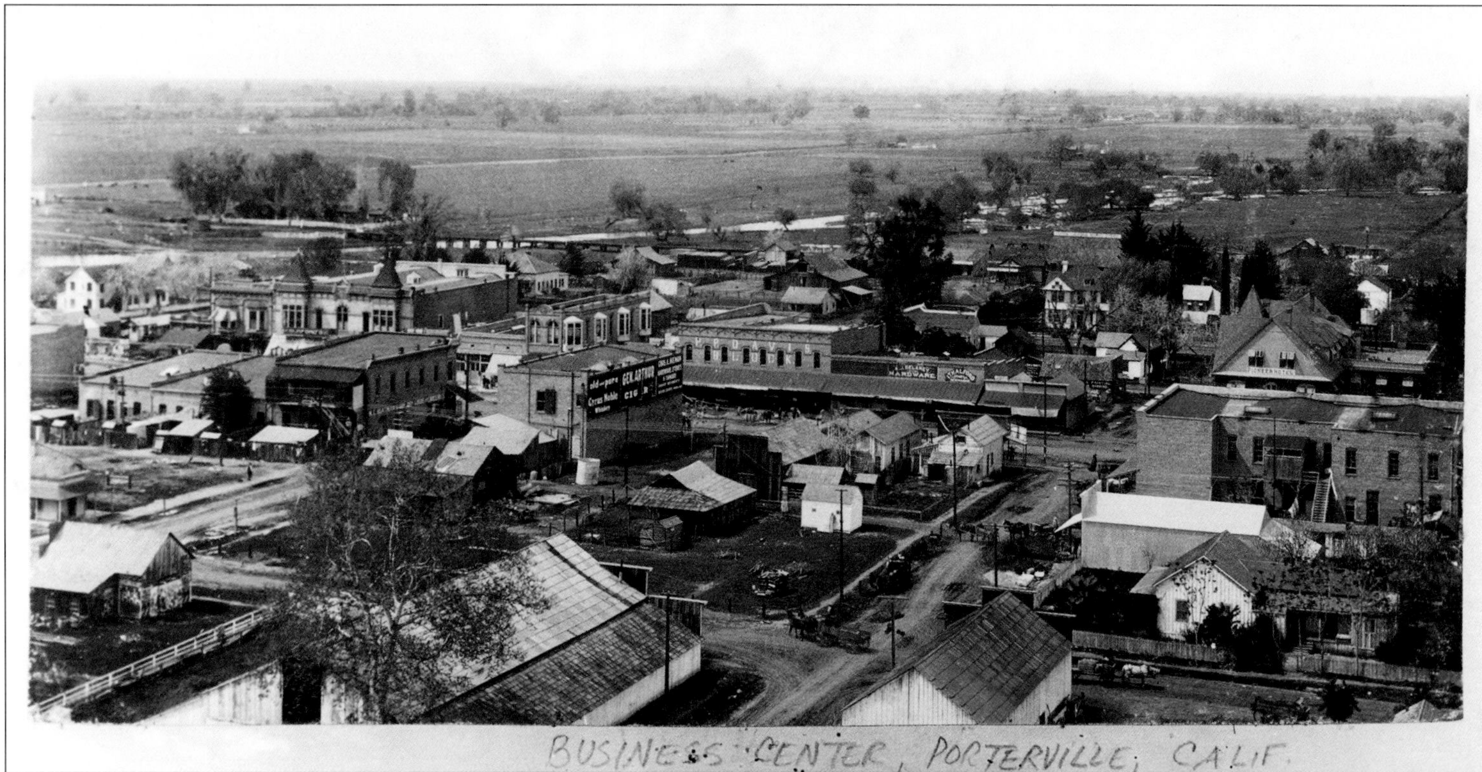

An important city with a waterway was Porterville, California. This later view, taken in 1900, still has many horse-drawn wagons and carts going about their business in the center of town.

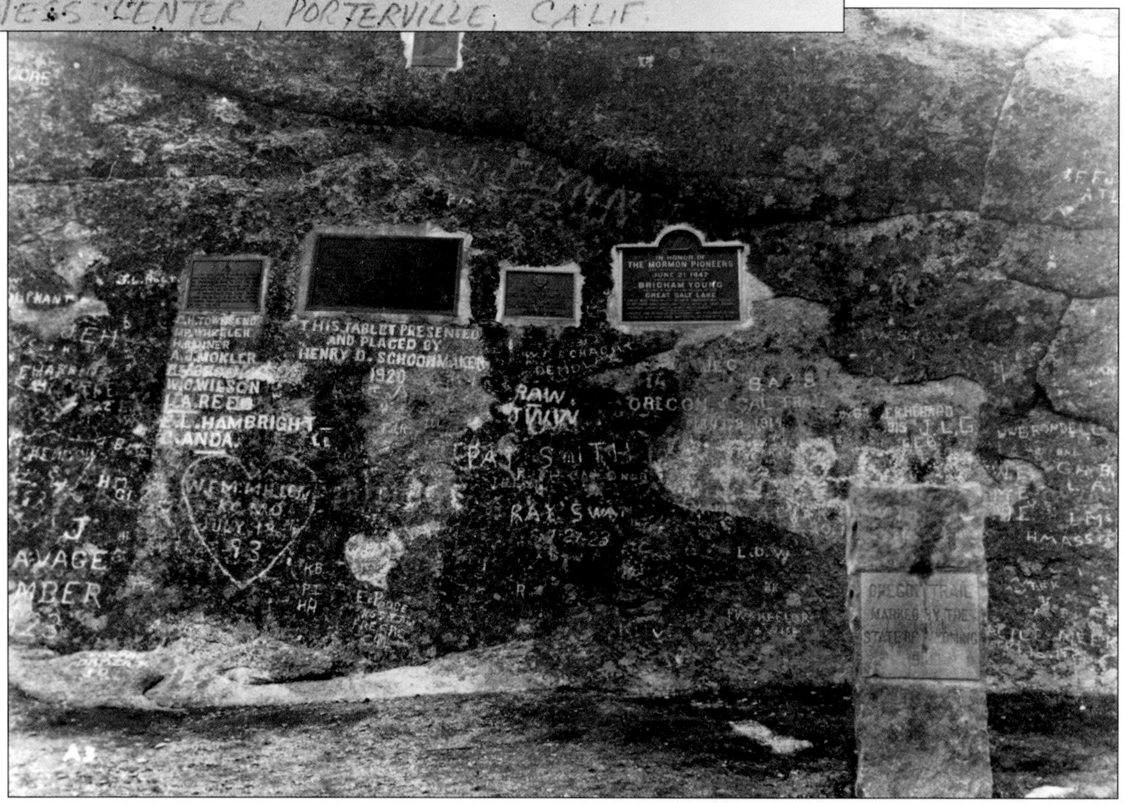

A lot of history has been attached to this rock, called, "The Independence Rock." Some fifty miles southwest of Casper, Wyoming, the tablets mark the Masons, the Oregon Trail, the Mormons, and at the top center "Ezra Meeker" is scratched on the rock. This photo was taken in 1931 by Emil Kopac of Oshkosh, Nebraska..

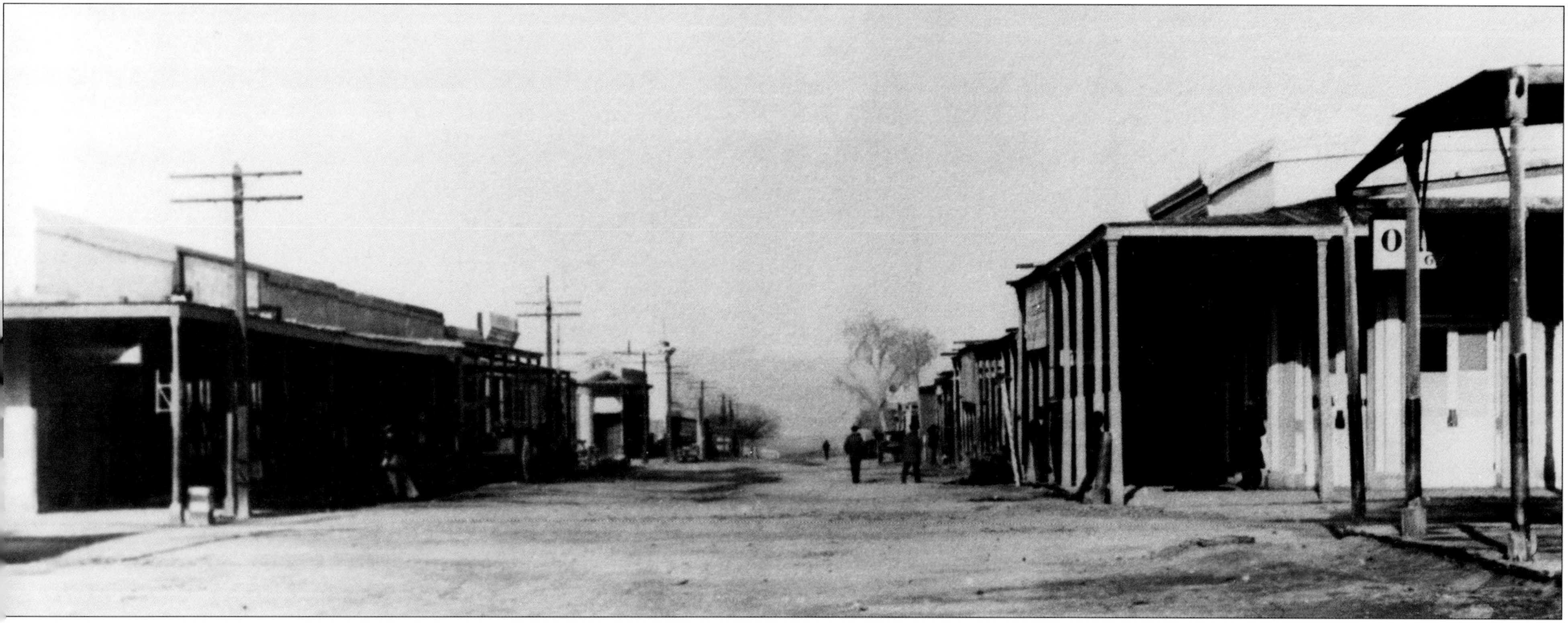

This was Tombstone, Arizona, in 1905. The town is almost deserted except for some folks who were walking the dirt street.

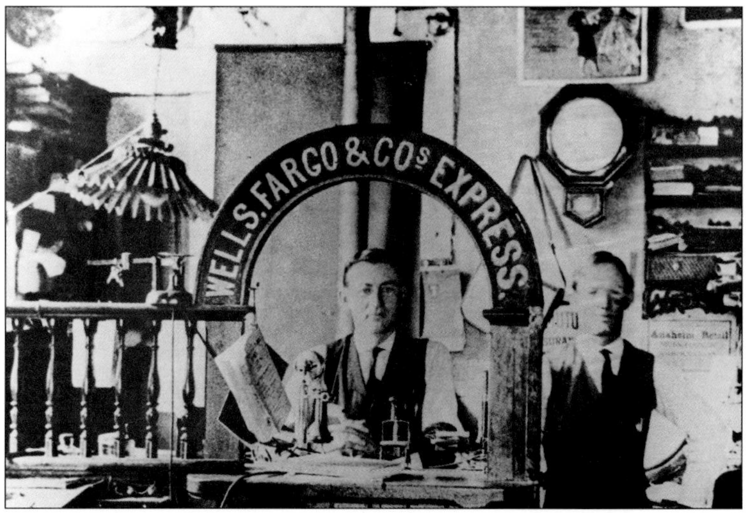

Anaheim, California's Wells Fargo Express office in early 1900.

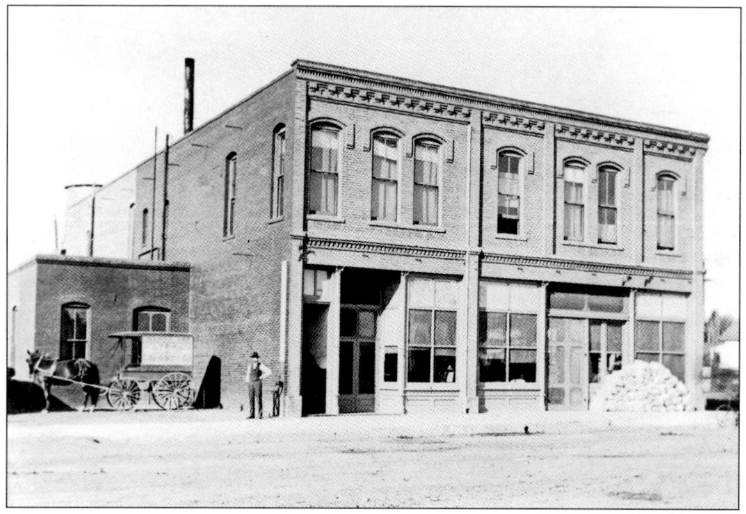

Santa Ana, California's lone laundry wagon, poses with the owner.

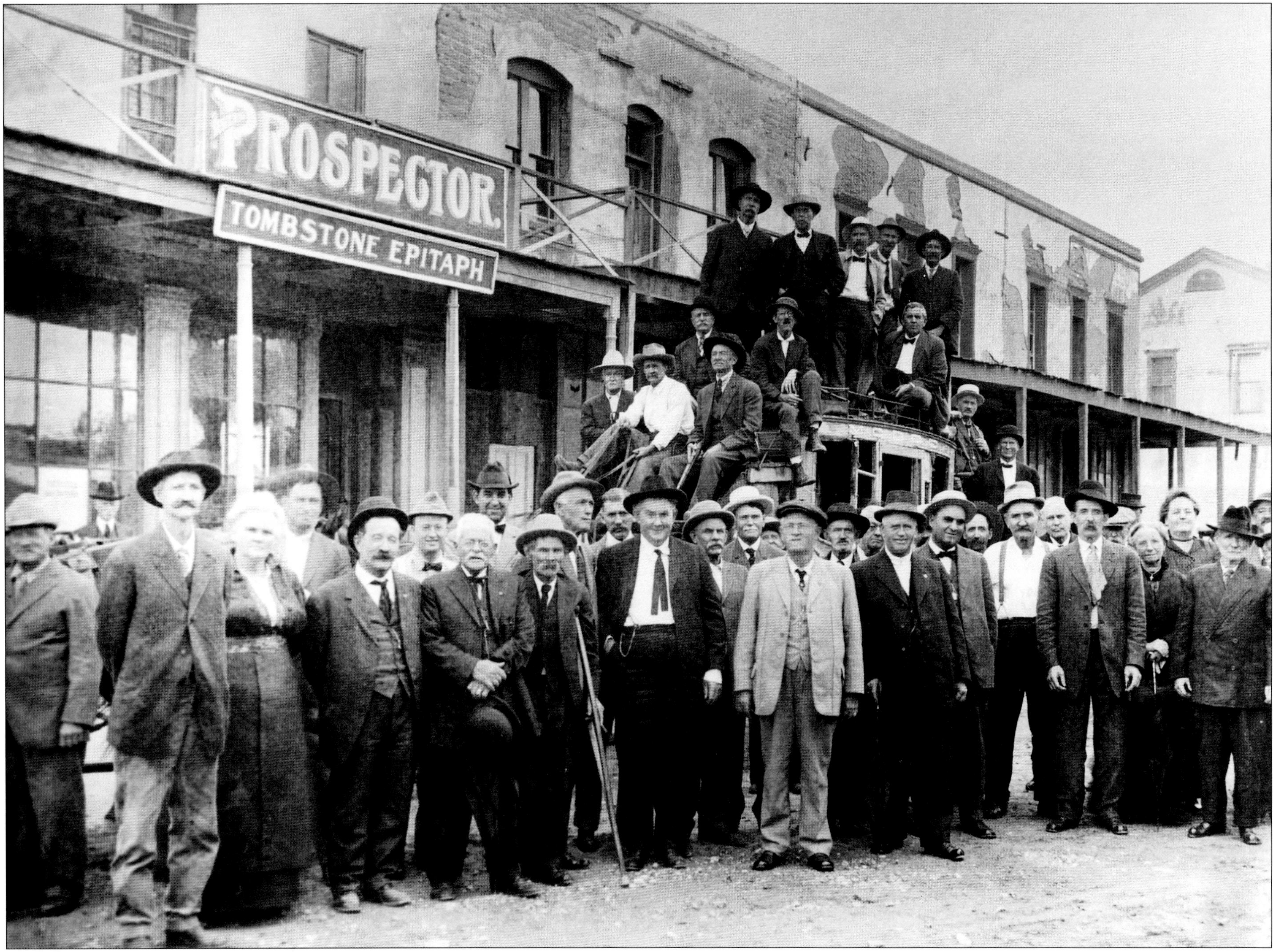

Standing beside the famous "Tombstone Epitaph" newspaper office, the entire town has come out for their portrait in 1912. The old stagecoach is used to good advantage by some folks who stand on its top.

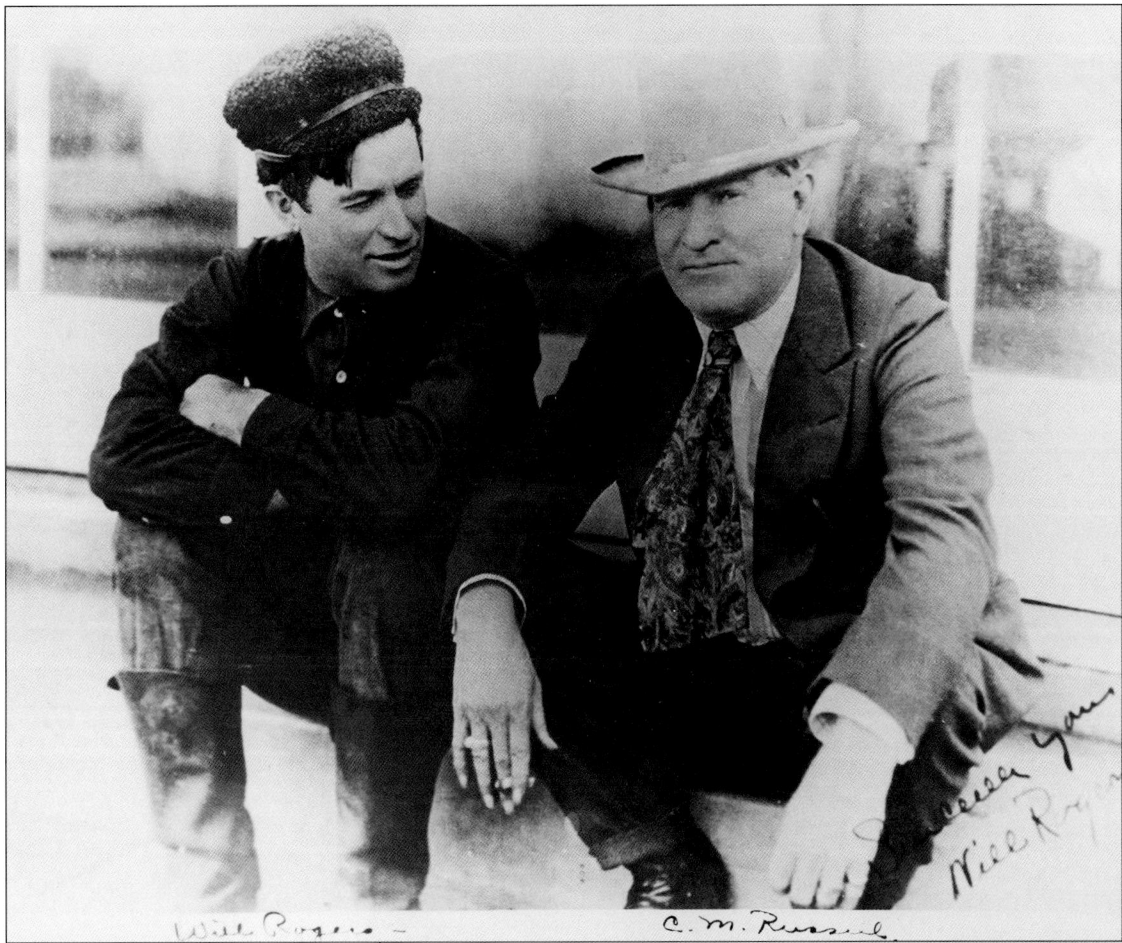

Two great western artists stop talking to have their picture taken. On the left is Will Rogers, a cowboy first, then a political speaker. Next to him is the artist Charles Russell whose work in painting, drawing, and sculpture are in every major museum in the country.

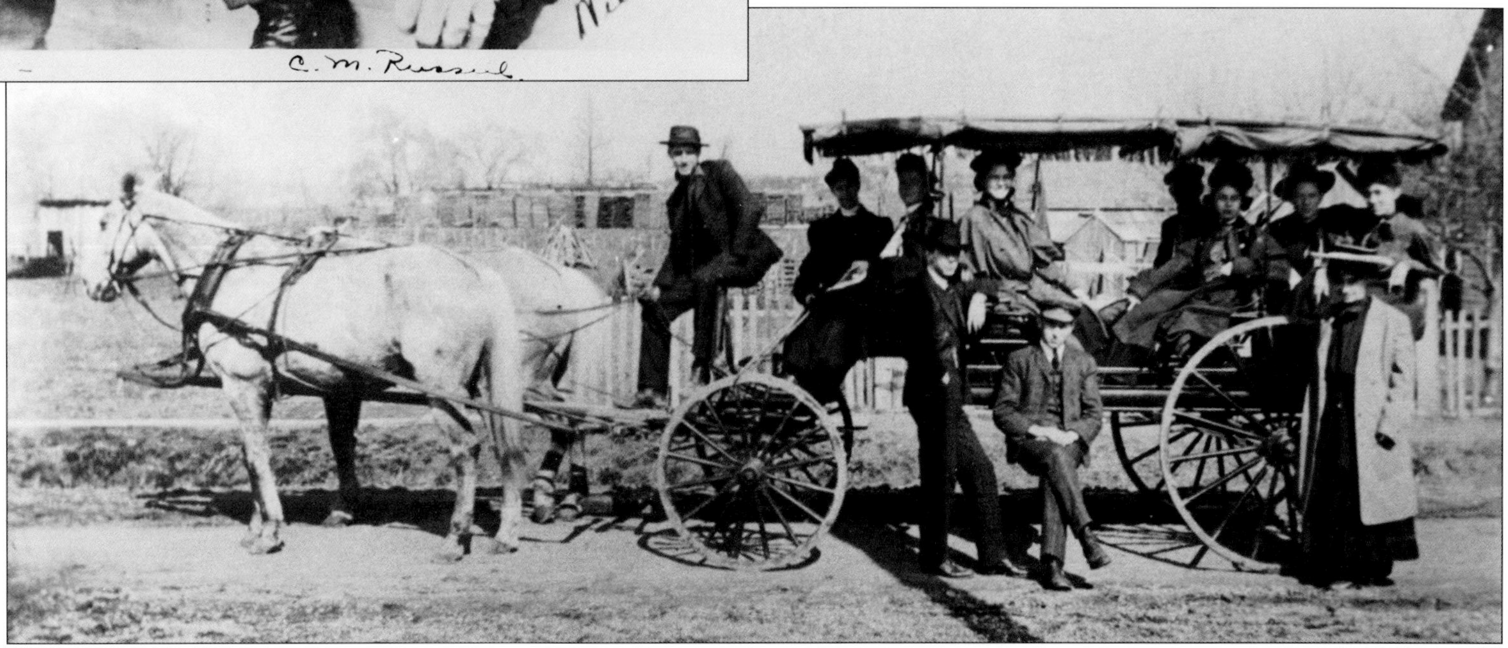

A long surrey with the fringe on top stops for its portrait. This unusually long surrey has the driver seated ahead of the normal coach's drivers seat. On the back of this mounted photo are the names of all the people in the photograph including miss Dorothy Gulch the chaperon. The comment was, "All had a Fine Time."

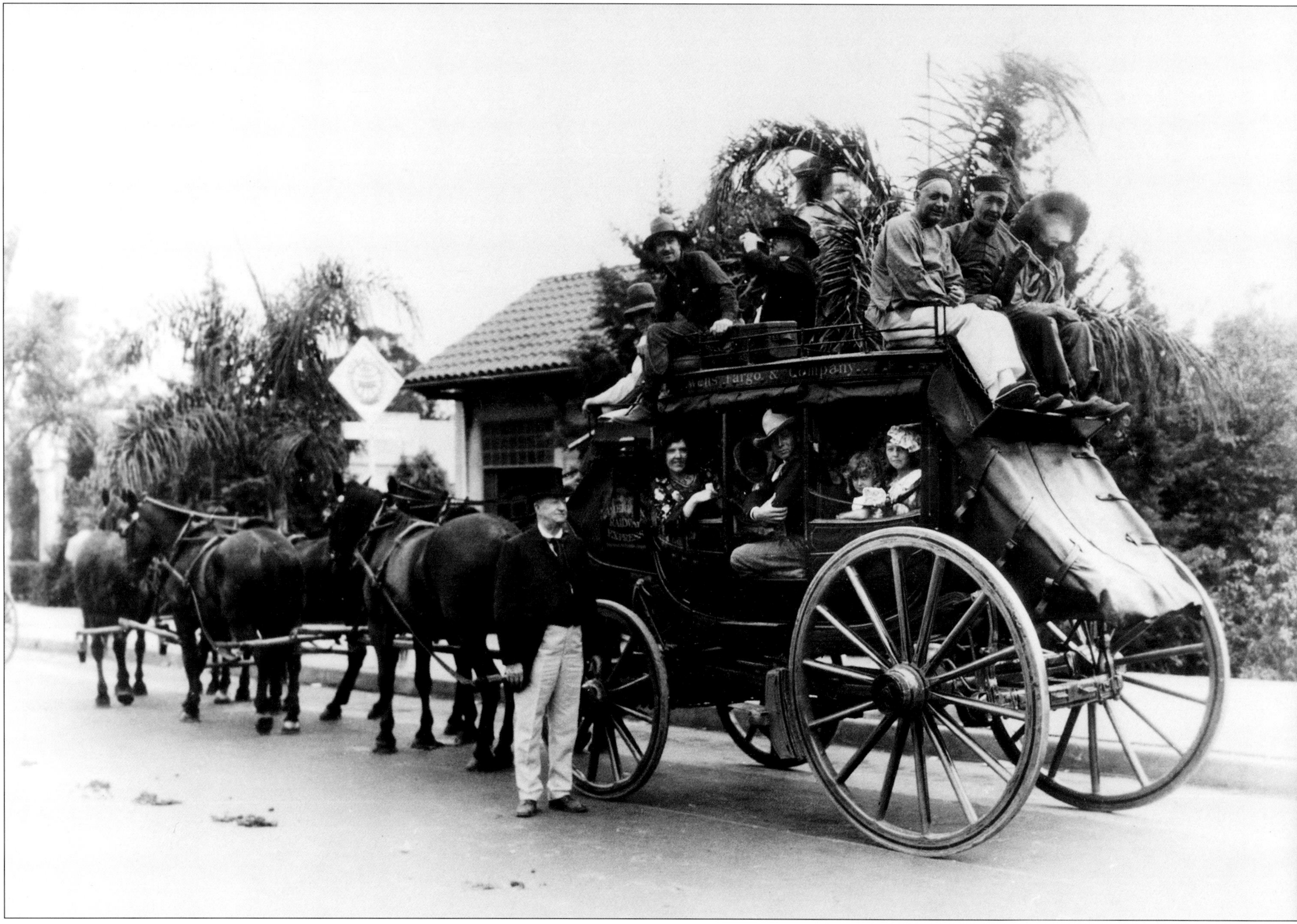

In Ventura County, the Wells Fargo stage stops
for its portrait with a full load of passengers.

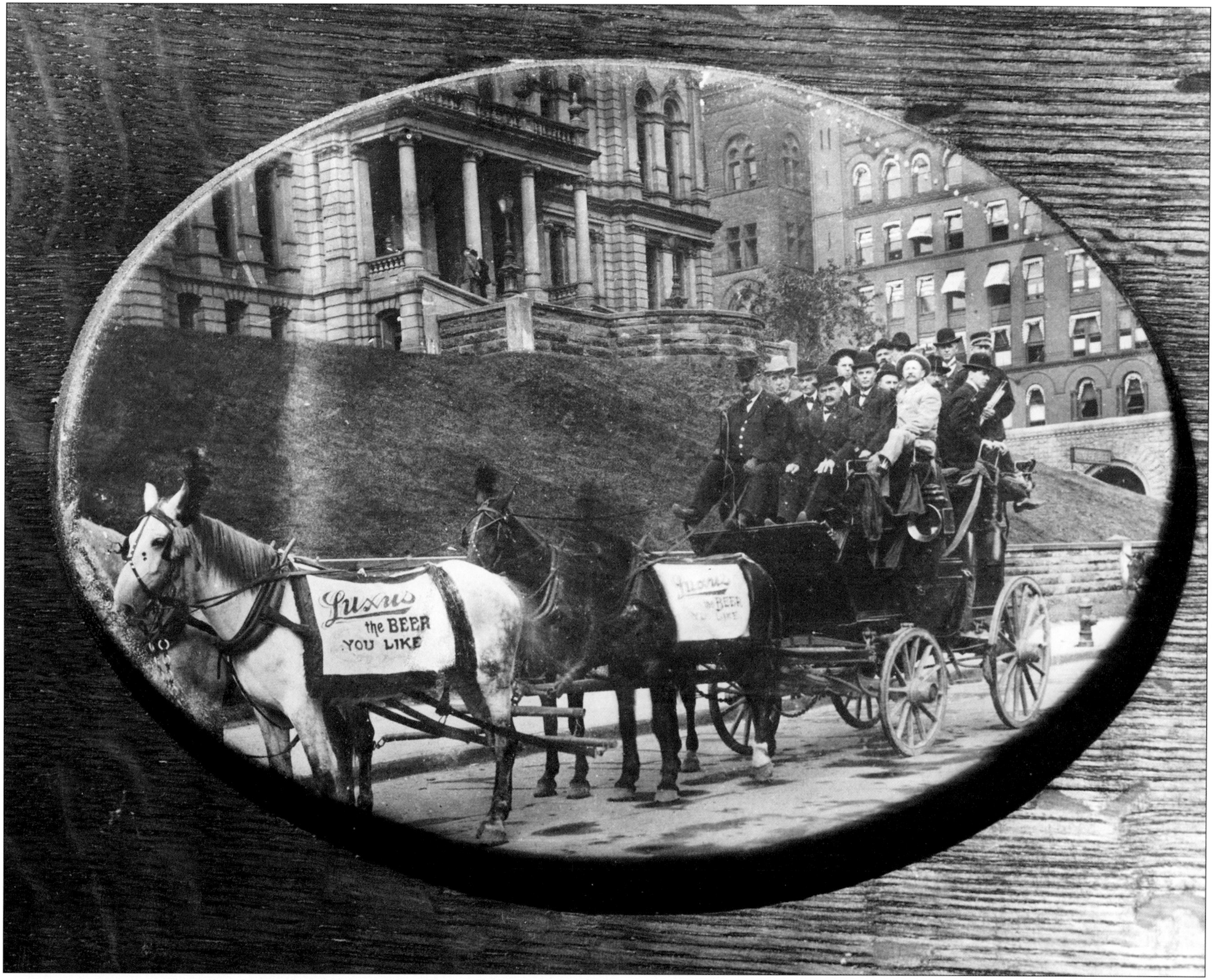

Advertising their Luxus Beer, the company's officers ride a stage around their town.

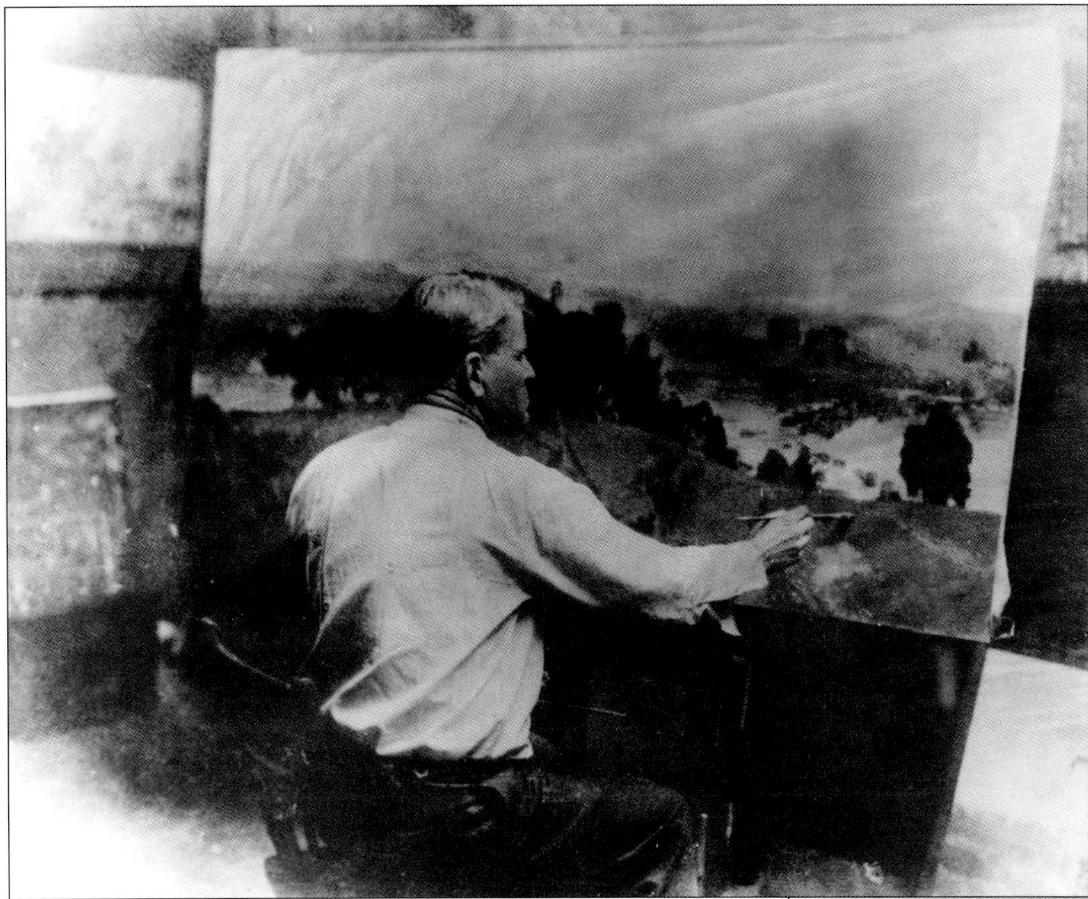

The artist Charles Russell working on a large canvas in his studio.

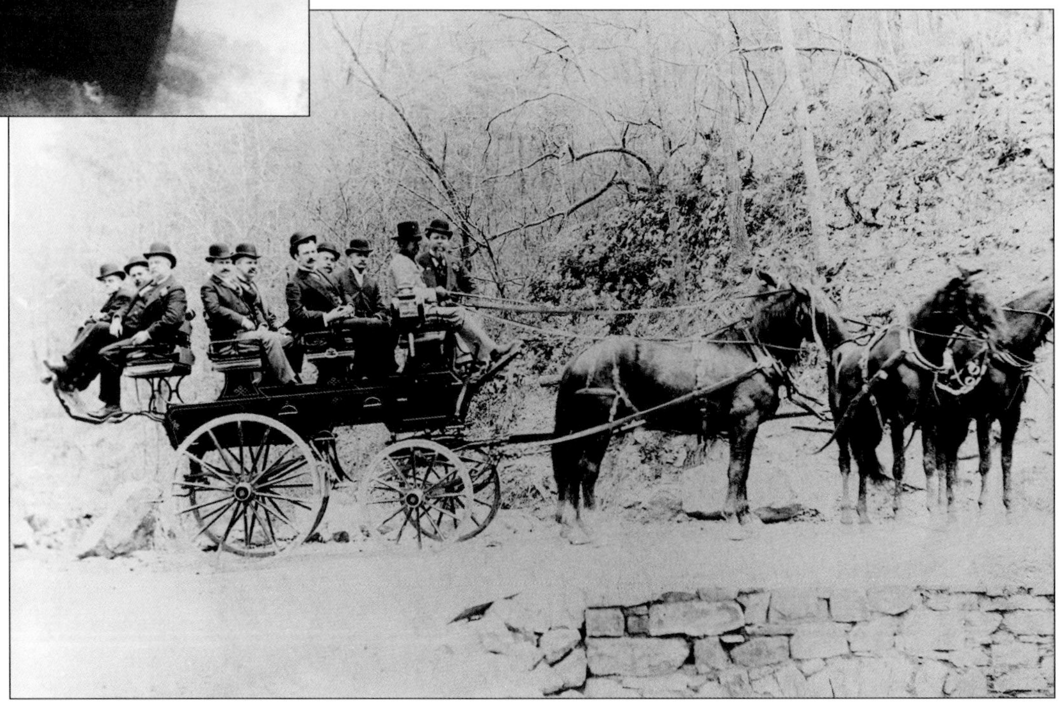

A large group, out for a good time, travels on the Boulder Creek Stage to Redwood Park, California.

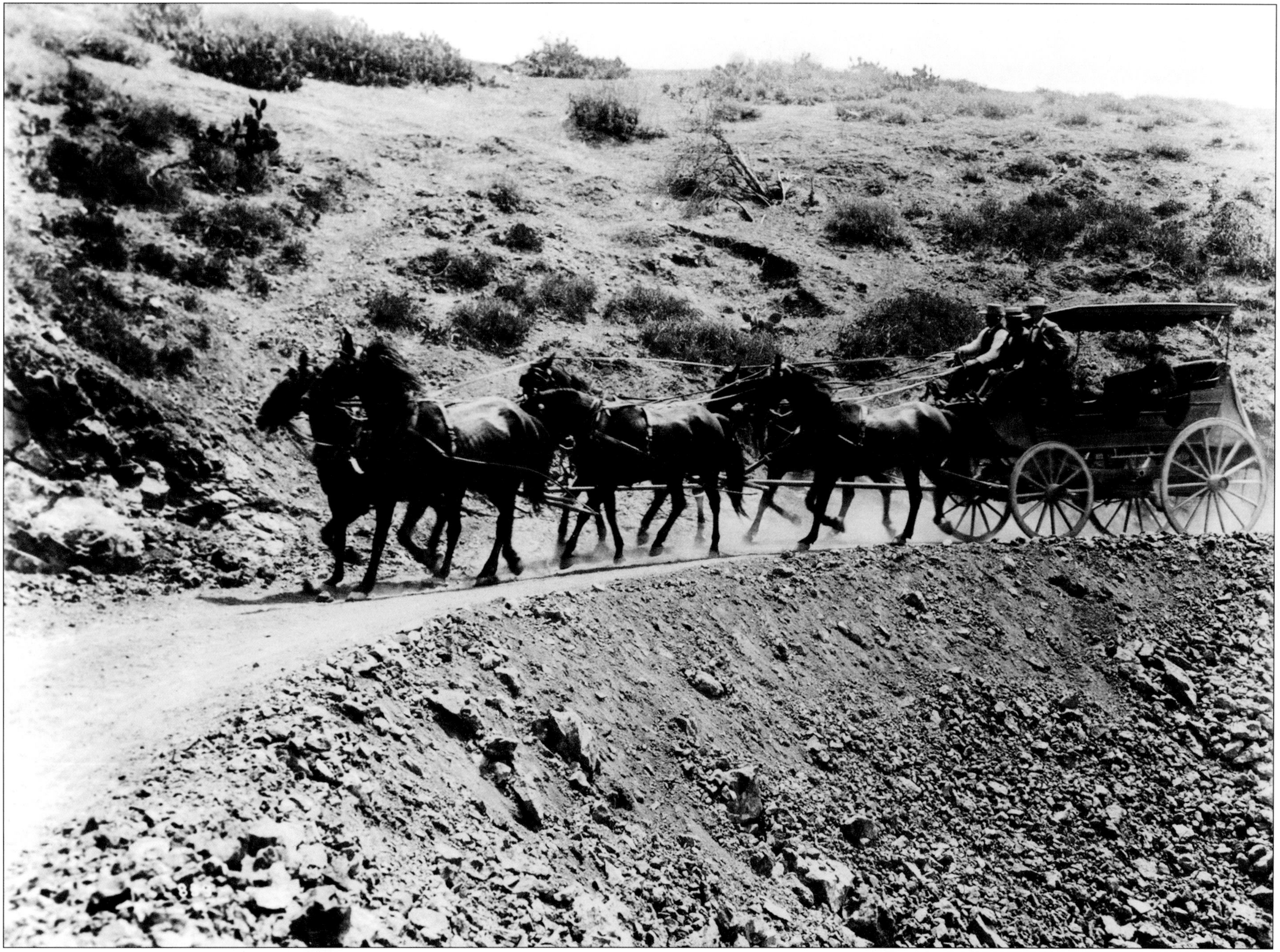

A great action photograph of Captain Banning driving the first stage around Catalina Island in 1887.

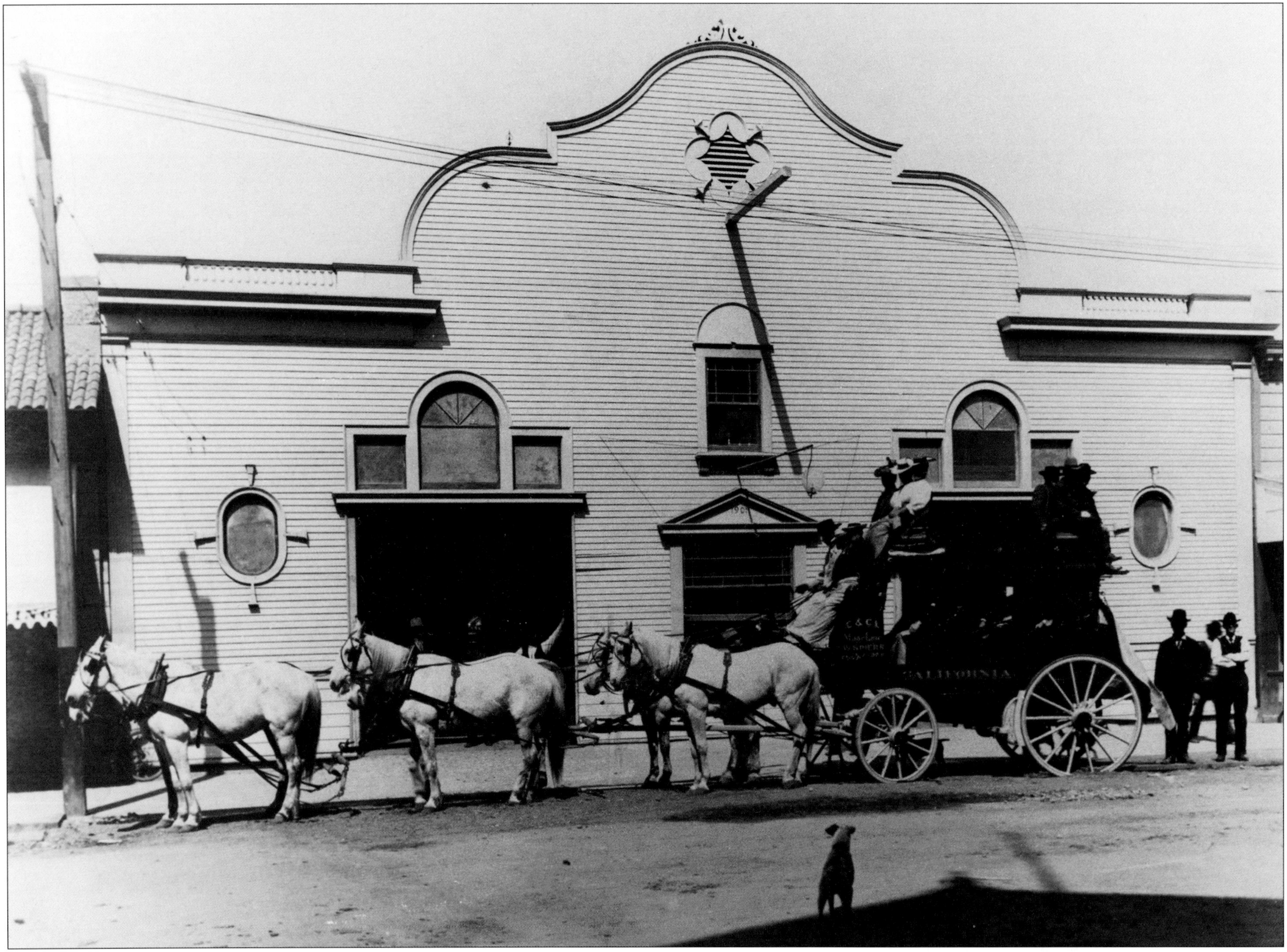

The C&CL Stage Line's six-horse coach is about to leave the depot.

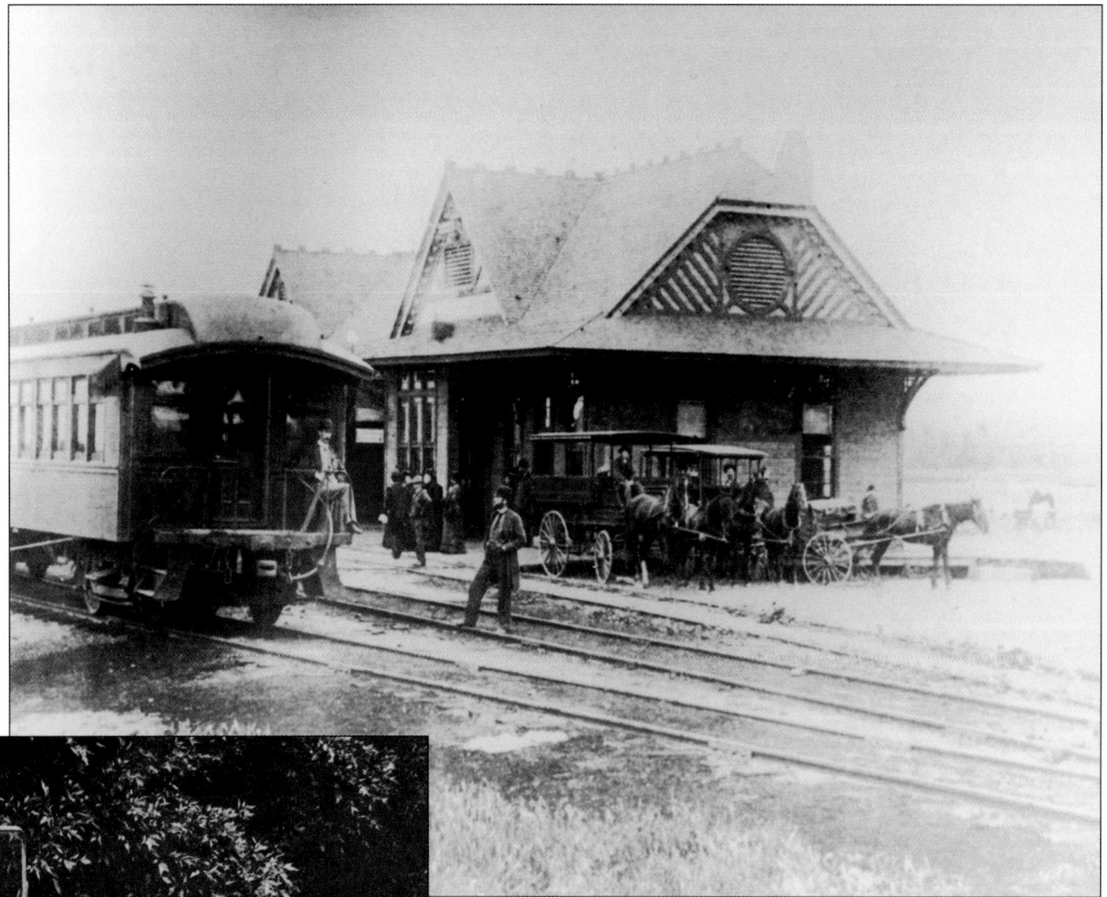

The carriages and stages line up at the Fullerton, California, railroad station.

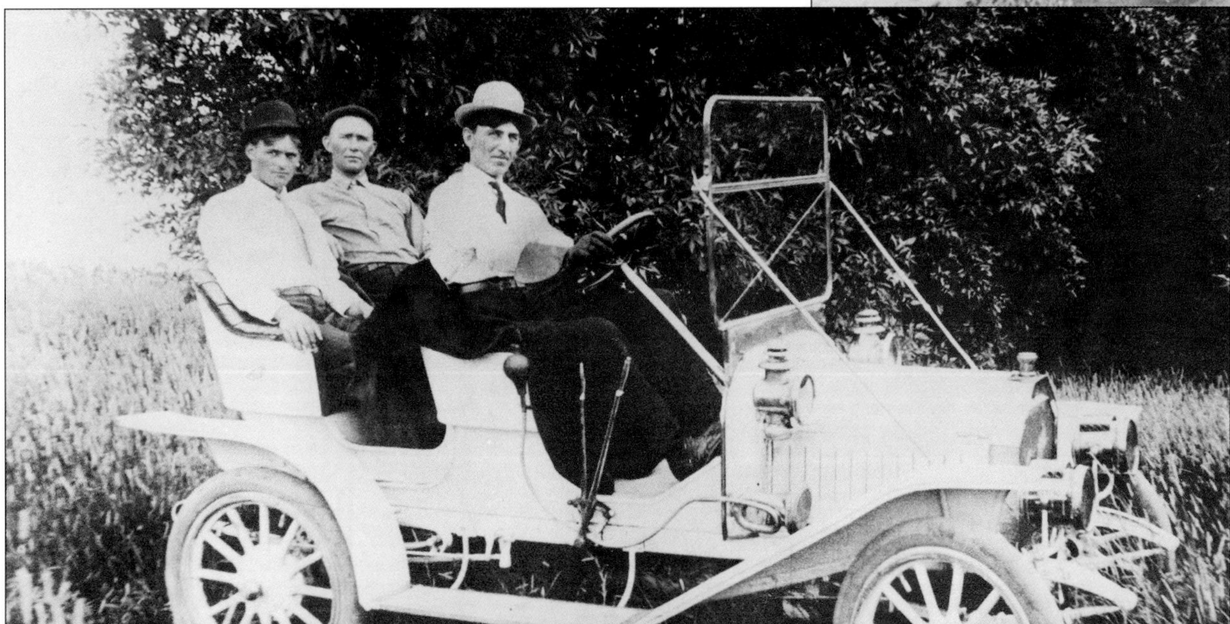

Edward Grafon, known was "the last stage robber," sits at the wheel of his automobile.

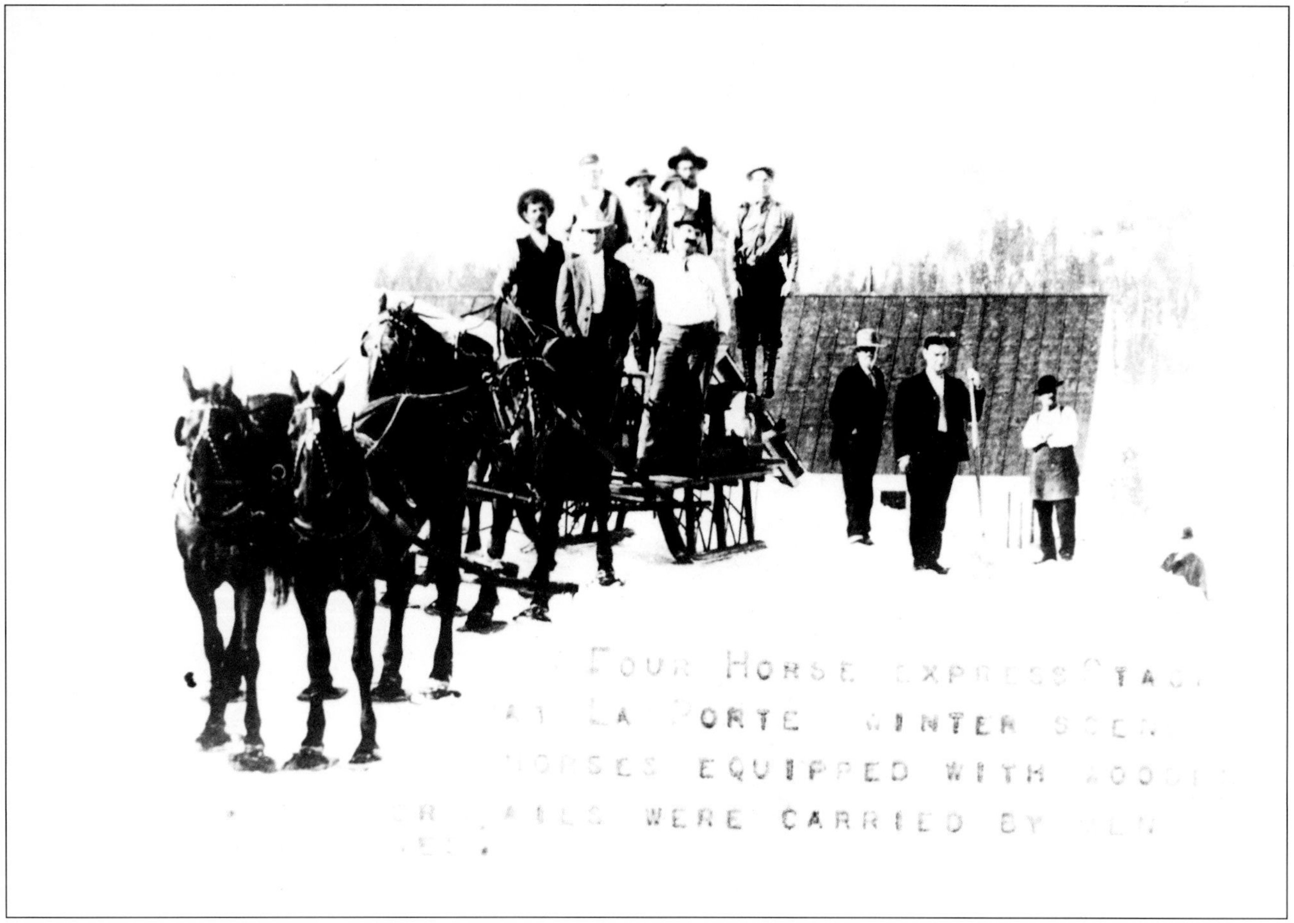

The title of this is "Four Horse Express Stage," at La Porte. The horses are equipped with snow shoes and a long sled offered its passengers transportation.

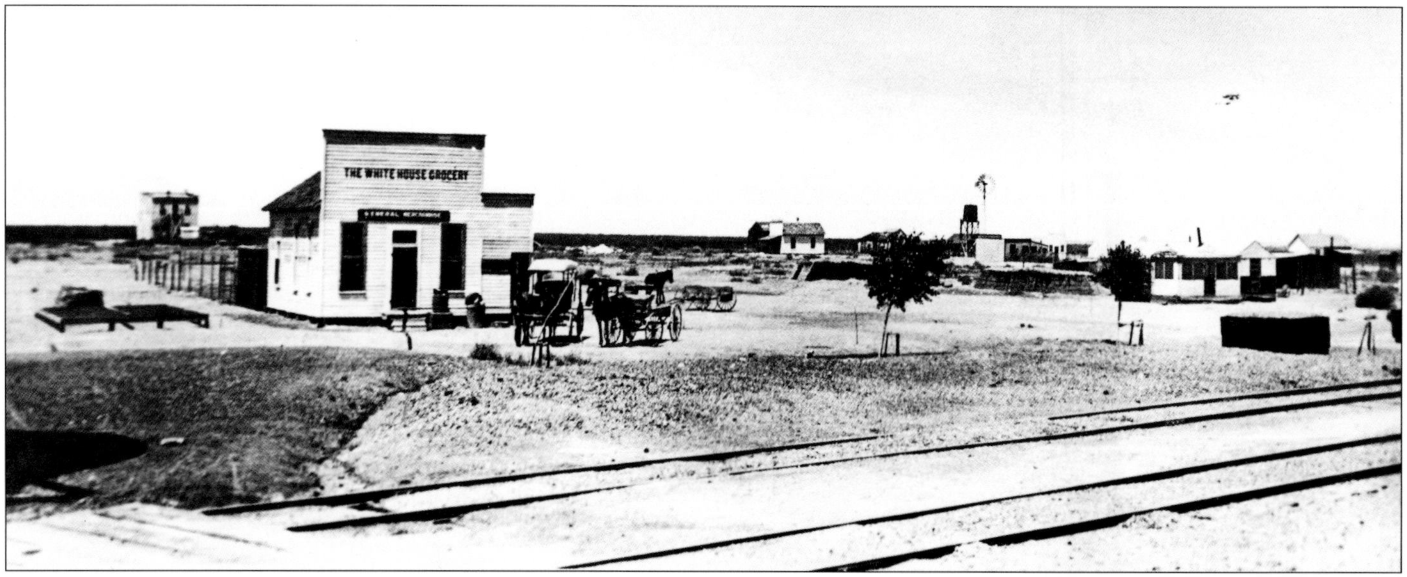

In Columbus, New Mexico, in 1910, a lone store called "The White House Grocery," stands along the railroad tracks. Several customers have left their carriages to shop inside.

Chapter 7

Wild West Shows, Parades, & Tourism

The Hiscock Photography Company recorded Buffalo Bill Cody's Wyoming Wild West. In this photo Cody is greeting tourists who have taken the stage to his "Town."

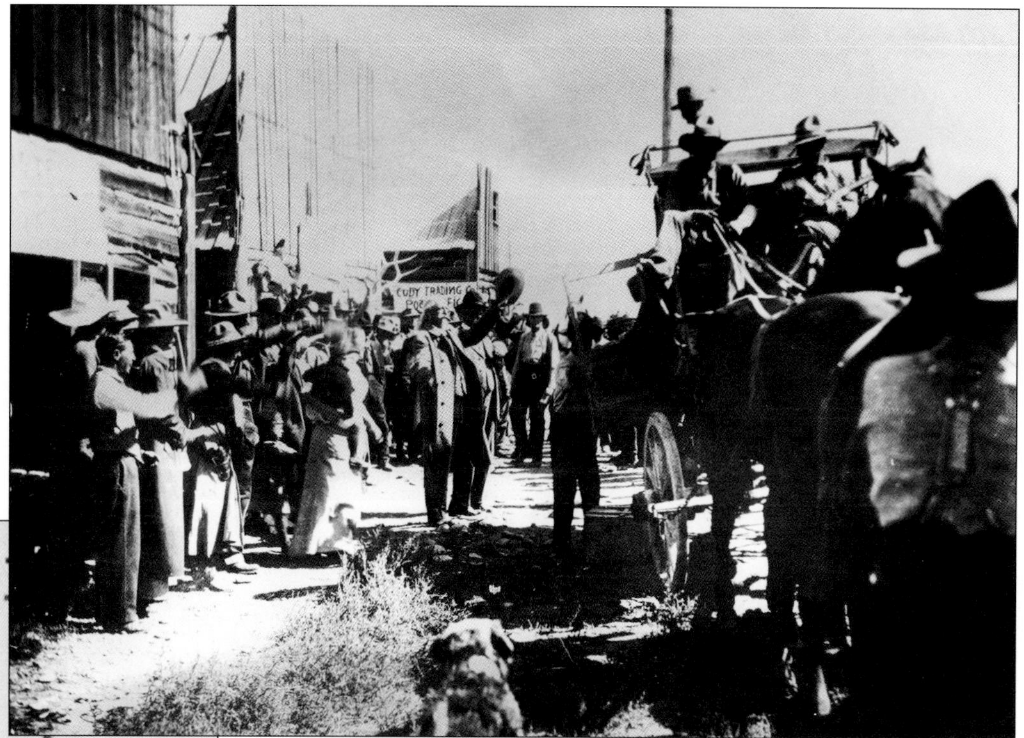

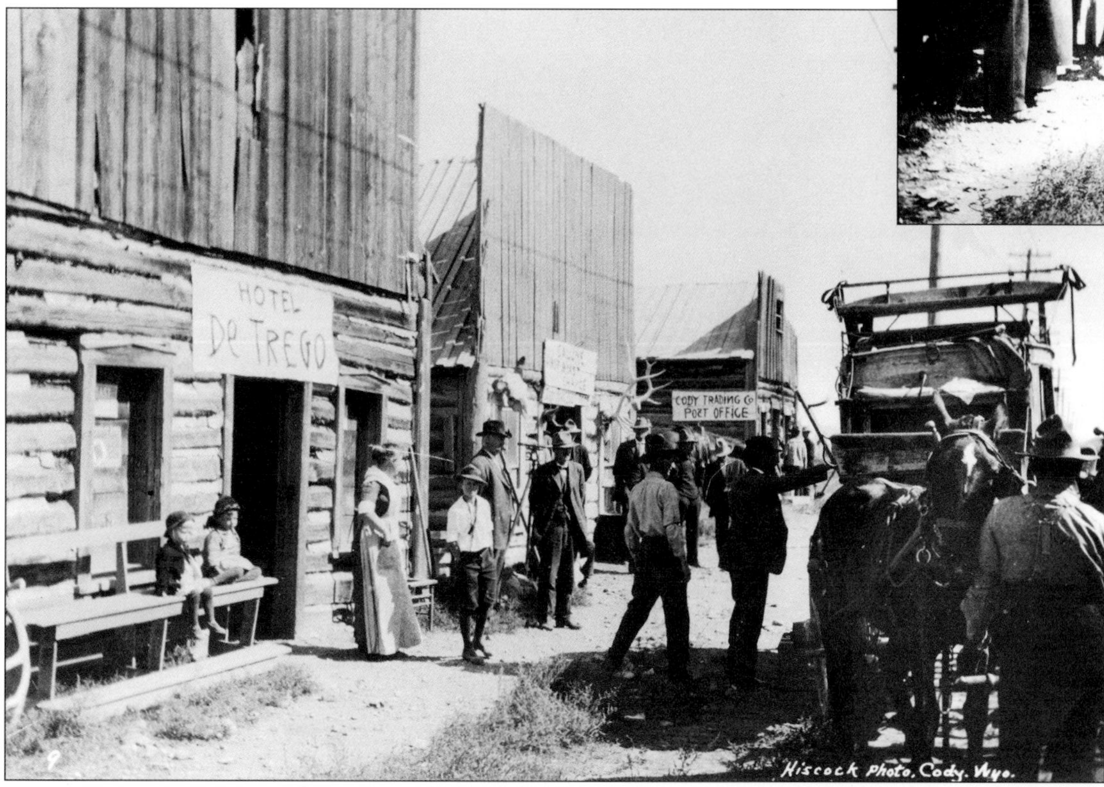

A photo of the Buffalo Bill Wild West Town where passengers are stopping at the "Hotel De Trego." Photo by Hiscock.

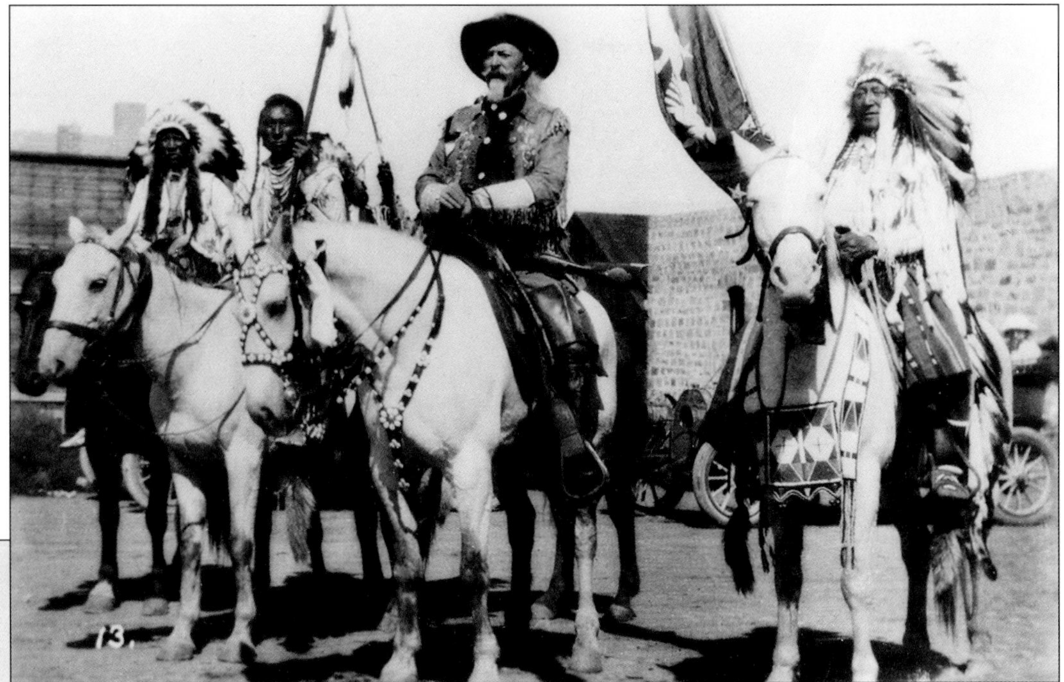

Buffalo Bill is surrounded by the Indians in one of his Wild West shows.

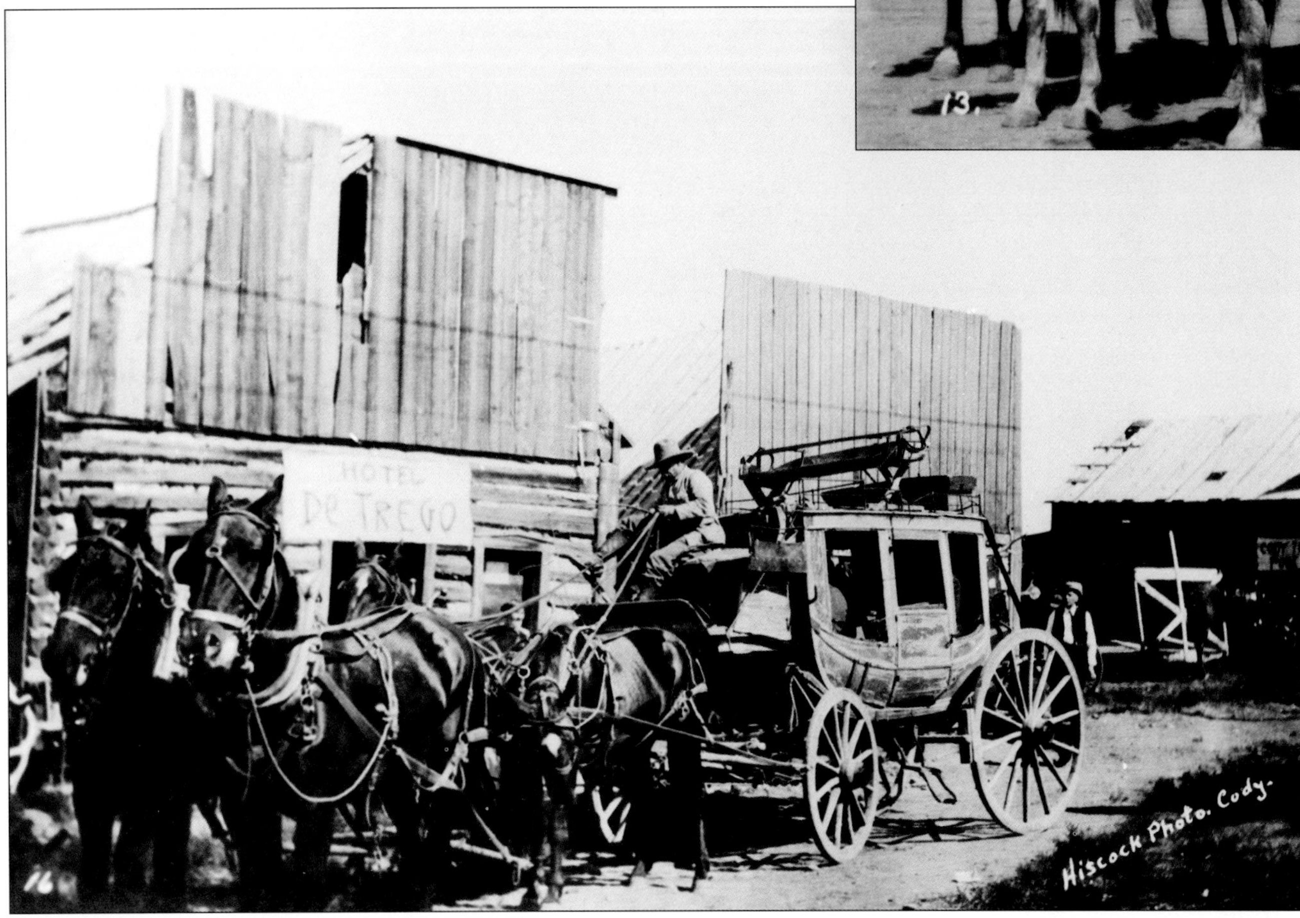

The Buffalo Bill Wild West Town's stagecoach has pulled up to the hotel to pick up passengers.

A stage is on the run in one of the Cody's Wild West roundup rodeos.

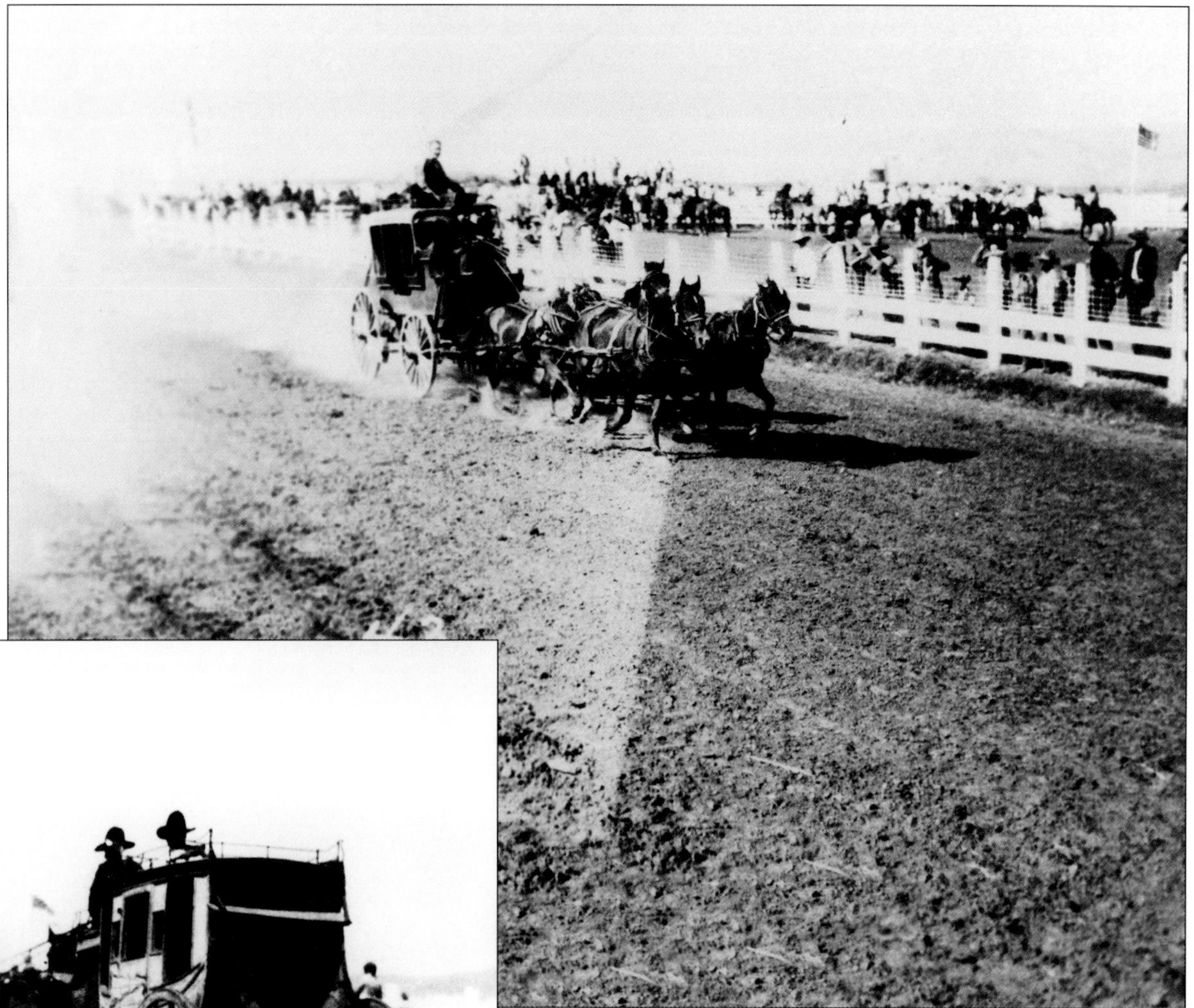

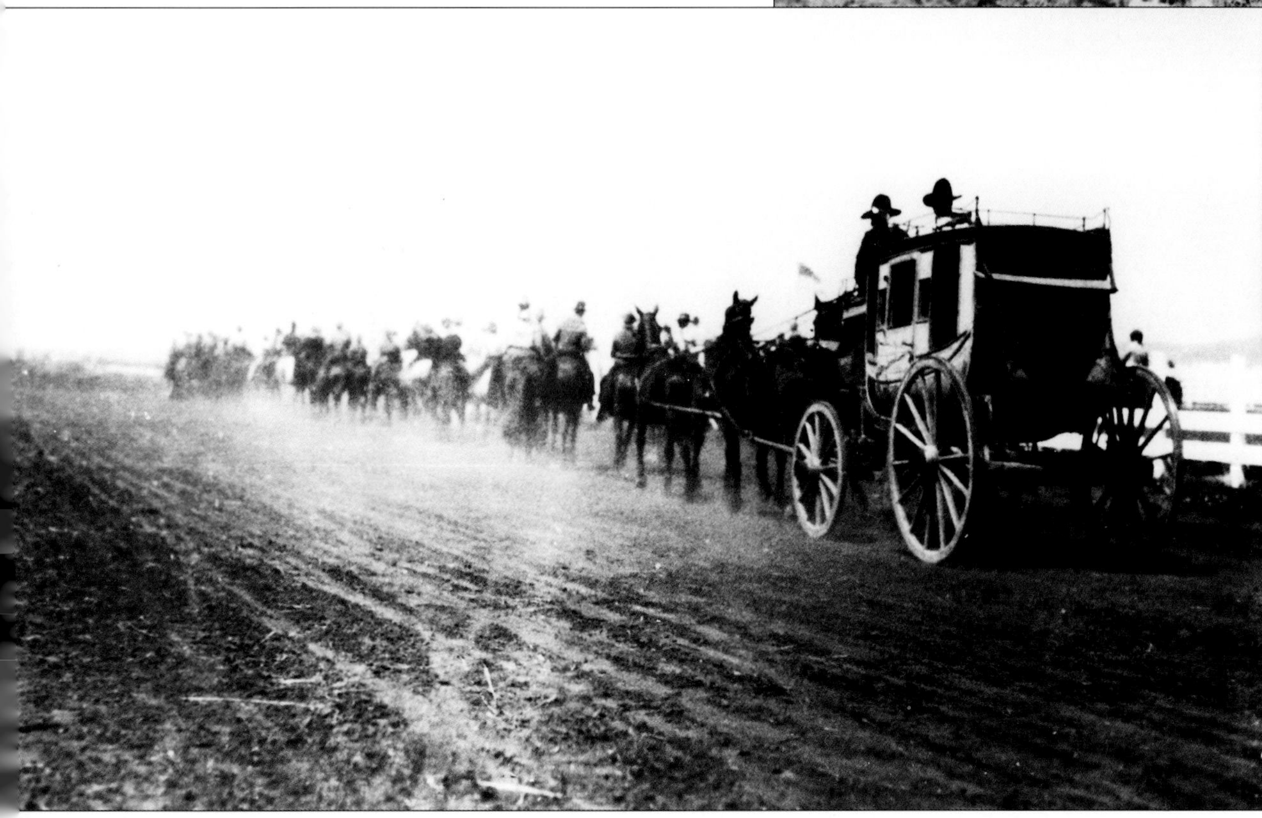

On parade in a roundup during a Wild West rodeo, a stagecoach follows a line of cowboys.

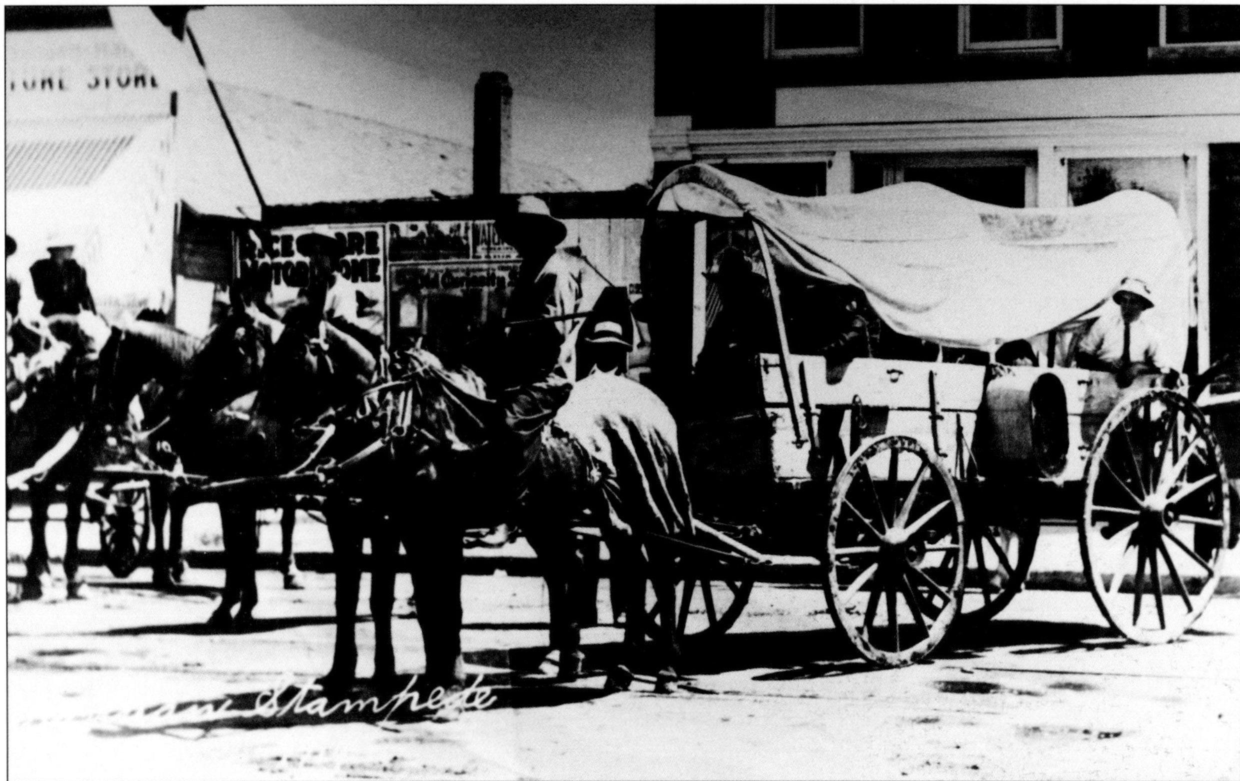

A covered wagon getting ready to participate in one of Oregon's Stampede rodeo's.

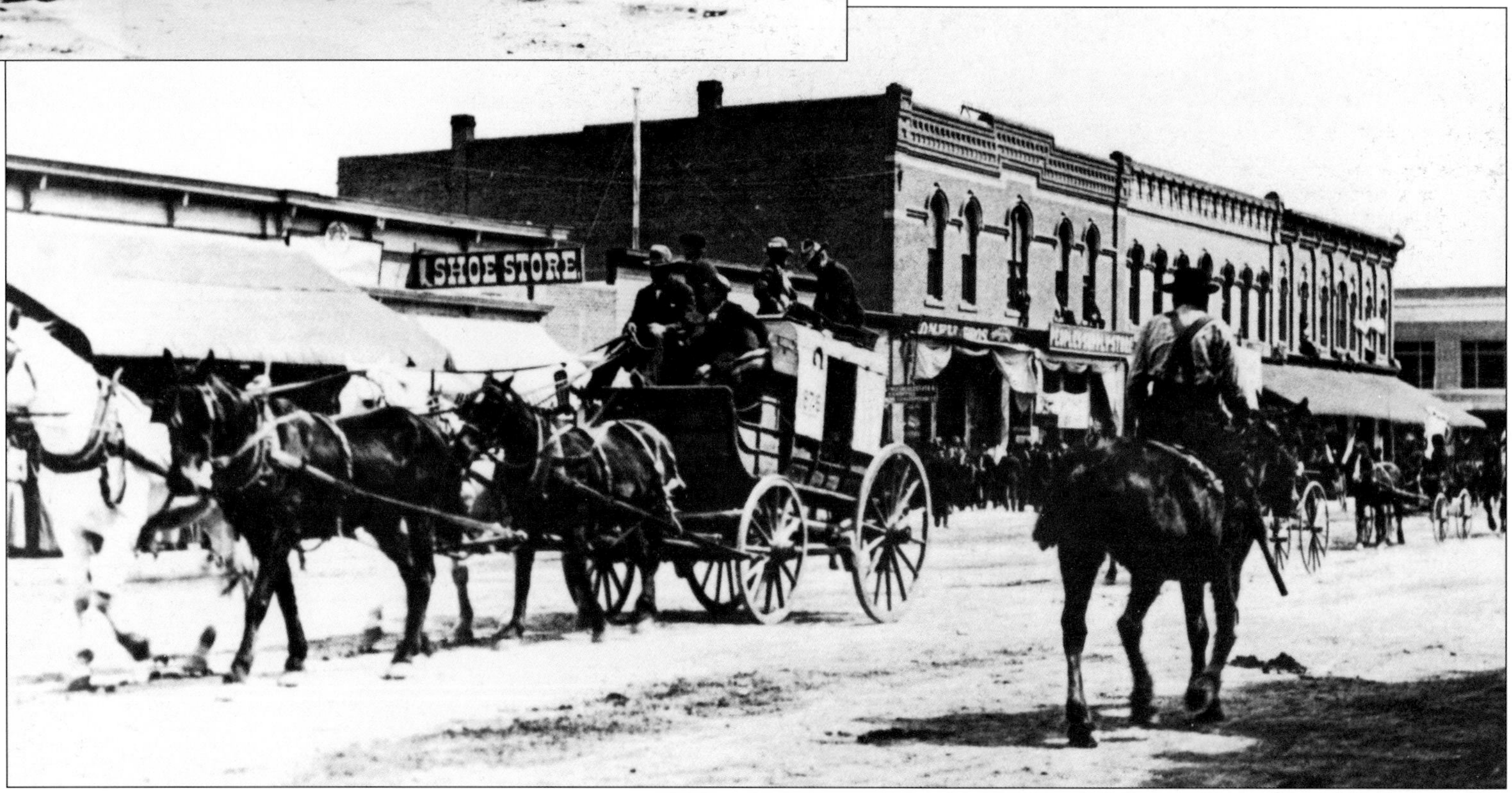

A parade during Stampede Days in Oregon.

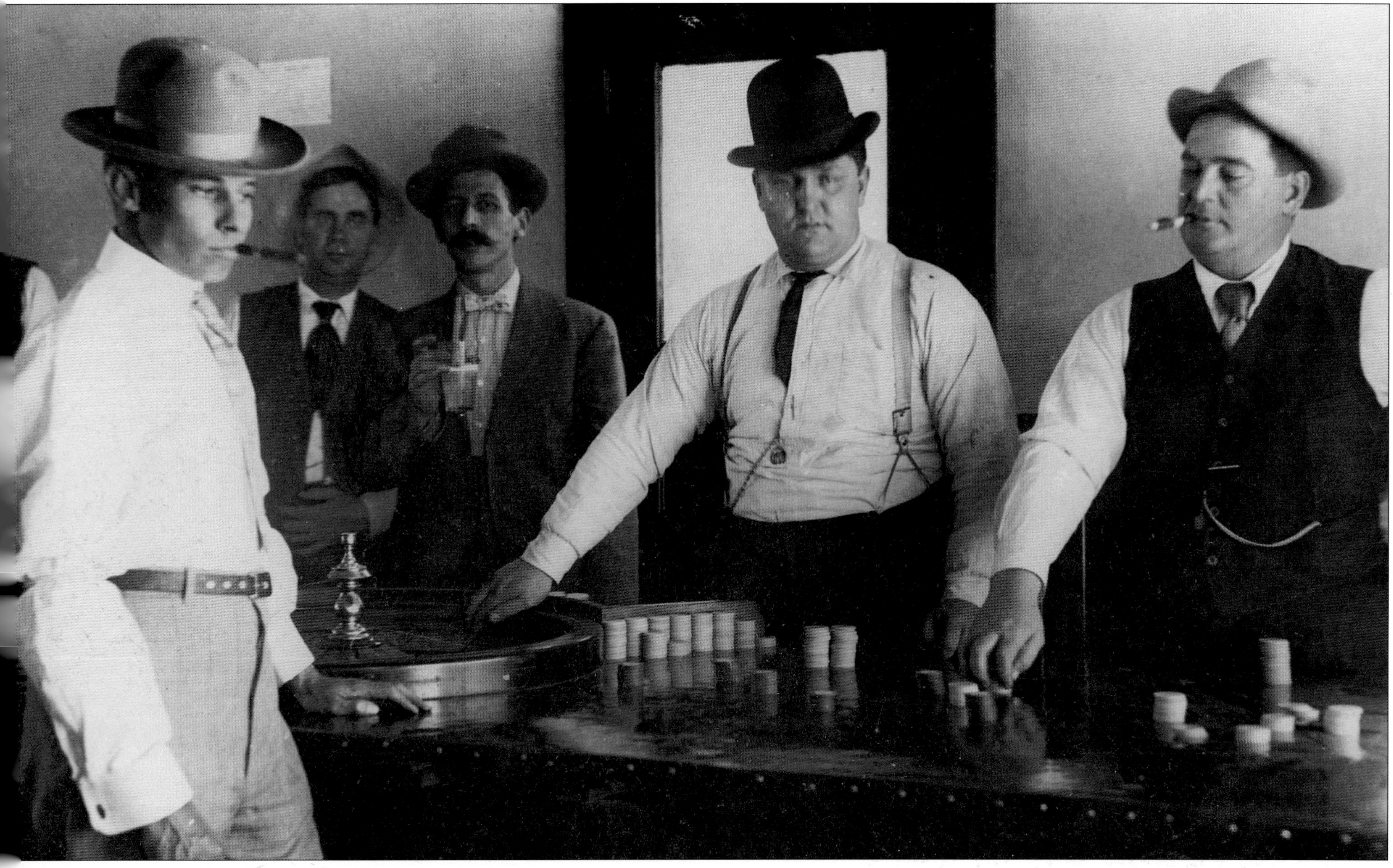

In 1905, these tough looking men ran the tables in Rawhide, Nevada.

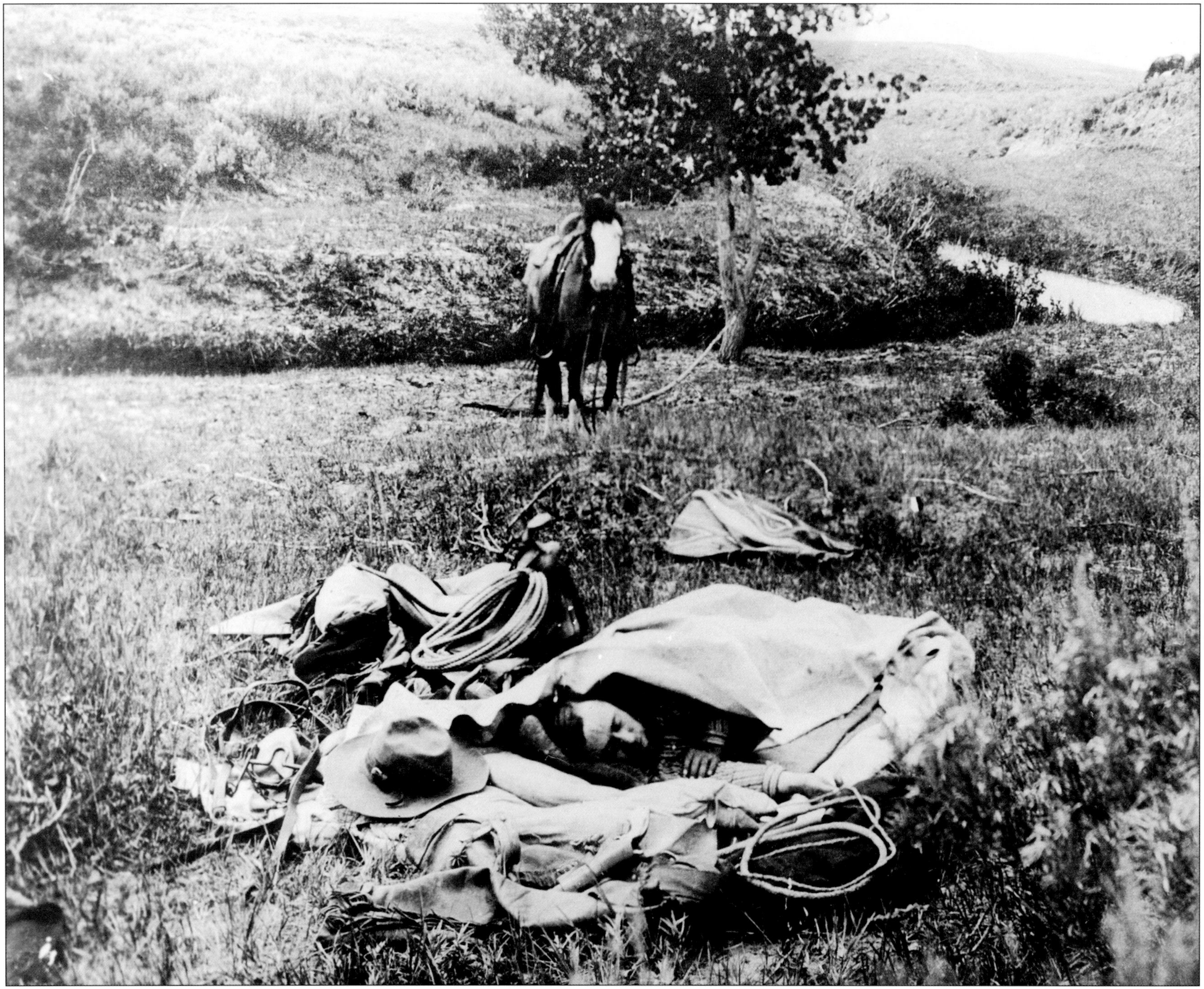

Out on the range, a cowboy would sleep in a rolled up blanket, after tying up his horse to a nearby tree.

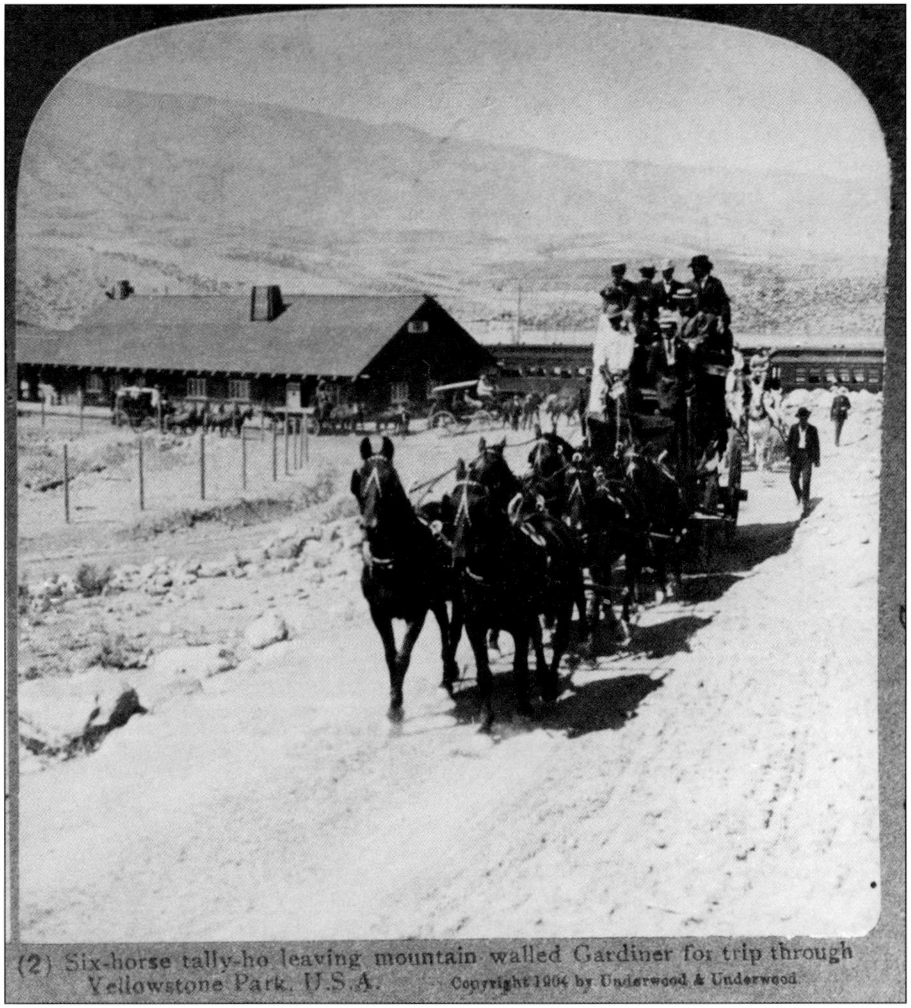

From a stereo card photograph taken at Gardiner, the stagecoach leaves for a trip through Yellowstone Park.

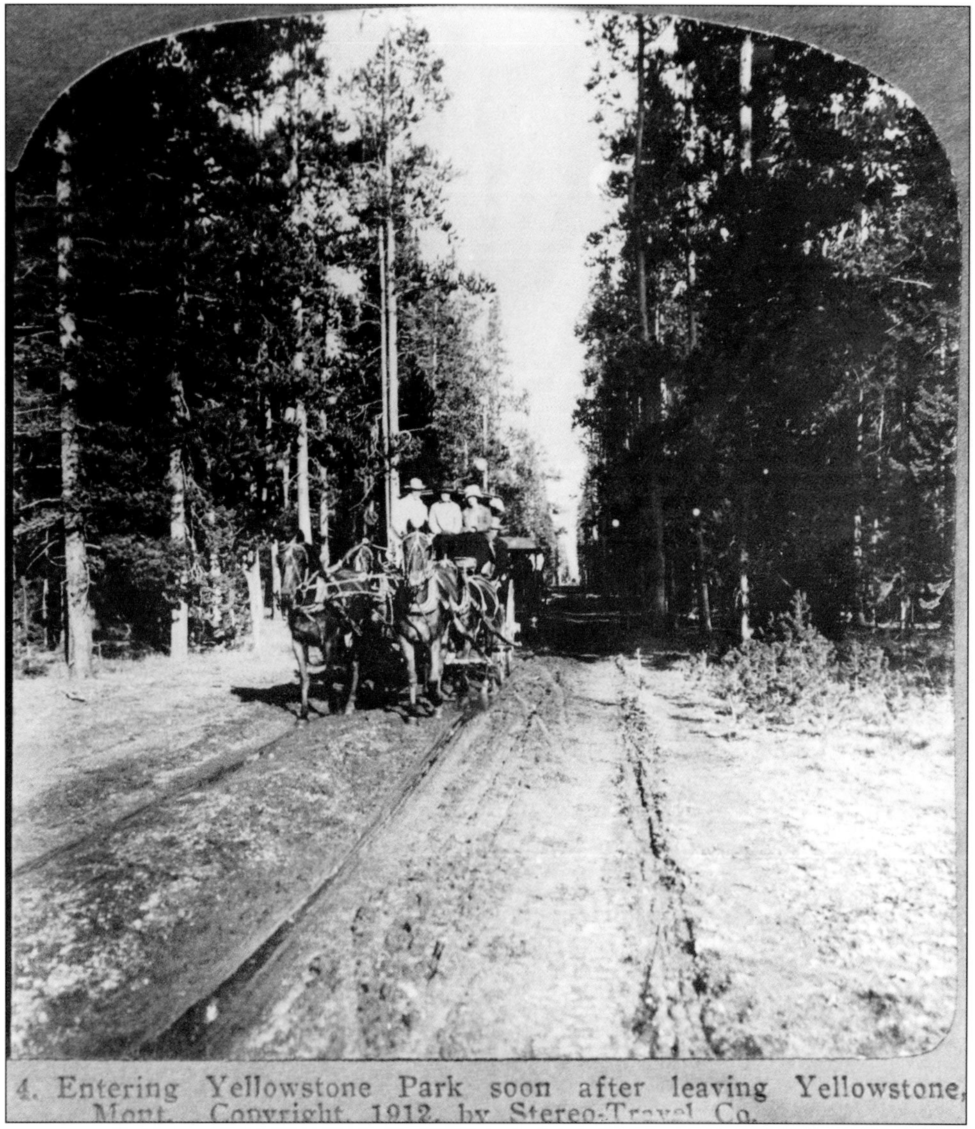

This is a stage entering Yellowstone Park, Montana. The photo is from a stereo photo card.

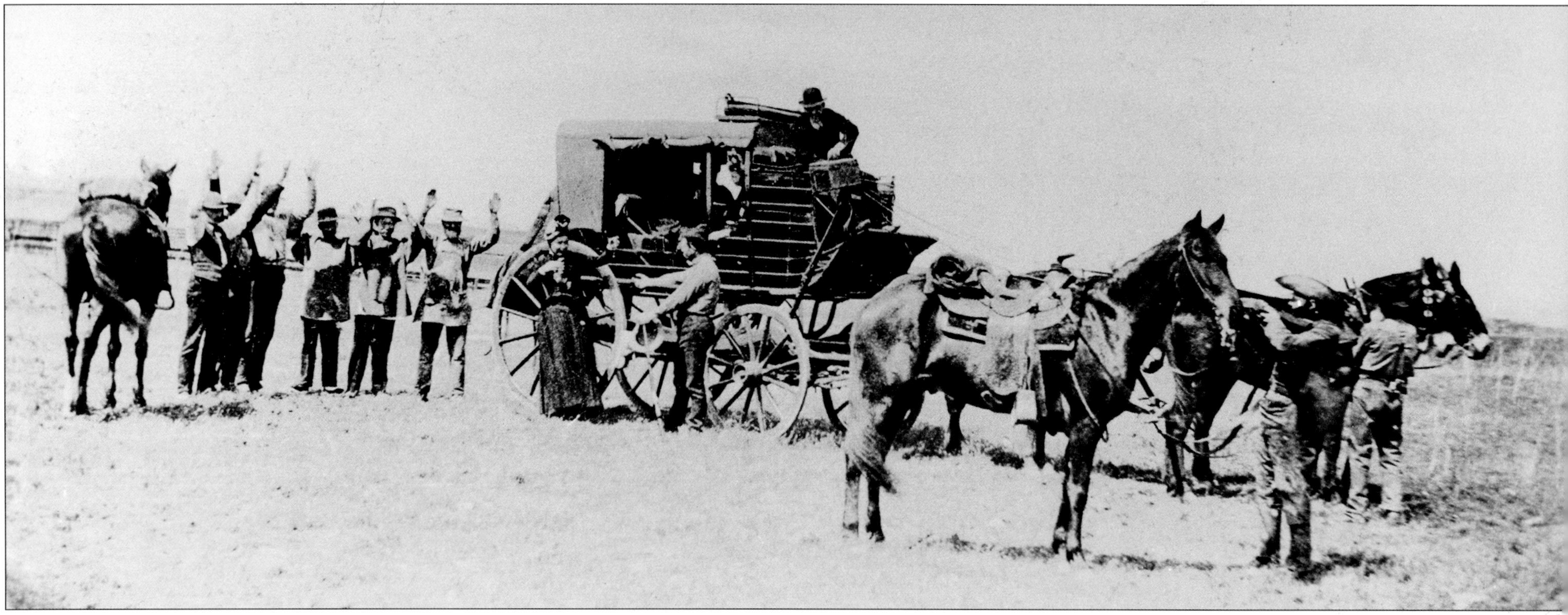

A staged hold up showing robbers with their guns drawn and passengers with raised hands up.

On the road to Silver Springs, Colorado, a group of Westerners show how they fought off the Indians many years ago.

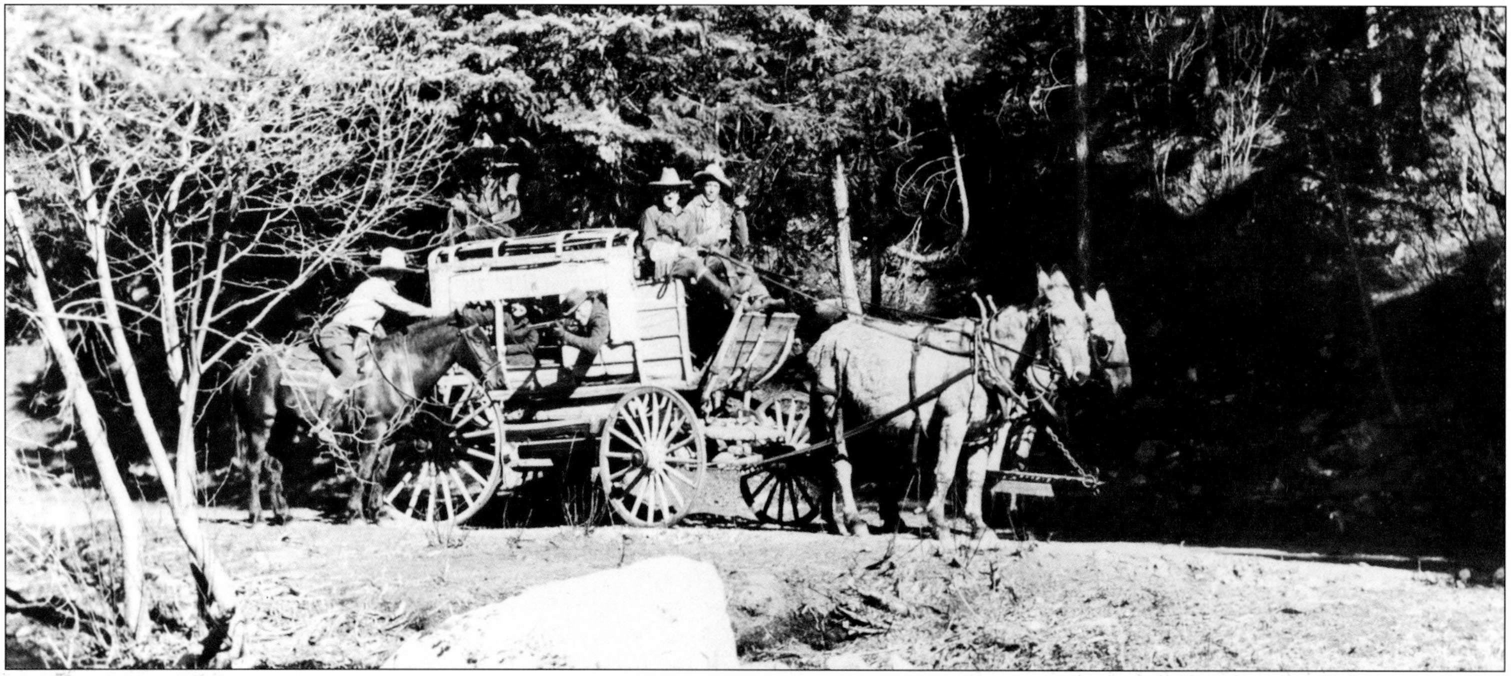

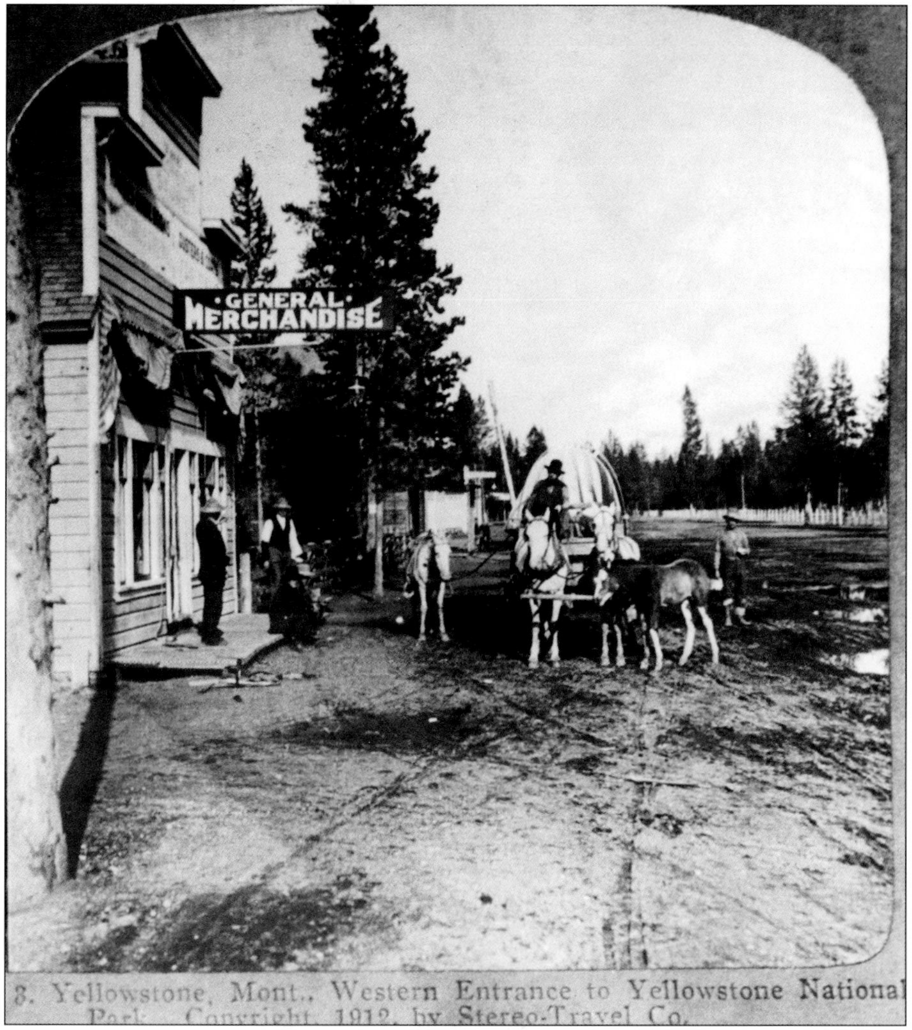

A stereo photo card showing the western entrance to Yellowstone Park. A supply wagon stops and the driver has some words with the store owners.

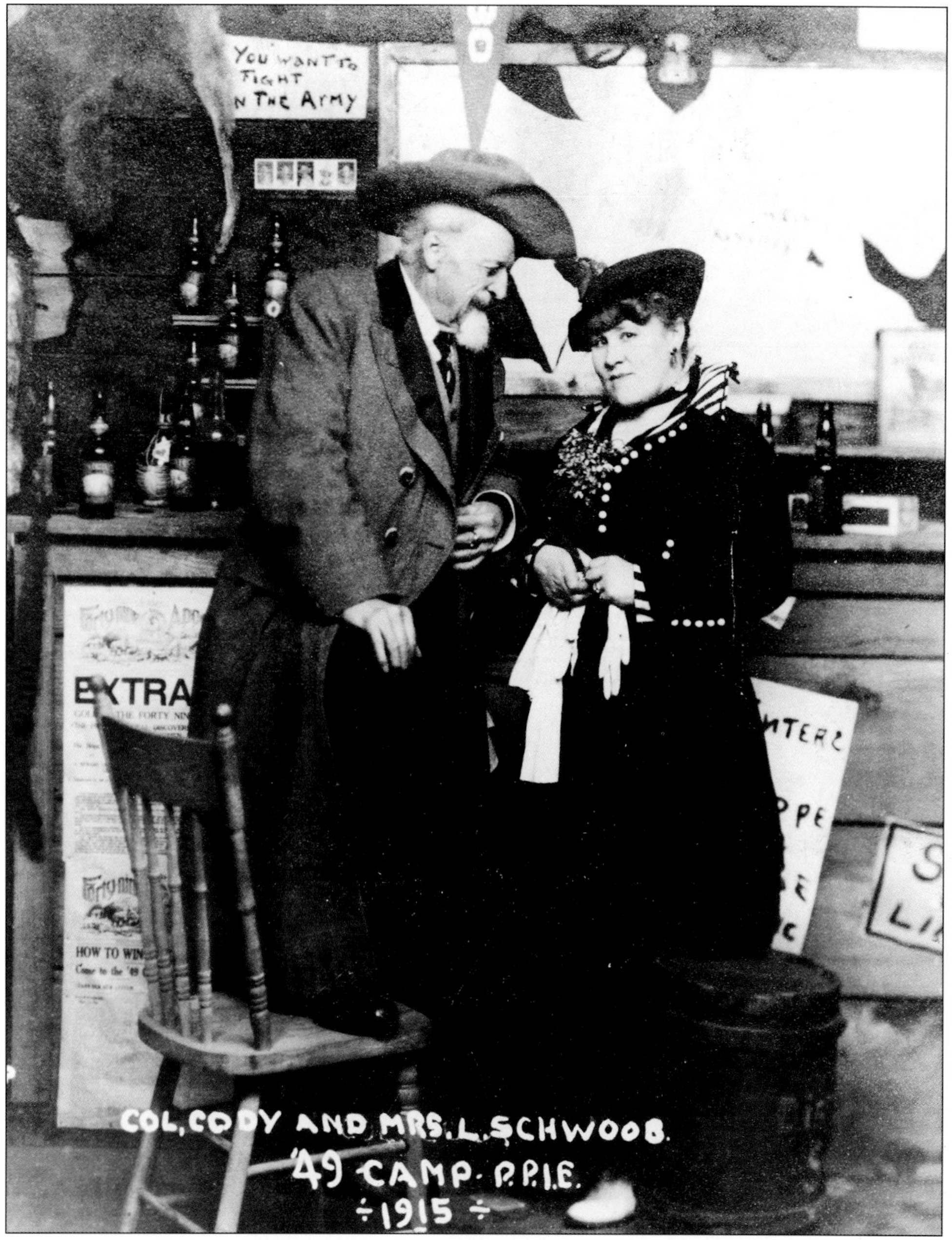

At the San Francisco World's Fair, Buffalo Bill Cody speaks to a Mrs. Schoob. This mock up of a saloon was a set for Cody to meet and talk to people about the wild west.

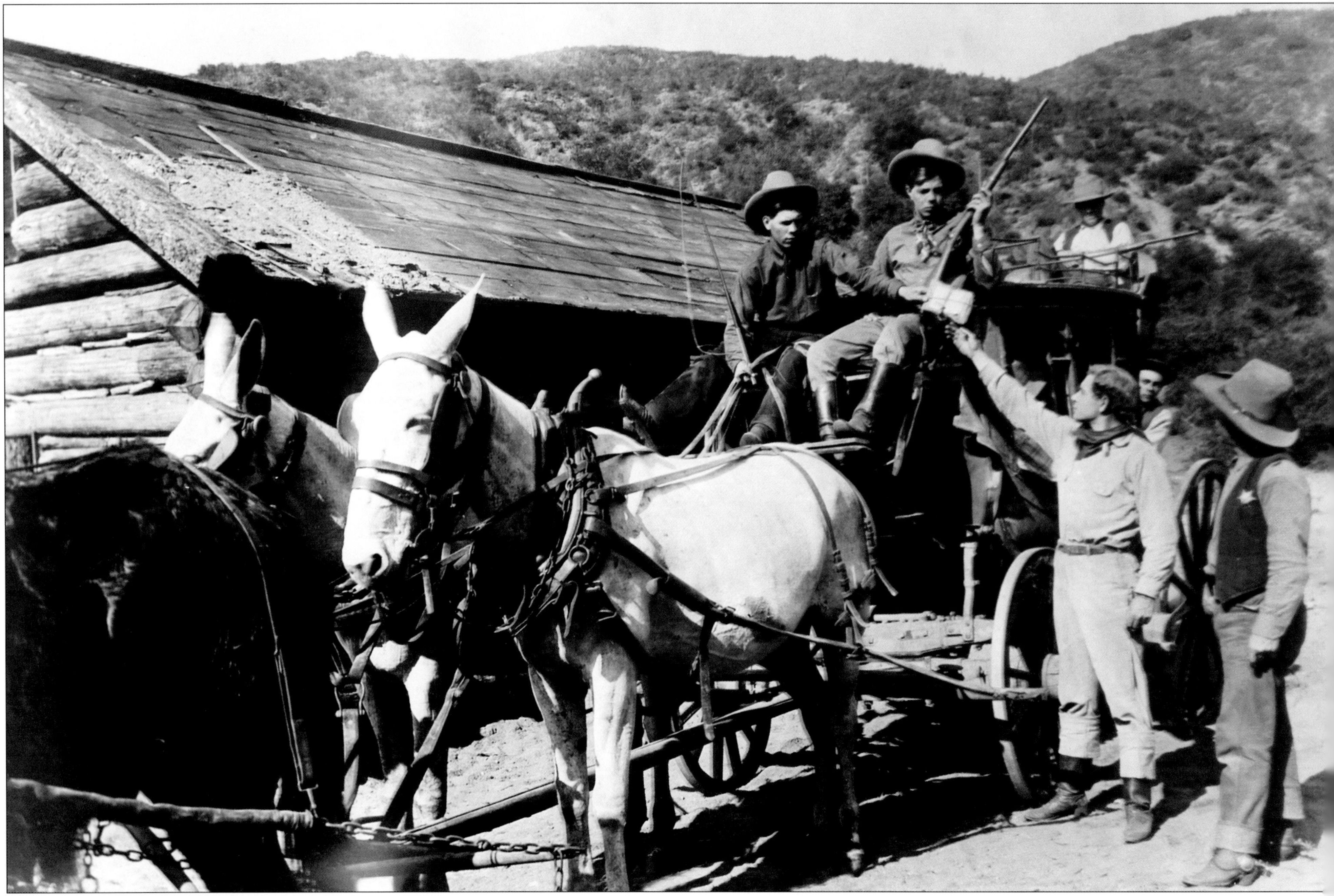

Made from a glass plate negative, this photo of an early western silent movie featured Hoot Gibson as the man riding shot gun on the out bound mail stage.

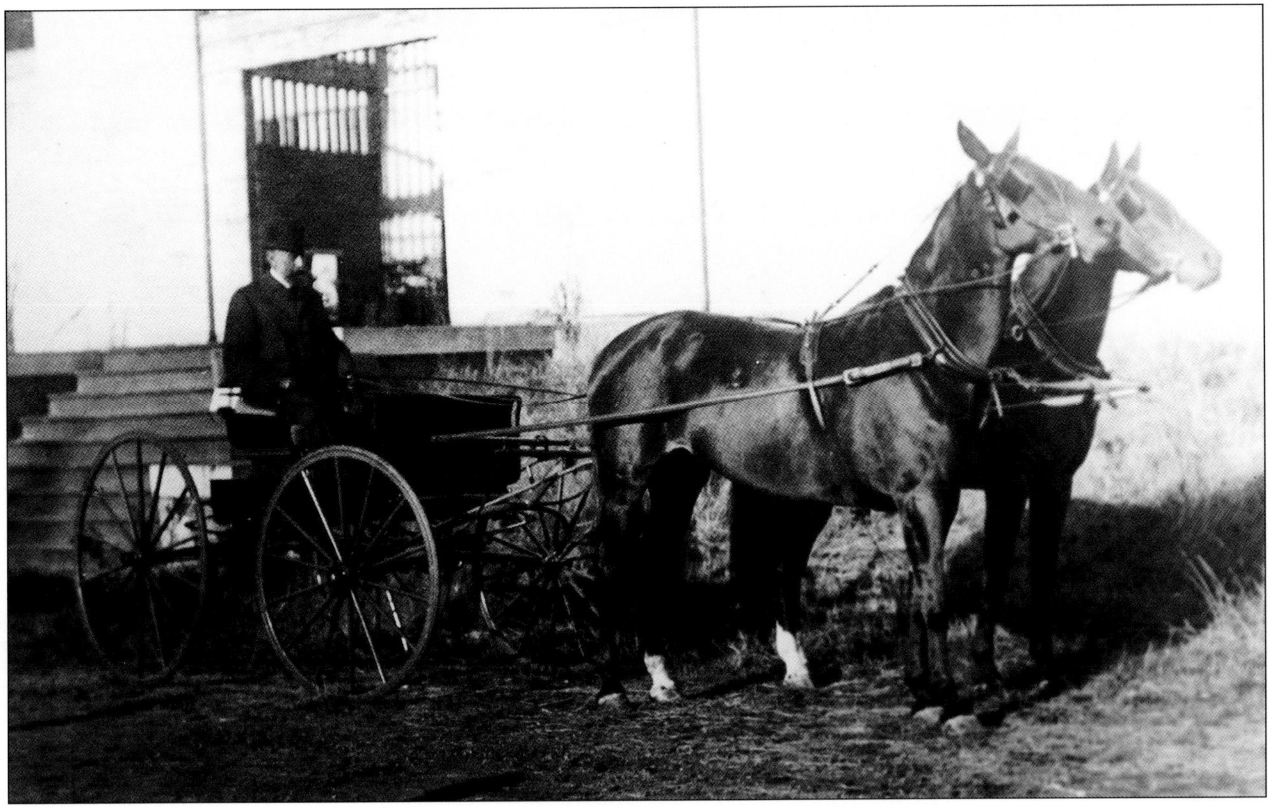

A fine example of a "runabout carriage" was photographed being driven by a unknown driver.

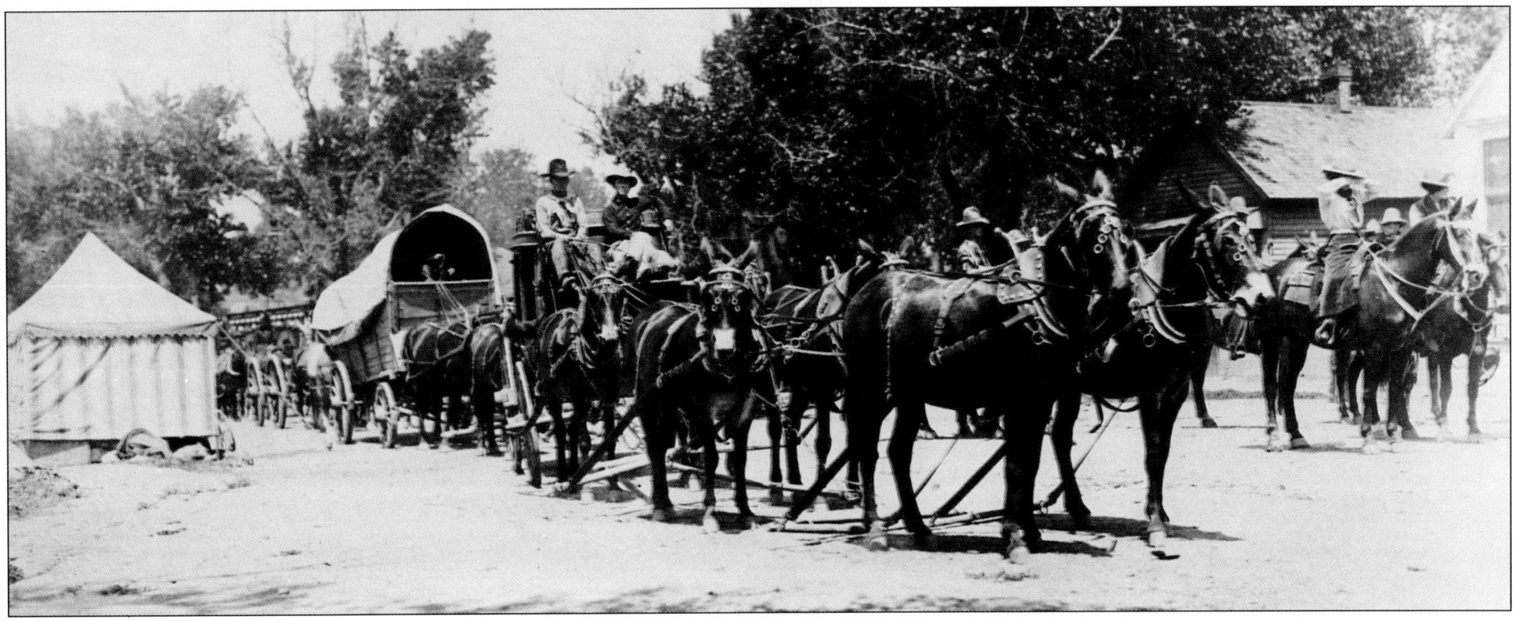

This mule train was all decked out for a parade in Placerville county, California.

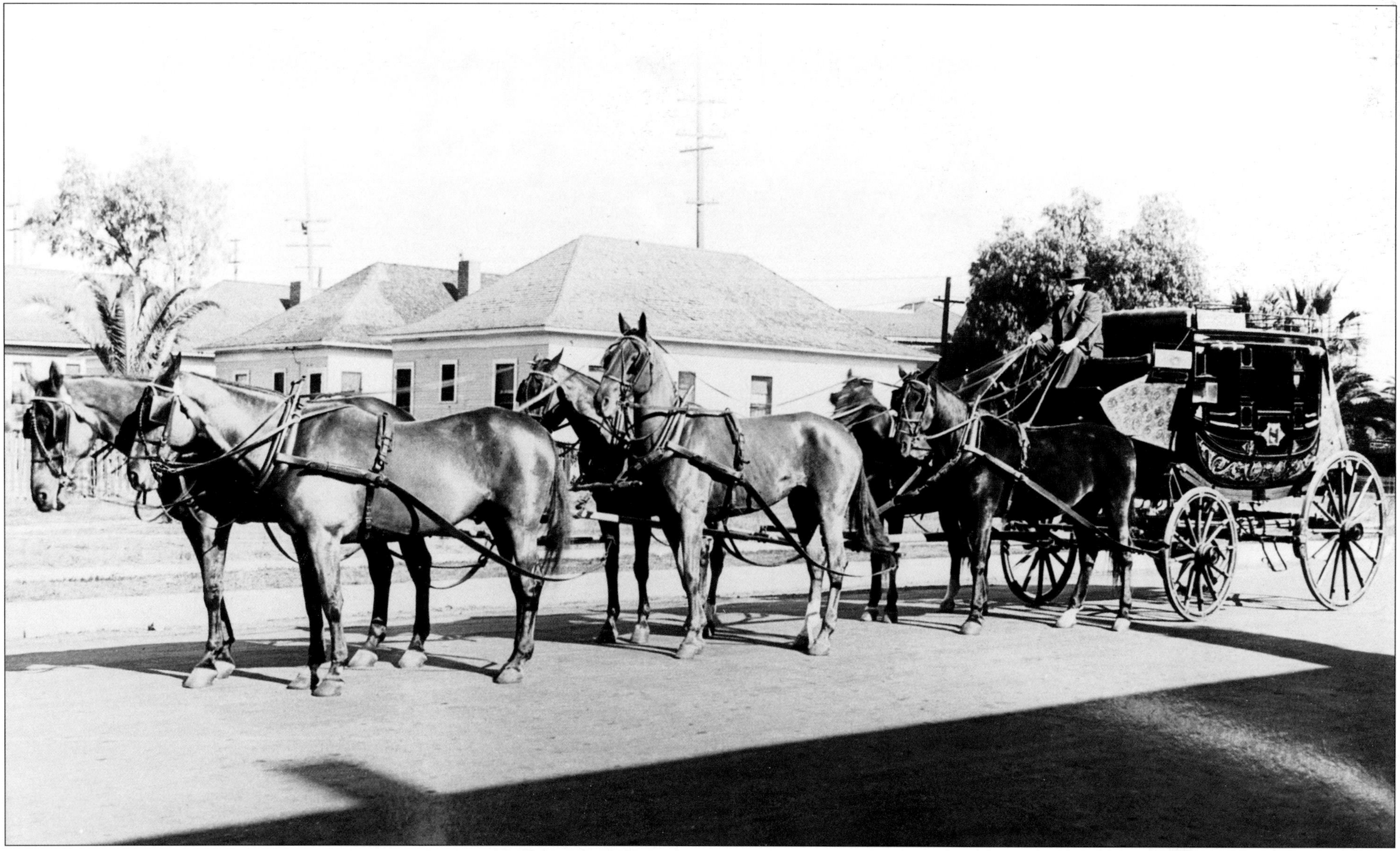

This fine photograph taken in Los Angeles, was given to Ben Powers by Captain William Banning who lived on Catalina Island at the time. It should be noted that the original coaches had plain leather boots, and no carving, but this coach has the original Concord harness.

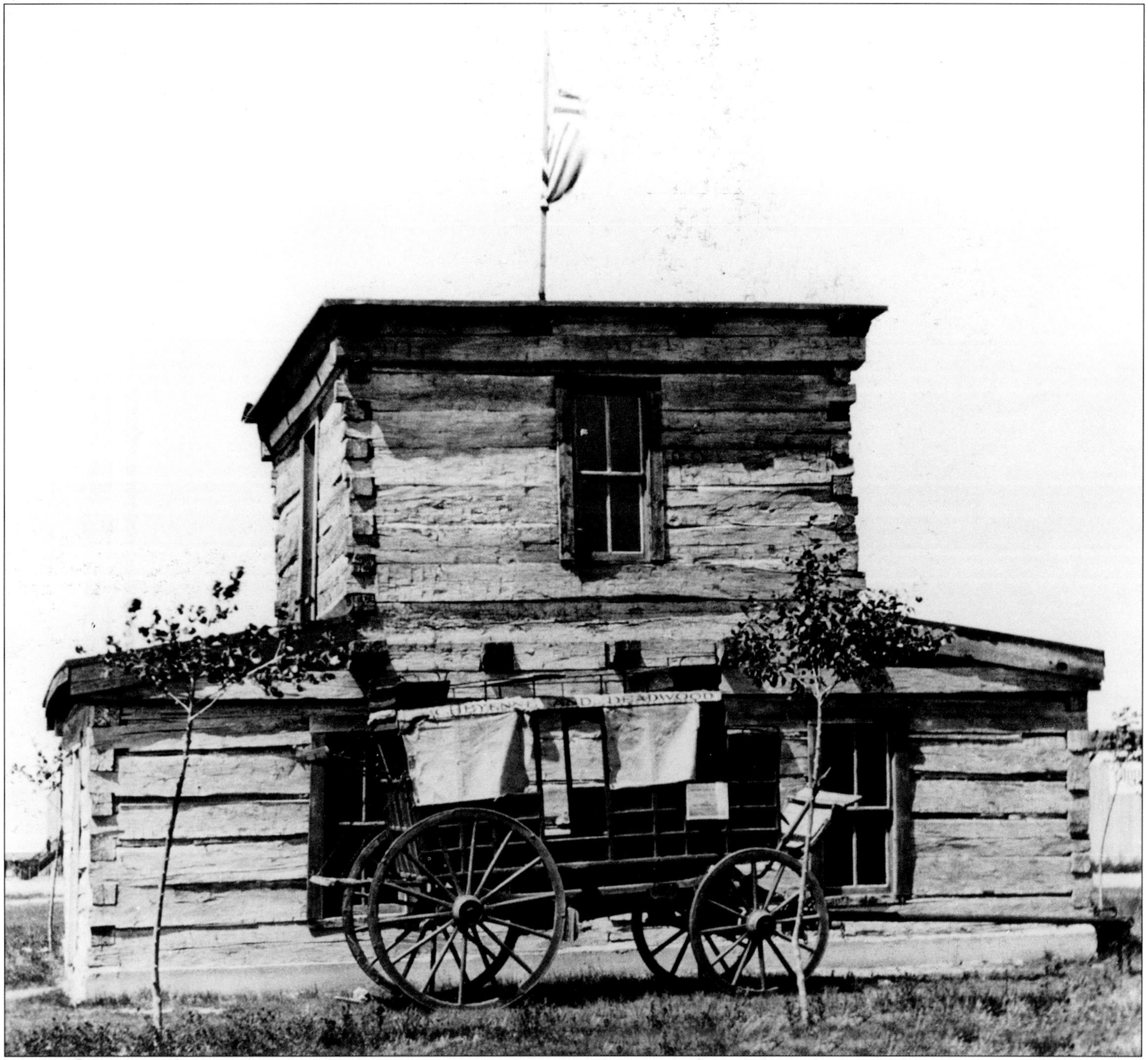

The Deadwood Dakota Stage is parked in front of a Jim Baker block house used in the early days and located at the fair grounds in Cheyenne Wyoming. The old Mudhen stage serves as a reminder of those early times.

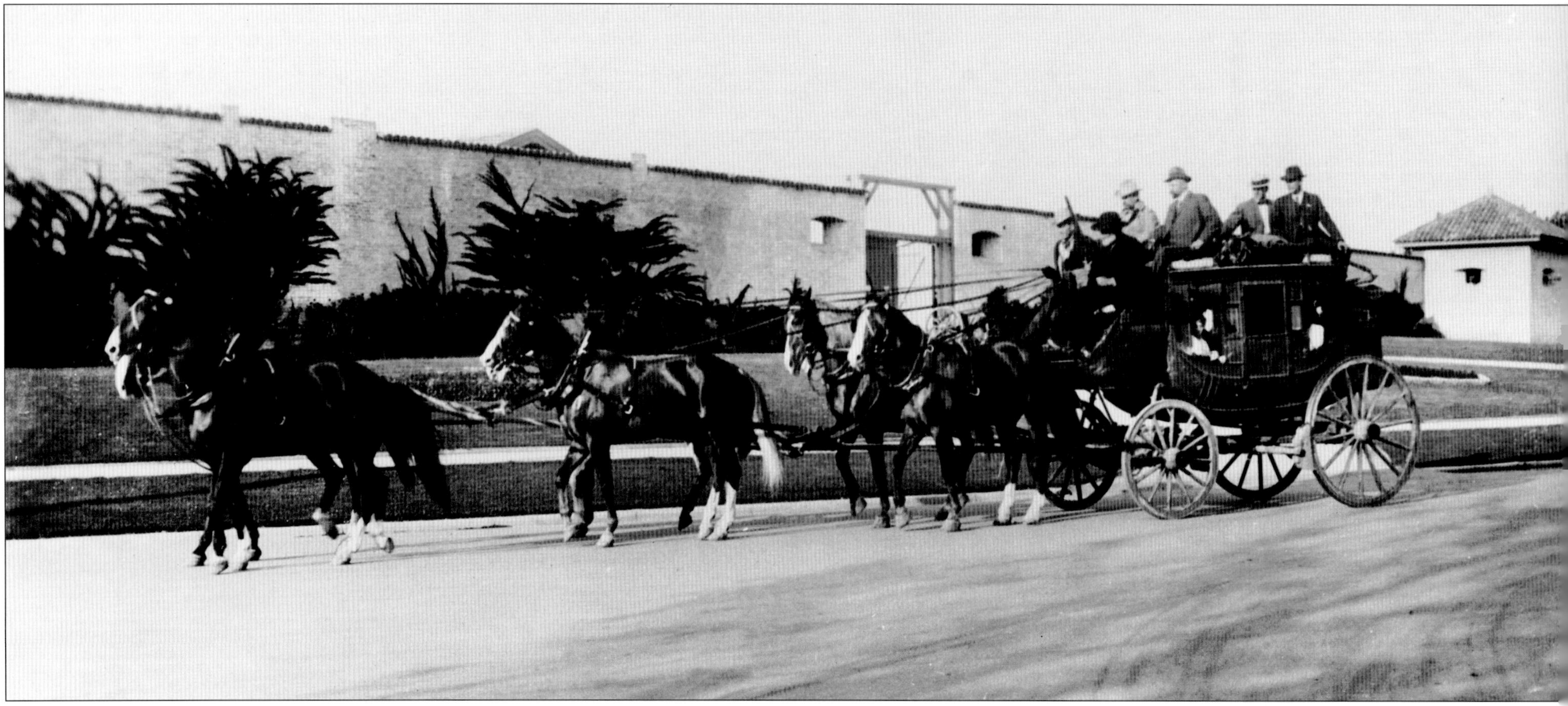

The Wells Fargo Stage, at old Fort Sutter in Sacramento, is driven by G. Christie. It was the Golden Jubilee Parade in October, 1912. The stage was built by Abbot and Downing Co., New Hampshire, in 1863. Shipped around the horn, it was nearly lost in a terrible storm off the Pescadero shores, about fifty miles south of San Francisco. This coach carried some famous people, including Mark Twain and Horace Greeley. Named on the iron plate in front of coach is W. A Knight.

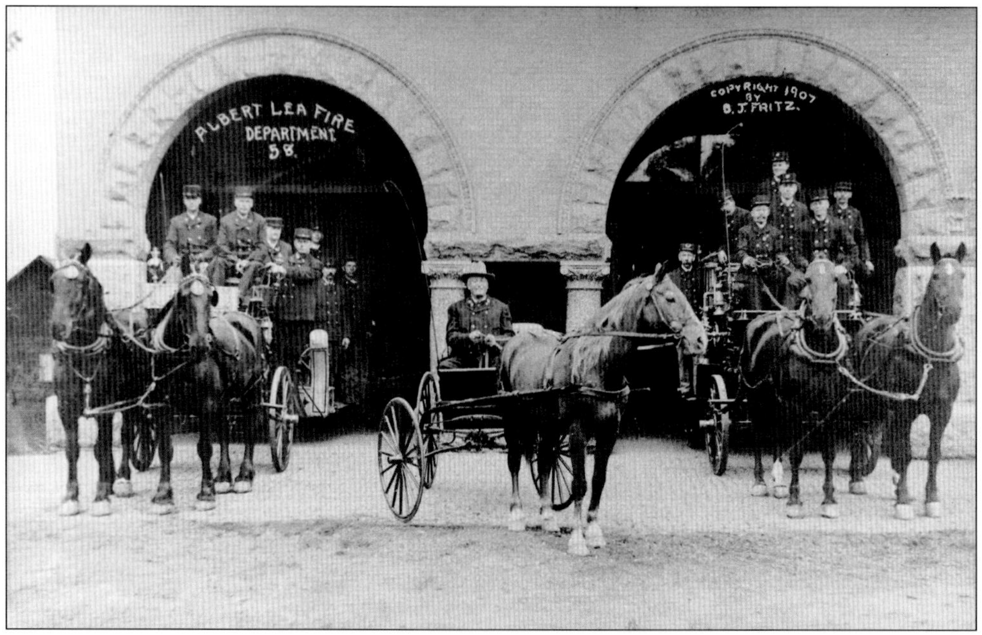

The Albert Lea Department's two horse-driven two wagons line up for their picture. The photographer has clearly written his name in the photo, B.J. Fritz. 1907.

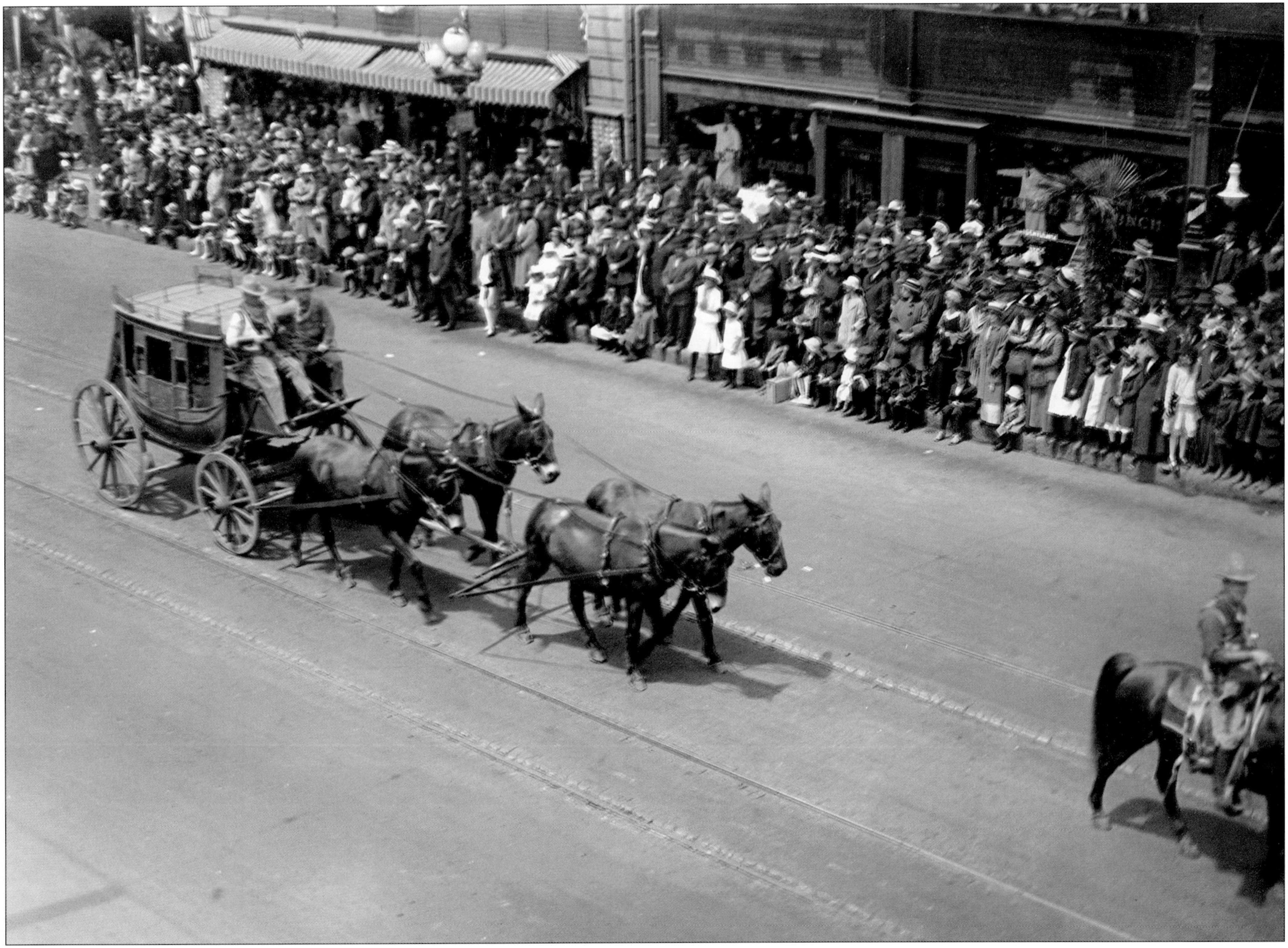

A early parade down main street in Los Angeles included an old Concord stage driven by two cowboys.

Chapter 8

Stage Coach Portraits

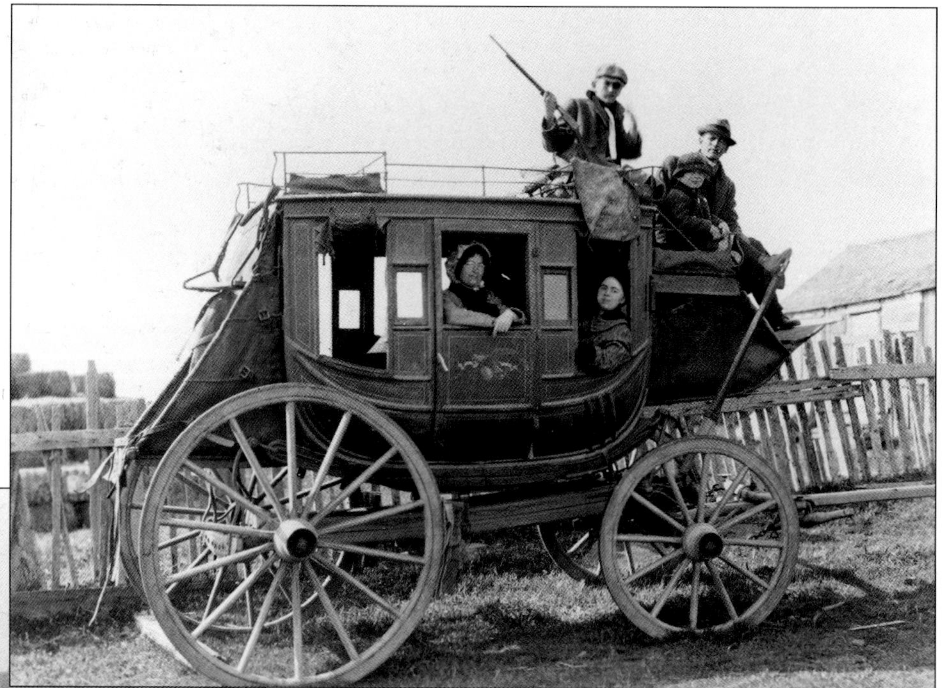

An old Concord stage in California. It was said to have burned up around 1922.

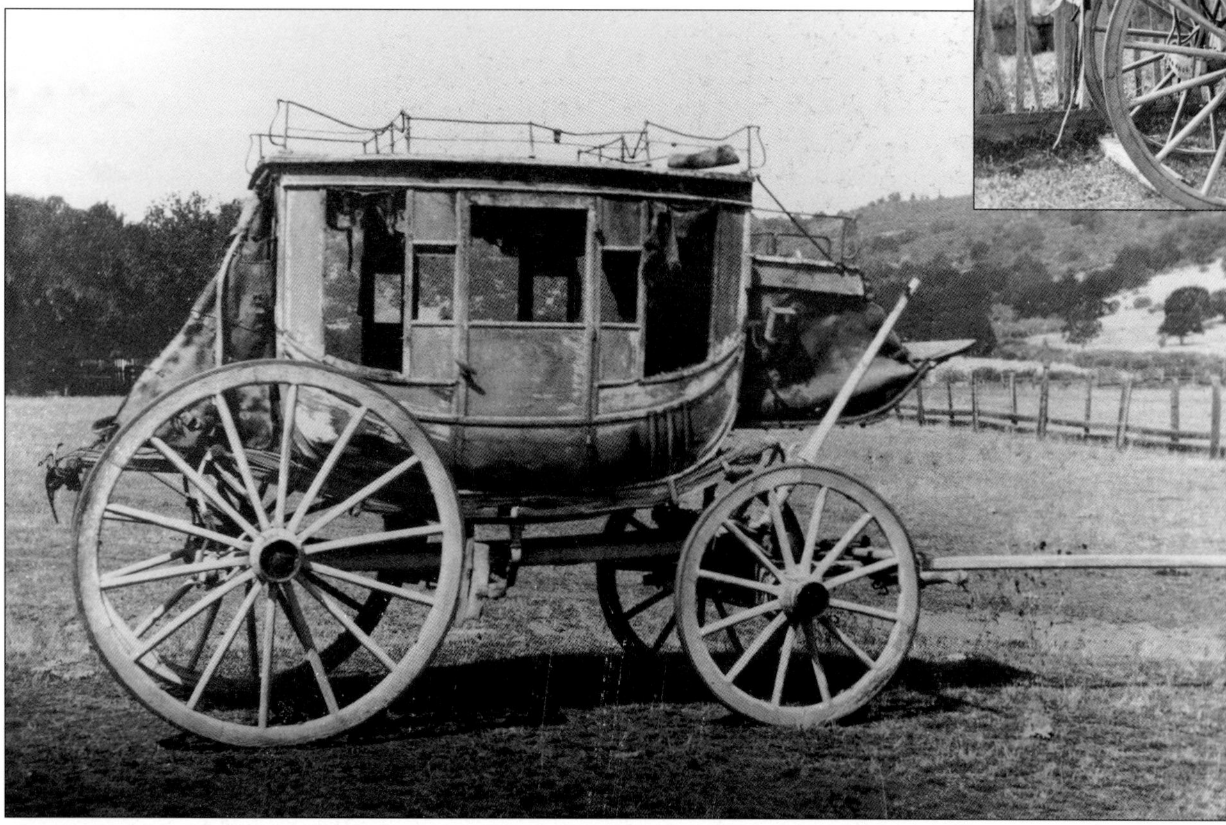

An Overland Stagecoach built by Abbot & Downing Co. in 1865. It was shipped to Ben Fisk, in Lexington Missouri in Oct. 1865 and hauled across the plains to the California Stage Company in Yureka, California. From there it went to Jacksonville, Oregon, and then on the Southern Pacific Railroad to Portland, Oregon, where it was restored in 1887. Sold at auction in Yureka, it was finally bought by Ben Powers in July, 1913.

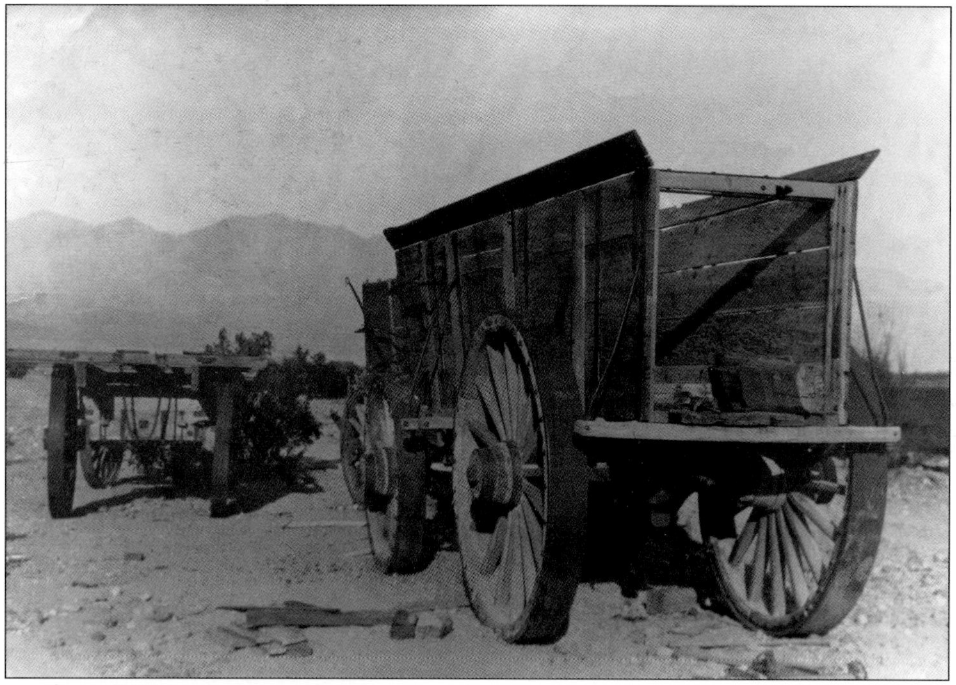

At Daggett, California, these twenty mule team mule wagons are left to decay in the hot sun.

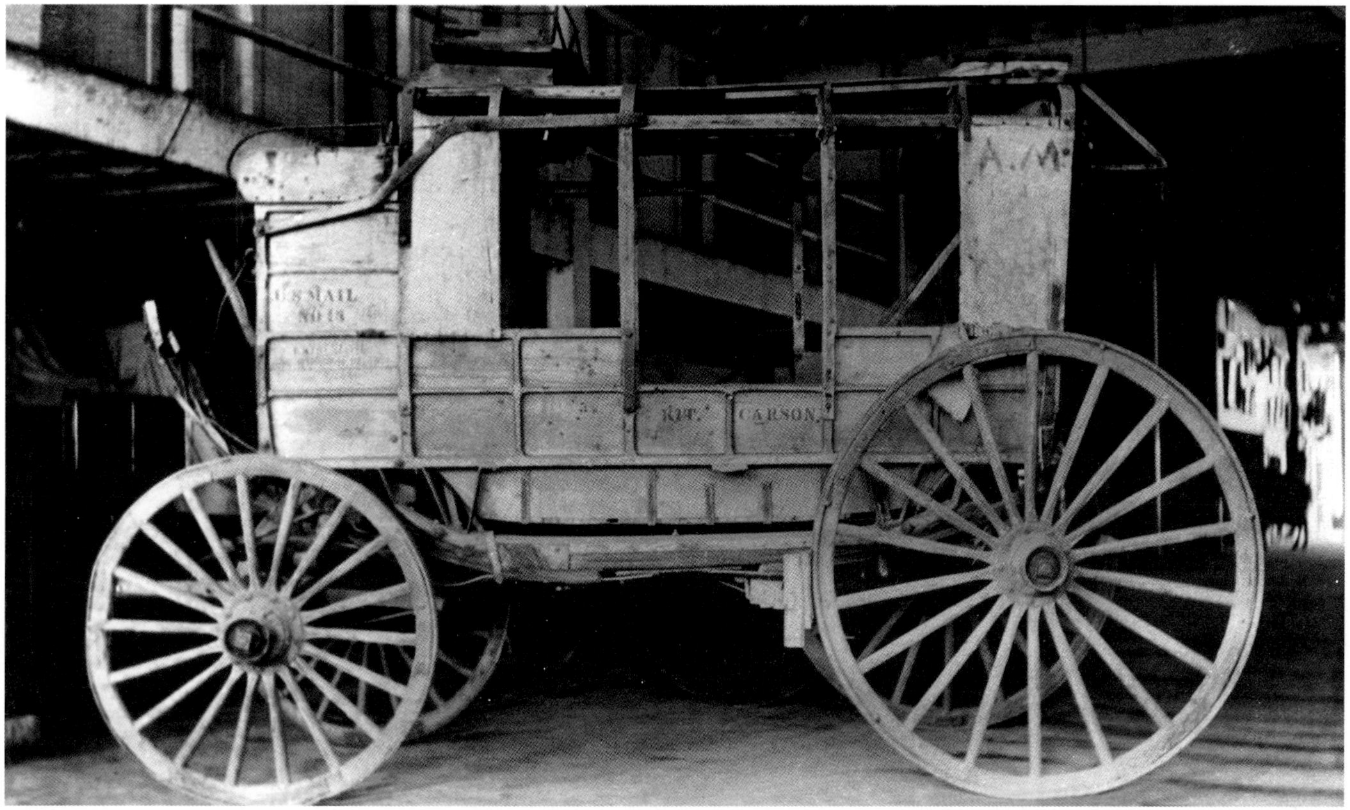

An old "Kit Carson" U.S. Mail wagon, now the property of Charles Irwin of Cheyenne. Irwin is the general agent of North Dakota at Cheyenne. Notes from Ben Powers dated 1924.

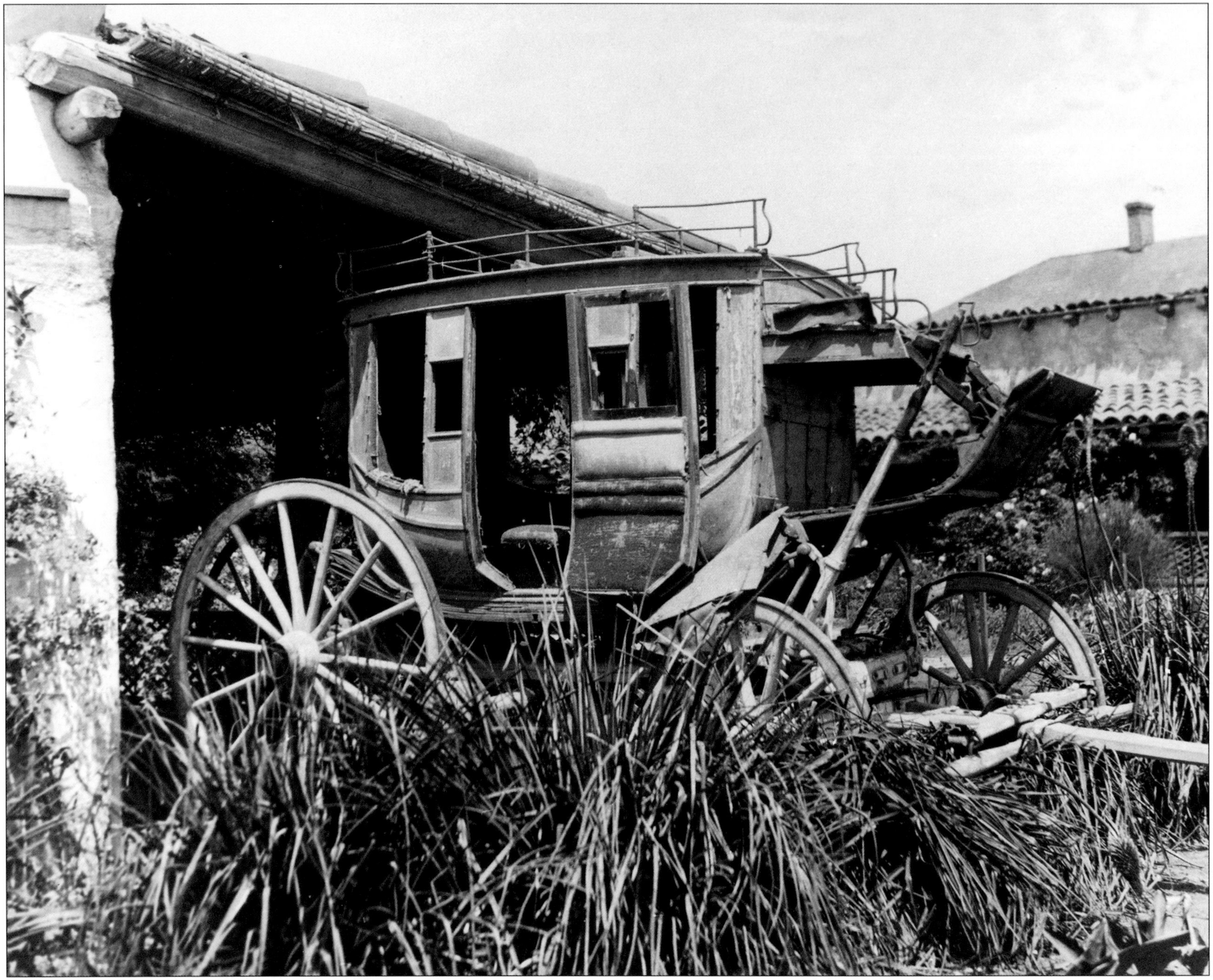

This old coach sitting among the tall grass has a lot of history to tell. It was brought to California by William Banning, who purchased it for $1600 and had it shipped around the Horn. It made its first run to Fort Yuma and back to Los Angeles.

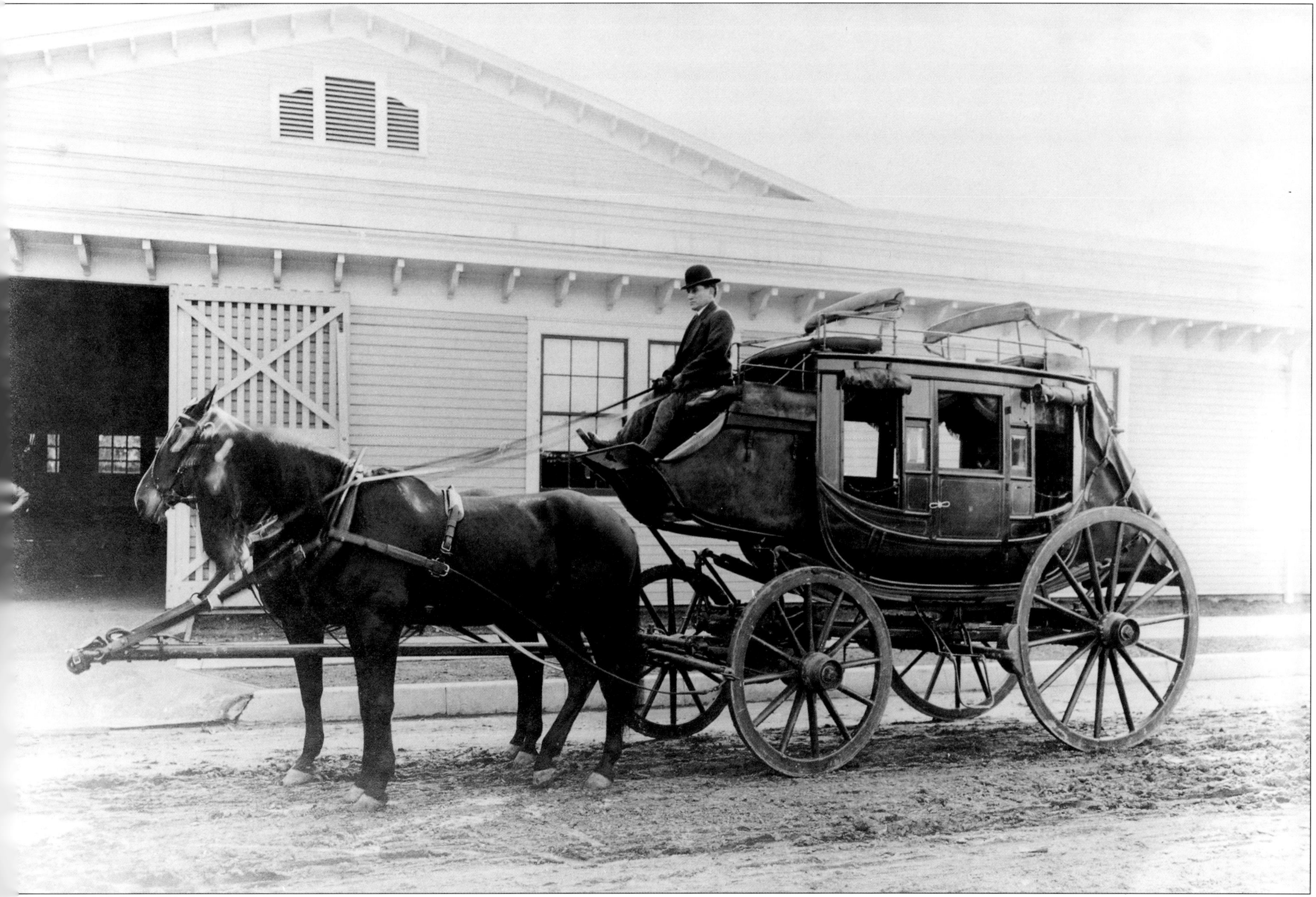

A fine example of an Abbot Downing stagecoach with "Tony" the driver on top. It was Captain Banning's personal stagecoach, but was burned in a fire at the paint shop.

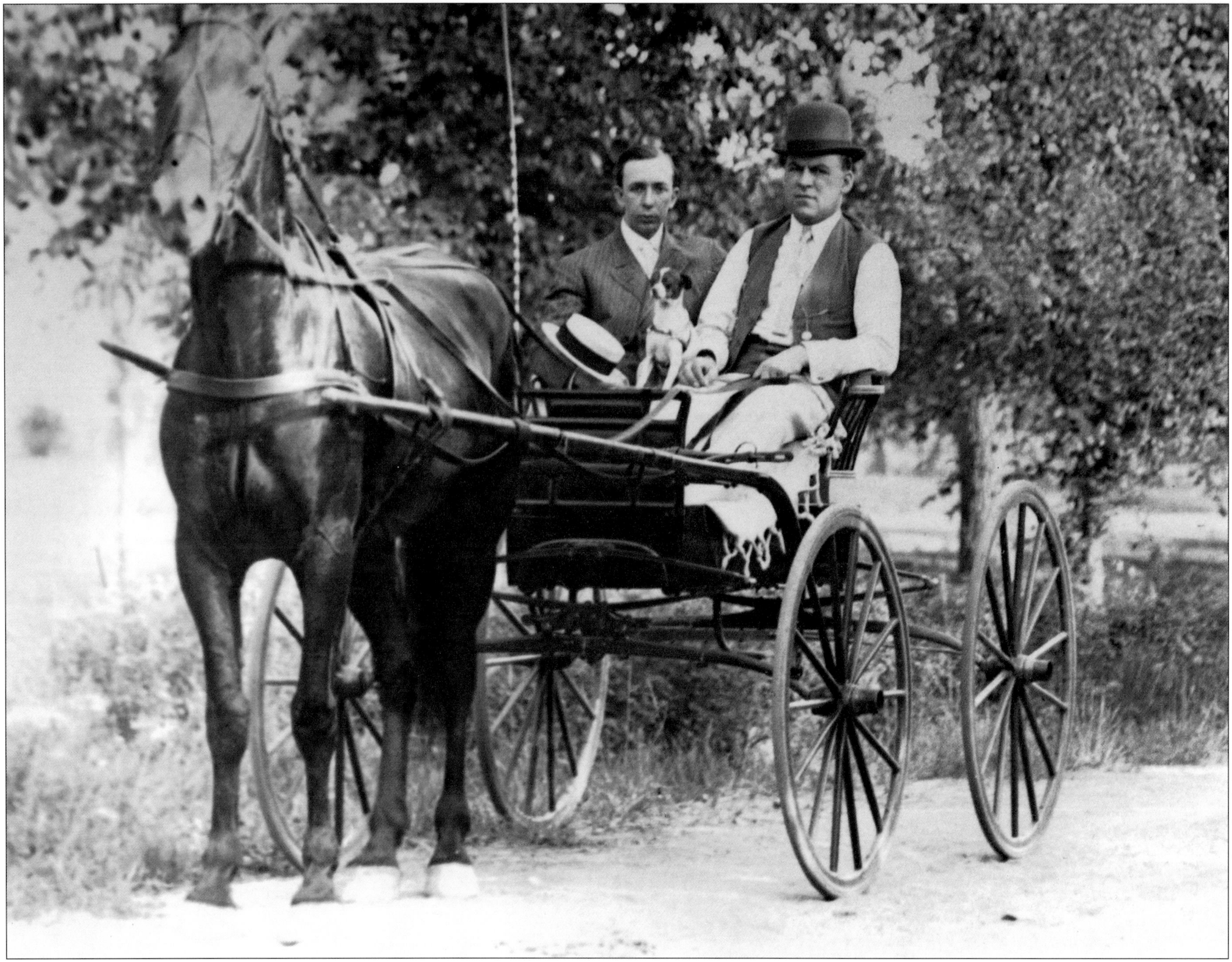

A fine example of a runabout with one horse. The owners proudly sit their dog in the center.

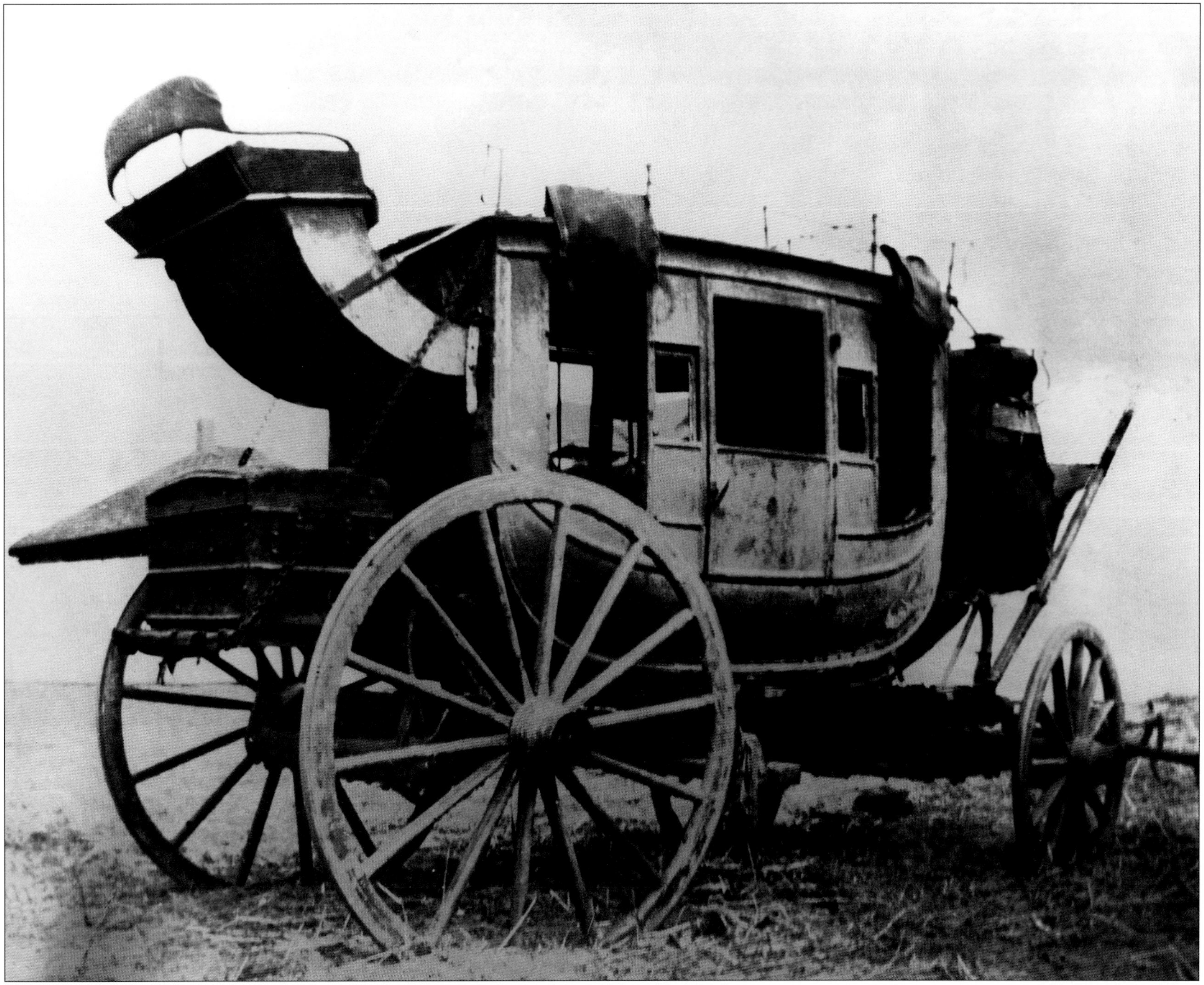

Taken in Buffalo, Wyoming, this picture is of the old Gidley coach that ran from Deadwood, South Dakota. It was sold by Gidley in 1885, who had, at that time, lost his stagecoach contract to Fort McKinney in Wyoming.

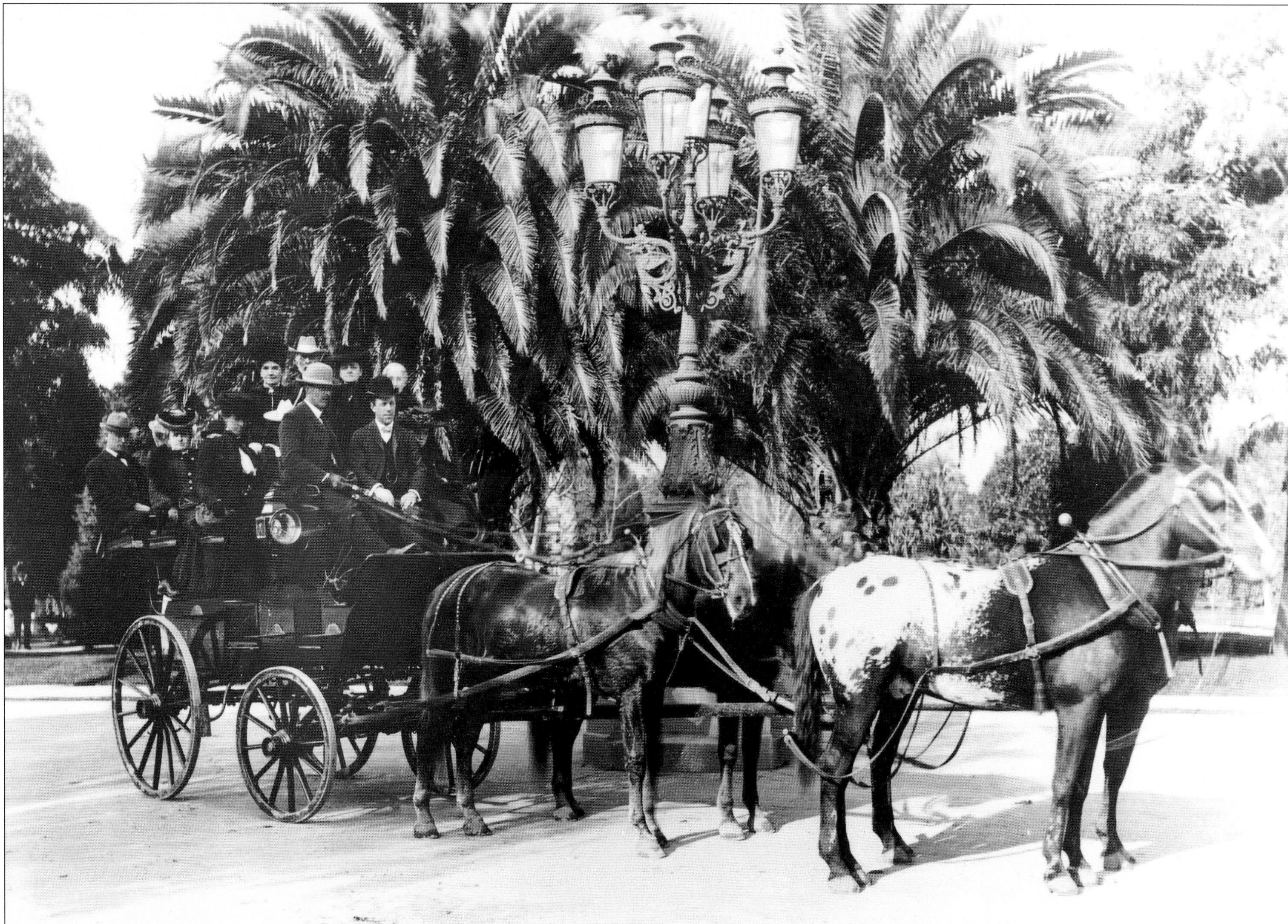

In Los Angeles, at James Park, the local women's club gets a ride on a stage celebrating Tally- Ho Day.

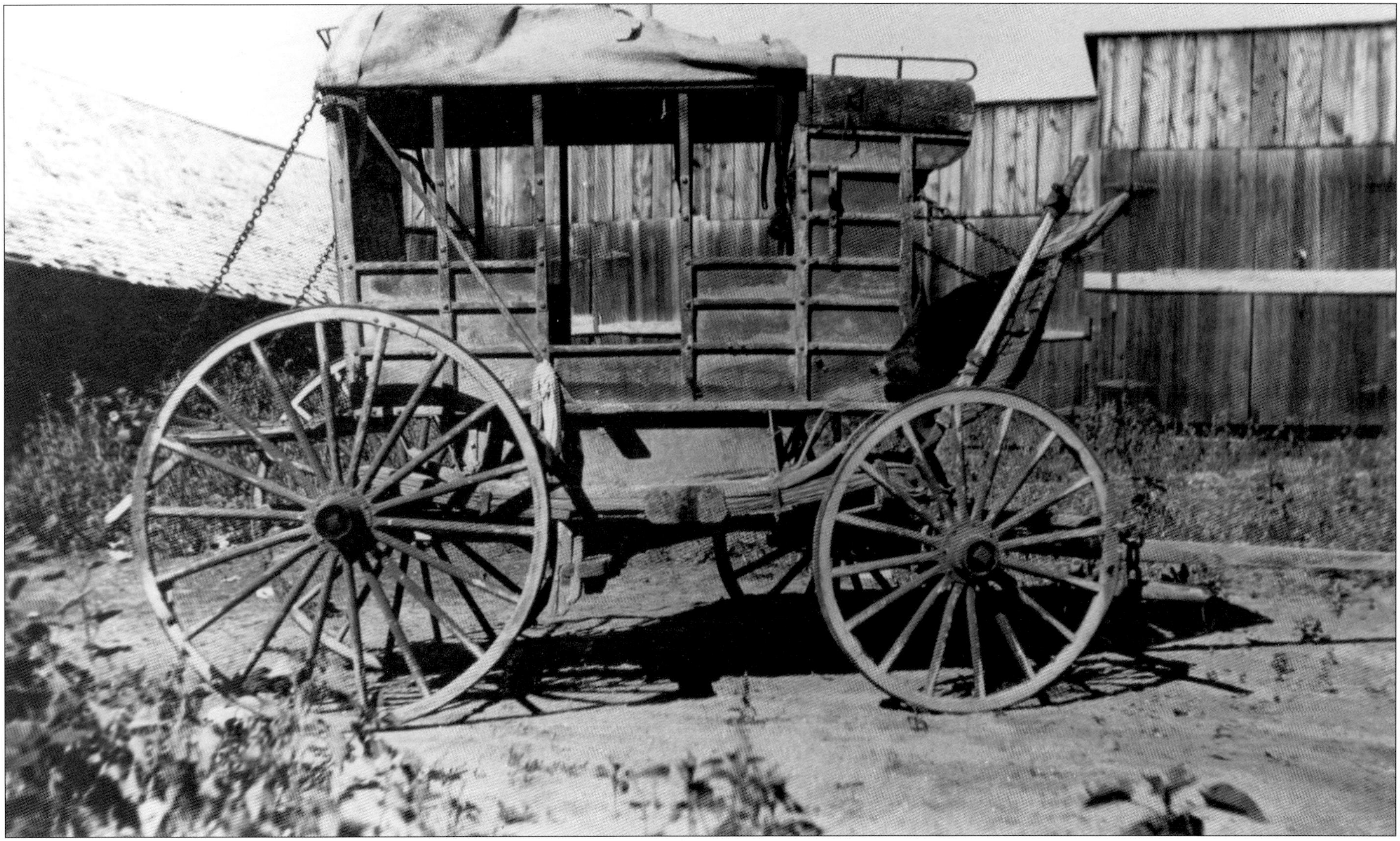

This old stagecoach formerly ran from Sommerville to Shelton, Arizona.

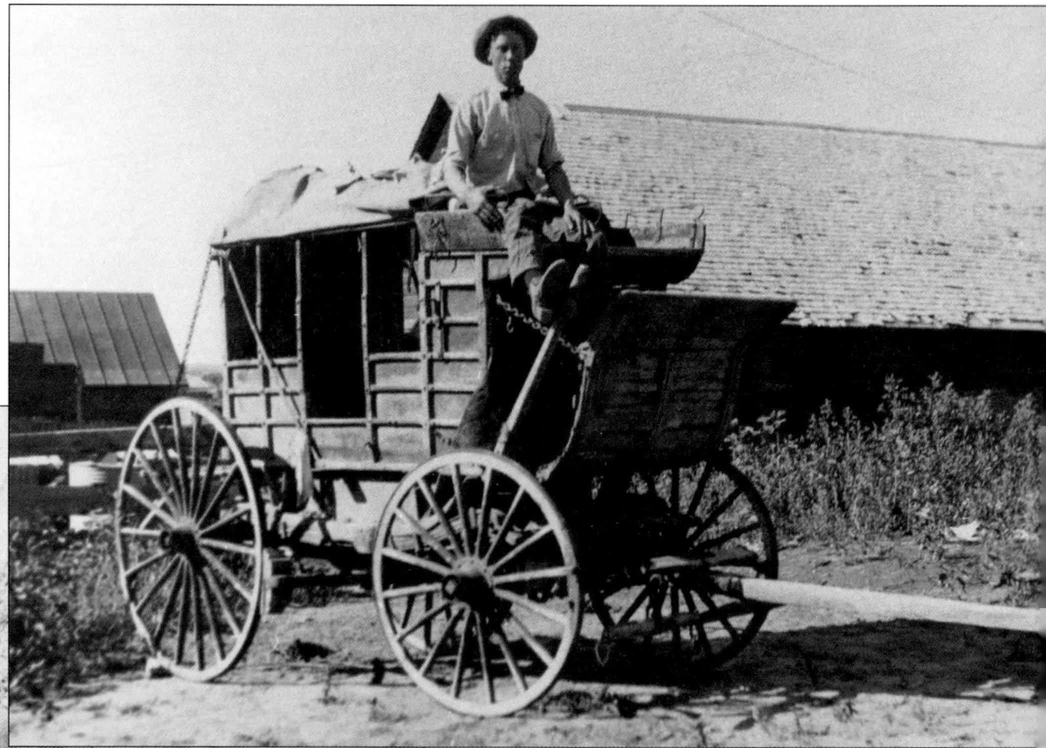

This stage, "Mudhen," was pulled out of a garage to have its picture taken.

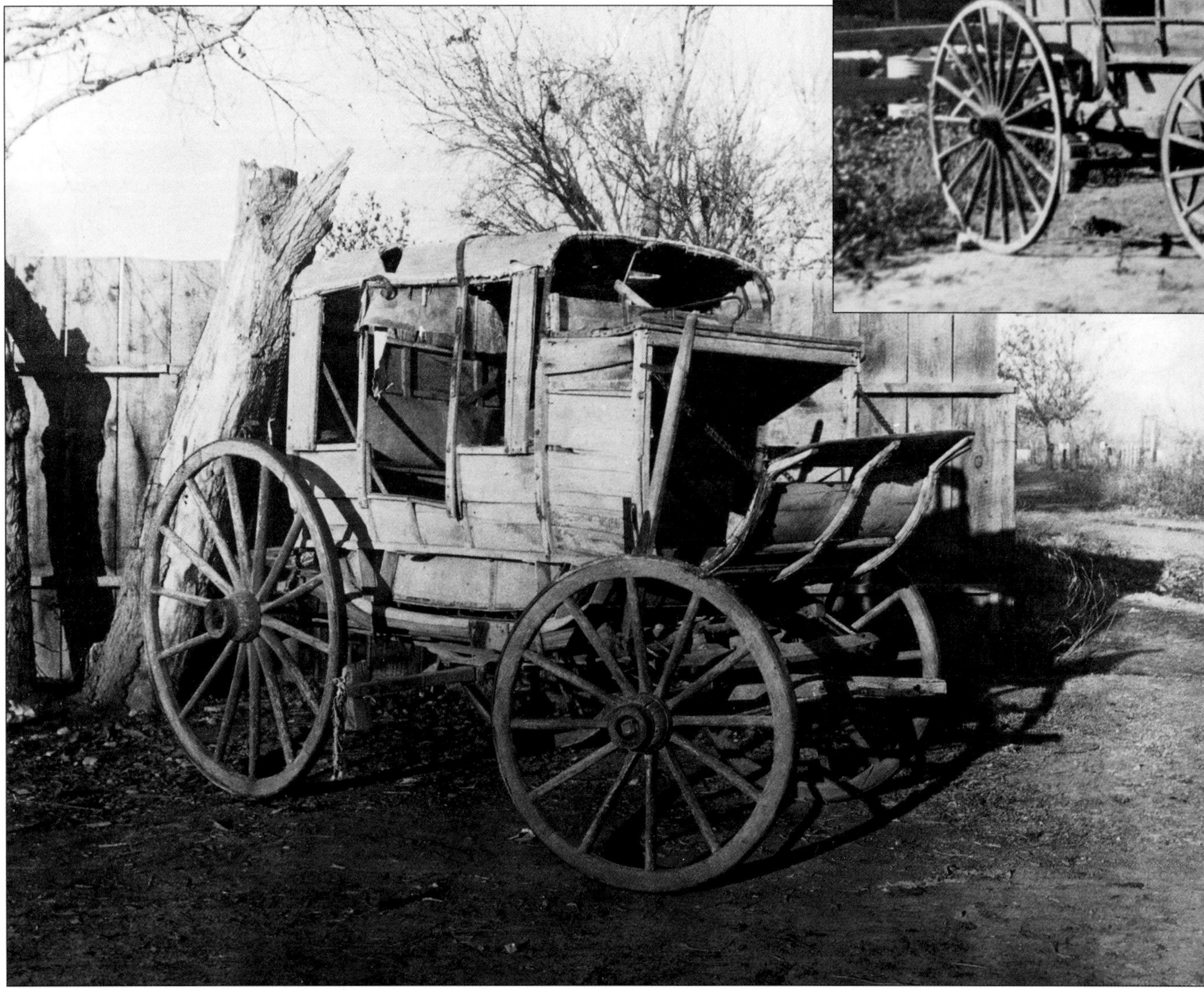

This old stagecoach was photographed at Newhall, California in 1920. It was used in a number of Tom Mix pictures and other silent movies.

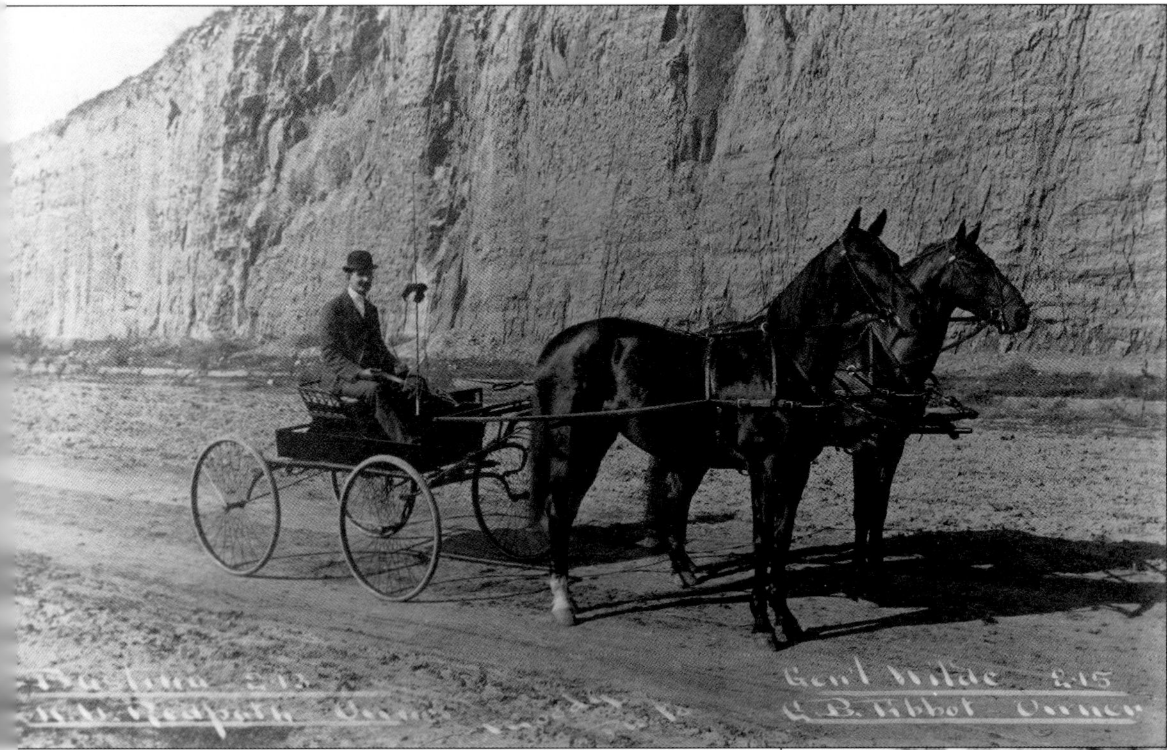

This Abbot stage was called a trotter. It is being driven by A. H. Redpath.

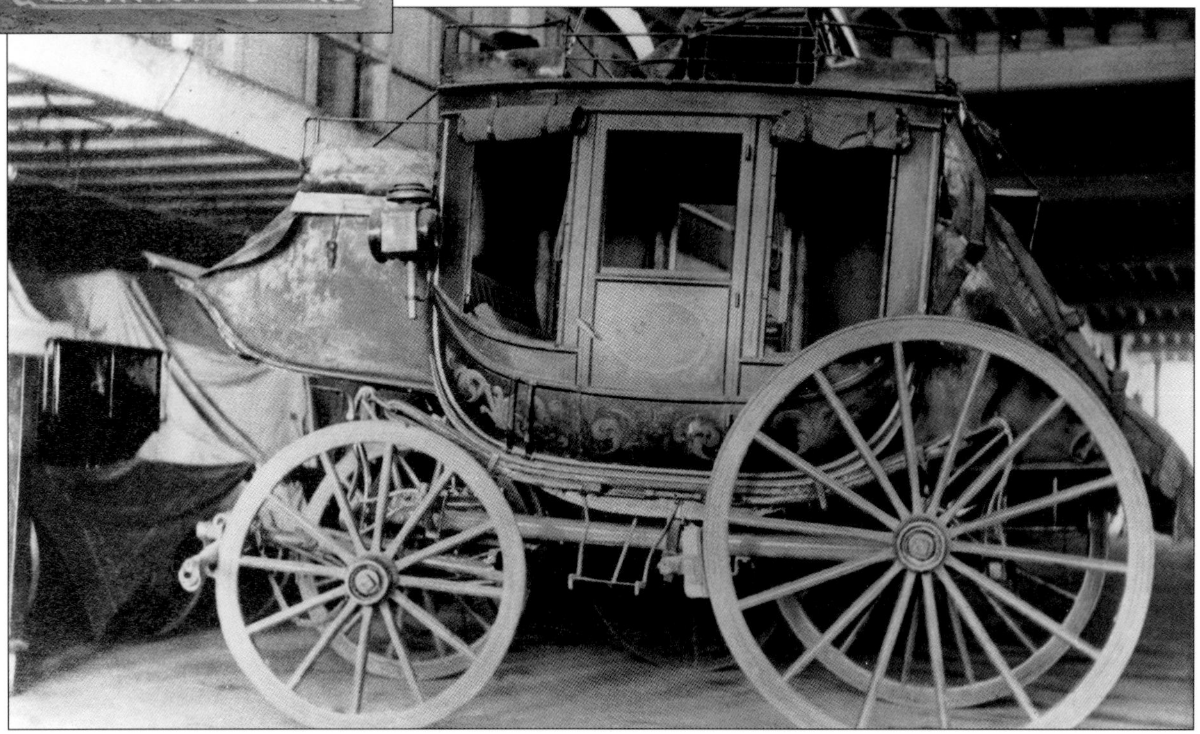

This small Concord belonged to the Denver Cab and Omnibus Company. Photographed by Kukindal.

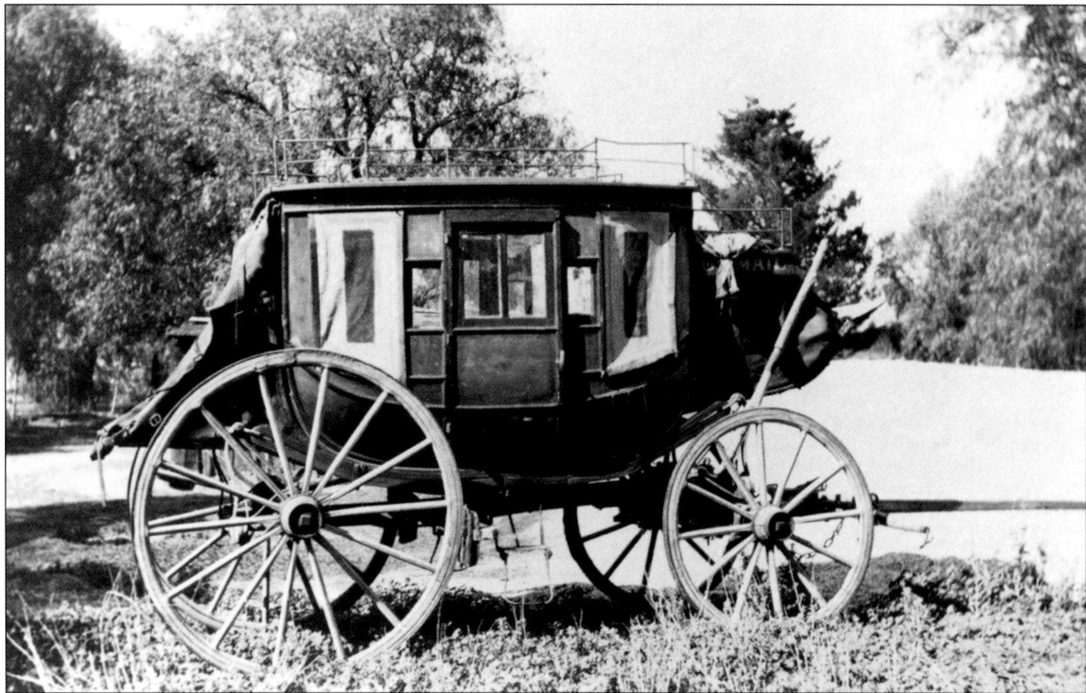

An old stagecoach parked in Yellowstone Park.

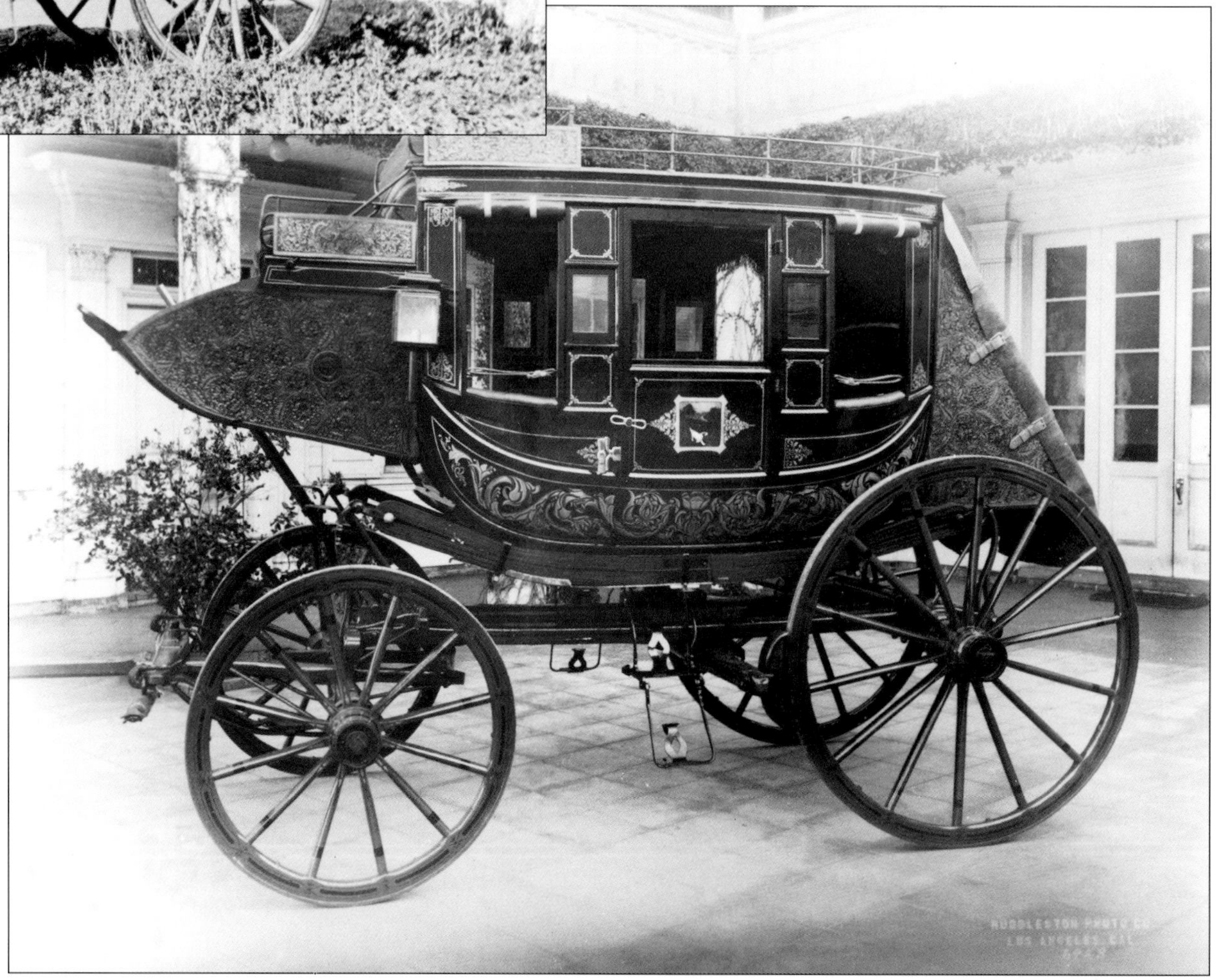

This Abbot Downing Concord Stage was built in November 1875. It was given to Capt. Wm. Banning by Abbot Downing to take the place of one that had burned in the paint shop fire. It was brought west by the steamer Avalon.

The following stage coach photographs and drawings are from a leather bound collection of stage coach photographs and pages from an original Abbot Downing catalog.

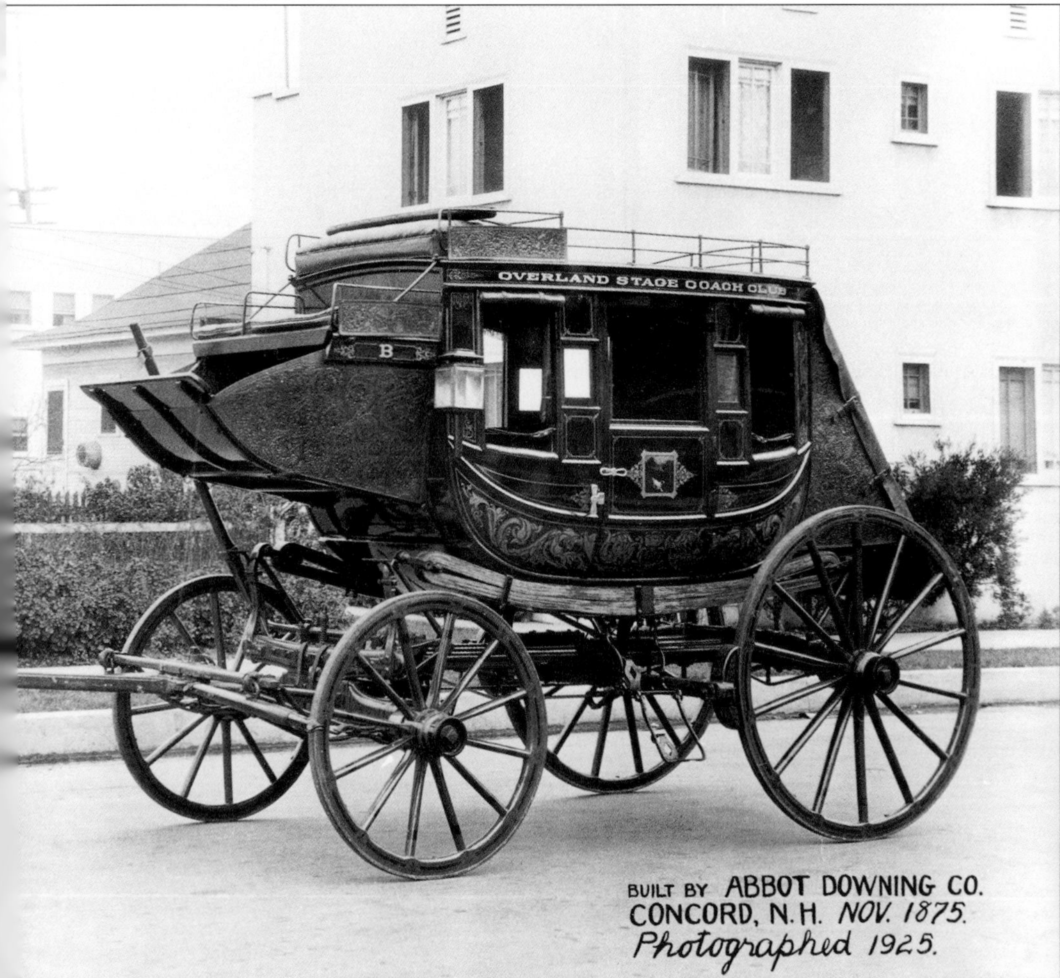

A restored version of the Banning coach described above; built in November, 1875. Photographed in 1925, part of the Overland Stage Coach Club collection.

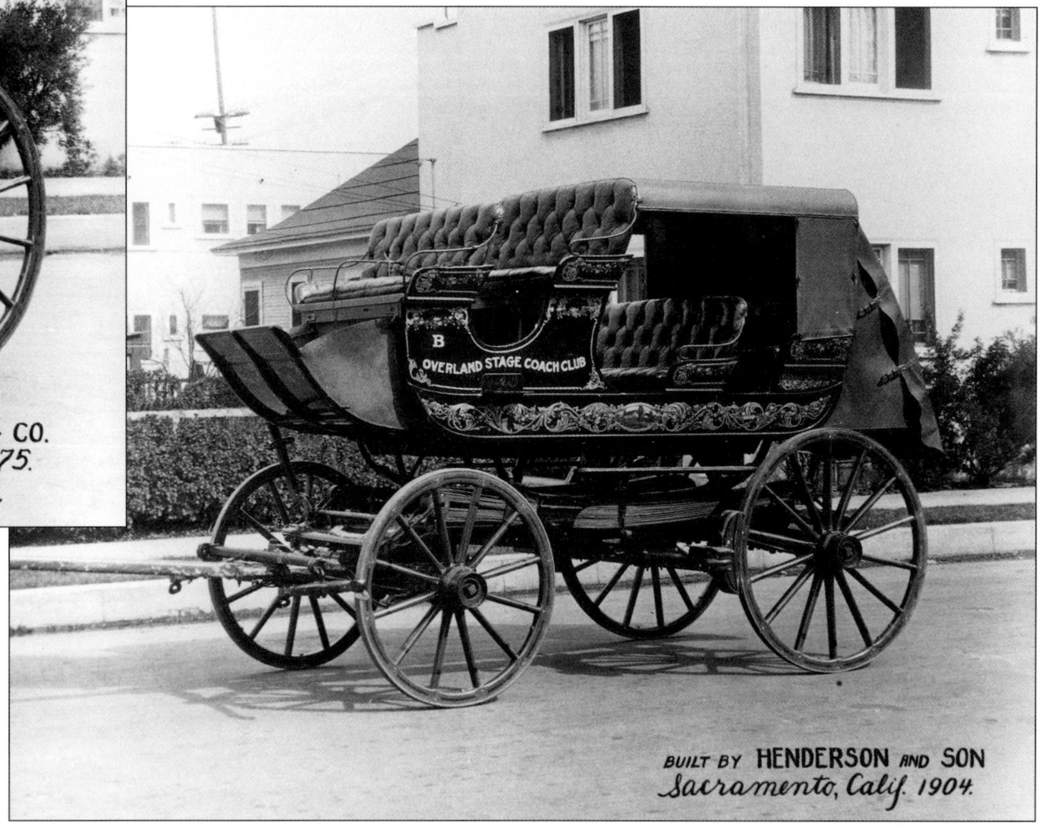

Stage coach built by Henderson & Son, Sacramento, 1904. Part of the Overland Stage Coach Club collection.

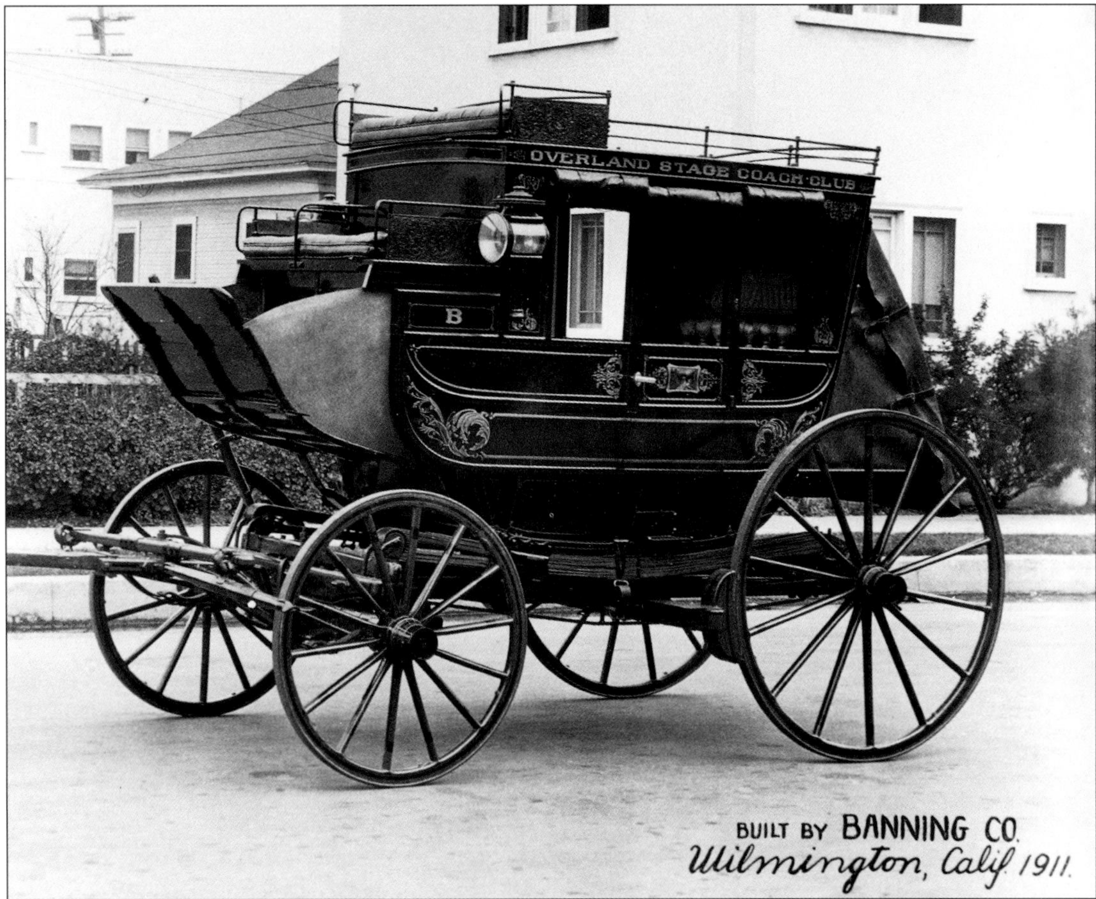

A Banning Co. stagecoach, Wilmington, California. 1911. Part of the Overland Stage Coach Club collection.

A wagon built by Banning Company, Wilmington, California, 1886. Part of the Overland Stage Coach Club collection.

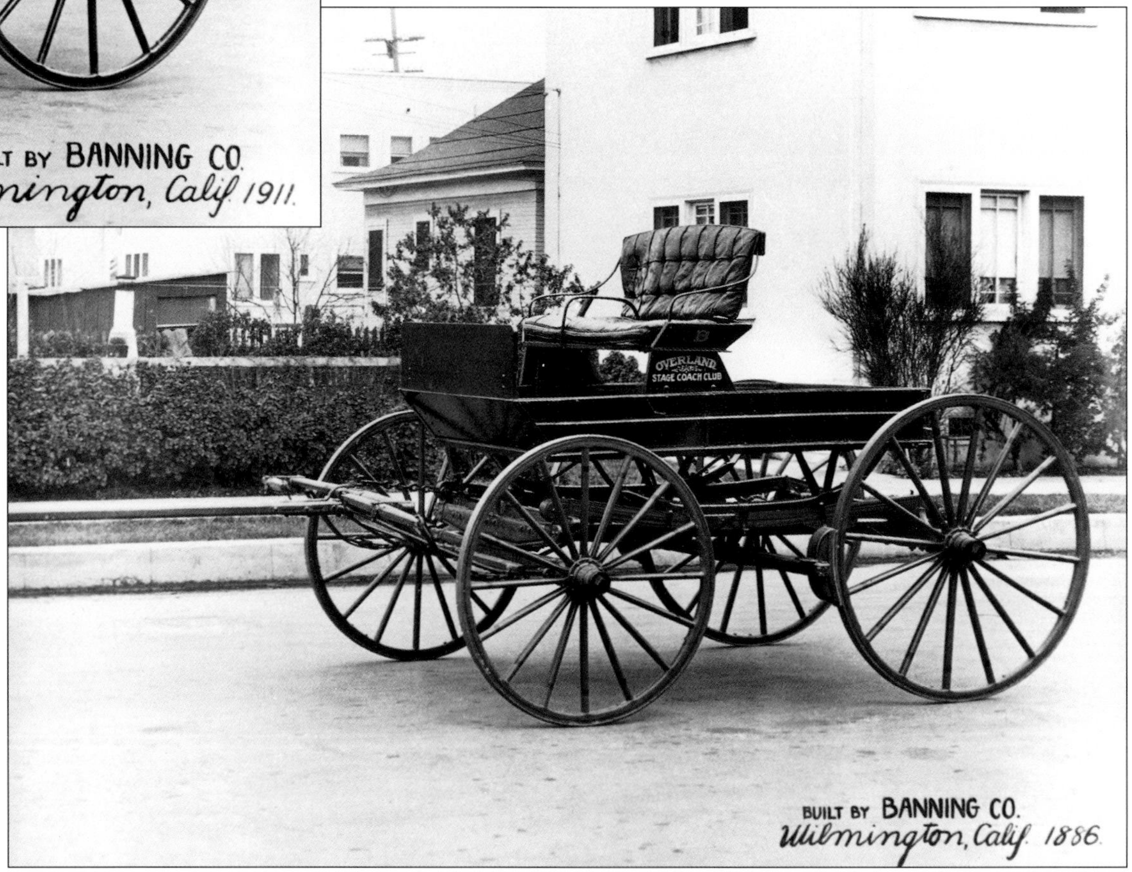

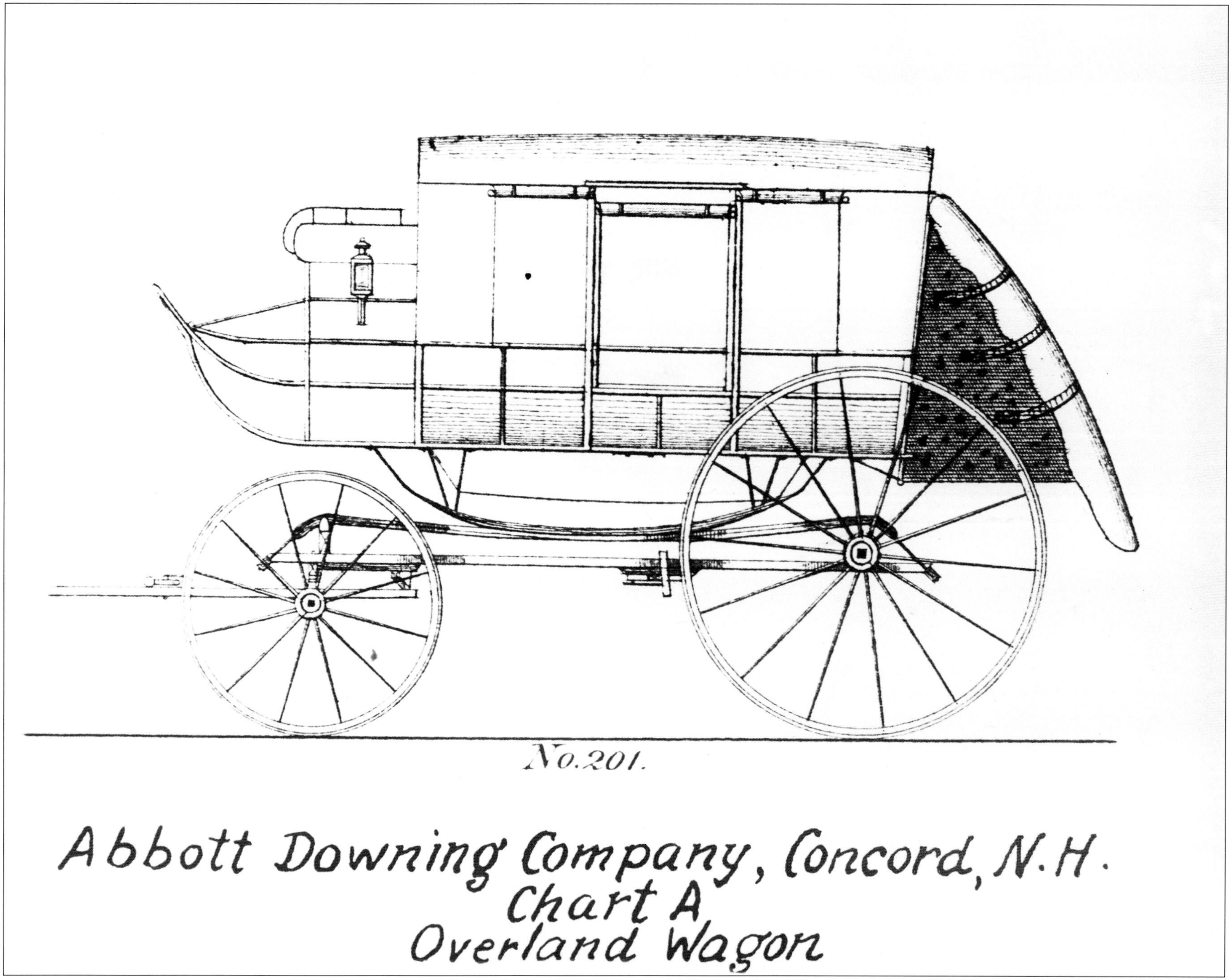

A line drawing of No. 201 of an Overland Wagon Chart A from the Abbot Downing Company catalog.

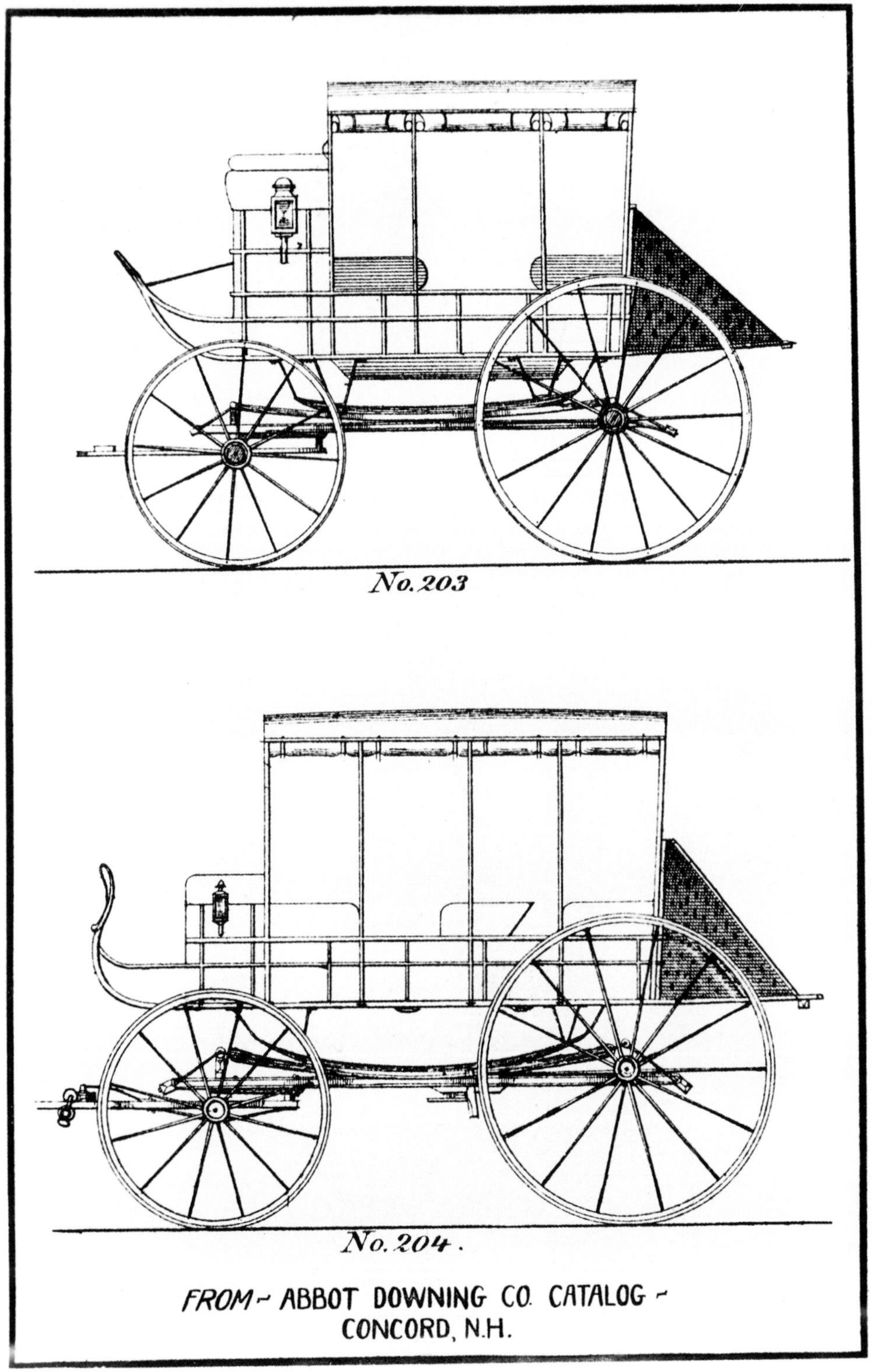

Line drawings of two coaches from Abbot Downing Co. Catalog No. 203 and 204

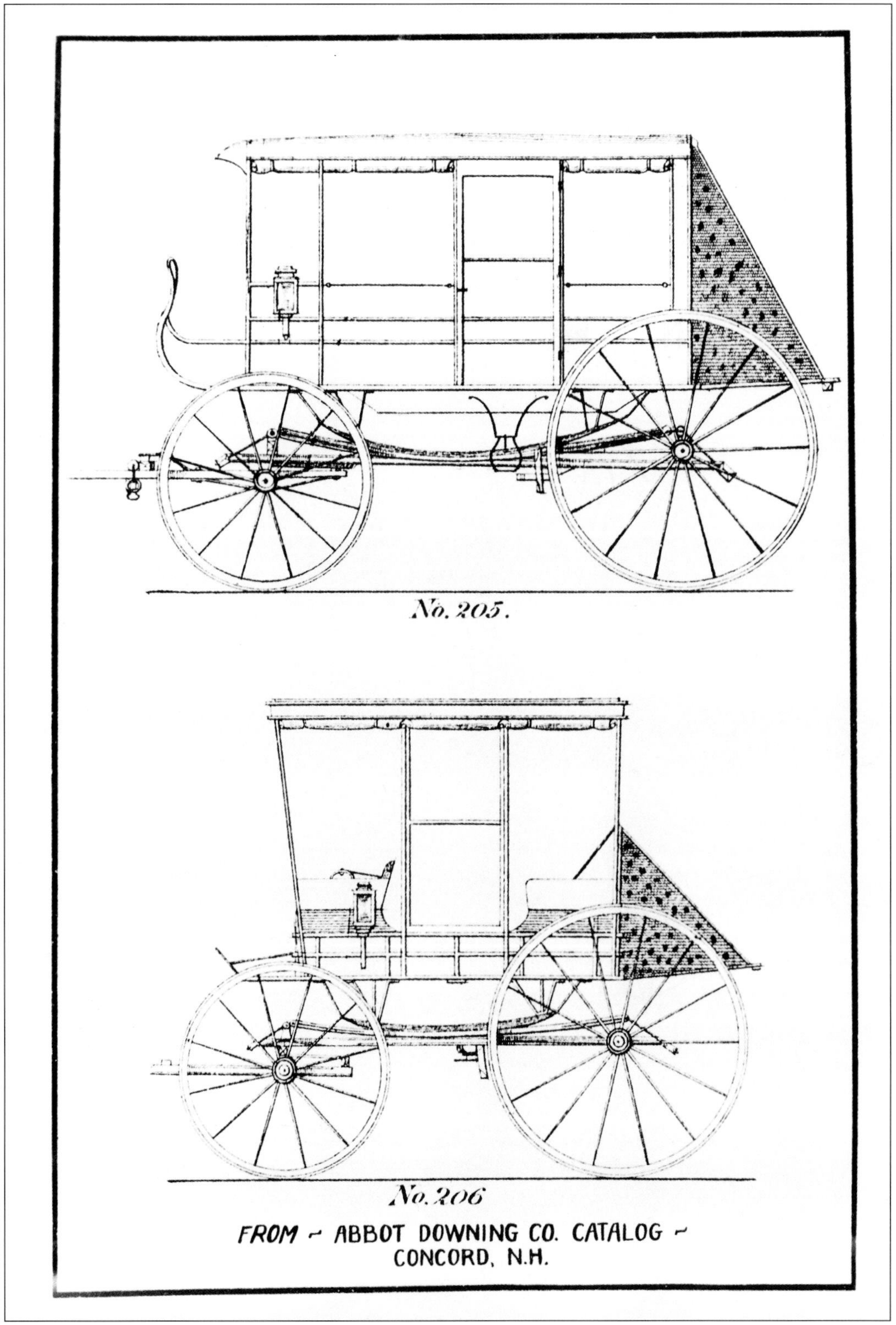

Line drawings of two coaches from Abbot Downing Co. Catalog No. 205 and 206

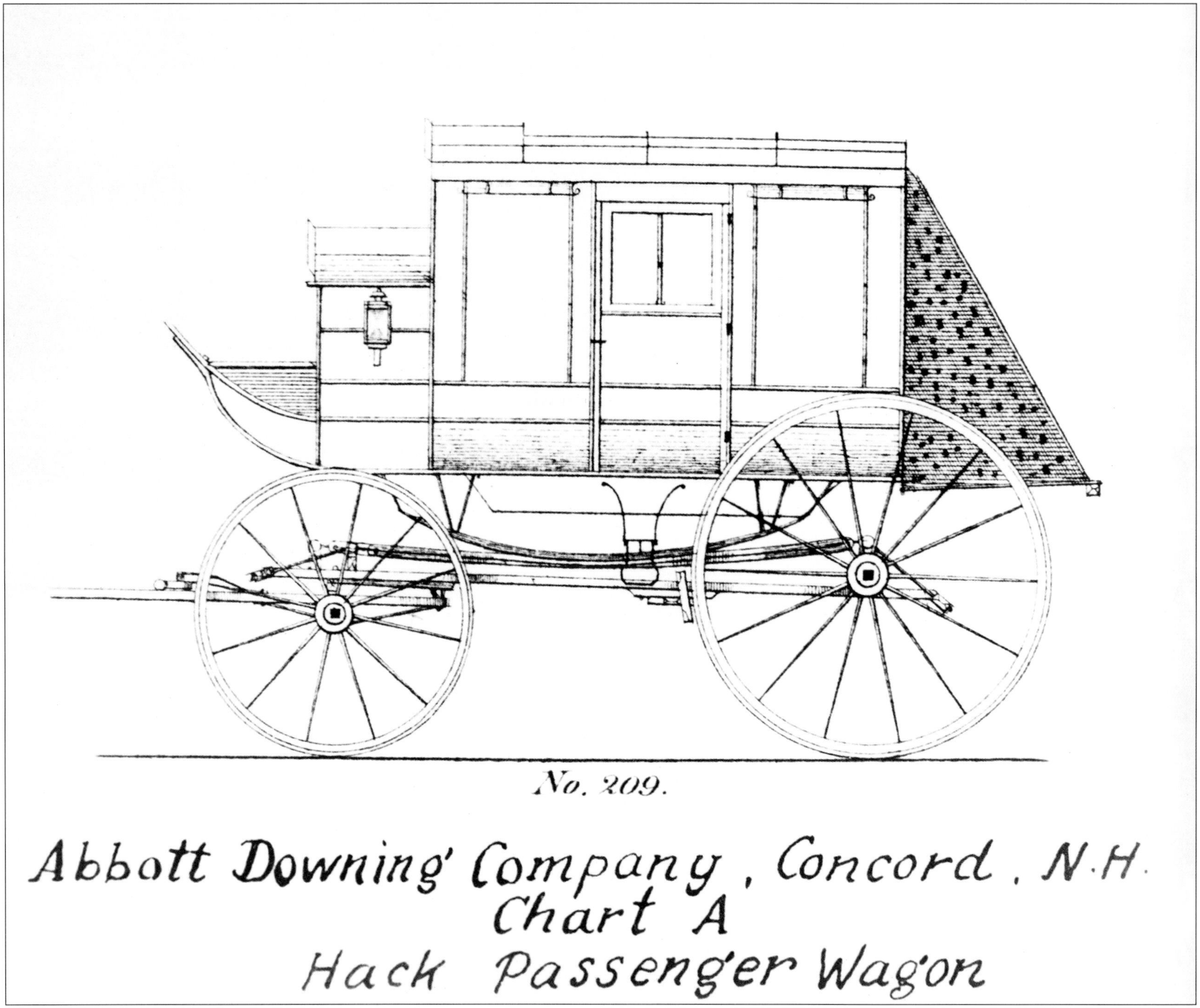

A line drawing of an Abbot Downing Company "Hack Passenger Wagon," No. 209

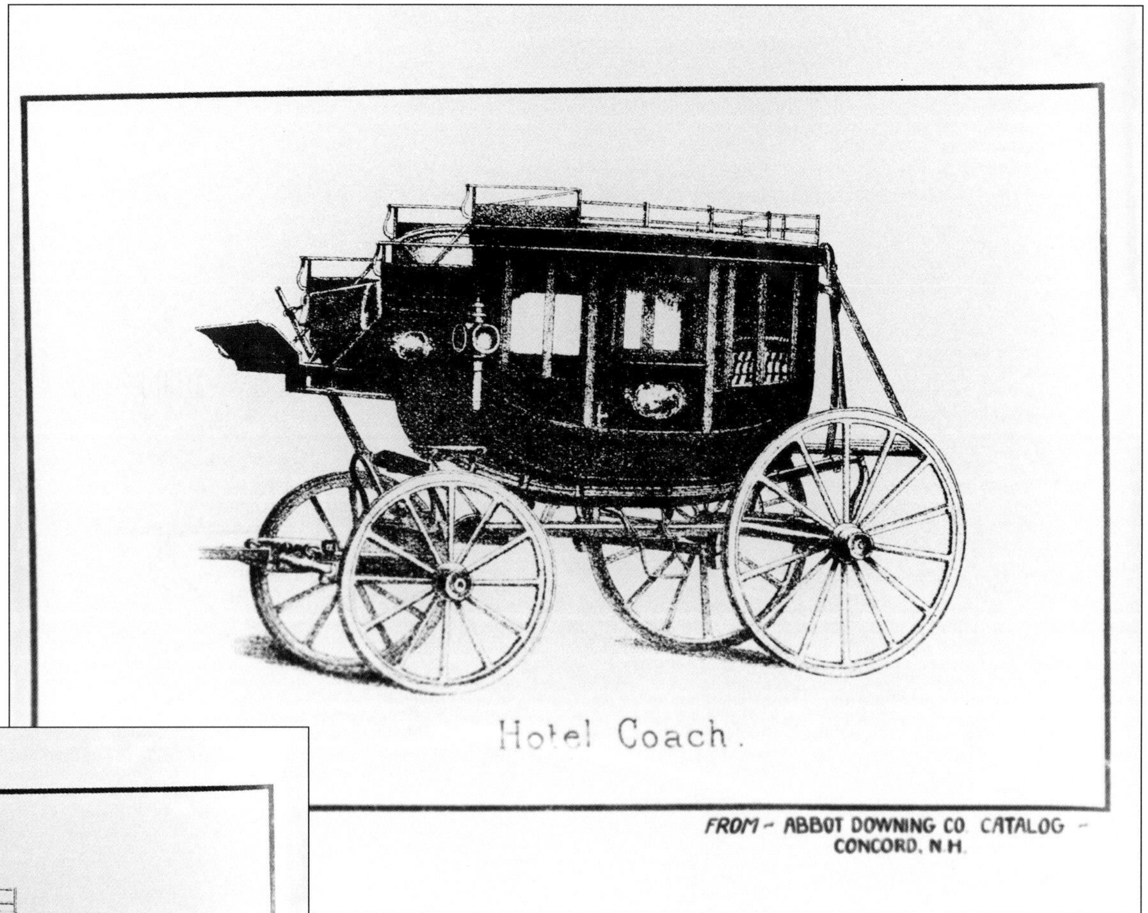

An engraving of an Abbot Downing Co. "Hotel Coach."

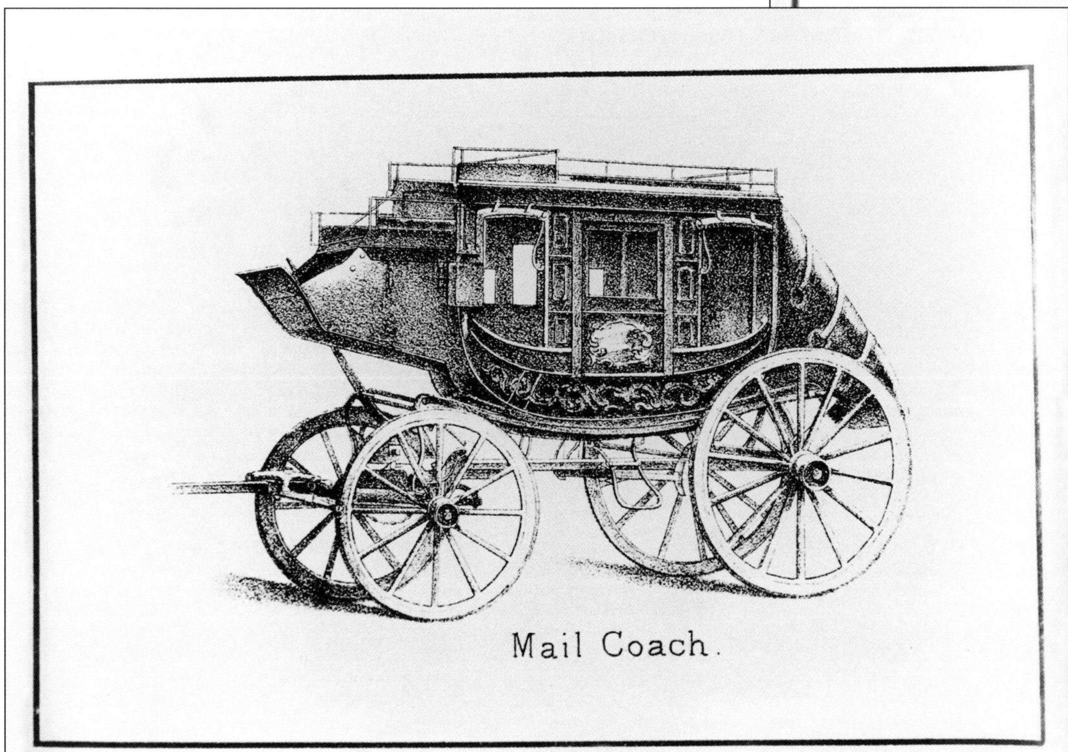

An engraving of a Abbot Downing Co. "Mail Coach."

Bibliography

The Country Paper published in Philadelphia, Pennsylvania, April 10, 1849. Story about attack and rockets against the Kioway Indian.

The Union newspaper Feb 2, 1849. Clipping about the arrangements of the government with troops to defend emigrants in their travel to California.

The Union newspaper, 1849. Clipping regarding the company that will host a emigrant party of wagons to California .

The Boston Daily, 1876. Clipping; mentions of emigrant travel To California.

Early Los Angeles newspapers. Clippings about Banning Stage Lines and L.A. Harbor information; clippings about China Town Riot.

1850 Report of the Secretary of War, from the Tenth Military Department's Lieutenant, G.H. Derby.

NOTE: There are many small clippings from very early newspapers in our collections. We have gone through a lot of them for the information contained in this book.

All photographs, prints, engravings, stocks, maps, and other materials in this book are from Sandor and Reva Demlinger's collection, collected over forty years.